WILLIAM GOLDING'S
LORD OF THE FLIES

A Source Book

$1.95

COMPLIMENTS OF

THE ODYSSEY PRESS · INC ·

55 FIFTH AVENUE   NEW YORK 10003

WILLIAM GOLDING'S LORD OF THE FLIES

A Source Book

WILLIAM NELSON
WICHITA STATE UNIVERSITY

THE ODYSSEY PRESS, INC. · *New York*

PREFACE

Interpretations of any current book are subject to a tentative quality that is unavoidable. When anyone attempts to predict the future importance of a book he is likely to find himself dangerously out on a limb. The history of literature is full of examples of current favorites which did not outlast a decade and which, in fact, now seem so obviously second-rate or insignificant that the modern observer can scarcely account for the hubbub. To do a source book on a work is to make some assertion about the lasting importance of that work. The author risks his critical acumen in claiming that this among current books is one which deserves to have the full panoply of scholarly examination—that it is, in fact, an important literary document.

On the other hand, the very fact that a book is read by a great many people is of significance in the history of letters, providing that the readers are not merely seeking some momentary anodyne against the pressures of living. William Golding's *Lord of the Flies* is being read by large numbers of college students and others. It is clearly not the kind of work that could be called an "anodyne." It does, in fact, make some rather opposite demands on the reader—that he can withstand some pain and that he forego some of the easier fictional conclusions, that of the compensatory universe, for example.

Because this novel raises a number of questions of a philosophical nature, I have thought desirable a collection of essays to guide the student to the lines of thought suggested by the novel. It is even better that there are divergent opinions as to the philosophical basis of the story. The essays here contain many contradictory conclusions about the novel; they should, therefore, provide the stimuli for many papers defending or attacking these positions. There are also discussions of the symbolism of the novel and some structural and technical speculations. The collection of essays correctly reflects the divided opinions and tentative judgements which must surround the contemporary work. Without the perspective of time and circumstances no one can finally pronounce judgement. Whatever the ultimate place of *Lord of the Flies* in our literature, such a collection should provide an interesting case study of a book which has already become a minor modern classic as well as a popular novel.

The page numbers of the sources are indicated thus /163/ at the point in the text where the original page ended. Some of the authors here quoted have desired modifications from their original texts; these have been gladly included.

My thanks are due the members of the Wichita University Research Council who were generous in providing me with a grant for this book. I also owe a debt of gratitude to Mr. Thoburn Taggart, Mrs. Marilyn Howard, and Miss Beatrice Paddock, all of the Wichita University Library, to Mrs. Del Smith of the English Department, and to my son, James, who read *Lord of the Flies* before I did.

W.N.

NOTE: The following is an inexpensive edition of the book which can be used with this study guide: William Golding, *Lord of the Flies* (Capricorn Books, New York. $1.25). For good introductory texts for the documented paper, see Cecil Williams, *A Research Manual*, 3rd Edition (New York: Harper and Row, 1963), and William Coyle, *Research Papers* (New York: The Odyssey Press, 1960).

CONTENTS

RELATED READINGS

INTRODUCTION

In the middle of the nineteenth century, R. S. Ballantyne published a boy's book entitled *The Coral Island.* His young heroes, Ralph, Jack, and Peterkin, are shipwrecked and land on a savage island; they make the best of it by rising to all occasions in good, manly, nineteenth-century boy's book fashion. In *Lord of the Flies,* William Golding's young characters, Ralph, Jack, and "Piggy," also project an attitude on the nature of boys—but a quite different one from their predecessors. The similarity of the names of the chief characters calls our attention to the earlier book and thus emphasizes the contrasting attitudes in the two novels concerning human behavior when ordinary social controls are absent. With Mr. Ballantyne, we had the prevailing of common sense and British pluck; with Mr. Golding, a horror both of Germany and of the soul.

However, in working with the philosophy involved, there are more profound sources of comparison for Golding's book than the rather superficial one of sentimentality versus horror. The climax of the novel presents the boys reverted to a savage state. Civilization is seen as a thin veneer quickly scraped away in the exigencies of living in a wilderness. And yet the abundance provided in the circumstances of these castaways does not permit the idea that hunger or the fear of hunger is the source of savagery in Golding's boys. It is clear that for him the savagery comes from forces which are barely concealed in civilized surroundings and are quickly released in the uncontrolled situation. These boys do not behave as did the traditional boy-hero of the story books. The boy-hero reflected the eighteenth century optimistic view of human nature—a view which has several facets. The first is the concept of the perfectibility of man, which includes the idea that evil is not inherent in man's nature but stems from the society which forms him. Another corollary idea is that of the noble savage. If man is by nature good, then it would seem that where he is found closest to the natural state he is at his most noble. Human beings in childhood or in a state of nature therefore presumably come closest to the ideal.

There are several sources for the ideas leading to the concept of the noble savage. The notion is implicit in much of the literature of the explorations of the western hemisphere—Columbus' narratives concerning the Caribbean natives probably doing much to start the idea. It was given further boost by such works as *Voyage of Sir Francis Drake from New Spain to the North-west of California,* and Raleigh's *Discourse of the large, rich and beautiful Empire of Guiana,* both of which have much to say about the physical beauty of the natives and of their pleasant and easy ways of living free of the corruption of more advanced nations.

More directly to the point for purposes of understanding the total perspective, however, are such humanitarian philosophers as Locke, Hume, and Rousseau. Each of these men, though not so extravagantly as they are sometimes interpreted, expressed a faith in the essential goodness of man's nature; they are responsible for the philosophical background for programs of humanitarian social progress in the nineteenth and twentieth centuries. Golding has been quoted as saying of *Lord of the Flies,* that his purpose "is an attempt to trace the defects of society back to the defects of human nature." The book, therefore, goes against the prevailing view of human nature since the time of the Enlightenment and instead expresses a view comparable to the Christian view of "original sin" and, in another realm of discourse, not incompatible with many recent insights of anthropology and psychology.

The material which follows consists of most of the periodical articles on *Lord of the Flies* from the early reviews down to the present. Included also are excerpts from *The Coral Island,* intended to make clear the use Golding has made of this earlier book. Finally, there are grouped at the end a selection of materials representing some views of man which are very much alive today. While by no means exhaustive of the subject, these articles should serve to introduce the religious, philosophical, and scientific controversies over the nature of man. It is on the view of the essential nature of man that much of the discussion of *Lord of the Flies* has centered.

ARTICLES ON WILLIAM GOLDING

NEW NOVELS
WALTER ALLEN

Mr. William Golding has found for his first novel a situation with which no one who writes as well as he does could go wrong. He has imagined a parcel of boys of roughly prep-school age—there is a cathedral choir school among them—set down and abandoned on an uninhabited Pacific island. "We are but little children weak"; but if Mrs. Alexander had written the hymn today she might have added "and polymorphously perverse into the bargain." Mr. Golding's boys are: under the stress of night-terrors and the leadership of a boy who in other circumstances might have been a modern Bully Flashman, they lapse into barbarism. Piggy, the clever boy of the outfit, lower-class, fat, asthmatic, short-sighted to the point of blindness, is killed, and Ralph, the responsible one, the born prefect, is hunted like an animal. *Lord of the Flies* is like a fragment of a nightmare, for all that it is lightly told. It commands a reluctant assent: yes, doubtless it could be like that, with the regression from choir school to Mau Mau only a step. The difficulty begins when one smells allegory. "There's not a child so small and weak But has his little cross to take." These children's crosses, it seems to me, were altogether too unnaturally heavy for it to be possible to draw conclusions from Mr. Golding's novel, and if that is so, it is, however skilfully told, only a rather unpleasant and too-easily affecting story. /370/

Walter Allen, "New Novels," *New Statesman*, XLVIII (September 25, 1954), 370. Reprinted by special permission.

NEW NOVELS

DOUGLAS HEWITT

It is clear from the start of William Golding's *Lord of the Flies*
(Faber, pp. 248, 12s, 6d) that it would be insulting to judge it by any
but the most rigorous standards. It concerns a number of schoolboys who are stranded on a desert island during a war; at first they
have great fun, but rivalries, jealousies, and fears rise inexorably to
the surface and soon they are living in a world of tribal superstitions and tribal warfare while some of them grope towards an
understanding of what is happening to them. The book is completely convincing and often very frightening. Moreover, Mr. Golding can suggest more than he says; this is perhaps most clear when
a dead airman, falling at night from a battle ten miles up, is held
upright by his parachute near the boys' signal fire so that they mistake him for a wild or supernatural beast and fly in panic. "That
thing squats by the fire," says one, "as though it didn't want us to
be rescued." The longer one considers the remark the farther do its
implications extend.

   The weaknesses of the novel may be summed up as a tendency to
be too explicit. At times the boys are less boys than archetypal
savages producing the correct taboos a little too promptly, at times
the metaphors—as in "authority sat on his shoulder and chattered in
his ear like an ape"—underline the sense a little too neatly. Perhaps,
too, the slaughtered pig's head adopts Beelzebub's name of Lord of
the Flies too easily in the mind of the delirious little boy and tells
him too dogmatically that the Beast which they all fear is a part of
themselves. But these reservations come only on reflection when the
book is subjected to the most exacting scrutiny; its progress from
the beginning when the little boy stands on his head in joy at being
on a real desert island to the end when, rescued physically, he weeps
"for the end of innocence, the darkness of man's heart" is magnifi-
cent. /4/

   Douglas Hewitt, "New Novels," *The Manchester Guardian*, LXXI (September
28, 1954), 4. Reprinted by special permission.

SMALL SAVAGES

LOUIS J. HALLE

The oldest of the English schoolboys was twelve and the youngest six. Finding themselves plane-wrecked on an uninhabited tropical island, without grownups, they had to manage for themselves. English political experience since Runnymede, however, made its contribution. An assembly was called, a leader elected, rules established, assignments distributed. Civilization had come down out of the sky with the children.

But so had savagery, and fear of the unknown brought it out. Parliamentary procedure, after all, cannot propitiate the beast in the dark. For that you have to paint your face with colored clays, chant incantations, dance ritualistically, and offer blood sacrifices. So the struggle between civilization and barbarism began.

William Golding tells all this in his first novel, "Lord of the Flies." One is impressed by the possibilities of his theme for an expression of the irony and tragedy of man's fate. Against his majority of little savages he places a remnant that convincingly represents the saving element of human heroism, thereby posing the eternal moral conflict. But he cannot quite find his meaning in his material. The heroes come to a bad end, having contributed nothing to such salvation as the society achieves. There is a great deal of commotion, and the last page is nothing more than a playwright's contrivance for bringing down the curtain. One is left asking: What was the point?

In 1929 Richard Hughes's "The Innocent Voyage" (also published as "A High Wind in Jamaica") set a standard for accounts of savage-civilized children (who are simply grownups more plainly written). The Bas-Thornton children were such fiends that even the pirates who captured them were shocked; but the angel still lay hidden in each. Hughes had simply turned the Victorian view of childhood upside down. The brutality with which he did this, however, revealed his humanitarianism. His inverted world was still a world for God's pity.

Louis J. Halle, "Small Savages," *Saturday Review*, XXXVIII (October 15, 1955), 16. Reprinted by special permission.

The integrity of "The Innocent Voyage" was perfect. It represented the single vision of a literary artist who knew human nature from personal experience. In Mr. Golding's novel, however, the novelist's vision conflicts with that of the textbook anthropologist. The novelist sees good opposed to evil; he recognizes the existence and the utility of heroes. But the social scientist deals only with amoral phenomena. In his termite society the novelist's heroes are social misfits who must come to a bad end, one suspects, to confirm the tacit assumption that maladjustment is undesirable. The intimidated novelist, thus opposed by the misplaced authority of science, dares hardly suggest even that his heroes save the honor of mankind. The best he can do, at last, is to find a meaningless fulfillment in thrills and horror. His rocket explodes in the air, spectacular for the moment, but leaving only the memory of a light that went out and the dead stick of an academic conception. /16/

ENGLISH SCHOOLBOYS IN THE JUNGLE

JAMES STERN

The title of this highly original first novel is the name given, symbolically, to the head of a wild pig which has been slaughtered for food by a horde of English schoolboys stranded on an uninhabited island somewhere in the Pacific. The noun "horde" is used advisedly, for by the time the pig's skull has been impaled on a stick, where it is promptly infested by flies ("black and iridescent green and without number"), the majority of these well-brought-up boys, none of whom has reached his teens, have retrogressed from the civilized state to the primitive. They have become, in a word, savages. Having slowly discarded the habits acquired at home and school, and discovered the "liberation" brought about by paint on the naked body, these children, faced by primeval conditions, are soon ready to torture, ready to kill. And not only animals.

As it is probably clear by now, "Lord of the Flies" is an allegory

James Stern, "English Schoolboys in the Jungle," *New York Times Book Review* (October 23, 1955), p. 38. Copyright by the *New York Times*. Reprinted by permission.

on human society today, the novel's primary implication being that what we have come to call civilization is, at best, no more than skin-deep. With undertones of "1984" and "High Wind in Jamaica," this brilliant work is a frightening parody on man's return (in a few weeks) to that state of darkness from which it took him thousands of years to emerge.

Fully to succeed, a fantasy must approach very close to reality. "Lord of the Flies" does. It must also be superbly written. It is. If criticism must be leveled at such a feat of the imagination, it is permissible perhaps to carp at the very premise on which the whole strange story is founded.

How did these children come to be on the island at all? And why, among them, were there no grown-ups? Although Mr. Golding's answer is simple, it may not convince everyone. The boys have been "dropped" in the "passenger tube" of a plane during an attack in an atomic war: the pilot has been seen to vanish in flames. This possibility once accepted, even the most skeptical reader will surely be carried away by the story's plausibility and power, by its skillfully worked-out progress, by the perfection of its characterization, dialogue and prose.

In an ovenlike and adultless jungle, clothes, of course, are the first things to be discarded. Slower to be shaken off are national characteristics: "After all we're English; and the English are best at everything. So we've got to do the right things." Faced, however, by brute Nature, by no power of authority and little hope of rescue, the "right things" seem particularly to the older boys (the "biguns"), to lose what purpose they may once have had. So two chiefs—Ralph and Jack—are appointed; meetings are held; rules drawn up. "Rules," says Ralph at last, "are the only things we've got!" To which Jack retorts: "*** to the rules!" And promptly authority is undermined, the common spirit split. Two camps are formed, and the fatal seed of rivalry, of hatred, is sown.

From the terror that follows one figure stands out, a character known to us all: the Fat Boy, commonly called "Piggy." This boy, however, has brains, and he is almost blind. And it is his blindness, by excruciating irony, that finally saves the lives of the surviving boys, while failing to save his own. Piggy is the hero of a triumphant literary effort. /38/

FIRST IDYLL, THEN NIGHTMARE
DAN WICKENDEN

William Golding, an English schoolmaster, has written a strikingly
original novel about a group of boys between six and twelve years
of age, from a comfortable middle-class background, who are isolated for a period of weeks or months on a remote tropical island
with no other human inhabitants.

In order to do so, he has had to posit a third world war, a mass
evacuation of children from England, and a plane crash that has
neatly disposed of all adults on board although the boys in their
charge have escaped unharmed and oddly unruffled. Rather too
many nagging questions remain unanswered, but the magic of a
born story-teller makes us forget our reservations, and *Lord of the
Flies,* engrossing from the first page, winds up by being almost too
persuasive.

For most of the boys the experience begins as a high adventure.
But all of them have been influenced by adult patterns, and soon
enough they are busy organizing, electing a chieftain, making rules,
establishing rituals. Then an ominous note, which has been faintly
audible from the start, rings out with increasing clarity. By degrees,
the miniature civilization breaks down; there is an accelerating reversion to savagery, and the idyll turns into a nightmare.

Mr. Golding focuses his attention on four boys. Ralph has been
chosen leader mainly because of his obvious physical superiority. He
is an instinctive administrator, but less intelligent than the bespectacled, asthmatic, despised fat boy nicknamed Piggy, who supplies the ideas that Ralph tries to carry into effect. Jack, a tall red-
head, has a more forceful personality than either of them; he turns
hunter, and once he has made his first kill it is obvious that the
latent rivalry between him and Ralph will eventually come into the
open and prove disastrous. But it is Simon, the seer—an odd and
skinny little boy, afflicted with fainting fits—who has the appalling
vision that supplies the novel with its title and underscores its meaning.

Dan Wickenden, "First Idyll, Then Nightmare," *New York Herald Tribune
Weekly Book Review,* XXXII (October 23, 1955), 6. Reprinted by permission of
New York Herald Tribune.

For *Lord of the Flies* is of course an oblique commentary on mankind's recurrently frustrated attempts to build a rational society. Unlike many novels of symbolic import, however, it is above all else an exciting and ultimately powerful narrative. The boys themselves are altogether convincing; the style is vivid and crystalline; the sense of mounting terror is brilliantly conveyed.

We are inevitably reminded of a famous and disturbing novel about children by Richard Hughes. Attempting rather more than *A High Wind in Jamaica,* Mr. Golding's book may achieve a little less, but it seems to this reviewer to belong on the same shelf. *Lord of the Flies* has its shortcomings, but all told it is a distinguished performance. /6/

SECOND READING

PHILIP DREW

' "I have made up my mind that it's capital,—first rate,—the best thing that ever happened to us, and the most splendid prospect that ever lay before three jolly young tars. We've got an island all to ourselves.' "

Peterkin Gay speaks these spirited words in the third chapter of *The Coral Island.* Later he says, referring again to the island on which he and his companions are wrecked, ' "My dear boys, we're set up for life; it must be the ancient Paradise—hurrah!" ' And indeed Ballantyne's three castaways live together on their island in a prelapsarian state of 'uninterrupted harmony and happiness'.

William Golding in *Lord of the Flies* (Faber and Faber, 1954) treats the same theme as Ballantyne. His chief characters are, like Ballantyne's, called Ralph and Jack; wrecked in the Pacific, they survive until they are rescued; the naval officer who saves them remarks ' "Jolly good show. Like the Coral Island." ' But *The Coral Island* is a romance, and in *Lord of the Flies* Mr Golding reconceives Ballantyne's story in remorselessly unromantic terms.

Philip Drew, "Second Reading," *The Cambridge Review* (October 27, 1956), pp. 79, 81, 83, 84. Reprinted by special permission.

His castaways are a party of English schoolboys whose plane has been shot down in flames. Left to govern themselves, for all the adults have been killed, they at first delight in their freedom and in the pleasures of the island. (One of them observes that it is like the Coral Island itself.) They elect as their leader a boy called Ralph, and under his guidance they agree to keep a fire burning as a signal, to summon assemblies by blowing a conch, and to allow a hearing to any boy holding the conch. Ralph and Piggy, a fat intelligent boy with asthma, arrange to build shelters, leaving foraging to a slightly older boy, Jack Merridew. As the leader of a group of choirboys who were among the castaways, he was envious of. Ralph's election; to pacify him Ralph suggested that the choir, led by Jack, should undertake to hunt the wild pigs living in the forests. Jack welcomes this and says that they will also watch the fire and keep a lookout.

However, the tedious duties of providing shelter and tending the fire soon pall, and it becomes clear that hunting is the real attraction. A ship passes, but the fire is out because the choirboys have gone hunting. Although Ralph and Piggy call frequent assemblies in which they try to rally the boys, the nerve of the party is broken by superstitious terror. When, at the last full assembly, Ralph unwisely disparages Jack's hunters, Jack goes off by himself. The rest of the novel tells how one by one the boys desert Ralph and Piggy, or are captured by the hunters and forced to join their 'tribe'. The tribe paint their faces, live under strict, almost military, discipline in a natural fortress at one end of the island, hunt the pigs by day, and leave the heads of their kill as a propitiatory gift for 'the beast'. Driven by fear, superstition and an obsession with hunting, Jack becomes increasingly tyrannical. Simon, an eccentric visionary choirboy, is done to death by the tribe in a ritual hunting dance, as he tries to tell them that they need have no fear of the beast on the mountain. Piggy is murdered by Jack's sadistic lieutenant Roger while he holds the conch, and Ralph is left alone. Goaded by Jack and Roger, all the other boys hunt him over the island, intending to sacrifice him when they catch him. They set the forest on fire, and just as Ralph must be killed either by the flames or by the spears of the hunters a cruiser sights the smoke and lands a rescue party.

Thus baldly summarised the plot sounds crude and sensational, but such is Mr Golding's skill and discretion in its deployment that the progressive disintegration of the group and degeneration of the individual are conveyed with subtlety and fidelity. Simply as narrative *Lord of the Flies* is exceptionally exciting and moving. But a deeper significance is implicit in the undertaking, and it is this which gives the novel its singular quality. By differing so sharply from Ballantyne's account of what happens when boys are left to their own devices Mr Golding implies a radically less sanguine view of human nature and civilization. More explicitly he uses his Pacific island to symbolize the condition of humanity. Having clinically insulated life on the island from the world and thus contrived a microcosm, he magnifies and inspects it. By this method, which is common ground to the great allegorists and satirists, he examines the problem of how to maintain moderate liberal values and to pursue distant ends against pressure from extremists and against the lower instincts.

Like the method the problem has exercised many writers of allegory and satire. In theme and treatment *Lord of the Flies* seems at first glance to resemble *1984:* in fact the books differ fundamentally. In *1984* Orwell is writing as a satirist. He is not concerned to symbolize man's condition or even the plight of modern man. His object is simply to record as forcefully as possible dangerous symptoms which he had already observed developing in Russia, America, and above all in Britain. To do this he exaggerated and extrapolated them, foreshortening the whole to bring his picture within the probable lifetime of most of his readers. *1984* is not about eternal values nor about the future of the world: it is about the sort of life we are living now. It has no allegorical or symbolic significance. To believe that it has is to weaken Orwell's satiric insistence that all the horrors of which he writes are not abstractions or imaginings but are *already* in the world. *Lord of the Flies* offers no such specific portrait of our own time. It is thus formally closer to *Animal Farm*, Orwell's timeless allegory of government, than to *1984*. It is not however the sort of allegory which depends on the establishment of neat one-for-one relationships between things inside and things outside the story.

Certain correspondences are nevertheless at once evident. For example, the conch which regulates the assemblies is a figure for the right of free speech in a free society. The fire which must be kept burning has a less rigid parallel—in the novel it represents a duty which must be done not for any immediate end but because it offers some hope of ultimate salvation. As Ralph says,

' "The fire is the most important thing on the island. How can we ever be rescued except by luck, if we don't keep a fire going? Is a fire too much for us to make?"

'He flung out an arm.

' "Look at us! How many are we? And yet we can't keep a fire going

to make smoke. Don't you understand? Can't you see we ought to—ought
to die before we let the fire out?" '   (Chapter 5)

At first the sole hope of rescue, keeping the fire alight gradually
becomes, even to Ralph himself, a symbolic duty. 'Ralph tried
indignantly to remember. There was something good about a fire.
Something overwhelmingly good.' (Chapter 10) In the novel attention to the onerous business of building and looking after the fire
is the mark of the more mature characters. While the task of maintaining the fire is the most obvious touchstone of the boys' quality,
the entire situation which Mr Golding has devised is a test of
their ability to survive by any but the most barbaric standards, /79/
and hence of the reality of civilization, and of Man's claim to be
an adult creature.

Similarly the individual characters, although they are fully real-
ised within the limits of their age, have symbolic value. Ralph and
Jack are, of course, the poles of the novel. Ralph is decent, though
not very intelligent, and has qualities of leadership, but it is Jack
who finally dominates the other boys. He is arrogant, brave, boast-
ful, unscrupulous and finally murderous. He and Ralph feel a
continual attraction and antipathy: in the last chapter Ralph realizes this fatal truth—'Then there was that indefinable connection
between himself and Jack; who therefore would never let him
alone; never.' On Ralph's side Piggy typifies thoughtfulness and
intelligence, the advanced side of man's mind which has made for
human survival and material development. His weakness is that
he cannot convince others or convey his ideas to a general audience.
When Jack steals his spectacles he at last finds words which strike
home.

'The shape of the old assembly, trodden in the grass, listened to him.
' "I'm going to him with this conch in my hands. I'm going to hold it
out. Look, I'm goin' to say, you're stronger than I am and you haven't
got asthma. You can see, I'm goin' to say, and with both eyes. But I don't
ask for my glasses back, not as a favour. I don't ask you to be a sport, I'll
say, not because you're strong, but because what's right's right. Give
me my glasses, I'm going to say—you got to!" '   (Chapter 11)

But it is too late to appeal to Jack, and Piggy is killed, hurled
from the cliff. 'Piggy fell forty feet and landed on his back across
that square, red rock in the sea. His head opened and stuff came
out and turned red. Piggy's arms and legs twitched a bit, like a
pig's after it has been killed.' (ib.) Simon, whom Piggy cannot understand, speaks always as the idealist. His faith and courage bring
him close to sanctity: his ritual sacrifice is a martyrdom. The other

boys think he is mad, and his advice is never heeded because it demands more of them than they can give. The twins, Sam and Eric, who speak antiphonally and act in concert, are types of the ordinary men of good will who do the decent thing as long as possible but eventually succumb to the opposition. They form a benevolent chorus to the action. The other boys are not sharply differentiated. Roger is vicious, Robert and Maurice are of Jack's stamp, but they are not clearly drawn. Nor is the number of boys ever precisely told—we are given a general impression of an island full of boys of various ages from six to twelve. We do not know how many there are, why they are there, or how fast time is passing. They are the common mass on which the leaders work, evasive and idle when the shelters are to be built, neglectful when the fire is to be watched, frightened of the dark and of their elders, but docile and well-disciplined when their faces are painted and they are members of the tribe of Jack's hunters.

A minor difficulty confronting the reader is to know what to make of the ending. In the simple context of the story it comes suddenly and arbitrarily at a time when Ralph is doomed. Since it springs from nothing in the book but comes like the waking out of a nightmare it is hard to attach any symbolic significance to it or to the final irony by which the boys hunting Ralph in fact kindle the fire that leads to rescue. This paradox and the final episode cannot be given a consistent allegorical status, but they may be accepted without strain as part of the narrative. The eye is, as it were, taken away from the microscope at the close, the boys become twelve-year-olds again, and the book ends in the naturalistic mode.

A more serious difficulty in exegesis is to determine how small Mr Golding's microcosm is, to decide, in other words, whether the island represents a society and the boys the various types and classes in that society, or an individual and the boys the various instincts or promptings in the mind or soul of a man. Although the former is the more obvious view, Mr Golding does not indicate directly whether one application is intended to exclude the other, and, if so, which is to be preferred. The result is that the reader finds himself called on at intervals to change his focus on the story, to see Jack and Ralph, for instance, now as types of two ways of life, now as opposed impulses or humours in one person. Moreover it is clear that the catastrophe occurs because the qualities of intelligence, address, bravery, decency, organization and insight are divided among Piggy, Jack, Ralph and Simon. Each of them lacks some vital gift: none of them is a complete person. The story

has thus on one level unmistakable moral implications for the individual. This blurring of the correspondences necessarily robs the
book of the hard satiric edge of, say, *A Tale of a Tub* or *Friendship's Garland,* and of the rigorous personal homiletic power of
The Purple Island or *The Holy War.* The effect is far more like
that of *The Faerie Queene* or *Moby-Dick,* for the symbolism of the
novel is not to be completely apprehended by the intellect but
exists as a reinforcement and deepening of the story.

The novel thus analyses the disintegration of a group, and the
symbolism exposes the desperate wickedness of the human heart:
it is evident that the story is grim, its incident macabre, and its
overtones, to say the least, not optimistic. Further it must be added
that the dominant tone of the book is unsavoury and depressing.
When Mr Golding writes in detail about life on the island it is to
emphasis [*sic*] its crudity, and the cruelty and intolerance of the
boys, so that his book is painful reading. He makes use of this, however, much as Swift makes use of obscenity. First it helps to convey
a sense of truth to life, to break down the Ballantyne picture of life
on a tropical island. The diarrhea, the sweat, the pig's blood and
the flies are set in powerful contrast to the pastoral life that Ballantyne describes on 'the beautiful, bright, green, coral islands of the
Pacific Ocean'. Secondly the emphasis on physical horrors arouses
in the reader a physical revulsion from savagery. This is especially
true of the pig's head which the hunters leave as a sacrifice to the
beast on the mountain, and which in one terrifying episode of delirium takes on the aspect of the Lord of the Flies himself. Thirdly,
it demonstrates most remarkably the lengths to which superstitious
terror drives the boys, and thus, by implication, the strength of the
terror itself. In *Lord of the Flies* indeed superstition is the most
powerful agent making for the degeneration of the individual. The
book's predominantly wry and unpleasant tone is therefore not a
mere flavouring, for in these three ways Mr Golding makes a vital
use of our reactions to dirt and brutality.

The basic procedure in *Lord of the Flies* is the same as that of
Mr Golding's second novel *The Inheritors*—the creation of sympathy for a group which in the face of opposition gradually dissipates. The result is inevitably despair and the disappointment of
one hope after another. Thus our compassion for the doomed
group is intensified; the deeper our sympathy the greater the force
of each successive failure and falling-off. In each book Mr Golding
takes a small group faced with extinction as a symbol of civilization
and humanity, but in each his examination leads to a different
conclusion. *Lord of the Flies* argues the precariousness of /81/ our

superiority to beasts and savages, the superficiality of our civilisation, and the impotence of good will and the forms of democracy against the instinctive savagery of man. It thus offers little inducement to optimism. Whereas in *Lord of the Flies* Mr Golding looks backward and observes how little man has advanced beyond the barbarity of his ancestors, in *The Inheritors,* which deals with the last days of the last of the Neanderthal men, he looks forward from the dawn of history and stresses, following Wells in some detail, the inevitability of the process of natural selection by which True Man has evolved. It may thus be held to imply a wary hopefulness.

There is, I think, a valid criticism that, although no Romantic, Mr Golding apparently endorses the Romantic fallacy that to examine the *nature* of a thing one must examine it in its most primitive forms. This leads him to use immature societies as his symbols of the community of man. With this reservation, however, it is true to say that he has devised in both books an apposite and original microcosm of humanity, a vehicle admirably fitted to bear the grave tenor of his philosophy. The strongest general criticism of his novels is not that they lack invention but that they lack copiousness. While the island in *Lord of the Flies* and the terrain of *The Inheritors* are acceptable as symbolic theatres of human experience they are not realized in comprehensive and concrete detail. Mr Golding, that is to say, does not convince as Defoe, for example, convinces, by proliferation of likely circumstance. The opposition in our own times is to Mervyn Peake, whose *Titus Groan* and *Gormenghast* are among the few post-war novels which are not diminished by a comparison with *Lord of the Flies.* Mr Peake's baroque fertility of incident and detail, his powers of characterization, and his exuberant wit are qualities which Mr Golding does not match. Instead he works with 'strict and adult pen,' tidily, economically, and dryly; with the exception before mentioned, he holds his allegory in steady focus, while the symbolic overtones of the Gormenghast books flicker excitingly but elusively beyond definition. Mr Golding's prose is plain but flexible. He writes sparely in short sentences about the island and the turbulent emotions of the boys, accurately reflecting their limited conversation. Now and then a vivid single word ('a clean flag of flame flying on the mountain', 'the concealing splendours of the sunlight') serves to save him from triteness and to brace the reader for the occasional passages of more complex writing. These occur mainly when he is describing Simon's ordeal and death, as for instance:

'Somewhere over the darkened curve of the world the sun and moon were pulling; and the film of water on the earth planet was held, bulging slightly on one side while the solid core turned. The great wave of the tide moved further along the island and the water lifted. Softly, surrounded by a fringe of inquisitive bright creatures, itself a silver shape beneath the steadfast constellations, Simon's dead body moved out towards the open sea.' (Chapter 9.)

Of course the failure to see the island as a whole, and the detached, even callous, descriptions of the successive brutalities are calculated effects of Mr Golding's narrative method, for he deliberately and skilfully limits his vision to that of the uncomprehending eyes of the boys, recording only what they may be supposed to have seen and felt. This shortening of the field of perception makes immediate the boys' lack of awareness of their own gradual deterioration, a blindness not without its image among men.

What I have said so far may convey that Mr Golding's /83/ novels in general and *Lord of the Flies* in particular are rather depressing books, arousing but not purging our terror and pity, and bedevilled with allegorical equivalences which carry, on the whole, pessimistic implications. No doubt there are those who find that reading Swift lowers their nervous tone. To these *Lord of the Flies* cannot be recommended. But for those who are prepared to learn even from so astringent and sceptical a tutor as Mr Golding it is possible to find in his work lessons not merely negative. Both his novels stress, and the second pivots on, the theme of communication. In each he isolates a society which is destroyed largely because its members cannot adequately express their thoughts either to themselves or to one another. Two quotations from critical points in *Lord of the Flies* serve to illustrate the importance of the theme.

' "They [Ralph and Jack] walked along, two continents of experience and feeling, unable to communicate.
' "If I could only get a pig!"
' "I'll come back and go on with the shelter."
'They looked at each other, baffled, in love and hate.' (Chapter 3.)

'The two boys [Ralph and Jack] faced each other. There was the brilliant world of hunting, tactics, fierce exhilaration, skill; and there was the world of longing and baffled common-sense.' (Chapter 4.)

It is not irrelevant to observe that much of *Lord of the Flies* is taken up with accounts of the assemblies and the attempts of Ralph, Piggy and Simon to make articulate and acceptable their pictures of what the boys must do to be saved. Man, therefore, cannot raise himself except in concert with other men. But from this, still without making Mr Golding an optimist, we may reasonably infer that if men do in fact understand one another there is some hope that they may live a better life and achieve a more stable civilization. Of mutual comprehension, indeed, one feels that Mr Golding would say what the scarred pirate in *The Coral Island* said of the Gospel:

'. . . I know that when any o' the islands chance to get it, trade goes all smooth an' easy; but where they ha'nt got it, Beelzebub himself could hardly desire better company.' (Chapter 23.)

In *The Coral Island* Beelzebub, the Lord of the Flies, finds his congenial prey in the unconverted natives. Mr Golding is less ready to divide the races of man. He writes more densely and more compactly than Ballantyne, combining in one island and one community, perhaps in one person the impulses Ballantyne separates and distributes appropriately between the savages and the manly British lads.

For since the book moves, as people live, on two levels, the individual and the social, what is true to Mr Golding of communication in a society is true also of individual self-knowledge and freedom from superstition, especially from the kind of unreasoning terror which takes shape in the book as the Lord of the Flies. Simon's peculiar strength is that he is not frightened of the island. Such a state of grace is not possible to all men, but there is hope in Ralph's gradual development to maturity. Although he is on the point of defeat when the cruiser arrives, he has learned steadily throughout the book. He learns to recognize the quality of Piggy's mind, to understand the minds of his enemies, to notice how far short he falls of his own standards, to think, to make rapid decisions, to realize that the rules must be obeyed 'because the rules are the only things we've got'. Like Lok in *The Inheritors* he grows by discovering more about himself and his fellows, but especially about himself.

Lord of the Flies, for all its clarity of outline, is a complex novel. Although it is immediately successful simply as narrative it draws its distinguishing power from its value as a symbolic representation. That is to say it is a parable whose truth must be recognized, not discovered intellectually, a sustained metaphor for human experience, for 'the end of innocence, the darkness of man's heart'. /84/

from LETTER FROM LONDON
WAYLAND   YOUNG

Golding is about forty, a schoolmaster in the tranquil and secluded
cathedral town of Salisbury. In the school holidays he navigates
large seas in small sailing vessels with his wife and children. He is
not seen at literary parties in London, does not review or broadcast;
he just teaches boys, navigates, and writes these diamond-hard and
diamond-exact novels.

His first novel, *Lord of the Flies,* came out in 1954. It has been
published already in America, France and Germany, and is to be
published in Italy. It made the sort of minor sensation here
("beautiful and desperate—something quite out of the ordinary")
which is made by some novel or other about once a month, and
which bore no relation to its very great excellence. He gives himself fifty or sixty small boys on a tropical island, survivors of an air
crash in which all the adults have been killed. They organize themselves to hunt and to keep a fire burning for passing ships to see.
But you realize after a time that the book is nothing less /478/
than a history of mankind itself; of its politics, its economics, its
religions, all its forms of existence except reproduction. The children quickly divide themselves into hunters and ordinary people,
and the hunters get out of hand; they forget that they are there to
feed the whole society, and give themselves up to the bloody joys
of killing. The fire which is to give a continuous column of smoke
—a symbol of prayer, though the specifically Christian element in
Golding's work is always subordinate to a generalized sense of
natural religion—is neglected and goes out. The most startlingly
beautiful part is about a Thing, a Beast, which terrorizes the citizens; it is seen on the mountaintop. One child, the *vas,* the artist,
perhaps the redeemer himself, goes up alone and faces the Thing.
He finds it is nothing more menacing than a dead airman whose
parachute is still attached to his shoulders so that he sits up and
regards, then slouches again, over and over, as the wind fills and
empties the parachute. The child who has understood brings down
his message to the others, and is killed by the hunters. The handling

Wayland Young, "Letter from London," *Kenyon Review,* XIX (Summer, 1957),
478-82. Reprinted by special permission.

here of the timeless story of fear, the tidings, and the blood sacrifice, is handled with a success as resounding, as complete, and as profoundly beautiful as anything in Western literature. This is a subjective judgment, of course, but I am measuring my words. The rest of the story is pessimistic, and deals with the extinction of civilization in war. The final chase in which the average bright citizen, the *enfant moyen sensuel* who was the leader of the ordinary people, is abandoned by his last adherents and pursued through burning undergrowth by the painted hunters going on all fours, is a ghastly tour de force.

The Inheritors (1955) is in my view less successful, though still highly interesting and original. It is a story about how one tribe of early man was defeated by another tribe of slightly less early man. You still feel that Golding has his eyes wide open to something concrete and very soberly imagined and objective, but it fails because he has set himself the task of conveying the sense of bewilderment felt by the more primitive people. The result is that sometimes the reader himself does not know what is going on. To bewilder your reader is a technique which many writers have tried, but I believe it always makes it harder to control the other things you want your reader to feel. This book also suffers from the shortness of the history which the reader and the characters have in common. So many things have happened to us which had not happened to the Neanderthal heroes and heroines that there is a feeling of shallowness, /479/ of short breath even. It has not yet been published outside England.

With *Pincher Martin* (1956) William Golding is back on the high road. Here he has narrowed the scene, and deepened it, to the confines of one man's mind. Pincher Martin is a wartime naval officer (in the Royal Navy certain surnames take invariable nicknames— Nobby Clark, Spud Murphy, Pincher Martin) torpedoed, and washed up on Rockall. Here he survives miserably for a few days, sick and hallucinated, eating algae and sea anemones. Then he dies. It is a fantastically narrow frame for a novel, and the pattern and symbolism is handled with fantastic rigor. Martin has not been a good man—Man has not been a good man either—and the memory of his little sins and little pleasures is deployed not so much to throw light on him alone as to spread out from that one scene— temporary lieutenant dying on beastly rock—and impose an organization of almost inconceivable precision and profundity on the chaotic content of all our lives. In this deployment, I should like to call it "lifework" on the analogy of Freud's "dreamwork," nothing is wasted, nothing is there for good measure, nothing is ever false, undigested, private to this or that sort of man. This "lifework," which is the moral and ecological substance of the novel, is set in a frame of descriptions of Martin swimming, being battered on rock, crawling about rock, collecting seaweed, eating seaweed, suffering fever, giving himself an enema with the filling tube of his Mae West, in short of Martin trying to survive, which are executed with a fine, heavy mastery of language.

Since I seem to be involved in a piece of straight criticism, I might as well try to say something about the aspect of Golding's work which most worries me, and many other people too; his endings. We can take first the ending of his latest work, a long-short story called *Envoy Extraordinary* published with stories by two other writers in a book called *Sometime Never.* This is a brilliant historical farce about an Alexandrian Greek who turns up in Imperial Rome having invented gunpowder, the steam engine, and printing. The Emperor enables him to try out the first two, and the consequent disasters are so overwhelming that instead of allowing him to try out the third as well he packs him off as ambassador to China. This is a beautifully witty trick, first because during all this uproarious cumulative destruction you are wondering how the hell he is ever going to put an end to it on the straight narrative level, and also because you are slightly worried all along by knowing very well that no Greek ever did turn up in Rome with these inventions. If he had, every- /480/ thing would have been so different. And then in one sentence he is sent off to China, and the thing connects up with real history.

Golding regularly uses the trick ending. In *Lord of the Flies* the hero, the *enfant moyen sensuel,* arrives at his last gasp of the burning forest onto the beach, and finds himself face to face with a naval officer who has seen the smoke of war and comes to take all the children off. In his presence they are able for the first time to weep naturally as children. What is it? Is it a straight happy ending? Or is it the second coming? We have already had something like the first coming in the episode of the dead airman and his parachute and the boy who understood and was put to death. But compared with the great narrative splendor of this, the arrival of the naval officer is strangely flat and cursory.

The ending of *Pincher Martin* is a major puzzle. When Martin is still swimming in the night sea, before he has been cast up on Rockall, he kicks off his seaboots to lighten himself. During his delirium on the rock he half remembers, half relives, a childhood experience when he half dreamed, half believed, that if he dared to go down to the cellar at night he would find the feet and knees of some gigantic effigies of gods. On the rock, he comes at last to prayer and atonement before something that might be a rock formation, or might be his own seaboots (though we are told that seaboots sink) but in any case bears a relation to the gods in the cellar. In the last chapter of the book we are translated to an island in the Outer Hebrides where the official who registers deaths comes to a lonely crofter and they look together at Pincher Martin's body, washed across two hundred miles of ocean. The crofter wonders if he suffered much before drowning, and the official says no: "he didn't even have time to kick off his seaboots." That is the last sentence in the book. What exactly has happened? He has somehow got his seaboots back on again. (And his Mae West.) On the level of sheer physical narrative, this is impossible. It is therefore a symbol of the supernatural. Are the seaboots the grace of God? If so, has the whole spell on Rockall been an allegory of purgatory? It may have, and a fine allegory too. But, and here's the rub, we never knew it, and the *lecteur moyen sensuel* can't take the shock of being suddenly told so at the end. This particular trick ending, the trickiest of them all so far, leaves one with a rather rebellious feeling.

For the moment, so much for William Golding. With luck he has thirty years of writing before him, and those who like me believe that he is a very fine writer will wait with the happiest attention to see what /481/ is the upshot of his unique blend of an anthropological approach and a vivid sense of redemption and atonement. /482/

THE FABLES OF WILLIAM GOLDING

JOHN PETER

A useful critical distinction may be drawn between a fiction and a fable. Like most worthwhile distinctions it is often easy to detect, less easy to define. The difficulty arises because the clearest definition would be in terms of an author's intentions, his pre-verbal

John Peter, "The Fables of William Golding," *Kenyon Review*, XIX (Autumn, 1957), 577-92. The "Postscript" to this article was kindly supplied by Mr. John Peter. Reprinted by special permission.

procedures, and these are largely inscrutable and wholly impre-
cise. For a definition that is objective and specific we are reduced
to an "as if," which is at best clumsy and at worst perhaps delusive.
The distinction itself seems real enough. Fables are those narratives which leave the impression that their purpose was anterior,
some initial thesis or contention which they are apparently concerned to embody and express in concrete terms. Fables always
give the impression that they were preceded by the conclusion
which it is their function to draw, though of course it is doubtful
whether any author foresees his conclusions as fully as this, and
unlikely that his work would be improved if he did. The effect of
a fiction is very different. Here the author's aim, as it appears from
what he has written, is evidently to present a more or less faithful
reflection of the complexities, and often of the irrelevancies, of life
as it is actually experienced. Such conclusions as he may draw—
he is under much less compulsion to draw them than a writer of
fables—do not appear to be anterior but on the contrary take their
origin from the fiction itself, in which they are latent, and occasionally unrecognized. It is a matter of approach, so far as that can
be gauged. Fictions make only a limited attempt to generalize and
explain the experience with with they deal, since their concern
is normally with the uniqueness of this experience. Fables, starting
from a skeletal /577/ abstract, must flesh out that abstract with the
appearances of "real life" in order to render it interesting and
cogent. *1984* is thus an obvious example of a fable, while *The
Rainbow* is a fiction. Orwell and Lawrence, in these books, are
really moving in opposite directions. If their movements could be
geometrically projected, to exaggerate and expose each other, Lawrence's would culminate in chaotic reportage, Orwell's in stark
allegory.

The distinction need not be limited to novels. *The Atheist's
Tragedy* by Tourneur is a fable, Shakespeare's *Troilus and Cressida* resembles a fiction, and perhaps an analogous (though
modified) difference can be detected between *Paradise Lost* and
The Prelude. Yet it has a particular value for the critic whose
concern is with novels, in that it assists him in locating and defin-
ing certain merits which are especially characteristic of novels,
and certain faults to which they are especially prone. Both types,
the fiction and the fable, have their own particular dangers. The
danger that threatens a fiction is simply that it will become confused, so richly faithful to the complexity of human ex   ce as
to lose all its shape and organization. This happens in Lawrence's
Kangaroo, for instance, and perhaps in some of Dostoevsky's work

also. My impression is that modern American novelists have often had to contend with this difficulty, not always successfully. The danger that threatens a fable is utterly different, in fact the precise opposite. When a fable is poor—geometrically projected again— it is bare and diagrammatic, insufficiently clothed in its garment of actuality, and in turn its appeal is extra-aesthetic and narrow. Satires like *Animal Farm* are of this kind.

It will be said that any such distinction must be a neutral one, and that the best novels are fictions which have managed to retain their due share of the fable's coherence and order. No doubt this is true. But it also seems to be true that novels can go a good deal farther, without serious damage, in the direction of fiction than they can in the direction of fable, and this suggests that fiction is a much more congenial mode for the novelist than /578/ fable can ever be. The trouble with the mode of fable is that it is constricting. As soon as a novelist has a particular end in view the materials from which he may choose begin to shrink, and to dispose themselves toward that end. Readers of *War and Peace* will remember the passage (at the opening of Book VI) where Prince Andrew Bolkónski drives past a bare oak in the forest on his way to visit the Rostóvs, and how on his return the oak has burst into leaf. The technique here approximates to the technique of fable, since the burgeoning of the tree is meant to symbolize his awakening feelings for Natásha, and it is curiously ineffective beside the fictional richness of the rest of the book. Compare it, for instance, with the idyllic account of the Rostóvs' country amusements in Book VII, which serves only a general purpose and is not fettered by pre-existing intentions, and it appears perfunctory and crude. To put it in another way, the old oak seen by Bolkónski is an author's prop, with none of the unpremeditated cogency of the wet birches beside the road down which, in Book IX, Nicholas Rostóv rides to the engagement at Ostróvna. These are barely mentioned, but they are *there*. The fact is that a novelist depends ultimately not only on the richness of his materials but on the richness of his interests too; and fable, by tying these to a specific end, tends to reduce both. Even the most chaotic fiction will have some sort of emergent meaning, provided it is a full and viable reflection of the life from which it derives, if only because the unconscious preoccupations of the novelist will help to impart such meaning to it, drawing it into certain lines like iron filing sprinkled in a magnetic field. Fables, however, can only be submerged in actuality with difficulty, and they are liable to bob up again like corks, in all their plain explicitness. It may even be true to say that they are best embodied in short stories, where economy is vital and "pointlessness" (except for its brevity) comparatively intolerable.

If this is so, and creative profundity less inaccessible in fiction, why should so many modern authors prefer the mode of /579/ fable? For many do, the results ranging from the puerilities of Rex Warner, through average work like Moravia's *The Conformist,* and respectable work like Orwell's, to the significant achievement of Franz Kafka. Part of the answer lies, no doubt, in our reluctance to admit that a particular and personal history can be as momentous as a symbolic paradigm. As Alan M. Boase put it some years ago, in introducing a play by Jean Cocteau to the British public:

> S'émouvoir en faveur des personnages fictifs qui n'ont pas une valeur symbolique paraît de plus en plus un abus de notre capacité de nous laisser attendrir dans une époque où l'atrocité du sort de tant d'êtres réels sollicite notre sympathie.

This is shrewdly observed. Nowadays we can only weep for King Lear after reassuring ourselves that he is less a man than Man, for our instinctive approach to Tragedy is quantitative, a matter not of depth but of scale. Then too, besides this, there is a special pragmatism in our approach to literature. We prefer our art applied, not pure, and are impatient with the indirectness of fiction and unsatisfied by the passive enrichment it can provide. The coherence of fable appeals to us as a moral tool, and its patterns become precepts. Much of this reasoning is obtuse, like the anxious student asking his instructor, "But sir, what is this Shakespeare play *about?*" but it is very prevalent. The upshot is that fable has heavily encroached on fiction in our time. Future critics, looking back, may well conclude that the best work of our generation was done in this mode, a compromise of proselytism and art like the literature of the Middle Ages.

These reflections are the result of a perusal of three books by an English writer, William Golding. Their titles are *Lord of the Flies, The Inheritors,* and *The Two Deaths of Christopher Martin* (or *Pincher Martin,* as it was called in the English edition). All three are recent, and generally speaking all have been very well received. This, to be sure, scarcely guarantees them. Reviewers in /580/ the English weeklies and Sunday papers are much given to acclaiming White Hopes of one kind or another, as the recent *furore* over Colin Wilson has again reminded us, and just at present young British novelists of any distinction are so rare that the practice of acclaiming almost anyone has sunk to a nervous habit. An empty and pretentious book like Iris Murdoch's *The*

Flight from the Enchanter has been saluted by all the best people
as a rich achievement, John Wain's reputation is already so
secure that it won praises even for his appalling second novel,
Living in the Present, and writers as incompetent as William
Cooper and as sterile as Anthony Powell are warmly and sometimes insistently recommended. Powell indeed has been made a
C.B.E. for his services to literature, and L. P. Hartley too, which
sets one wondering what porridge D. H. Lawrence had. Fables
apart, the one young man with anything like a fresh talent
(significantly reflected in his ability to write a racy, individual
prose) is Kingsley Amis, who is usually grouped with Wain and
Miss Murdoch and reproved for not being more like them. He
has had more than his share of officiously avuncular criticism,
though there are encouraging signs in his second novel, *That
Uncertain Feeling,* that he is able to ignore it. In the circumstances public praise cannot be thought to count for much; yet
Golding's books are well worth the attention they have had, and
rather more. On the one hand he can be taken as a diagnostic
example, reflecting the interests of our time in several important
ways; on the other he is a good enough writer for a preoccupation
with his work not to seem precious or misdirected. Since he is
not well known on this side of the Atlantic an introduction to
his books may not be out of place. I take them in the order of
their appearance.

Lord of the Flies, which appeared in 1954, is set on an imaginary
South Sea island, and until the last three pages the only characters
in it are boys. They have apparently been evacuated from Britain,
where an atomic war is raging, and are acci- /581/ dentally stranded
on the island without an adult supervisor. The administrative
duties of their society (which includes a number of "littluns," aged
about six) devolve upon their elected leader, a boy of twelve named
Ralph, who is assisted by a responsible, unattractive boy called
Piggy, but as time passes an independent party grows up, the
"hunters," led by an angular ex-choir leader named Jack Merridew.
This party, soon habituated to the shedding of animal blood, re-
cedes farther and farther from the standards of civilization which
Ralph and Piggy are straining to preserve, and before very long
it is transformed into a savage group of outlaws with a costume
and a ritual of their own. In the course of one of their dance-feasts,
drunk with tribal excitement, they are responsible for killing the
one individual on the island who has a real insight into the problems of their lives, a frail boy called Simon, subject to fainting fits,
and after this more or less intentional sacrifice they lose all sense

of restraint and become a band of criminal marauders, a threat to everyone on the island outside their own tribe. Piggy is murdered by their self-constituted witch-doctor and torturer, the secretive and sinister Roger, and Ralph is hunted by them across the island like the pigs they are accustomed to kill. Before they can kill and decapitate him a naval detachment arrives and takes charge of all the children who have survived.

It is obvious that this conclusion is not a concession to readers who require a happy ending—only an idiot will suppose that the book ends happily—but a deliberate device by which to throw the story into focus. With the appearance of the naval officer the bloodthirsty hunters are instantly reduced to a group of painted urchins, led by "a little boy who wore the remains of an extraordinary black cap," yet the reduction cannot expunge the knowledge of what they have done and meant to do. The abrupt return to childhood, to insignificance, underscores the argument of the narrative: that Evil is inherent in the human mind itself, whatever innocence may cloak it, ready to put forth its strength as /582/ soon as the occasion is propitious. This is Golding's theme, and it takes on a frightful force by being presented in juvenile terms, in a setting that is twice deliberately likened to the sunny Coral Island of R. M. Ballantyne. The boys' society represents, in embryo, the society of the adult world, their impulses and convictions are those of adults incisively abridged, and the whole narrative is a powerfully ironic commentary on the nature of Man, an accusation levelled at us all. There are no excuses for complacency in the fretful conscientiousness of Ralph, the leader, nor in Piggy's anxious commonsense, nor are the miscreants made to seem exceptional. When he first encounters a pig Jack Merridew is quite incapable of harming it, "because of the enormity of the knife descending and cutting into living flesh," and even the delinquent Roger is at first restrained by the taboos of "parents and school and policemen and the law." Strip these away and even Ralph might be a hunter: it is his duties as a leader that save him, rather than any intrinsic virtue in himself. Like any orthodox moralist Golding insists that Man is a fallen creature, but he refuses to hypostatize Evil or to locate it in a dimension of its own. On the contrary Beëlzebub, Lord of the Flies, is Roger and Jack and you and I, ready to declare himself as soon as we permit him to.

The intentness with which this thesis is developed leaves no doubt that the novel is a fable, a deliberate translation of a proposition into the dramatized terms of art, and as usual we have to ask ourselves how resourceful and complete the translation has been, how fully the thesis has been absorbed and rendered implicit in the tale as it is told. A writer of fables will heat his story at the fire of his convictions, but when he has finished the story must glow apart, generating its own heat from within. Golding himself provides a criterion for judgment here, for he offers a striking example of how complete the translation of a statement into plastic terms can be. Soon after their arrival the children develop an irrational suspicion that there is a predatory beast at /583/ large on the island. This has of course no real existence, as Piggy for one points out, but to the littluns it is almost as tangible as their castles in the sand, and most of the older boys are afraid they may be right. One night when all are sleeping there is an air battle ten miles above the sea and a parachuted man, already dead, comes drifting down through the darkness, to settle among the rocks that crown the island's only mountain. There the corpse lies unnoticed, rising and falling with the gusts of the wind, its harness snagged on the bushes and its parachute distending and collapsing. When it is discovered and the frightened boys mistake it for the beast the sequence is natural and convincing, yet the implicit statement is quite unmistakable too. The incomprehensible threat which has hung over them, is, so to speak, identified and explained: a nameless figure who is Man himself, the boys' own natures, the something that all humans have in common.

This is finely done and needs no further comment, but unhappily the explicit comment has already been provided, in Simon's halting explanation of the beast's identity: "What I mean is . . . maybe it's only us." And a little later we are told that "However Simon thought of the beast, there rose before his inward sight the picture of a human at once heroic and sick." This over-explicitness is my main criticism of what is in many ways a work of real distinction, and for two reasons it appears to be a serious one. In the first place the fault is precisely that which any fable is likely to incur: the incomplete translation of its thesis into its story so that much remains external and extrinsic, the teller's assertion rather than the tale's enactment before our eyes. In the second place the fault is a persistent one, and cannot easily be discounted or ignored. It appears in expository annotations like this, when Ralph and Jack begin to quarrel:

> The two boys faced each other. There was the brilliant world of hunting, tactics, fierce exhilaration, skill; and there was the world of longing and baffled commonsense. /584/

Less tolerably, it obtrudes itself in almost everything—thought, action, and hallucination—that concerns the clairvoyant Simon, the "batty" boy who understands "mankind's essential illness," who knows that Ralph will get back to where he came from, and who implausibly converses with the Lord of the Flies. Some warrant is provided for this clairvoyance in Simon's mysterious illness, but it is inadequate. The boy remains unconvincing in himself, and his presence constitutes a standing invitation to the author to avoid the trickiest problems of his method, by commenting too baldly on the issues he has raised. Any writer of fables must find it hard to ignore an invitation of this kind once it exists. Golding has not been able to ignore it, and the blemishes that result impose some serious, though not decisive, limitations on a fiery and disturbing story.

The Inheritors, published in 1955, is again an indictment of natural human depravity, though to its author's credit it takes a quite different form. This time the central characters are a group of hairy, simian pre-humans, much like Yahoos in appearance but in other respects very different. The people, as they call themselves, are as intelligent as their experience permits them to be, they are warm-hearted and reverent—quite simply, good—and Golding invests them with a quite extraordinary charm. The group is only a remnant, those who have survived a forest fire, and the story tells of their encounter with other creatures whose existence has hitherto been unknown to them, men and women. Their instinctive reaction to these strangers is one of admiration and affection (it is typical that they should at first regard the poisoned arrows shot at them as gifts), but for their part the humans hate and fear them, killing them on sight. Inevitably they are destroyed. The narrative closes with a last survivor, Lok, in his death-throe, howling his grief for the companions he has lost, for the inexplicable misery that has possessed him, while the humans row away in their dug-out down the lake.

Like its predecessor *The Inheritors* is a disturbing book to /585/ read, passionate, often moving, and with a rich command of irony. There is a passage in Sir William Walton's recent opera, *Troilus and Cressida,* that might stand for irony at its laconic best—when the lovers' duet in gratitude to Aphrodite for having answered their prayer and brought them together is immediately and tartly succeeded by Pandarus's theme from the orchestra. Golding's irony seems not a whit inferior when, after one of their number has disappeared, he shows the people's bewilderment and anxiety, allows them to take comfort from the thought that the missing Ha will have been befriended by the humans, because "People understand each other," and appends the sentence: "The people considered this and shook their heads in agreement." But this adroitness is not confined to isolated passages. The narrative relies heavily on irony for it pungency, and even the title and the epigraph were clearly chosen for their ironic force. The title reminds us that it was the meek who were to inherit the earth. The epigraph (a passage from Wells's *Outline of History,* suggesting that the ogre of folk-lore may derive from "the dim racial remembrance" of "gorilla-like monsters, with cunning brains, shambling gait, hairy bodies, strong teeth, and possibly cannibalistic tendencies") is tellingly reinterpreted in what succeeds, where all doubt as to who are monsters and who not is soon dispelled. The very core of the book is ironic, for its purpose is to play off against our smug prejudices—like those of the epigraph—a representation of their grounds that is as humiliating as it is unexpected. Irony of this kind is always valuable to an author who wishes to be challenging, as Swift knew when he put Gulliver in Brobdignag, but what gives it a special value here is its capacity to function instead of an explanatory commentary. We are sufficiently familiar with the ways of men and women to form an adequate idea of the motives of the humans, but their actions are presented through the eyes of Lok and his companions. Thus a persistent discrepancy is maintained between appearances and realities, and it is across this gap that the sparks /586/ of irony can crackle most sharply. No explicit comments are needed, for even an inattentive reader can see what is going on, and how it is being misinterpreted. The effect is that propositions pass quite smoothly into plastic terms, leaving no unnecessary residue to clog the prose.

Golding's skill and assurance can be seen throughout *The Inheritors,* both in this implicit exposition and in the approach he takes, beginning with the people and, by initiating us into their mental processes, establishing their full claim on our sympathy. Only at the end is the viewpoint altered to allow us to identify ourselves with the humans, after seeing Lok from the outside as "the red creature," and by then of course it is too late. The conclusion has something in common with the last pages of *Lord of the Flies,* when the naval officer makes his appearance, but the effect here is poignant as well as interpretative: Lok sits weeping for Liku, with her doll clasped in his hand, a more pathetic figure than any man could be because of his simplicity. It might be argued that all these effects are built on a basic fallacy, and that if all humans were as slenderly endowed with pity and benevolence as those in the book it would be unintelligible to its readers; but this is only a debater's point, itself fallacious and in any case altogether divorced from any honest response to the story as it is told. Again, a fable so intimately concerned with semi-mythical creatures might easily seem sketchy or incredible. Yet it is sensuously and persuasively rendered and seems unquestionably real. The people's existence is remote from any conception of existence we possess but its physical conditions are carefully re-created, and any thinness in its subjective texture is naturally referred to the limited awareness they enjoy. Since there is no equivalent to the boy Simon, the irony serving to replace him, the book is also more strictly faithful to the canons of its aesthetic type. It seems to me a marked improvement over *Lord of the Flies* and that in itself is no mean praise.

The new novel, which appeared as *Pincher Martin* in 1956, /587/ is again a species of fable, though its thesis is much more difficult to infer than those of its predecessors. This obscurity is partly stylistic, the outcome of a prose which has grown progressively cryptic through the three books, but it is also a result of the book's construction, the unprecedented obliquity with which the author's drift appears. Christopher Martin, precariously afloat in the sea after being torpedoed, is able to clamber exhaustedly on to Rockall, the bare tooth of rock in the North Atlantic, and there he keeps himself alive for six days while memory, and in time delirium, gradually gnaw away his consciousness. Unlike Crusoe, he is never rescued. Unlike Crusoe also, he is by human standards despicable. As his memories unfold we learn that he is a vain *poseur,* obsessively selfish, a thief, a cheat in examinations and in personal relationships, an adulterer, a rapist, and (in intention at least) a murderer too. The bleakness of his solitude offers no security against introspection and, as his selfishness comes to comprehend the self it serves, his personality disintegrates. Inexorably, as he has eaten others, the rocky teeth in the sea eat him. He goes mad and dies during an apocalyptic storm, his vision tormented by the hallucinations engendered by fever and self-disgust.

So, at least, the few reviews I have seen maintain. As we have observed, however, the endings of Golding's books are always significant, and here a brief final chapter is appended in which we learn that Martin's body, washed ashore, still wears the seaboots of which he had divested himself on the fourth page of the story—a revelation which is all the more portentous for being reserved until the very last sentence of the book. He has not been out of the water, whether on Rockall or anywhere else. What does this extraordinarily belated disclosure involve?

In the case of most of Golding's contemporaries what it involved would be simple ineptitude. If the plot were what ostensibly it is, with no rescue and no redeeming features in the protagonist, it would inevitably trail away into nullity or infini-/588/tude, in effect disappearing below or above the level of feasible dramatization, and the last sentence would be a meretricious attempt to vivify and complicate it, an endeavor (to adapt Golding's own metaphor for voracity) to eat one's corpse and have it too. But this novel is on a quite different level of achievement from *The Flight from the Enchanter,* for example, and in fact the disclosure about Martin's boots is both crucial and integrally related to what has gone before. Myself, I found that it necessitated reading the book again, and only when this had been done did the subtlety of the design begin to reveal itself. It is indeed so subtle, being to *Lord of the Flies* and *The Inheritors* much as symbolism is to allegory, that it cannot be satisfactorily translated or paraphrased. I attempt some translation here to dispel the false impression which the reviewers may have given, lest the figure in the carpet—more, the carpet itself—should go altogether unappreciated.

The essential point is that this is a story about a dead man. It is about a consciousness so self-centered and so terrified of the infinite that it creates for itself, even in death, a fantasy existence which, however arduous and painful, nevertheless still permits it the luxury of personal identity. Dead as he is, Martin clings savagely to the idea of survival, inventing a rocky outcrop on which he can exist, inventing the conditions of that existence, re-creating his naval identity disc to prove that he is still himself, continually applying the intellect of which he is so impiously proud to obliterate and deny the fact of death.

I won't die.
I can't die.
Not me—
Precious,

he thinks at the outset, and in a sense, for a time, he does not. But the existence he enjoys is a figment of his own will only, and in the most secret recesses of his being he remains horrifiedly /589/ aware of its unreality. This is why he is afraid of sleep, with its surrender of control, and appalled when he discovers that he has seen a red lobster in the sea, or forgotten that guano is insoluble. His intellect, commissioned to establish a mode of life for him, has made mistakes about these details, and the errors force him to admit, for a searing moment, that his whole environment is as imaginary as the dissolved guano or the lobster. I think the ambiguity here is masterly, for at first one supposes that his fear is simply a fear of insanity. Yet, as later appears, Martin is not afraid of insanity. He even courts it for himself, destroying his water-supply and shouting "Mad! Proof of madness!" when it is gone. The fact is that when his imagined existence begins to dissolve there is only one alternative to death remaining to him, only one last crevice in which he can hide: either he *is* dead, or he is insane. So terrified is he of "the positive, unquestionable nothingness" that he seizes on the alibi of insanity to deny it; and already, characteristically, he is slopping about in self-pity, dramatizing himself as a "Poor mad sailor on a rock," his fraudulent mummery brilliantly indicated in the enfeebled lines he misremembers from *King Lear*. When, towards the end, he creates an image of God dressed as a mariner, and defies it—"I have created you and I can create my own heaven"—the figure replies soberly, "You have created it." He has indeed, out of the resources of his own being, but these are so utterly impoverished that it cannot endure. The absolute black lightning of which his friend Nathaniel Walterson had spoken, the instrument of divine vengeance for all who lack "the technique of dying into heaven," comes to annihilate the theatrical paper world he has made for himself, and he lapses into the death he has repudiated, the compassion (as Golding expresses it) that is timeless and without mercy.

The book seems to me, in all seriousness, as brilliant a conception as any fable in English prose. Perhaps the execution is not absolutely faultless, but it is impressive, with the interest finely /590/ sustained through nearly two hundred pages of ambiguity. Yet the novel is more than a technical *tour de force*. It has the organization of a poem and, like a good poem, its ultimate power lies less in the resources of its parts than in its scope as a whole. The symbols that it uses—black lightning, eating, the Chinese box—may not be uniformly compelling but they are integrated into a pattern which is, a pattern where the meaning is difficult to exhaust. This is where the book differs from its predecessors, in a sense transcending the mode of fable itself. In the earlier books the thesis to be conveyed is comparatively specific: however trenchantly expressed, however sensitively embodied, it remains finite and in consequence limited, what oft was thought but ne'er so well expressed. This one is richer because exploratory, a configuration of symbols rather than an allegory, and for this reason it will bear an intensity of attention that its predecessors could not sustain. Perhaps because it *is* exploratory it lacks a little of the clarity, and more of the warmth, of *The Inheritors*. The alternative to Martin's self-worship has to emerge

by negative implication, where the goodness of Lok and the people
appeared directly, and the human agents of the fable (Nathaniel
and Mr. Campbell, though not Pete) sometimes come uncomfort-
ably close to the Simon of *Lord of the Flies.* There is a degree of
obscurity too about the symbol of the cellar, representing childhood terror, which seems to me either unnecessary or indicative
of a limited but lurking incoherence. And there is some tenuity
here and there, the result of conciseness, in the flashes of reality
glimpsed in Martin's memories. But there are niggling criticisms.
What impresses, beyond the qualification of any minor weakness,
is the profundity and power of the emerging pattern, and the
assurance that has left it to speak for itself. The book is arresting,
with an originality all its own. It is also a penetrating comment on
corruptions of consciousness which, however inveterate, are particularly in evidence today—some of them indeed, the less noxious,
associated with our preference for fable over fiction. /591/

This brings me back, uneasily, to my original point, that fable
tends to tie a writer down within his conscious purposes, restraining
him, while the freedom of fiction can draw him out beyond his
ascertained abilities. In view of the level of Golding's achievement,
especially here, it seems futile to insist that he will never be a major
novelist, but the doubt must remain to taunt an admirer like myself. Obviously a man has to write in the vein that suits him best,
so that it would be impertinent, and probably destructive, to urge
a maker of fables to apply himself to fictions. But it is easy to
imagine some critic of the future assessing Golding's case, and deploring the conditions for literature which drove a talent so
egregious into the narrow province of fable, instead of enlarging
and enriching it. To such a critic a moderate success in the mode of
fiction, like Angus Wilson's *Anglo-Saxon Attitudes,* may well seem
preferable to any fables contemporary with it, however finely done.

Judgments of this kind are not predictable, however, and in the
interim work like Golding's deserves much more than casual praise.
I mentioned Walton earlier and am reminded of Sir Donald Tovey's
comment on his Viola Concerto, composed when he was a young
man of 27: "This seems to me to be one of the most important
modern concertos for any instrument, and I can see no limits to
what may be expected of the tone-poet who could create it."
Though the limits are clearer, of Golding something very similar
might be said. To have published three such books as these in as
many years, to be capable alike of the compassion of *The Inheritors*
and the brilliance of *Christopher Martin,* to be able to write with
the art and the succinctness that almost every page reveals—capaci-

ties of this order, in lean times like ours, inspire something close to awe. Already, working in a recalcitrant mode, he seems to me to have done more for the modern British novel than any of the recent novelists who have emerged. More, it may be, than all of them. /592/

POSTSCRIPT

(to "The Fables of William Golding")

.   Victoria   College
                                                     Victoria, B.C.

Although on publication this essay took the form of a review article on *The Two Deaths Of Christopher Martin* it was written some months before the American title for *Pincher Martin* was announced, and later editorially adjusted to this form. If the second title was designed to dispel the incomprehensions of critics, as seems likely, it came too late to benefit me at all, except in its corroboration of my reading of the book.

As to the symbol of the cellar, which I criticised as obscure, Mr. Golding's comments in a private letter are very pertinent and deserve to be quoted here:

> The cellar in *Pincher Martin* represents more than childhood terrors; a whole philosophy in fact—suggesting that God is the thing we turn away from into life, and therefore we hate and fear him and make a darkness there. Yes, very confused but surely legitimately confused because at that depth these aren't ideas as much as feelings. Pincher is running away all the time, always was running, from the moment he had a persona and could say 'I'.

That this significance is fully conveyed in the book I am not sure, but that it would be integrally related to the rest of the tale is obvious. Golding may sometimes assume too ready a comprehension in his reader, and perhaps he does so here; but to speak of incoherence, even tentatively, as I did, is to do him an injustice.

John Peter

SECRET PARABLES
V. S. PRITCHETT

The essence of the novelist's art—especially the English novelist's—is the quotidian. From the moment Crusoe domesticates and diarises his desert island, the novel reflects the confidence the individual derives from the society he lives in. The risks of romance are gone; he is safe in the realist's nest: Selkirk was lonely, but Crusoe is the least lonely man in the world. This confidence has lasted in our tradition. But when we look up from our books into the life around us today, we wonder how the prosaic observer in realistic fiction can be so certain of himself. The quotidian art goes on describing and describing and, as far as externals are concerned, we cannot complain that the modern realist fails to describe the features of a changing, violent or collapsing society. But he is the spectator, in some lucky way insured and untouched; rarely does the novelist find the point at which we are involved or committed; rarely does he touch the quick, so that for once the modern alibi—'it is beyond the power of the imagination to grasp, etc., etc.'—does not work. The imagination will never grasp until it is awakened; and facts will not awaken it. They merely strengthen opinion; and there is nothing so apt to shut us off from the world as the correct opinion about it. The imagination can be awakened only by the imagination, by the artist who has the power to break us down until the point of secret complicity is reached. It was this point which the writer of romance, undeterred by the day's events, and lost in his world of dramatic wishes, once knew how to reach.

Mr William Golding is an artist of this kind. His three books, *Lord of the Flies* (1954), *The Inheritors* (1955) and *Pincher Martin* (1956) are romance in the austere sense of the term. They take the leap from the probable to the possible. *Lord of the Flies* has a strong pedigree: island literature from Crusoe to *Coral Island, Orphan Island* and *High Wind in Jamaica*. All romance breaks with the realistic novelist's certainties and exposes the characters to transcendent and testing dangers. But Golding does more than break; he bashes, by the power of his overwhelming sense of the

V. S. Pritchett, "Secret Parables," *New Statesman* (August 2, 1958), pp. 146-47. Reprinted by special permission.

detail of the physical world. He is the most original of our contemporaries. Many writers have been concerned, as a matter of argument, with what is rhetorically called 'the dilemma of modern
man', and have given us, as it were, lantern slide lectures on the
anarchy of a poisoned future; they are really essayists sitting in
comfort. Golding, on the contrary, scarcely uses an argument or
issues a warning. He simply shakes us until we feel in our bones the
perennial agony of our species. By their nature, his subjects—prep-
school boys on a desert island in a world war, the calvary of a sailor
who gave the right order but whose half-conscious body is being
washed about the gullies of an Atlantic rock, the conflicts of a handful of Neanderthalers could easily become the pasteboard jigsaw of
allegory, pleasing our taste for satire and ingenuity; but the pressure
of feeling drives allegory out of the foreground of his stories. He is
a writer of intense visual gift, with an overpowering sense of nature
and an extraordinary perception of man as a physical being in a
physical world, torn between a primitive inheritance and the glim-
mer of an evolving mind. A dramatic writer and familiar with the
strong emotions that go with the instinct of self-preservation—blind
love for his kind, hatred, fear and elation—he is without hysteria.
He is not cooking up freakish and exotic incident; he is not
making large proclamations about man against nature, God, destiny
and so on; he is seriously and in precise, individual instances
gripped—as if against his will—by the sight of the slow and agonis-
ing accretion of a mind and a civilised will in one or two men,
struggling against their tendency to slip back, through passion or
folly, and lose their skills in panic. And there is pity for the pain
they feel.

Pain is the essence of Mr Golding's subject. In *The Inheritors*
it is the obscure pain of a baffled and dying group of ape men who
see themselves supplanted by the more skilful new being called
Man. The ape man experiences the pain of the grunt, of trying to
communicate from one poor mind to another—'I have a picture.
Can you see my picture?'—and also the pain of trying to distinguish,
for a moment, what is inside from what is outside himself. From
his tree he sees Man who is not afraid of water, as he is, who gets
drunk on honey, who has invented love-play; he sees with a kind
of grieving as an animal might grieve. In *Pincher Martin,* the tale
of a modern sailor whose broken body is washed about the Atlantic
rock, who eats limpets, is poisoned by his store of food and who
eventually goes mad and dies, the pain is in the fight against physical hurt and loss of consciousness, in the struggle to put his educated will against his terrors. It is also in the Job-like protest against

a defeat which wrongs everything he has believed in. In *Lord of the Flies*—the first and, I think, the best of these books—a group of schoolboys re-enact the *Coral Island* story and the pain is in the struggle between the boys who revert through fear to the primitive and turn into savage hunters, and those who are trying vainly to preserve foresight and order. In the end, the boys are rescued, but not before they have lived through the modern political nightmare. (I hope this book is being read in Germany.)

Mr Golding's sensibility to pain is the spring of his imagination and if, in all three stories, the heroes are smashed up, he is by no means a morbid or sadistic writer. The chest of the creature, running in terror from its enemies, scorches, the calves cramp, the skin tears, the body has to endure what animal panic lets it in for. Pain is simply the whole condition of man; it is the sign that he is awake and struggling with his nature, and especially with the terror which so suddenly scatters the mind. *Lord of the Flies* contains one episode of great horror. The rotting body of a dead parachutist is blown across the island in the night, almost stepping on the trees and the beaches, until it is taken out to sea. The sight is the final and clinching argument to the very young boys that a devouring Beast has really been among them; and one might conclude that this is a decisive symbol of human defeat and the meaninglessness of the struggle. The idea is irrelevant. Mr Golding's imagination is heroic. Against the flies that buzz round the dangling scarecrow must be put the elation of the adventure, the love of natural life, the curiosity of the eye, that run through the writing. And the compassion.

It is natural to compare *Lord of the Flies* with *Coral Island*—and then with *High Wind in Jamaica*. In *Coral Island* we see the safe community. A century without war and with a settled sense of the human personality has produced it. In Richard Hughes's book, we saw the first sign of disintegration: the psychologists have discovered that children are not small fanciful adults, but are a cut-off, savage race. In *The Lord of the Flies* we understand that the children are not cut-off; anthropology, the science of how people live together, not separately, reflects the concern of the modern world which has seen its communities destroyed. The children in *Lord of the Flies* simply re-enact the adult, communal drama and by their easy access to the primitive, show how adult communities can break up. Of course, Mr Golding's improbable romances remain improbable; they are narrow and possible. The modern romancer has the uncluttered chance of going straight to the alienation of the individual and to the personal solitude that is one of the forgotten subjects. In our world, which is so closely organised we are hardly aware of what we are privately up to. We use large words like calamity, disaster, racial suicide, devastation; they are meaningless to us until an artist appears who is gifted enough to identify himself with a precise body being washed up against a precise collection of rocks, a precise being sniffing the night air for his enemy or feeling the full force of a particular blow. Until then, we are muffled in our alibi: 'the imagination cannot grasp'.

Lord of the Flies is the most accomplished of Mr Golding's novels. Its portraits of the shipwrecked boys and its understanding of them are touching and delightful and he is master of a rich range of scene and action. In this book his spirit and his serenity are classical. *Pincher Martin* is more chock-a-block, but it has fine descriptions of the roaring, sucking, deafening sea scene on the rock which we know stone by stone. He is a modern writer here in that his eyes are pressed close to the object, so that each thing is enormously magnified. We see how much a man is enclosed by his own eyes. The important quality of all Golding's descriptions is that they are descriptions of movement and continuous change and are marked by brilliant epithets. (One remembers: 'three prudish anemones'.) There is this picture of the swimming sailor, almost at the rock:

> Ropes held him, slipped and let him go. He saw light, got a mouthful of air and foam. He /146/ glimpsed a riven rock face with trees of spray growing up it and the sight of this rock floating in mid-Atlantic was so dreadful that he wasted his air by screaming as if it had been a wild beast. He went under in a green calm, then up and was thrust sideways. The sea no longer played with him. It stayed its wild movement and held him gently, carried him with delicate and careful motion like a retriever with a bird. Hard things touched him about the feet and knees. The sea laid him down gently and retreated. There were hard things touching his face and chest, the side of his forehead. The sea came back and fawned round his face, licked him. He thought movements that did not happen. The sea came back and he thought the movements again and this time they happened because the sea took most of his weight. They moved him forward over the hard things. Each wave and each movement moved him forward. He felt the sea run down to smell at his feet then come back and nuzzle under his arm.

But this book succeeds less when it takes us into the sailor's chaotic recollections of his life. It contains some flashes back to scenes of jealousy and rivalry which are hard to grasp. It may be that Golding's sense of theatre—often strong in writers of romance—has overcome him here. (He is the author of a witty satirical play, *The*

Brass Butterfly, which is excellent reading.) But in making us feel in the current in the modern world, instead of being stranded and deadened by it; in providing us with secret parables; in unveiling important parts of the contemporary anguish and making them heroic, knowable and imaginable, he is unique. /147/

CORAL ISLANDS

FRANK KERMODE

Ballantyne published *The Coral Island* in 1858. It is still reprinted, and the copy in the local children's library seems to be taken out at least once a fortnight, from what strange motives of pubescent piety or hypocrisy I do not understand. Ralph Rover, the narrator of the story, addresses himself 'especially to boys, in the earnest hope that they may derive valuable information, much pleasure, great profit and unbounded amusement from its pages,' but adds this warning: 'if there is any boy or man who loves to be melancholy and morose, and who cannot enter with kindly sympathy into the regions of fun, let me seriously advise him to shut my book and put it away.' For Ralph and his Bible go cheerfully to sea. The ship is full of jolly, clean-spoken tars, but they are all drowned through lack of common sense when the ship strikes a coral reef. Ralph and a ghastly comic boy called Peterkin are saved because they take the advice of Jack, an imperturbable leader-type. 'You see it is impossible,' he explains as the ship founders, 'that the little boat can reach the shore, crowded with men. It will be sure to upset, so I mean to trust myself rather to a large oar. I see through the telescope that the ship will strike the tail of the reef, where the waves break into the quiet water inside; so, if we manage to cling to the oar till it is driven over the breakers, we may perhaps gain the shore.' This they do, conversing the while in semi-colons. Under Jack's benevolent discipline they have small difficulty in leading civilised lives on the island; he understands the flora and fauna, knows how to light fires with bowstrings and spyglasses and can

Frank Kermode, "Coral Islands," *The Spectator*, CCI (August 22, 1958), 257. Reprinted by special permission.

hunt and kill pigs with much ease and a total absence of guilt, or indeed bloodshed. They are all Britons—a term they use to compliment each other—all brave, obedient and honourable. There is much useful information conveyed concerning tropical islands, including fieldworkers' reporting of the conduct of cannibals; but anthropology is something nasty that clears up on the arrival of a missionary, and Jack himself prevents an act of cannibalism by telling the flatnoses not to be such blockheads and presenting them with six newly slaughtered pigs. The parallel between the island and the Earthly Paradise causes a trace of literary sophistication: 'Meat and drink on the same tree! My dear boys, we're set up for life; it must be the ancient paradise—hurrah! . . . We afterwards found, however, that these lovely islands were very unlike Paradise in many things.' But these 'things' are non-Christian natives and, later, pirates; the boys themselves are cleanly (cold baths recommended) and godly—regenerate, empire-building boys, who know by instinct how to turn paradise into a British protectorate.

The Coral Island could be used as a document in political, social or educational history, but also in the history of ideas. It belongs to the period preceding the breaking of that great wave of primitivism which has so altered the features of the modern mind; and in 1954 Mr. William Golding had the idea of studying Ralph and Jack against this altered landscape. (Peterkin is replaced by a fat, asthmatic, shortsighted butt called Piggy, who is nevertheless one of the two wise men of the book.) The device is interesting in itself; but rereading *Lord of the Flies* after the publication of two more major novels by its author we should be able to keep it in perspective. It is interesting, certainly, that so evident a master should want to use it; Mr. Golding, who knows boys well enough to make their collapse into savagery perfectly plausible, has, strangely, a profound and tragic interest in what interests them. Among the half-dozen really potent boyhood myths there are two he dwells on; the old one, of an individual or group facing natural problems unaided by adults, and a newer one, of prehistoric fantasy—steaming swamps and megatheria and men primitive in language and techniques. The first makes for tragedy, the second for its explanation; enormously refined, they come together as an animating conviction which is essentially close to Rousseau's *l'homme est un animal dépravé*.

The price of human consciousness, of technical and linguistic power, is guilt. This theme is not centrally placed in *Lord of the Flies*, which is therefore much illuminated by *The Inheritors*, a novel about the supersession of an innocent predecessor by *homo sapiens.* The intellectual superiority which enables this victory is precisely measured by the cruelty and guilt invented in the process. Man, who cooks, makes drawings, alcohol and love, can think; he replaces with language that picture-dialect, guiltless of all abstraction, which the victim used, and which is found in *homo sapiens* only in certain pathological conditions. *The Inheritors* is Mr. Golding's most perfect book, ambitious in design and of terrific imaginative force, though, since it is concerned only with the Fall and not with the Last Things, it offers a less complete account of the Golding world than *Pincher Martin.* Together, these later books suggest that the author is much concerned with redemption. It cannot be had by retreat to primeval innocence; this we know from the superb conclusion of *The Inheritors.* Nor can the intellect, any more than the pig's snout, command death and hell, or, when the stolen fire destroys, blame its source; but that evil is human, and would vanish if the mind could alter its theme, is what the queer religious Nathaniel tells Prometheus-Pincher in the last Æschylean novel. It is also what Simon, the sick visionary, discovers in *Lord of the Flies.*

Once more, then, Ralph the Rover and Jack the leader and Piggy the fool drop—this time from the stratosphere—into the Earthly Paradise, where 'flower and fruit grow together on the same tree.' Once more, every prospect pleases, but the vileness proceeds, not from cannibals, but from the boys, though Man is not so much vile as 'heroic and sick.' Unlike Ballantyne's boys, these are dirty and inefficient; they have some notion of order, symbolised by the beautiful conch which heralds formal meetings; but when uncongenial effort is required to maintain it, order disappears. The shelters are inadequate, the signal fire goes out at the very moment when Jack first succeeds in killing a pig. Intelligence fades; irrational taboos and blood-rituals make hopeless the task of the practical but partial intellect of Piggy; his glasses, the firemakers, are smashed and stolen, and in the end he himself is broken to pieces as he holds the conch. When civilised conditioning fades—how tedious Piggy's appeal to what adults might do or think—the children are capable of neither savage nor civil gentleness. Always a little nearer to raw humanity than adults, they slip into a condition of animality depraved by mind, into the cruelty of hunters with their devil-liturgies and torture; they make an unnecessary, evil fortress, they steal, they abandon all operations aimed at restoring them to civility. Evil is the natural product of their consciousness. First the smallest boys create a beastie, a snake—'as if it wasn't a good island.' Then a beast is created in good earnest, and defined in a wonderful narrative sequence. The emblem of this evil society is the head of a dead pig, fixed, as a sacrifice, on the end of a stick and animated by flies and by the imagination of the *voyant*, Simon. But Simon understands, and this is the wisdom Golding treats with awe, that evil is 'only us'; he climbs up to where the dead fire is dominated by the beast, a dead airman in a parachute, discovers what this terrible thing really is, and rushes off with the good news to the beach, where the maddened boys at their beast-slaying ritual mistake Simon himself for the beast and kill him. As Piggy, the dull, practical intelligence, is reduced to blindness and futility, so Simon, the visionary, is murdered before he can communicate his comfortable knowledge. Finally, the whole Paradise is destroyed under the puzzled eyes of an adult observer. Boys will be boys.

The texture of Mr. Golding's writing is highly individual and proper to the heroic scale of his fictions. He keeps one aware of many contexts, his men live in a world of rock and sea and amoebae heaving in the pull of the moon, refusing to be locked fast by human imaginings of good or evil, obstinately talking its own language of sucking, plopping and roaring, against the human language which gives it another kind of life. The difference of this world from Ballantyne's simpler construction from similar materials is not merely a matter of the incomparability of the two talents at work; our minds have, in general, darker needs and obscurer comforts. It would be absurd to suppose that the change has impoverished us; and it will not do so provided that Ballantyne's Jack, confident in some laboratory, can exist side by side with Golding's Simon, crouched in his horrible solitude, observing and naming the beast. /257/

THE NEW REALISM: THE FANCY OF WILLIAM GOLDING

RALPH FREEDMAN

I

More, perhaps, than he knows, William Golding represents the Inheritors. Without Osborne's impatience or Amis' easier wit, he has presented us with several workable alternatives to the Symbolist approach to fiction. For the Romantic heritage, crystalized in the symbolic patterns of *Ulysses* and *The Waves,* had reached a mode of expression beyond which it was impossible to go without being imitative or dull. There had been, of course, other alternatives to Joyce and Woolf: D. H. Lawrence's fervor, the existential symbology of Graham Greene, the Trollopian visions of Cary and Snow, the survival of satire in Huxley, Orwell, or Waugh. But a generation of men, who had entered their manhood early in World War II, have introduced new forms. They have returned us to the origins of the English novel: the eighteenth century.

A self-conscious use of wit, of pseudo-picaresques, of ironic distortions, recalls Fielding and Swift. But in the hands of William Golding (and to some extent also of John Wain), these techniques have freed the concept of self from the Coleridgean vision which underlies the novel of subjectivity: that of the self as recreating the world in its internal perceptions. For though Golding is as passionately involved in the nature of self as Virginia Woolf had been in *Mrs. Dalloway* or Joyce in *A Portrait of the Artist,* his vision has consistently focused on the self as distinct from the universe of characters and objects. The psychological notion of sensibility becomes the epistemological notion of cognition; the aesthetic problem of objectifying internal perception in art becomes the existential problem of identity. Instead of being the means of attaining mystical recognitions, self acts as the inviolable core matched with and defined by a gross but external reality.

The contours of Golding's phantastic vision are clear enough. In a manner reminiscent of Kafka and Swift, without undue borrow-

Ralph Freedman, "The New Realism: The Fancy of William Golding," *Perspective,* X (Summer-Autumn, 1958), 118-28. Reprinted by special permission.

ings, he plays tricks with our capacity to empathize. Each of his three novels—*Lord of the Flies, The Inheritors,* and *The Two Deaths of Christopher Martin* (or, in its original title, *Pincher Martin*)—presupposes a metamorphosis of reality in which his themes are embedded.* In *Lord of the Flies* we are asked to identify with a group of school boys—/118/ evacuees from atom-bombed Europe whom a mishap had landed in a benevolent tropical island —succumbing to their innate corruption in the absence of "civilization" or adult control. In *The Inheritors,* we enter the minds of pre-rational animals, near-human Neanderthal men, whose gentle and sweet-natured savagery is marred by failures in understanding and memory. In *Pincher Martin,* the best of Golding's novels, we follow a tale about a ship-wrecked sailor ambiguously exiled in a world which presupposes death, struggling against hostile physical nature and the hallucinatory compulsion to identify his universe with himself.

Each of these novels deals with an eighteenth century concept or situation: the savage child, the "noble" savage, Robinson Crusoe's triumph of reason and ingenuity over hostile external nature. But in each novel a significant distortion tends to subvert the eighteenth century premise. The civilized child turns savage in a benevolent world of nature in which there are no threats except its own disposition to evil. The noble savage is nobler than his more "civilized" adversary only because his lack of wit entails an incapacity for guilt which prevents him from understanding his own moral decline. Robinson Crusoe is rewarded for his ingenuity and moral awareness by becoming a decomposing bulk which no living man wishes to touch. For the answers Golding gives to the question he poses—what is the essence of human nature?—belong in the twentieth century. The Swiftian balance of reason and passion becomes for Golding the tension between identity and primal impulse produced and varied by deliberate changes in a hypothetical but distinct reality which his heroes seek to control.

II

Each of Golding's novels begins with a significant change: the drop into the tropical paradise by the boys in *Lord of the Flies*; the mysterious disappearance of the "log" (vouchsafing passage over taboo water) in *The Inheritors,* the "first death" or ambiguous and provisional rescue in the second terrifying life of Christopher Martin. In other words, Golding defines his "unreal" or hypothetical

* The most complete and perceptive appraisal of these three novels in this country is John Peter's review-article in *Kenyon Review* (Autumn, 1957).

world through a moment of change, a traumatic break from one reality into another of distorted experience from which his protagonists expect to be "rescued." The children in *Lord of the Flies* immediately make a fire to attract rescuers. The Neanderthal protagonists Lok and his more intelligent mate Fa fail in their attempts to rescue the children who were to guarantee their survival. All of Pincher Martin's thoughts are crystallized in the self-saving formula: "I shall be rescued." This need for rescue underlines the predicament of Golding's heroes. It suggests that in an ordinary state man has no need to define himself. But in a changed universe in /**119**/ which normal habits are interrupted and experience relates to unknown and untried conditions, he must take full measure of himself in his present and past.

The motif of rescue suggests the evident inspiration of *Robinson Crusoe* in the first and last of Golding's novels and the criticism of a naive Rousseauistic view of the state of nature in the second. But it also emphasizes sudden change and its traumatic consequences which is reminiscent of Kafka's *Metamorphosis* and the opening chapter of *The Trial*. In *Lord of the Flies,* the jolt caused by the changed conditions necessitates adjustments which pre-enact the entire novel. In the first chapter the two boys, Ralph and Piggy, who, between them, represent order, meet and obtain leadership; the arrival of Jack Merridew and his black-robed "choir" anticipates the disastrous attempt to kill in which the knife is fixed as the symbol of corruption. In *The Inheritors* the changes likewise make disintegration inevitable. The absence of the log induces the death of the patriarch Mal and heralds the human presences. But the force of the metamorphosis is nowhere more clearly demonstrated than in *Pincher Martin*. As has been rightly suggested the ending leaves open the question whether we have witnessed a "real" struggle for survival or a hallucinatory extension of such a struggle into a man clinging for existence after death. The ambiguity is clear enough, the sea boots Martin abandons at the beginning of the novel are found on his body in the end, but the question itself is very much like the question whether Gregor was "really" a bug. The ambiguity teases our imagination and brings the hero's struggle for identity against the invasion of solipsism into even sharper relief. For what remains is the transformation from one state of being into another, from life into death-in-life or life-in-death, followed by recognition, shock, and adjustment.

Man's first job is to control his changed conditions by imposing order. In this respect, both *Lord of the Flies* and *Pincher Martin* follow the eighteenth century pattern. The children, a collective

Robinson Crusoe, follow their leader and organize their world, an order which is afterwards destroyed in solipsistic orgies. Martin's entire second life is a series of attempts to organize and control his environment, to be obliterated in hallucination and madness. And in an inverse way, control is also the subject of *The Inheritors*. The Neanderthals, with relatively little persistence, memory, or rational awareness of self, cannot control their environment. The humans, more corrupt because basically more aware of guilt, can do so and inherit the earth.

Control, therefore, means awareness. It requires the kind of rational self-awareness which exists only through the recognition of that which /120/ is external to self. The dénouement in each of the three novels is the obliteration of such a sense of identity based on an awareness of distinction between self and "other."

III

Self-awareness, then, in corruption or identity, proceeds through the awareness of "other"—of objects and persons in their changed perspectives. In *Lord of the Flies,* revelation, or cognition, of a world external to self is symptomatic of order; failure to recognize such a world becomes symptomatic of moral decay. The hopeful early chapters, despite the ugly foreshadowings of the future, all relate to identification, identity, and discovery. The two boys through whose point of view much of the novel is seen, perceive and name the world around them, orient themselves, and exchange names. They then find the conch-shell with which to call the boys scattered throughout the island, to have an organizing meeting, to take roll-call and census. Part of their immediate need to explore and control their universe is to know themselves and that which is beyond them. As the plot turns to the disintegration of the colony, attention is focused more and more away from what is "out there" to what cannot be seen or heard, to what is imaginary or hallucinatory, to what is part of an inner compulsion occasioned by events which are misinterpreted. The real distinction between the "conch-shell" and the "Lord of the Flies" is that one is a real object, accepted in the light of reason and dedicated to social control, while the other is an object endowed with mystical qualities, embodying hallucination and fear and dedicated to social extinction.

Recognition, indeed, awareness and acceptance of "other" is also the theme of *The Inheritors*. When Ha, the less practical but more intelligent member of the Neanderthal group, disappears and no explanation can be found, the group is mystified because they agree that there can be no "other." Indeed, one of the most important themes in *The Inheritors* is that of primitive solipsism. The "people's" disavowal of the reality of "other" until it is too late produces the ultimate disaster. By contrast, the human beings who are seen only through the eyes of the Neanderthal men except for the concluding chapter, live and survive through their awareness of other, their determination to eliminate, classify, and control "other."

If *The Inheritors* is a *tour de force* in primitive solipsism, *Pincher Martin* is a well-structured argument for the definition of self in relation to a world the hero confronts in a state of forced isolation. For Martin struggles to the end against being swallowed up by primitive solipsism. The world remains that of "other" in present and past. One of Golding's /121/ great achievements is that he makes us believe in this struggle for identity and definition even as he ambiguously suggests the possibility of utter hallucination. The "story" is the second life, the life on the rock. What we find out about his past—and fortunately for the novel we are never given enough of these trailers to turn our interest from the rock to the theatrical "first life" of Chris Martin—are individual scenes which, never continuous, define the hero's conscious and unconscious states. Martin is always alone, faced with himself. His dreams do not entertain him by peopling his world; they define him.

Throughout the novel, Martin, though alone, seeks to define himself exclusively through "other." During the calm, relatively sane days between the storms, when he names his world, secures his livelihood, ponders his chances for survival, Martin also takes stock of himself. The first thing he does is to undress and inspect the body; the next thing he does is to inspect his soul. Memory figures become objects of awareness, not to permit a higher insight, like that of Proust's Marcel, but to become tangible figures to which, in his search for identity, Martin can relate.

This sense of awareness of self through "other" is augmented by painstaking attention to details of perception, particularly the perception of objects. The children in *Lord of the Flies* organize by perceiving objects, becoming aware of them, naming them. (The primal act of naming is a continuous by-product of humanity in Golding's work.) Awareness of objects and naming through association with the familiar is part of the process whereby the struggle between intelligence and unreason proceeds in *The Inheritors*. Each encounter of the Neanderthals is portrayed through sensations and objects—trees, logs, water, sticks (arrows), animals—and many of the same perceptions are repeated through the more rational minds of the human beings. The first chapters of *Pincher Martin* abound with perceptions of objects apprehended for the purpose of civilized control: rocks, algae, sea water, rain water, sea gulls, fish. In a moving scene, Martin's inspection of his body makes of his body an object. When in hallucination there occur shifts in the "reality" of objects—most notably in the appearance of a red lobster and other impossible natural phenomena—he becomes increasingly aware and afraid of losing identity and mind.

Perception, organization, and naming, which are means of rational control, are expanded through the conscious and unconscious endowment of objects with symbolic values. In *Lord of the Flies,* objects like the conch-shell and Piggy's eye-glasses on the one hand, and sticks, rocks, and knives on the other, are respectively, symbols of states of /122/ control through reason and through brutality or "darkness." The characters are usually aware of the symbolic import of the few objects in their possession. Piggy struggles to save the conch-shell and blinds himself by losing his remaining eye-glass. The public school boy clothes in which they arrived—their shirts and shorts and windbreakers with zippers—the dark cloaks of Jack's military "choir," the disintegrating rags, the hunters' garb worn later in mockery of civilized clothes, are symbolic of their respective states and positions. In *The Inheritors,* the dim semi-darkness of mind in which the Neanderthals live forbids the conscious awareness of symbolism in objects, but in *Pincher Martin* the recognition and naming of his world means human control through the symbolic import of language. With it, Martin endows the few objects of his circumscribed universe with deliberately symbolic meanings with which to make his world more habitable. Most significant here is Martin's compulsive concern with his clothes (oilskins, jacket with braids, sea boot socks), with his papers, and his identity disk.

In addition, Golding also works with unconscious symbolism, but his method can be clearly distinguished from a Symbolist approach. Unconscious symbolism is taken in the Symbolist sense: as an intuitive awareness of meanings which unconsciously reveal not the properties of the object in question but qualities in the self which they objectify and render universal. But Golding deliberately identifies this type of symbolism with degradation, with the gradual submergence of man in his undifferentiated substratum. In both *Lord of the Flies* and *The Inheritors,* for example, fire and water are symbolic. Cleansing water becomes brine-covering, filth-bringing stuff which taints the children. Rescuing fire, becomes, as we have seen, the fire of orgy and death (in a primitive ritual Jack's hunters steal the fire). The Neanderthals carefully nurture fire which their matriarch carries along on their pilgrimage; its extinction is their extinction, but Mal's apocalyptic vision also recalls the gigantic fire which had destroyed most of their race. For rational man, who can control fire by being able to light it without preserving a spark left by nature, fire is the soaring flame of passion and chaos. Similarly, men and Neanderthals are distinguished by their attitudes towards water. The river is taboo for the "people"; submergence in water for them is equivalent to death. Refusing to cross the arm of water that separates them from the humans, they can neither attack their island nor be successful in their attempts at rescue. When at last they find a safe way the humans elude them in boats. But in banishing the Neanderthals into darkness of forests and caves and in seeing themselves as governing the light and the water, the human be- /123/ ings apprehend consciously the symbolism which has been unconscious in the Neanderthals, and utilize it in their attempt to organize and control.

In *Pincher Martin,* unconscious symbolism is expressed by the "center," the inmost "center" of being which is opposed to the verbalizing, rationalizing "mouth." But being neither child nor near-animal, Martin, the twentieth century man to whom unconscious symbolism is available as a concept, struggles to clarify and make meaningful the unconsciously induced symbols he encounters. In his increasingly feverish, increasingly distorted mind, even at the point of madness, he gropes for rational control to convert that which is within him to "other" and thus to return from primitivism to civilization. In this way, flabby sensations, orifices, sea weeds, gull, women-shaped rocks and vaginal crevices are made meaningful with the aid of memory and reason. Rendering unconscious symbolism conscious is in all three novels the attempt to rise from undifferentiated humanity to rational, differentiating man.

IV

The eighteenth century conflict between reason and passion is thus translated by Golding into a tension between the undifferentiated basic human impulse (man's nature conceived in anthropological terms) and individuated man. The opposition itself has also been dramatized by Coleridge and Novalis, Lawrence and Joyce. But if writers of Romantic or Symbolist traditions have viewed man as suspended between dissolution and re-integration of self, for Golding the "state of nature" (of dissolution and unconscious symbolism) is exclusively chaos which must be overcome. For man's tragic failure is the failure to distinguish, to blend the world with himself and to vivify it with his hallucinations. Only reason ensures identity; only awareness of *integritas* can be rewarded with recognition.

The undifferentiated impulse is, of course, revealed through Golding's most obvious theme: that of the corruption of innocence. Order and chaos, innocence and guilt are juxtaposed in *Lord of the Flies,* but no boy is left untainted by the loss of innocence in the end. Even Ralph is made responsible for murder because he emotionally participated in the orgiastic dance after first viewing it with horror. As a lush nature corrupts their senses of self, of cleanliness and order, so their own inner nature (their collective evil) must destroy their paradise in the end. Fascinated with the idea of man's progress through the anthropological stages of evolution, Golding puts these English school-boys from 6 to 14 through the two most significant moments in human development. The /124/ Lotus Eaters are taken over by the Hunters. Similarly, Lok and Fa lose their *raison d'etre* as noble savages when after viewing two orgies of human beings they inadvertently intoxicate themselves with stolen mead and thus lose their innocence. Drawn with curiosity to the orgies they observe, they are ultimately involved and corrupted.

The Lord of the Flies, the decomposing Pig's Head as the symbol of primitive passion, reveals itself to the frightened but perceptive Simon in the same way as the stag dance of the men appears to the observing Neanderthals. It becomes a supernatural force which, in his ironic surrender to hallucination and loss of identity, Martin creates for himself at the concluding moment of his second life. But up to this point Martin's civilized consciousness, like that of Piggy and Ralph, had sought to control and clarify the corrupting force of nature—physical as well as human. It is here that the significance of the memory trailers becomes most incisive. They reveal the chaos beneath the closed surface of twentieth century man and permit him to deal with it. Scenes which exhibit each of his irrevocable betrayals—of his friends, of his mistress, of his colleagues—and which show him seeking to control others for the sake of satisfying himself alone, expose him as adolescent and primitive. In this way, the monstrous pictures of a feverish mind transcend hallucinations to become moments of moral awareness which lead to identity. If in the most monstrous of hallucinations—God appearing to him as a sailor of his own creation—this identity is finally submerged, this does not negate his persistent struggle to retain it, to rise from general or archetypal to individual or moral consciousness. Intelligence, then, becomes the individuating, moral quality of self with which the urge to darkness can be opposed, pitting Houyhnhnm against Yahoo in twentieth century terms.

Intelligence is the key to *The Inheritors* which provides its weird fascination. Golding has succeeded with peculiar conviction not so much in making us believe in this small Neanderthal family—

their softness, their desire to cuddle, their adoration of femininity, their near-animalistic rituals—as in making us accept his portrayal of the state of semi-intelligence. "Thought" is self-conscious and mystical contemplation which few can master and none can sustain. "Memory" and "imagination" are activities which consist in calling up "pictures." The moments when thought and pictures fail are the moments when identity is lost. Therefore, even the most adept among them are no match for the truly intelligent human beings. For this reason even their corruption loses its moral force because it is not accompanied by guilt. Memory and awareness produce the sense of identity through which guilt in human beings /125/ (Ralph, Piggy, Jack, Martin) is fixed and identified.

Self as differentiating and sustaining intelligence is the core of *Pincher Martin*. If his first life had been marked by moral degradation, his second life reconstitutes the self in moral awareness. Capable of being verbally aware of his world, within and beyond himself, he communicates the saving formula *education and intelligence* to an indifferent universe. Although these tools proved ultimately as ineffective as the life-preserver had been treacherous, they permit him to maintain himself, to exist, unified and whole, up to the last phase of his final destruction. But as he approaches the moment when he must give in to the chaos of madness, he senses more and more the underlying ambiguity of human existence. Partly struggling for lucidity, partly submerged by the chaotic sea, there appears to him a catalogue of equivocations: "Sensations. Coffee. Hock. Gin. Wood. Velvet. Nylon. Mouth. Warm, wet nakedness. Caves, slack like a crevice or tight like the mouth of a red anemone. Full of stings. Domination, identity." Three key words—*mouth, domination,* and *identity*—express the ambivalence of Martin's state. The verbalizing and rationalizing mouth of reason becomes the sensuous mouth of chaos; domination or control of environment which had regulated his present becomes the compulsive need to dominate which had informed his past; identity achieved through rational control becomes irresponsible domination through the senses by which he is destroyed.

Like Lear, whom he misquotes in his delirium, Martin must divest himself of all the symbols of his manhood and individual humanity: shedding all his clothes, he sees "the last glimpse of gold braid," the sea-boot stocking, and he succumbs not only to the storm but also to the undifferentiated human impulse against which he had struggled in his search for identity. Stripped of reason and memory, man is Jack Merridew; he is expressed by the symbols of the pig's head and the dance of the rutting stag; he must see Piggy's

spattered brains on the rocks. Soft, sensuous, governed by sensation
and the primitive need to dominate, he loses his ability to control
and becomes the "poor forked animal," the victim of external pressure.

It would seem from these similar conclusions that "light" does
not triumph in Golding's universe. But in each novel, amazingly
parallel in construction, "light" is restored in a counterpoint. In
Lord of the Flies the rescuing naval officer restores identity and
order. Though he cannot obliterate the destruction of intelligence
and remove past unreason, he can restore the perspective of the
day. In *The Inheritors,* our attention shifts from the "people,"
corrupted at last, to the humans, who though /126/ corrupt, are
rationally aware and capable of taking over control and reorganiza-
tion of the world. But in *Pincher Martin* the counterpoint fulfills a
different function, although it serves similar ends. Having met
Martin in two deaths, we now confront him in a third. In the calm
light of day, which aptly contrasts with the darkness and madness
we have just passed through, two officers are faced with the problem
of living with and identifying Martin's shattered and decomposing
body. Mr. Campbell, the man who had found him ashore and had
"lived with him" for several days, is alert to the horror of death and
wonders if there is an identity beyond that of a broken human
shell. But Mr. Davidson, the graves registration officer, merely replies with the cryptic sentence: "whether he suffered or not . . ."
"Then don't worry about him. You saw the body. He didn't even
have time to kick off his sea-boots." Since, as we know, he had
kicked them off before the "second life" began, this sentence suggests not only obtuseness to the ways of dying; it also illuminates
retroactively the Gothic distortion through which the entire second
life becomes a *tour de force* in a world of possible but hypothetical
action; it makes of the conflict between "mouth" and "center"
which had compelled our attention, the hypothesis it must be. But
with bizarre irony, these words also comment upon man's state
which reduces his attempt to triumph through his identity to an
abrupt moment of dying. The officers, like Conrad's judicious com-
mentators, have spoken their post-mortems. But in his particular
universe of discourse, Martin had defined himself.

V

Despite their great differences in setting and theme, it appears
that all Golding's novels are variations of a similar idea—that of
the opposition between individual identity, obtained through
reason and memory, and a dim, pre-historic consciousness. The

eighteenth century contrast of civilization and primitivism is restated in twentieth century terms. These terms, couched in the phantastic visions of the Lord of the Flies, the Neanderthal Ogre (so ironically different from H. G. Wells' projection), and of Christopher Martin, are highly appropriate to a mid-century consciousness. For Golding renders a modern interpretation of what is human which could not have been accepted twenty or thirty years ago.

What is essential to man? Freud and Jung, both working within the Romantic tradition, viewed man's humanity as an inner conflict between the need for rational and social control on the one hand and the basic animal impulse, in an individual or collective sense, on the other. Being /127/ necessarily aware of both, Golding goes beyond them to approach the techniques of Kafka's *Metamorphosis* and Camus' *The Plague*. For after a significant transformation in his world, each of Golding's figures—the collective heroes of *Lord of the Flies* and *The Inheritors* and the individual hero of *Pincher Martin*—is stripped down to his essentials, his humanity. Confronting the self with hypothetical shifts in the universe of action, Golding forces it to demonstrate its capacity for rational control through which identity and existence can be assured. For to the recognitions of the thirties—that man's nature is sensuous and dominating, corrupt and cruel—he opposes the acts of intelligence and memory through which his individual manhood can be manifested.

The phantastic fancy of William Golding is not Coleridge's imagination. His encounters are not those of *The Ancient Mariner* or *Heinrich von Ofterdingen* or Hesse's *Steppenwolf*. They are not symbolic manifestations of inner states. Golding's fancy links up matters of fact in the most varied poses and presents them to the self as external, if distorted, objects of perceptual and moral awareness. For his fantasy works through distortion in the manner of the eighteenth century Gothic which deliberately changes the world while accepting its rational distinctions. Thus, in his novels as well as in his shorter work (like *The Brass Butterfly* recently produced as a play), Golding introduces significant changes in an external universe through whose control the self can define its existence. As a realist in a philosophical and in a literary sense, Golding reveals a fancy which rests on the separation of subject and object, quality and substance, self and other, to recreate a universe which a mid-century audience can accept.

from ONE MAN'S MEAT, THE IDEA OF INDIVIDUAL RESPONSIBILITY

JOHN BOWEN

---

*   *   *

William Golding has also written about cruelty, and there are those who see in his first novel *Lord of the Flies* only a social allegory of the way in which, when the civilized restraints which we impose upon ourselves are abandoned, the passions of anger, lust and fear wash across the mind, obliterating common-sense and care, and life once again becomes nasty, brutish and short. The book may certainly be read in this way, but it is also a religious allegory. The boys under Jack, the dark, handsome angel who used to lead the choir, not only kill Piggy, the "sage" who is blind without his glasses, and hunt Ralph, the confused ordinary boy who wants to do right but is not sure how; they also "sacrifice" Simon, the only one among them who has gone up to the top of the mountain and discovered the truth.

*   *   *

In *The Inheritors*, his second novel, Mr. Golding set himself what was primarily a technical problem. He took as his protagonists beings who expressed themselves in pictures, not in ideas, and described the action almost entirely from their point of view. Even in this book one may find a religious statement if one looks for it (but I am chary of making much of this; a critic can find almost anything if he looks for it), since the Neanderthal people of *The Inheritors*, who lack any ideas at all, lack among them the idea of sin and exist in primal innocence, while the more evolutionally advanced people who destroy them are certainly capable of sin. What is perhaps more important to realize about the people of *The Inheritors* is that they are destroyed chiefly because those who destroy them do not recognize that they are men at all.

Mr. Golding's third novel, *Pincher Martin*, is an overtly religious book, and cannot be read in any other way. The book is a piece of

John Bowen, "One Man's Meat, The Idea of Individual Responsibility," *Times Literary Supplement*, 2997 (August 7, 1959), xii-xiii. Reprinted by special permission.

subtle construction, so that it is not until near the end that we discover that what seems to be a factual account of a physical struggle for survival by a shipwrecked sailor on a lonely rock in the Atlantic is in fact being carried on entirely in the mind of the man himself as he drowns. The first moment when we begin to realize what is happening to him is when he recognizes that the rock is the exact shape of a decaying tooth in his own head. In the short space of time that it takes him to drown, Pincher Martin fights with God, making the affirmation that man can help himself, that man has the equipment to survive and to *be* man, and only when everything has failed does he, as an act of will, make his surrender.

Obviously Mr. Golding is not a very orthodox Christian, but equally obviously his religious views are not close to those of Mr. Wilson. But Pincher Martin's surrender is an /**xii**/ individual act of will, and so is Meg Eliot's decision to leave her brother; neither group religion nor group morality has anything to do with those decisions. /**xiii**/

BENDING OVER BACKWARDS

JOHN BOWEN

Let the novelist speak:

It seems to me that there's really very little point in writing a novel unless you do something that either you suspected you couldn't do, or which you are pretty certain nobody else has tried before. I don't think there's any point in writing two books that are like each other. . . .

I see, or I bring myself to see, a certain set of circumstances in a particular way. If it is the way everybody else sees them, then there is no point in writing a book.

Those two remarks were both made by Mr. William Golding to Mr. Frank Kermode in a discussion broadcast by the Third Programme. They illustrate both a strength and a weakness in Mr. Golding's work. On the one hand there is a curiosity, a sense of discovery, a continual pushing and questing to widen his own

John Bowen, "Bending over Backwards," *Times Literary Supplement*, 3,008 (October 23,1959), 608. Reprinted by special permission.

technical range and the range of the novel. We may get bad work
from Mr. Golding, but we are unlikely to get second-rate work,
because he is not interested in copying a style or moving predictably
over the rails of a familiar theme. On the other, there is a weakness
for the "gimmick," and an inability to recognize that all human
beings, all writers, are individuals, and that, provided one writes
from one's *own* vision and through one's *own* observation (which
are not at all the same), even the most conventional ideas will be
coloured by one's individual appreciation of them. Shakespeare,
after all, borrowed many of his ideas, as well as his plots.

In any case, although each of William Golding's novels has been
set within the framework of a different technical problem, now
that, with the publication this week of *Free Fall*, we have four of
them, it is possible to look at the total work and to try to find a
unifying principle in it. Perhaps, deceived by Mr. Golding's way
of growing, we have thought that the themes of these books have
been more different than they are. Other good novelists have grown
by a steady widening and deepening of their technical resources.
Mr. Golding has tried to put down a pattern, like a child playing
battleships, and to join it up. But at the centre of the pattern (or
behind, if you will, the pencil that makes it) there is only one
child, one Mr. Golding.

Lord of the Flies, Mr. Golding's first novel, and in many ways
his most successful with the public, took Ballantyne's *Coral Island*,
said, "Nonsense! It couldn't ever have been like that," turned it on
its head, and stuffed its pockets with meaning. On one level, *Lord
of the Flies* was a straightforward, terrifying tale about the way in
which the patterns of civilized life break down when civilized checks
(the grown-up world) are removed, and original savagery begins to
stir again. On the level of metaphor, the book told how sin destroys
the garden of innocence and kills the saints—for Ballantyne's
Peterkin has become Simon (Simon called Peter), who tries to tell
the truth and is slaughtered as a beast. Mr. Golding himself has said,
"Originally I think in metaphor," and, although the imposition of
patterns of metaphor upon work in which it was unintended or
at least unconscious is a great game for academics, we must allow it
for Mr. Golding's work.

The second novel, *The Inheritors*, was already more difficult. Up
to the last few pages, the whole novel was written from the point
of view of a people (Neanderthal Man) to whom a logical sequence
of thought was not natural; they thought in pictures and in conditioned memory. For those who admired the book, it was easy for
an appreciation of the technical achievement to get in the way of

what the technique was conveying. For those who were not prepared to make the effort of entering the minds of its characters (it
was not a great effort, but those whose interests are more social and
conventional than personal may have found it so), it was easy
to write the book off as science fiction, in which the same sort of
technical problem is often met though seldom so successfully
solved.

But once we look at the *what* of *The Inheritors* and forget the
how, we see that already the difference between it and *Lord of the
Flies* is not so great. Once again, something has been stood on its
head—after *Coral Island*, H. G. Wells's *Outline of History:* Wells
and Ballantyne, you see, have got it wrong, and must be put right.
And again there is a preoccupation with innocence. Mr. Kermode,
in the discussion which has already been quoted, has suggested:

> It seems to me that *The Inheritors* develops a theme which is extremely
> original and for which you can scarcely have any kind of literary support
> in the past . . . which is the idea . . . that the man who meditates is a
> guilty man, that the power of meditation, in the sense in which we under-
> stand meditation, is an aspect of human guilt, and that human guilt is
> inseparable from a particular kind of human development (Golding:
> "Umm! Umm!").

Once again sin is something which has come out of the nature of
man *as he now is,* and has defiled and destroyed the garden. It is a
twisting of Rousseau to a godly end.

There is an ambiguity in this view of things, an ambiguity which
becomes more apparent in Mr. Golding's third novel, *Pincher
Martin,* and it is an ambiguity of which he himself may not be
entirely conscious—as Mr. Angus Wilson has recently pointed out,
also in a Third Programme discussion, it is precisely this sort of
unconscious ambiguity which gives the English novel a textural
richness which we do not always find in those of the more lucid
French. Mr. Golding himself has said, "I regard myself as a religious, but possibly incompetently religious man." In *Lord of the
Flies* not only Simon was hunted by the wicked; so was Ralph, the
hero, who stands in a childish way for the values of the developed
man, the absent adult world; and Piggy, the rational boy, was killed
as Simon was killed. In *The Inheritors,* a sudden shift of viewpoint
at the end shows us the new kind of men as they appear to themselves. It is another characteristic these four different books have in
common, that each has a "gimmick" end (the word is Mr. Golding's)
in which the viewpoint is shifted, and the reader is wrenched suddenly from the identification he has made so far.

The wrench is strongest in *Pincher Martin,* perhaps because the identification has been strongest. Mr. Golding has said of Pincher:

> "He's fallen man, yes. Very much fallen—he's fallen more than most, you see. . . I went out of my way to damn Pincher as much as I could by making him the most unpleasant, the nastiest type I could think of, and I was very interested to see how critics all over the place said "Well, yes. We are like that."

Pincher is a pincher; he has stolen everything in his life, both things and ideas from other people. But his real name is Christopher and it is by this name that God calls him at the end.

What could be clearer than this story of a man being stripped of all that he has stolen before he can bring himself to accept, as an act of will, the call of God, the Father? But it is not simple; it is not clear. In his struggle for survival on that rock, in his struggle *against* God, Pincher becomes Prometheus, becomes an incarnation of fallible, torturing and tortured, ordinary man, fighting his individual, courageous, haphazard, improvising fight against God, against the rocks, against the sea. It seems not to have been intended, but it is there as surely as it is there in *Moby Dick,* and perhaps Mr. Golding's "incompetently religious" novels are the fruit of an internal struggle with God which can be reasonably compared with Melville's. "To a large extent," he has said, "I've cut myself off from contemporary literary life, and gained in one sense by it." There, too, it might be Melville speaking.

Mr. Golding's publishers tell us that his latest novel, *Free Fall,* is set in the present, but this is not really so; the action of the book moves from the 1920s to the Second World War, and none of the topical preoccupations of the 1950s is to be found in it. Nevertheless, there is, as we might expect, a new technical task, though not such a very difficult one. This is Mr. Golding's first social novel. The boys' society in *Lord of the Flies* was isolated, almost experimentally so. Lok and Fa in *The Inheritors* had only the society of a tiny tribe. Pincher Martin was alone on his imaginary rock. But Sammy Mountjoy (again you will notice the importance of the names) was born in a Kentish slum, went to school, made friends and enemies, was adopted by a High Church homosexual rector, seduced one girl and married another, went in and out of the Communist Party, became a painter and did well at it, went to war, was captured, and betrayed his comrades—or was prepared to betray; it is not quite clear which, but the distinction is unimportant. He tells his story (again a difference) in the first person, and the effect of this is not to make Sammy more real but to spoil the effect of the usual "gimmick" ending, in which the shock does not shock because, as long as the same person is telling his own story, the viewpoint cannot really be changed.

Again the theme is innocence and retribution. The book is all flashbacks, as Sammy casts back into his memory to discover the moment when he first sinned—the first "important" sin by which he lost his innocence and committed himself to something worse which must inevitably follow. Sammy's "fall" is free, just as Adam did not have to (surely no behaviourist could say so?) eat the apple, and just as the fall was free and had to be paid for, so a return to grace could be freely made by confession and the admission of error. The casting-back process in the novel reminds us more of the psychologist's couch than of the confessor's box, but although the technique of *Free Fall* may have some kinship with free association, the attitude is more Catholic than Freudian.

But the book, unfortunately, is a disappointment. Of course it should be read; of course there are good things in it. Mr. Golding's understanding of children has always been good, and these children take their places as living beings within the pattern of the novel. The sense of fairness is there, which gives us a lovable (but essentially wrong) rationalist, and a hateable (but essentially right) teacher of Religious Knowledge, and which understands that nasty people are imprisoned in their own nastiness and why. The set-pieces of imaginative powerful writing are there, and we are taken frighteningly, believably enough, into a mind which is about to break down. But statements like, "If man is his own creator, then good and evil is decided by majority vote," are question-begging statements, and only beg the question even further by being part of a first-person narrative. And the climax of the book, Mountjoy's act of betrayal against himself and another self, the act which every successive remembered incident has led towards ("Here?" he asks himself, and the reply comes back, "Not here."), becomes oddly unimportant and obvious, unimportant in any real sense to Mountjoy, obvious to us.

It is as if Mr. Golding has been trapped by *hubris*. He has said he is not interested in writing what has been written before, as if all his fellows walking their more usual technical paths but lighting them with their own personal lights were doing something he scorned to do, and now he has written a social novel (which has been done before), a novel of memory (which has been done before), and has done it less well than some of his fellows; Joyce Cary

could have done better. Nevertheless, the book continues to extend
Mr. Golding's range. It is possible to profit from this sort of defeat.
The reader can profit, since even poor Golding is better than most
other novels published nowadays. And Mr. Golding may profit,
simply by having learnt from it—by having learnt humility among
other things, and humility can be a great source of strength. /608/

THE STRANGE CASE OF MR GOLDING
AND HIS CRITICS

IAN GREGOR AND MARK
KINKEAD-WEEKES

*'On an occasion like this, it is more than a moral duty to
speak one's mind. It becomes a pleasure'!* (WILDE)

I

On October 23rd, 1959, Mr William Golding's novel *Free Fall*
was published. The occasion is worth recalling. It was distinguished,
in the first place, by its publicity—leading articles in all the 'serious'
newspapers and journals, photographs of the author, radio and
television discussions. Not for some considerable time had an
English novel enjoyed so conspicuous a launching. Unfortunately,
the ceremony was not really a happy one. Mr Golding was an
'important' novelist, but *Free Fall,* it seemed, was a failure. He had
reached his greatest publicity only to find his artistic fortunes at a
low ebb. There is no reason why a novelist's career, however important, should necessarily be a record of gradually unfolding genius, but the curious feature in Mr Golding's case was that *Free
Fall* was the logical culmination of the earlier novels, which the
reviewers were recalling with intellectual nostalgia. Further, though
nearly everyone was clear that *Free Fall* was a failure, no one
·seemed quite clear just what the novel was about.

Ian Gregor and .Mark Kinkead-Weekes, "The Strange Case of Mr. Golding
and His Critics," *The Twentieth Century,* CLXVII (February, 1960), 115-25.
Reprinted by special permission.

The present article has been prompted by two reflections arising out of these circumstances. The first one to try and say quite simply what *Free Fall* seems to be about and why it takes the shape it does. The second, to offer a small anthology of contemporary novel reviewing, in a case where a considerable number of leading reviewers had been brought together because, in Mr Toynbee's words, 'Mr Golding has become a novelist to be scrutinized with the utmost respect and to be /115/ interrogated with the sharpness which respect should earn'. This article is offered as a gloss on Mr. Toynbee's salutary admonition.

II

Free Fall is Mr Golding's fourth novel and it allows us to see in a new perspective what Mr Golding was up to in its predecessors. The three tales—*Lord of the Flies, The Inheritors, Pincher Martin*—were deliberate and self-contained attempts to pin-point a single target, a number of radar stations giving Golding the shape of what he wanted to fire at and the range. *Free Fall* is a frontal attack on a target long since determined. This implies a different kind of equipment and a different kind of plan.

In the earlier novels we find the deliberate isolation of strongly defined subjects from the mesh of complicating circumstance that surrounds them in 'real life'. All the novels ask, fundamentally, the same question 'What is man?' and their myth-like structure enables Golding continually to direct our attention to Man, rather than 'a man' or the relationships of men. In *Lord of the Flies* (1954), Mr Golding occupies Ballantyne's Coral Island, and declares its way of seeing life to be 'unrealistic' because it fails to take into account the evil inherent in the nature of man. Ballantyne's adventure story becomes the basis of an expanded metaphor about human existence. In *The Inheritors* (1955) Mr Golding again goes to literature to provide himself with a setting. Taking the chapter on Neanderthal man in Wells's *Outline of History*, which Mr Golding regards as 'the rationalist gospel in excelsis', Mr Golding treats it in a way similar to his treatment of *Coral Island*. It is again unrealistic, fathering on to our predecessors *our* base passions and cruelties. Mr Golding reverses the account. Just as the boys in *Lord of the Flies* are the prey of their own natures, not as in Ballantyne of pirates and savages, so 'homo sapiens' in *The Inheritors* expresses the evil already within him in his destruction of his innocent predecessors. 'Innocent' because they have not had to pay the price of human consciousness, which is guilt. In *Lord of the Flies* and *The Inheritors* the main emphasis is on the presence of evil as concomitant with the nature of man, in other words, on a state of being; with *Pincher Martin* (1956) the emphasis shifts to the consequences of such a state. Ostensibly concerned with a drowning /116/ sailor in mid-Atlantic, the novel's real purpose is to show what happens when a man whose whole nature has been centered on himself, dies. The murderous nature lives on, fighting for its own identity in face of the mercy of God, a pair of claws clutched together in defiance of love, which can be seen only as a black lightning of destruction. Christopher, the Christ-bearer, has turned into Pincher, the epitome of greed and self-will. Man has constructed his own hell.

It is under these three different lenses that Mr Golding has examined the nature of man. *Lord of the Flies* gives a grim endorsement to the child as 'father of the man'; *The Inheritors* sees man in relation to the life which preceded him, *Pincher Martin,* in relation to the life that awaits him. What has been carefully excluded is the central relationship of Man in relation to Man. It is precisely to this subject that Mr Golding addresses himself in *Free Fall.* The autonomy of the book is not compromised by saying that the three novels which preceded it have created the meaningful space into which it must fit. Inevitably, it takes up and re-orchestrates themes from the earlier novels. *Lord of the Flies* makes its ghost-presence felt in the school-room world; *The Inheritors* in the distinction between 'the innocence' of Johnny Spragge and 'the evil' of Philip Arnold; *Pincher Martin* in Samuel (the chosen one of God) becoming Sammy, using people for his own pleasure, turning the spiritual Beatrice into Miss Ifor, another creation of the murderous self.

These deliberate echoes of the earlier novels are employed here for a new purpose, a purpose which seeks to enrich Mr Golding's conception of myth. He seeks to invest contemporary, naturalistic scene with the cosmic implications that his previous isolated and remote settings were designed to evoke. Mr Golding, with these three novels behind him, looks in *Free Fall* at the nature of man with the lens of a social novelist. This gives the novel the *appearance* of a psychological fiction. Essentially, however, the book is composed of the same material as the earlier novels, only this time instead of choosing a coral island, or prehistory, or a drowning sailor, Mr Golding selects a number of archetypal naturalistic situations in the twentieth century and gives them a sufficiently realistic top-dressing, not so much added to the myth, as a condition of its growth. The reason is surely to convince us of the centrality and urgency of his mythical account to modern experience. The fiction in *Free* /117/ *Fall* is an amplifier built into the perennial myth that Golding has constantly sought to explore and understand—the myth of paradise lost.

III

We are presented in the first paragraph of *Free Fall* with 252 of its 253 pages in miniature.

> I have walked by stalls in the market place where books, dog-eared and faded from their purple, have burst with a white hosanna. I have seen people crowned with a double crown, holding in either hand the crook and flail, the power and the glory. I have understood how the scar becomes a star, I have felt the flake of fire fall, miraculous and pentecostal. My yesterdays walk with me. They keep step, they are grey faces that peer over my shoulder. I live on Paradise Hill, ten minutes from the station, thirty seconds from the shops and the local. Yet I am a burning amateur, torn by the irrational and incoherent, violently searching and self-condemned.

The first response to this is likely to be that it is unbearably pretentious, overblown Dylan Thomas. But the second response should be, strengthened by every page of the book, that it is a figure in which every element of the 'myth' that explains Sammy Mountjoy is crisply sounded. These are the elements which the whole 'fiction' of his life will develop into full vision for us, and will embody in experience. The 'book' that Sammy writes will contain the Lenten purple and the white hosanna of his life, will reveal the crook of the Shepherd and the flail of justice operating on him. It will show how scars may become stars, how a man may experience through his tears the transfiguration of the pentecostal vision. It records a knowledge of an old myth made new by being actualized and realized in experience.

But the paragraph also reveals an irreconcilable dichotomy between the 'real' world of the flesh and the equally 'real' world of the spirit. It reveals a mind which is conscious of both but cannot make them fuse. Most important of all, this is a mind that cannot escape from its own sense of guilt, a mind haunted by the grey faces of its past. The pattern of the myth is true, but it does not include forgiveness. To get the point of this first paragraph is to get the point of the whole book. /118/ Sammy has already some insight into the truth of the fall, the judgement, and the transfiguration of the earth through tears; but in seeking to realize the myth in its full implications in his own life, what he is looking for is forgiveness and reconciliation. It is precisely because he cannot reconcile the two halves of his split world that he is a 'burning amateur'. It is precisely because he is self-condemned and cannot find forgiveness that he is 'violently searching'. The 'monstrous consciousness' that we set out to actualize and explore is the experience of a split world, in which spiritual insight has only entered to condemn.

The search falls into three movements. It distorts chronology because its logic is not the logic of time, but of spiritual insight, in which certain truths can only be grasped *after* certain others have been realized—however the events that embody them may be ranged on the chronological scale.

The first movement, given the monstrous consciousness, asks 'Where did it begin?' In chronological time the laws of cause and effect operate, and we can explain a man in terms of his heredity and environment. But Sammy knows, with Milton, that man is not ultimately determined, that he is created 'sufficient to have stood, but free to fall'. So, the question formulates itself, where, hidden inscrutably in the facts of the case, is the point at which the infant Samuel, living God's work on earth on Paradise Hill, chose to become Sammy Mons Veneris, the destroyer, violently self-condemned? He examines his childhood and finds it innocent. The two-foot view of Rotten Row shows a filthy slum, but a community, shows woman as Ma, earthy and amoral but unexploiting, and an Evie whose sexuality is innocent fantasy. Man is Johnny and Sammy, brutal gang leaders without brutality; two starry-eyed ragamuffins who experience tragedy and transfiguration without understanding either. The world is sordid, ugly; contains death cruelty, suffering and wrong. Sammy steals, bullies, tries to desecrate an altar. But across his childhood lies the colour of innocence where there cannot be evil because it cannot be chosen or understood. Only Philip is evil, because he is conscious, and because he is conscious he was never a child. Moreover, innocence has nothing to do with the grey faces. Because it cannot understand it needs no forgiveness, and is incapable of forgiving.

Yet, at the point when Sammy entered decisively on his seduction of Beatrice, crossing a red light on a bridge, he sees /119/ that he was already determined. That relationship is the source of the grey faces of guilt and condemnation, but freedom to choose had already been lost. There is no moral relativity in the treatment of this episode, the experience is seen in both its sordidness and its sadness . . . the moral chaos of the Communist Party, the sexual frustration, the baffled attempt to love and communicate, the running away. There is an emphasis on the girl's inability to respond, but the inadequacy of Sammy's understanding of her is firmly placed for us as his artist's eye picks out the aura of blessedness, which his sensual eye chose to ignore. But there is no blame, for the Sammy who did these things was already incapable of acting otherwise. The agonized search for the exact location of the point of choice breaks down. *'Here? Not here?'* In childhood it is too early, by the beginning of the desecration of Beatrice it is already too late.

The search breaks down because insight into the beginning can only come *after* insight into the end. Sammy has to work *backwards* from the experience out of which the insight of the book's opening paragraph originally came. It was in a prisoner of war camp that the full enormity of what he had chosen to become, was first revealed to him. Interrogated by a Gestapo psychologist, Sammy is made to see himself as a man who can neither believe in the Spirit, nor in disbelief. Therefore, the temptation to betray himself and his fellow men is a parody of the temptation of Christ. Christ could be tempted because he could say 'yes' or 'no'; could refer temptations to standards good or bad. Sammy can be neither a villain nor a hero because he does not know what he believes, does not know what he knows. He simply cannot answer, so he is thrown in pitch darkness into a cell in which there is only himself. In his terror he uses his imagination to torture himself, and what the torturing imagination reveals is the true nature of the mind that imagines. At last we realize that for Sammy there is only one central reality—sex—and consequently only one overwhelming fear, the fear for his privates. *This* is what he has become. The revelation is symbolic in two ways. The worst thing that he can imagine put into the cell to torture him is the multilated male organ which he thinks he finds in the centre of the floor. But the gruesome thing is also a reflection of himself . . . that, severed from complex humanity, is what he has chosen to be. Dr Halde, 'Dr Slope', has taken him up to the pinnacle of the temple to plunge him down into the cesspit of himself. In a /120/ scream of horror, Sammy cries out of the depths of his being to a place he did not know existed, 'Help me'. And the cell door opens.

In the most beautiful and solidly realized chapter of the book, Sammy staggers out, blinded by the tears of shame and horror, into the world of the camp. It is sordid and dusty, evidence of man's inhumanity to man. But through the tears of shame the world is transfigured, becomes startlingly and miraculously beautiful as though it had just issued from the hand of the Creator. It is seen with blinding love through the dead eyes of a destroyed self. Sammy's fellow prisoners are seen as the 'Kings of Egypt' who had always been his image of the glory of man. (But they are kings of Egypt not of Israel, seen by one who has just staggered out of the Red Sea.) Dead to himself in shame, suffused with love for God's world and loathing for himself, Sammy Mountjoy knows the pentecostal vision. 'I was visited by a flake of fire, miraculous and pentecostal; and the fire transmuted me, once and for ever.'

Only now that the re-experiencing memory has thoroughly grasped the exact nature and significance of the fall, is Sammy free to locate it and explain it. The confused guilt surrounding the grey face of Beatrice, the accusations from his frustrated love that blurred the image of his sin, are brought beneath a sharper focus. Sammy can see through them to the deeper truth of the exact nature of his choice, and its significance.

The choice was both partly conditioned, and ultimately free. It was conditioned by the views of reality presented to him by his teachers; the ordered physical universe of scientifically predictable cause and effect that Nick Shales taught; and the spiritual world of Miss Rowena Pringle's scripture lessons on Moses and the burning bush. But Sammy chose between them, not as they were, but as they were presented. He chose Nick's instinctive goodness and love which formed no part of his philosophy; he rejected the tortured and torturing spinster who foisted her sexual nastiness on him and constantly belied her teaching. Yet no complexity of conditioning accounts for the choice. The fall *was* ultimately free. For Sammy, aflame with desire for Beatrice Ifor, took from his teachers only what he needed, in order to deny any realities beyond that desire. Having chosen Nick's goodness rather than his philosophy he used the philosophy to deny the goodness. On the other hand, Nick's failure to relate sex to goodness is seized on and used in a /121/ deification of lust. (Nick, as his name implies, is another form of the Tempter without meaning to be. He offers Sammy the opportunity to choose evil.) The final condition of freedom in Sammy's choice is, however—rising sheer away from his intellectual and moral confusions—the certainty of his *own* knowledge of what Beatrice is like. Knowing fully that she is a *fusion* of the spirit and the body, that she is both Beatrice and I-for, he chooses to deny her blessedness and impose on her complexity, the simplicity of his lust, the ultimate selfishness. He chooses freely to deny God and good and affirm lust, exclaiming in parody of Milton's Satan, 'Musk, be thou my good'. His headmaster has told him, 'If you want something enough you can always get it, provided you are willing to make the appropriate sacrifice'. Sammy is willing. What he is prepared to sacrifice is 'Everything'.

Yet there was a sting in the tail of the headmaster's advice. 'But what you get is never quite what you thought; and sooner or later is always regretted'. The result of 'Musk, be thou my good' for Sammy himself, was the revelation of the cell. The last experience of the reality of the myth is the realization of what the result of choice looks like outside himself. He finds Beatrice again only to find that she is no longer Beatrice, whom he rejected, but purely Miss Ifor, what he chose. What Miss Ifor *is* is an inmate of a lunatic asylum, is mindless and animal, like the little Mongol Minnie of his schoolboy memory who was only minimally human. (Beatrice, like all the other characters, is there not as a personality in her own right but as a focus on Sammy. This is not psychological fiction, the function she serves is to actualize myth in a carefully limited human complexity. She is mainly there—though she is psychologically explicable to some extent—to focus sharply the proposition 'To choose Ifor and reject Beatrice is ultimately to choose Minnie').

The book has filled out its opening paragraph, so that it no longer seems merely rhetorical. Having fully understood the nature of what he chose to become, having located the choice and explained it, and having formulated its results, Sammy sums up again with crystal clarity the elements of his myth. (He has lived the world of the flesh and been smitten by the insight of the spirit. He has looked at the world through eyes transfigured in shame, but turned inward they cannot forgive the nauseous reality of himself. We can see now the tragedy of his early formulation: 'Yet who but the injured can forgive an /122/ injury? And how if the lines at that particular exchange are dead?') At the top of the last page of the novel, Sammy has *not* succeeded in reconciling his tragically dual world, or in finding forgiveness. 'For this mode which we must call the spirit breathes through the universe and does not touch it; touches only the dark things, held prisoner, incommunicado, *touches, judges, sentences, and passes on*. . . . Both worlds are real. *There is no bridge*'. (Our italics.)

But *Free Fall* does not end at the top of its last page. It ends, as all Mr Golding's novels do, with a 'gimmick' ending that is far more than a gimmick because it asks the reader to look at the whole book again with different eyes. Sammy has left out of the whole shuffle and coil of his search the one vital incident which alone can complete it and make it meaningful, as an account of the facts of human experience. His memory now gives it back to him, and we leave him puzzling over its meaning. But to us the meaning should be clear. In the agony of his self-knowledge he cried out for help, *and the cell door opened.* He found himself facing not the Judge he expected, but Pity, which knew, though it spoke cryptically in comic guttural English that the judge is less than the whole truth about life because he 'does not know about peoples'. He heard a voice say 'Heraus', go forth in freedom from the cell of yourself. He was asked 'Have you heard?' which we ought to be able to interpret 'Have you heard that you are free, forgiven?'

In fact we can now see the whole point of the book has been to make us realize the *gap* between the myth of fall and judgement and the whole truth of human experience, and take the leap across it ahead of Sammy. It is like a jigsaw puzzle with one piece missing; the eye cannot rest on the pattern but is compelled remorselessly to the missing shape which the incomplete pattern defines. No other method could do this quite so forcefully. And the fact that this is presented so cryptically, and we leave Sammy puzzling, is not a gratuitous difficulty. It is supremely tactful. *Is* it not a greater mystery than the 'Sphinx's riddle' of the nature of man, that the Sammy-Mountjoy-in-man can be forgiven? He offers his tragic duality and receives an incredible gift. It is the miraculous operation of grace abounding that alone can fuse Sammy's split world and offer forgiveness, though he cannot see the fusion or accept the grace. Yet its evidence is *there* and the whole purpose of the book is, precisely, to point to it. /123/

IV

This then is the kind of book the leading reviewers of virtually all the 'serious' press and periodicals found lying on their tables one week at the beginning of last October. What they made of it must surely have serious claims to be considered a 'locus classicus' in the annals of irresponsible reviewing. The ineptitude of the comment was rivalled only by the bland confidence with which it was delivered. It was possible to read eight reviews of the novel and be left with the impression that Mr Golding had written an ambitious, incoherent novel, written it badly and injected it, for good measure, with gratuitous difficulties. And this, about a novel which has the demonstrable precision and purpose of a finely jewelled watch. (Only Mr Kermode's review in *The Spectator* and Mr Malcolm Bradbury's in *Punch,* both brief, were perceptive and helpful about *Free Fall.*) Unfortunately, we have no space to docu-

ment the reviewing in detail, but perhaps the following 'flori
legium' will suggest its drift and tenor.

The first group of quotations indicate the way in which certain
'difficulties' in reading are translated simply as 'blunders'. The
question 'why' seems never to have been asked. Of the time-sequence

> Chronology . . . is played about with in a way that creates deliberate
> difficulties for the reader, but it is *impossible to see* (our italics) that this
> device serves any purpose.' (Mr Philip Toynbee—*The Observer*.)
> . . . there is a central obscurity about what happens in the prisoner of
> war camp. (Mr Graham Hough—*The Listener*.)

On the style

> Mr Toynbee took the carefully 'fugal' opening paragraph, placed
> against it a plain passage of narrative and commented, 'the obvious
> clothed in purple followed by the obvious wearing nothing at all'

On the point of view

> But statements like 'If man is his own creator, then good and evil is
> decided by majority vote' are question-begging statements, and only beg
> the question even further by being part of a first person narrative.'
> (*The Times Literary Supplement*.)
> Like most painters, Sammy is no great shakes as a thinker. This is un-
> fortunate, because most of the book is Sammy thinking. (Mr Duval Smith
> —*New Statesman*.) /124/

And then we have the completed judgements, as interesting in
their tone as in their content:

> Mr Golding may have walked with kings, but he has lost the common
> touch which is particularly appreciated by English readers. (Mr J. D.
> Scott—*The Sunday Times*.)
> So far as the theme is concerned, everything is inconclusive. Mr Golding
> has been unable to hand down the tablets, to give us decisive answers.
> (Mr Roy Perrott—*The Guardian*.)
> Where did he lose his way? The novel has no answer to this question
> which is easily arrived at. And that's why you'll remember the book
> once you've read it. (Mr Rees—*Time and Tide*.)
> This book seems to me a failure in almost every direction. . . . The
> book is dull, and dull in the most disturbing way—dull as Charles Mor-
> gan's *The Fountain* is dull. That is to say that the machinery of lan-
> guage, presentation and form is large and noisy out of all proportion
> to the work it is doing. . . . Can he now retreat from this misfortune in
> order to advance on his own path? (*The Observer*.)
> It is possible to profit from this sort of defeat. The reader can profit,
> since even poor Golding is better than most novels published nowadays.
> And Mr Golding may profit simply by having learnt it—by having learnt

humility among other things—that humility can be a great source of
strength. (*The Times Literary Supplement*.)
Some of the congregation are staring curiously at the preacher. Why
does the perspiration stand out so? they wonder. Why is he shouting?
What does it signify that wild look in his eye? (*New Statesman*.)

If indeed there is a 'wild look' in Mr Golding's eye, the reason
would certainly not be far to seek. /125/

NOVELS OF A RELIGIOUS MAN

SAM HYNES

"I think of myself," William Golding said recently, "as a religious
man." This is in itself not a very unusual statement; there must be
many novelists who, in their private hearts, think of themselves
as religious. But Golding is unusual, perhaps unique among English
novelists, in the degree to which his religiousness informs the fabric
of his novels. For the English novel has not been, traditionally, a
medium for the expression of religious ideas; its strength has been
rather in its representation of society. The English, it has been
said, are afraid of metaphysics, and this is nowhere clearer than in
their fiction: they have their Fielding and their Dickens, but they
have no Dostoevski, no Melville, no Mann, no Camus.
    Or at least they didn't have until Golding appeared; by which I
don't mean to suggest that Golding has achieved what these great
masters achieved, but simply that he shares with them certain basic
and "un-English" themes, that like them he is concerned not with
man in relation to society, but with man in relation to his universe, and to himself. The problems which are central in his novels
are the eternal questions of the religious man: the nature of good
and evil, guilt and responsibility, the meaning of death, and free
will. His concern with such questions, and the ways which he has
found to pose these questions in fiction, set him apart from other
English novelists, and make his work both interesting and important.
    The essential technical problem for a "religious novelist" is a

    Sam Hynes, "Novels of a Religious Man," *Commonweal*, LXXI (March 18,
1960), 673-75. Reprinted by special permission.

simple one (though the answer is far from simple). The form which religious fiction has traditionally taken in English literature is allegory—as in *Everyman* and *Pilgrim's Progress.* Allegory has the advantage of being clear and easily interpreted; but it has the disadvantage of being dead. Except for the odd beast fable, like Orwell's *Animal Farm,* it has not been a possible form for fiction since Bunyan. The modern reader expects in his fiction a surface of literal action, credible characters, and a believable human situation, and allegory provides none of these. But on the other hand, if the religious novelist is to realize his theme lucidly and wholly, he must find a way of avoiding the clutter and irrelevance of ordinary existence, of what Forster called "the world of telegrams and anger."

Golding has attacked this problem in a number of ingenious ways; indeed his technical ingenuity is in itself enough to make his work worth reading in a time when novelistic technique seems otherwise to have come pretty much to a halt. In his first three novels, Golding isolated his characters either in time or in space, placing them in primitive situations from which the telegrams and anger would quite naturally be excluded, and in which the immediate problem would be simply survival. Then by manipulating action and symbols, he made it clear that survival must be taken to mean more than the preservation of life; the castaway on his island might first ask "What must I do to be saved?" and mean it quite literally, but he could not prevent the question expanding to its full religious dimensions.

By carefully preserving the primitive simplicity of the literal action, Golding was able to create in these three books narratives which are essentially myths, which strike through to the deepest roots of our existence—to fear, to hunger, and to the will to survive. And because these roots are universally in men, he has managed through them to give fictional form to religious themes, and to make them at once immediate and timeless. For it is through myths, after all, that the substance of religious belief is most directly communicated.

Golding's first novel, *Lord of the Flies,* is the story of a plane-load of choir boys, being evacuated from some unspecified war, who crash on an uninhabited island, and of their efforts to survive in a world without adults or the rules of adults. Golding has used the framework, and the innocent expectations, of a boy's adventure story (the boys in the novel recognize the similarity of their situation to that in Ballantyne's *Coral Island),* but has turned the whole thing upside down, by adding the one element which boys in adventure stories never have—evil, the will to destroy.

As the boys begin to realize their situation, they begin to retro-
gress from the civilized, rational actions of a human society to the
savage and irrational actions of a pack. The process by which the
choir boys become murderous, blood-thirsty animals is a terrifying
one, and it is most terrifying because one sees that the savages
existed all the time, under the choir robes, and /673/ that the conflict which the novel sets between "the world of hunting, tactics,
fierce exhilaration, skill" and "the world of longing and baffled
commonsense" is a fundamental human struggle which never ends.
The story, that is to say, is a myth of man's dual nature.

No intelligent reader would have much trouble taking the novel
this far, but Golding would like the interpretation of the myth
to be even more specific. For example, he places on the top of his
island's mountain a dead parachutist; the boys, seeing the body
and the billowing chute in half-light, think it some hideous monster, "the Beast," and fear it and make blood sacrifices to it. One
may be momentarily troubled by the probability of the parachutist's
being up there, but symbolically the Beast works very well; it is
important, for instance, that the Beast should be in reality human,
for what the boys fear is in fact in themselves. But Golding apparently meant even more than this; in a recent interview he described the body on the mountain as representing "history, the
past," though it is hard to see how a reader could arrive at such a
conclusion. Similarly, he would wish us to understand of a boy
called Simon, who has a vision in which the Beast tells him, "I'm
part of you," who discovers what the Beast really is, and who is
orgiastically murdered by the other boys when he tries to tell them
the truth, that he is Simon-called-Peter, a saint, "somebody who
voluntarily embraces his fate." But this is putting a great deal of
weight on a name, and without the specific association the meaning
of Simon's knowledge and death is clear enough. These examples
give some indication of the density with which Golding has constructed his myths; but they also indicate a danger which must be
always present for the myth-maker—the temptation to impose local
and arbitrary meanings beyond what the myth will bear.

Golding has said, "I don't think there's any point in writing two
books that are like each other," and so far he has managed in each
of his books to set himself a new and difficult technical problem. If
the problem of *Lord of the Flies*—to make a myth of human duality which will at the same time be a true version of schoolboy
consciousness—seems difficult, the problem of his second novel, *The
Inheritors,* seems impossible. For here he assumed as his point of
view the pre-consciousness of Neanderthal man.

These creatures, "the people" as they call themselves, are first seen seeking survival in a new hunting-ground. There they discover, for the first time, "the new people," men, and are in the end destroyed by them. The people, being pre-human, are essentially instinctual, and use their minds only with great difficulty; they are the innocent. The new people can use their minds to reason, to make weapons and utensils, and to kill; they are the inheritors of paradise, human and therefore touched by evil and guilt. One might say that the novel is an alternative Garden of Eden myth, using the materials of anthropology instead of the Book of Genesis—a myth in which the Original Sin is man's first premeditated act.

Golding handles his Neanderthal point of view with superlative skill, and as a *tour de force* the novel is a brilliant technical achievement. But the reader must not be lulled into thinking that this is all irrelevant far-away-and-long-ago whimsy; and to make this point clear Golding shifts, in the last chapter, from the last innocent creature, grieving alone, to one of the new people, whose mind, full of anxieties, fears, and lust, and haunted by the death of innocence, we must recognize as our own.

When Golding changed the title of his third novel from *Pincher Martin* in the English edition to *The Two Deaths of Christopher Martin* in the American, he seemed to be acknowledging a weakness in the conception of the book. For though the book is about two deaths—a material one and a spiritual one—this is not made clear until the very last sentence of the novel, at which point one is compelled to go back and re-read the book in the light of the new information.

What happens is this: as the novel begins, a man is struggling in the sea, where he has apparently been blown from his torpedoed destroyer. He is determined to survive; he goes through the proper survival procedure—kicks off his sea boots and inflates his life jacket —and at last reaches a barren rock, on which he attempts to save himself. The rest of the novel is an account of his efforts at survival there, interspersed with flashbacks to his past. We gradually learn that he is an entirely vicious man, one who devours experience and people, a depraved appetite of a man, and we recognize a certain appropriateness in his hungry fate on the tooth-like rock, as he is gradually reduced, by exposure to the elements and to the truth of his own nature, from humanity to a pair of hideous, lobster-like claws.

Then, in the last chapter, a naval officer visits a remote Scottish island to pick up a body which has been washed ashore; the body

is Pincher Martin's. An old fisherman asks the officer if the dead
man had suffered, and the officer replies, "He didn't even have
time to kick off his seaboots." But we thought we saw him kick
them off on page two. This means that everything from that page
on that we have been taking as a literal survival story has happened
in fact *after* Martin's death, and must be taken as an account of
another kind of attempt at survival, the survival of a soul before
God.

Martin is a pincher, a devourer, and even after death he is determined to preserve his mortal identity. Martin's torments on the
rock, then, are the torments of a soul as it is stripped to its essential
nature—symbolized for Pincher Martin by the terrible lobster /674/
claws. In his last scene, he sees God in the figure of a great sailor,
who asks him, "What do you believe in?" "The thread of my life,"
Martin answers. God says, "Consider," and Martin retorts, "I will
not consider! I have created you and I can create my own heaven."
To which God replies, "You have created it." The rock and the
lobster claws are Pincher Martin's eternity.

The Two Deaths of Christopher Martin is the most difficult of
Golding's books, perhaps because it is the most mythic and symbolic, perhaps because eschatology is the most difficult aspect of
religious belief. It is a satisfying book, in the way that a profound
and intricate poem is satisfying—that is, it requires effort, but it
also rewards effort, and one acknowledges that the difficulty is
necessary to the subject.

Among Golding's first three novels there is a certain obvious
kinship; they are all "religious," they are all deeply serious, and
they are all quite remote from the traditional forms of the English
novel. *Free Fall,* his latest novel, has some of these attributes, but
not all of them, and where it is least like the others it is least successful. *Free Fall* is, unlike the first three, a novel of more or less
ordinary modern English society; the narrator, Sammy Mountjoy,
is a painter who has risen from a slum to a position of professional
success, and we see this rise at various stages—his early childhood,
his school life, his first love affair, his imprisonment as a prisoner
of war. So far, it sounds like just one more novel in the maturing-
of-a-sensibility school, like *Of Human Bondage* or *The Portrait of
the Artist as a Young Man.* But *Free Fall* is different in this, that
it is, like Golding's previous novels, an investigation of a religious
concept—in this case, as the title suggests, freedom and the loss of
freedom through sin. Sammy looks back on his experience, asking
"When did I lose my freedom?" and after each remembered scene
asks "Here? Not here" until he reaches the recognition scene, in

which he learns that in his freedom he has destroyed another human being.

Although *Free Fall* is much more of a history than any of Golding's other novels, it is not organized chronologically, but ranges back and forth over Sammy's past as he thinks back to his lost freedom. This organization rarely seems to have any structural necessity, and is sometimes simply confusing; it seems, in fact, to be a gratuitous difficulty thrown in to do the work of the genuine, organic difficulty of the earlier books. But a more basic weakness is that there is not, in the history of Sammy Mountjoy, any mythic pattern to give to the difficulty order and significance. The events of his life are only events, and his own philosophical comments on them seem pretentious and shallow substitutes for the direct meaning of symbolic action.

One might trace the failure of *Free Fall* back to Golding's statement that there is no point in writing two books that are like each other. Apparently Golding has taken this principle to mean that no two books should be in any formal way alike; the result is that he has forced his talent out into the world of the social novel, a world in which it is obviously not at home. Because Golding's is a robust and marvelously inventive talent this brief excursion out of its element is not likely to hurt it much—indeed, it probably helps a serious and gifted writer to know by experience what he can't do well. The knowledge should not depress him or us; no novelist can do everything, and Golding must certainly find solace in the fact that he can do brilliantly what no one else writing in England can do at all—he can write the novels of a religious man. /675/

DISTASTE FOR THE CONTEMPORARY

MARTIN GREEN

William Golding already has a considerable, but unofficial, reputation in this country. There has been one article about him—in the *Kenyon Review*—but the charge carried by his name in literary

Martin Green, "Distaste for the Contemporary," *The Nation*, CXC (May 21, 1960), 451-54. Reprinted by special permission.

conversations is out of all proportion to that. To some degree, the
lack of published criticism may actually increase that charge: to
say the right thing about Golding is the most searching of current
tests of one's sophistication. The recent flustered review of *Free
Fall* in *The New York Times Book Review* was one example of this
nervous excitement.

The achievement claimed for him is that he is the most original
and profound of the postwar novelists in Britain, the one with
something new to say; *The Lord of the Flies* (1955) has been re-
issued in a highbrow paperback series alongside Rilke, Shaw and
Whitehead. The exact nature of this achievement is indicated by
the vocabulary of his admirers; he is said to write *fables,* to make
brilliant use of *symbolism,* to deploy the findings of modern thought
about *man-in-society,* to have a vision of the *evil* inherent in human
nature. He is compared to Conrad.

The outlines of his career are quickly given. William Golding
was born in 1911, studied science and then literature at Oxford,
was a naval officer during the war, and since then has taught and
written. He has produced some poetry and a play, *The Brass Butterfly,* but he is best known for four novels, *The Lord of the Flies, The
Inheritors, Pincher Martin* (published over here as *The Two Deaths
of Christopher Martin*) and now a new one, *Free Fall.* Of these,
the best known, and the best, is the first. It deals with the moral
evolution of a group of British schoolboys, about twelve years old,
wrecked on a tropical island by an airplane crash; their life together
develops in two directions, one toward a civilized, rational, parliamentary discussion of common problems, in imitation of the
society they were born into, the other toward tribal superstitions
and rituals, orgiastic hunting, dancing and human sacrifice. The
two tendencies clash, and the first is defeated (this, of course, is
the book's big shock and challenge), but just as the last representative of civilized behavior is about to be hacked to pieces by his
companions, the adult world returns, in the shape of a British
naval officer just landed on the island, and in a flash all the boys
revert from howling savagery to the mundane classroom obedience
which was all they had been capable of until a few weeks before.
This ending, and the relief it brings, is ironic, for the officer is
himself engaged in a war of far more appalling savagery than the
one he interrupts. The whole action, moreover, is an ironic reversal
of a well-known Victorian boys' book, R. M. Ballantyne's *Coral
Island,* still favorite children's reading in England, in which three
boys wrecked on a tropical island solve all the problems of primitive living in a jolly-romantic way, with of course no uneasy stir-

rings of the primeval in them. Golding has given his main characters the same names as the protagonists of *Coral Island;* Ralph, the thoughtful narrator of the Ballantyne book, is here the leader of parliamentarism, the one about to be tortured and slain by his companions at the end; Jack, the brave and dashing hero, is here the leader of those who revert to savagery; and winsome Peterkin (in Golding called Piggy) is a fat, bespectacled, sweaty boy, the butt of the group, who insists on debate and formality because he can get his rights only in an adult world. He is one of those killed by Jack's group.

The other books do not deserve such elaborate summary. *The Inheritors* takes us inside the minds of those beings who preceded us in the evolutionary process; we follow the adventures of a tribe of these, and see the advent of the first human beings (an unattractive group) from their point of view. The creatures whose consciousness we share cannot be said, strictly, to have any thoughts or feelings, so the book is a tour de force technically. *Pincher Martin* is the record of the feverish reminiscences and efforts at survival, during the few days between his shipwreck and his death, of an unscrupulous and treacherous naval officer, alone and resourceless on a meager mid-Atlantic rock. At the end of the story we realize, by another technical sleight of hand, that the whole thing has been a horrible illusion in the mind of a drowning man, and that he never reached the rock in the first place. *The Brass Butterfly,* it is worth noting, is in the mode which is so often the obverse of the mode of these three novels; it is an elegant, mannered, frivolous story of a Roman emperor's court in the third century A.D., with an ultra-civilized, ripely wise, old emperor (Maurice Chevalier type), his brilliant-effete poet grandson (the play was first presented at Oxford, and this character can best be described as a British undergraduate) and figures obliquely symbolizing modern science and Christianity. The play's effective sympathies are all with civilization and paganism, the emperor and the grandson.

It is clear, from even this summary, that Golding is not importantly original in thought or feeling. He sees life in the categories which have been most common among writers, especially in Britain, since the First World War; which by now are perceptibly losing vigor and conviction. His world view, that is, closely resembles that of T. S. Eliot, Graham Greene, Evelyn Waugh and a dozen other typically modern authors.

And I think it can be demonstrated, even from his new book, that he is not a significant artist. His admirers will protest that he must be judged rather by *Lord of the Flies*. It is true that is a much more successful piece of work, but it is so for highly special reasons, and its success does not, after all, transcend the limitations of Golding's talent; it is not, after all, about the evil inherent in human nature, but about how brutal twelve-year-old boys can be to each other, and the specious extension of that conviction (profoundly, obsessively felt) to an attitude to life is no insight but a trick. *Free Fall* is a better test case. It is a life story and self-interrogation, told in the first person, by a man Golding's own age, an artist, with an intellectual and religious history presumably very like his creator's. In this freest of forms, though complete artistic success may be difficult, whatever a /451/ writer has to offer can find expression; at least as a test of a writer's power of experience this may be taken as fair. And a poverty of experience, a poverty of imagination, is exposed in every line of *Free Fall*.

Golding is a rigidly disciplined writer—his poverty is not unconnected with that—and the structure of *Free Fall* is beautifully clear. Each part can be grasped as a thing in itself, and in its relation to the whole; a relation which is, mechanically, very economical and efficient and harmonious. The narrator tells us his early history, before he lost his freedom and his innocence, for eighty pages; then jumps a few years, to describe his cruelty and compulsion in a love affair, after he had lost that freedom, for fifty pages; then fifty pages about the experience of torture as a prisoner of war which reduced him to self-contempt, returned him to God and started this process of self-interrogation; then forty pages on the crucial intervening period of adolescence, the influences on him of science and religion, and the decision to rebel against his better self which, he realizes, lost him his freedom.

The prose bears the marks of the same rigid discipline. On the whole it is simple and flat, with contemporary colloquial phrases, and metaphors drawn from scientific technology. "He was specialized and soulless as a guided missile"; that sees as at the atom furnace, by reflection." The images are sensually realized and fully worked out. At other times there is an odd archaism about the diction: "Shall I choose a Roman Catholic *to* my father? . . . I may communicate in part; and that surely is *better than utter* blind and dumb." And there are passages of violent imagery, like the opening sentence: "I have walked by stalls in the market place where books, dog-eared and faded from their purple, have burst with a white hosanna." In every mood, the prose bears the marks of a scrupulous craftsman.

But it is not the prose of a successful artist. There is no life in his language; it is all ingenuity, intention and synthetics. The colloquialisms are never the perfect expression of complex meaning; the elaborate imagery is never assimilated into a natural speaking voice. Ideas are worked out too mechanically. A character described as "skimped in every line of his body by a cosmic meanness," has all the details of his physique accounted for in the same metaphor.

> His hands were in his lap, his knees together. His hair was of a curious indefinable texture—growing all ways, but so weak that it still lay close to his skull like a used door-mat. It was so indeterminate that the large, light freckles blurred the hair-line on his sloping forehead. His eyes were pale blue and seemed curiously raw in that electric light for he had neither eyebrows nor eyelashes. No, madam, I'm sorry, we don't supply them at that price. This is a utility model.

Details are often flatly commonplace, though at the same time exaggerated, in a way that is not really redeemed by the author's indication that he knows they are. Beatrice is described as having "huge, unutterable eyes." And when he escapes the commonplace it is by invoking the eccentric. "Now I saw the very water of sorrow hanging honey-thick in eyelashes or dashed down a cheek like an exclamation mark at the beginning of a Spanish sentence." Most limiting of all, an obsessive ugliness of experience reveals itself continually in casual metaphors. "In winter you can see the soil smeared away from the chalk like the skin from a white skull. . . . That potency which is assumed in all literature was not mine to use at the drop of a knicker."

Some of these effects make one believe that Golding uses other writers' interpretations of experience as his basic material. The physical description quoted above, for instance, must surely remind one of Dickens. One is reminded of some other writer on nearly every page of *Free Fall*. The intellectualism which dominates it all, especially in would-be Rabelaisian scenes, is very like Joyce Cary's; for instance, the figure of Ma, and the scene of her emerging from the lavatory. The vision of life (the people, places, events, seen as characterizing contemporary experience) is very like that of Wells. The hero's character and his life story are very like those of *Tono-Bungay* and *The New Machiavelli;* above all, the two women in his life, one passive, slow-minded, sexually alluring, a victim; the other energetic, ambitious, rough-talking, an aristocrat, these are Wells's two kinds of women. All this is not a simple kind of imitation; the various reminiscences dovetail together beautifully, and offer themselves quite convincingly as Golding's own view of life. But there is so little new experience here, or new interpretation; so much re-interpretation. The figure of the rector, for example, is *judged* differently from how Wells would judge him, but he is seen with Wells's eyes. And where there is no vividness of experience, the reader can have no vividness of response.

The other source of trouble is that the experience in the book which *is* vivid—the repeated discovery of meanness and nastiness in others and in oneself—is so much on one note of pain; so much of the thinking is a repeated demonstration of this one ugly fact of life; the other things seen and reported /452/ seem to have been all vitiated for the writer—at least his report is vitiated for the reader—by this early obsession. In consequence, everything in the book, language, characterization, symbolism, ideology, etc., divides itself between the commonplace and the nightmarish. Here, for instance, is a description of the alarm clock going off in the hero's bedroom, while he was still a child, his security still unshaken:

> All night it had ticked on, repressed, its madness held and bound in; but now the strain burst. The umbrella became a head, the clock beat its head in frenzy, trembling and jerking over the chest of drawers on three legs until it reached a point where the chest would begin to drum in sympathy, sheer madness and hysteria.

The intention seems to be richly imaginative; the effect is both dull and disturbing. Or here is a description of a near-mystical discovery of beauty:

> The trunk was huge and each branch splayed up to a given level; and there, the black leaves floated out like a level of oil on water. Level after horizontal level these leaves cut across the splaying branches and there was a crumpled, silver-paper depth, an ivory quiet beyond them.

Here it is not so much the ugliness of the oil image as the deadness of the crumpled silver-paper and ivory which is oppressive.

The large experiences described take on the same characteristics. The love affair between the hero and Beatrice is presented as notably dull and commonplace, but at the same time as so painful that it deranged them both, mentally and morally. The book's naturally evil figure (the one skimped in every line of his body) becomes a minister of the Crown and "he finds life as easy as breathing"; the naturally good figure dies very young—he is last shown riding a motorcycle at 100 m.p.h. up over the brow of a hill and turning round to kiss the girl riding pillion as he does so; again everything is both too predictable and too exaggerated. The hero's membership in the Communist Party is dismissed as the simplest kind of self-delusion; the only working-class comrade had joined as a move to better himself socially; the others were all either fools or knaves. He sums up his pre-religious experience as a whole as the discovery that "Sex is everything and is a poor return for birth, for the shames and frustrations of growing up."

The handling of ideas is similar, too predictable and too exaggerated. The attack on hygiene, liberalism, rationalism, progress, and the return to mysticism and dogma, both have nothing new in them. "And this is my cry; that I have walked among you in intellectual freedom and you never tried to seduce me from it, since a century has seduced you to it and you believe in fair play, in not presuming, in being after all not a saint." Such sentiments, in such diction and rhythms, in 1959, can only seem like a summary and an echo. The big themes, of memory and time, of free will and compulsion, of sin and regeneration, are summaries and echoes. The treatment of memory and time is the flattest textbook application of a narrative method we are now all familiar with. There is a mechanical rigidity in the treatment of sin (some characters are "good," others "evil," and the hero stops being "good" and becomes "evil," in one clear-cut, irreversible, eternally binding gesture) which is very inappropriate to the theme of free will. And the technical tours de force, like the discovery at the end that the Gestapo cell (where the hero had suffered the solitary confinement that led to his religious experience) was really only a broom closet, convey a disrespect for the reader and for the art of fiction.

The Lord of the Flies succeeds much better because Golding is genuinely involved in that experience, has some complexity of knowledge and vividness of feeling about boys' brutality to boys; also because the simplification and formalization which can alone disguise his lack of other experience is uniquely appropriate to those characters and that form (the ironic comment on an earlier fiction). But even there you may easily detect the author loading the dice, prejudicing the issue, insuring the triumph of greed, savagery, slyness and panic.

In other words, Golding is a belated recruit to the ranks of those writers who have rediscovered for this century man's essential savagery; who have triumphantly rejected science and hygiene, liberalism and progress; who have, in any account of contemporary conditions, alternated between effects of commonplaceness and effects of nightmare. He is so belated as to inherit these themes in their decrepitude. It is not Conrad he should be compared to, but Graham Greene.

In *The Brass Butterfly* the wise emperor exiles the representative of modern science to China, and thus wins the West a thousand years' reprieve from gunpowder, the printing press, steam, etc., and from all the "unrest, ferment, /453/ fever, dislocation, disorder, wild experiment and catastrophe" which they will bring. This should corroborate Sir Charles Snow's recent thesis of the hostility active between the literary and the scientific cultures, and of its consequences for modern writers. Golding is perhaps the most extreme example of that sullen distaste for the contemporary which Snow describes as cankering modern literary intellectuals and as deriving from their rejection of science.

LORD OF THE FLIES
C. B. COX

William Golding's *Lord of the Flies*, published in 1953, is a retelling in realistic terms of R. M. Ballantyne's *The Coral Island*. A group of boys, shot down during some kind of atomic war, are marooned on an island in the Pacific. In contrast to the boys in Ballantyne's story, who after a number of exciting adventures remember their time on the island as an idyllic interlude, the children in *Lord of the Flies* soon begin to quarrel, and their attempts to create an ordered, just society break down. On one level the story shows how intelligence (Piggy) and common sense (Ralph) will always be overthrown in society by sadism (Roger) and the lure of totalitarianism (Jack). On another, the growth of savagery in the boys demonstrates the power of original sin. Simon, the Christ figure, who tries to tell the children that their fears of a dead parachutist are illusory, is killed in a terrifying tribal dance. The Lord of the Flies is the head of a pig, which Jack puts up on a stick to placate an illusory Beast. As Simon understands, the only dangerous beast, the true Lord of the Flies, is inside the children themselves. Lord of the Flies is the Old Testament name for Beelzebub.

Lord of the Flies is probably the most important novel to be

C. B. Cox, "Lord of the Flies," *Critical Quarterly*, II (1960), 112-17. Reprinted by special permission.

published in this country in the 1950s. A story so explicitly symbolic as this might easily become fanciful and contrived, but Golding has mastered the art of writing a twentieth century allegory. In contrast to the medieval audience, the general reading public today does not believe that correspondences exist between the material and spiritual world, and they do not automatically expect every incident or object to have symbolic importance. No conventions of allegory exist, and the writer cannot introduce colours, animals, flowers or any of the other emblems which were available for the medieval writer. In these circumstances, many novelists have given objects an arbitrary symbolic meaning. In Iris Murdoch's *The Bell*, for example, there is no inherent reason why the bell under the lake should represent absolute values, and so her fanciful developments of plot to illustrate this meaning often appear rather forced. This type of allegory can fully succeed only if the literal sense is dramatically coherent in its own right, as in Camus's *The Plague*. There are other methods of writing twentieth century allegory, of course, as in Kafka's use of fanciful situations to explore psychological and religious experiences; but if a story based on real life is used, then there must be no unlikely situations or fanciful embroidery. A modern audience will accept the underlying meanings only if they are conveyed in a completely convincing, true to life series of events.

To find an exciting, stimulating plot which is both dramatically credible and capable of allegorical interpretation is exceptionally /112/ difficult. The idea of placing boys alone on an island, and letting them work out archetypal patterns of human society, is a brilliant technical device, with a simple coherence which is easily understood by a modern audience. Its success is due in part to the quality of Golding's Christianity. He is neither puritan nor transcendentalist, and his religious faith is based upon his interpretation of experience, rather than upon an unquestioning acceptance of revelation. Although his four novels deal with the depravity of man, he cares deeply about the condition of human life, and shows great compassion for men who suffer and men who sin. His religious sense does not make him turn from life in disgust, but proves to him the dignity and importance of human action. In development of plot, descriptions of island and sea, and treatment of character, he explores actual life to prove dramatically the authenticity of his religious viewpoint.

Lord of the Flies is a gripping story which will appeal to generations of readers. It is easy to despise the power of a good story, and to think of moral implications as an alternative to the obvious devices of surprise, suspense and climax. But to succeed, a good story needs more than sudden deaths, a terrifying chase and an unexpected conclusion. *Lord of the Flies* includes all these ingredients, but their exceptional force derives from Golding's faith that every detail of human life has a religious significance. This is one reason why he is unique among new writers in the '50s, and why he excels in narrative ability. Typical of the writers of the '50s is an uncertainty about human values, a fundamental doubt about whether life has any importance whatsoever. In contrast, Golding can describe friendship, guilt, pain and horror with a full sense of how deeply meaningful these can be for the individual. The terrible fire which kills the young children, the fear of Ralph as he is pursued across the island, and Piggy's fall to his death on the rocks make us feel, in their vivid detail, Golding's intense conviction that every particular of human life has a profound importance. His children are not juvenile delinquents, but human beings realising for themselves the beauty and horror of life.

This faith in the importance of our experiences in this world is reflected in Golding's vivid, imaginative style. He has a fresh, delightful response to the mystery of Nature, with its weird beauty and fantastic variety. The conch, which Ralph and Piggy discover in the lagoon and use to call the children to assemblies, is not just a symbol of order. From the beginning Golding does justice to the strange attraction of the shell, with its delicate, embossed pattern, and deep harsh note which echoes back from the pink granite of the mountain. When towards the end of the story the conch is smashed, we feel that sadness which comes when any object of exquisite beauty is broken. The symbolic meaning, that this is the end of the beauty of justice and order, is not forced upon us, but is reflected through our emotional reaction to the object itself. /113/

In this way Golding expresses his passionate interest in both physical and moral life. His narrative style has an unusual lucidity and vitality because he never forgets the concrete in his search for symbolic action:

> Now a great wind blew the rain sideways, cascading the water from the forest trees. On the mountain-top the parachute filled and moved; the figure slid, rose to its feet, spun, swayed down through a vastness of wet air and trod with ungainly feet the tops of the high trees; falling, still falling, it sank towards the beach and the boys rushed screaming into the darkness. The parachute took the figure forward, furrowing the lagoon, and bumped it over the reef and out to sea.

With admirable simplicity this passage conveys a multitude of effects.

The incident is part of an exciting story, a surprising climax to the murder of Simon; at the same time the dead parachutist is the 'beast' to the children, a symbol of adult evil, which, by their own act of killing, they have shown to be part of themselves. But the passage achieves its strong emotional impact because it is so firmly grounded in physical awareness. Water cascades from the forest trees, the parachutist 'furrows' the lagoon. These precise words describe with physical immediacy a situation which is real and dramatically poignant. And the picture of the man treading the tops of the high trees recalls the mystery of human life, with its incredible inventions, and yet also makes us feel deep compassion for the ungainly feet, the horror of death.

The island itself is boat-shaped, and the children typify all mankind on their journey through life. In the opening scenes the island has the glamour of a new-found paradise. With the green shadows from the palms and the forest sliding over his skin, Ralph is overcome by wonder. He lolls in the warm water, looking at the mirages which wrestle with the brilliance of the lagoon. But soon the terrifying fire transforms the island, and illusion gives way to reality. In nightmares the children begin to be afraid that this is not a good island; they become accustomed to the mirages, "and ignored them, just as they ignored the miraculous, throbbing stars". The beauty of the earthly paradise grows stale to their eyes. At the end they leave behind them "the burning wreckage of the island", whose loveliness has been degraded by their presence.

As his attempts to discipline the boys begin to appear hopeless, Ralph, on a search for the illusory beast, sees beyond the lagoon out to open sea:

> The lagoon had protected them from the Pacific: and for some reason only Jack had gone right down to the water on the other side. Now he saw the landsman's view of the swell and it seemed like the breathing of some stupendous creature. Slowly the waters sank among the rocks, revealing pink tables of granite, strange growths of coral, polyp, and weed. Down, down, the waters went, whispering like the wind among the heads of the forest. There was one flat rock there, spread like a table, /114/ and the waters sucking down on the four weedy sides made them seem like cliffs. Then the sleeping leviathan breathed out—the waters rose, the weed streamed, and the water boiled over the table rock with a roar. There was no sense of the passage of waves; only this minute-long fall and rise and fall.

This creature becomes a part of Ralph's consciousness, a symbol of a reality he tries to avoid. As he watches the ceaseless, bulging passage of the deep sea waves, the remoteness and infiniteness of the ocean force themselves upon his attention. By the quiet lagoon he can dream of rescue, but the brute obtuseness of the ocean tells him he is helpless. It is significant that the two boys who are killed, Simon and Piggy, are taken back to this infinite ocean.

As the waves creep towards the body of Simon beneath the moonlight, the brilliantly realistic description of the advancing tide typifies all the beauty of the world which promises eternal reward to those who suffer:

> Along the shoreward edge of the shallows the advancing clearness was full of strange, moonbeam-bodied creatures, with fiery eyes. Here and there a larger pebble clung to its own air and was covered with a coat of pearls. The tide swelled in over the rain-pitted sand and smoothed everything with a layer of silver. Now it touched the first of the stains that seeped from the broken body and the creatures made a moving patch of light as they gathered at the edge. The water rose further and dressed Simon's coarse hair with brightness. The line of his cheek silvered and the turn of his shoulder became sculptured marble. The strange, attendant creatures, with their fiery eyes and trailing vapours, busied themselves round his head. The body lifted a fraction of an inch from the sand and a bubble of air escaped from the mouth with a wet plop. Then it turned gently in the water.

Here we become aware of the Christian meaning underlying the story. For Ralph the sea typifies the insensitivity of the universe, but this is to see it from only one point of view. The multitudinous beauties of the tide promise that creation was not an accident; after our suffering and confusions are over, a healing power of great beauty will solve all problems. The advancing waves are like moonbeam-bodied creatures, gently washing the body of Simon free from all stain, and dressing him in pearls, silver and marble in token of the richness of his love for the other children. Instead of seeking to introduce ancient myths into the modern world, Golding creates his own, basing his symbols on the actual wonder of life itself. The intricate beauty of the waves is not merely a pleasing arrangement of light and matter, but an incredible manifestation of the wonder of creation, with a valid life in our consciousness. As Simon's body moves out to open sea under the delicate yet firm lifting of the tide, it seems impossible that his sacrifice has had no ultimate meaning.

The island, the sea and the sacrifice of Simon all show Ralph the /115/ truth of the human situation. His mind finds the burden of responsibility too great, and he begins to lose his power to think coherently: "He found himself understanding the wearisomeness of this life, where every path was an improvisation and a considerable part of one's waking life was spent watching one's feet". Jack's re-

turn to savagery, taking all the children with him, is portrayed
with frightening realism. The lust for killing grows too strong, and
Ralph's inadequate democratic machinery cannot keep it in check.
Behind their painted faces, the children can feel a security, a lack
of personal responsibility for the evil they perpetrate, and this desire explains the growth of Jack's prestige. When he tells them they
will not dream so much, "they agreed passionately out of the depths
of their tormented private lives", and he is amazed by their response. Only the intelligence of Piggy is not tempted by the tribal
dances, and his character is presented with great compassion. His
fat, asthmatic body is a natural butt for children, and continual
mockery has taught him to be humble and to enjoy being noticed
even only as a joke. But he has a powerful belief in the importance
of civilised order, and gradually Ralph learns to appreciate his
value. His death is a poignant reminder of the unjust treatment
given by society to so many good men.

Simon is perhaps the one weakness in the book. We see his
friendship for Ralph, when he touches his hand as they explore
the island, and his love of all people when he ministers to the dead
body of the parachutist, but alone among the characters his actions
at times appear to be motivated not by the dramatic action, but
by the symbolic implications of the story. At the beginning, when
he withdraws at night from the other children, his motives are left
uncertain. But the scene where he confronts the lord of the flies
is most convincing. In this pig's head covered with flies, he sees "the
infinite cynicism of adult life". He has the courage to face the
power of evil, and, knowing that the beast is in all of them, he
climbs the hill to find out the truth about the dead parachutist.

The whole story moves towards Simon's view of reality. The
growth of savagery forces Ralph to make strange speculations about
the meaning of human identity. When they hold an assembly at
nightfall, he is surprised at the different effect made by the darkness:

> Again he fell into that strange mood of speculation that was so foreign
> to him. If faces were different when lit from above or below—what was
> a face? What was anything?

He faces the possibility that there is no absolute perspective to
human life, and that all experience may be meaningless. He longs
to return to the world of adults, and the irony of this illusion is
shown when, after a battle in the skies, the dead parachutist comes
down "as a sign from the world of grown-ups". At certain stages
of the /116/ story, Golding deliberately makes us forget that these

are only young children. Their drama and conflict typify the inevitable overthrow of all attempts to impose a permanent civilisation on the instincts of man. The surprising twist of events at the end of the novel is a highly original device to force upon us a new viewpoint. The crazy, sadistic chase to kill Ralph is suddenly revealed to be the work of a semi-circle of little boys, their bodies streaked with coloured clay. But the irony is also directed at the naval officer, who comes to rescue them. His trim cruiser, the submachine gun, his white drill, epaulettes, revolver and row of gilt buttons, are only more sophisticated substitutes for the war-paint and sticks of Jack and his followers. He too is chasing men in order to kill, and the dirty children mock the absurd civilised attempt to hide the power of evil. And so when Ralph weeps for the end of innocence, the darkness of man's heart, and the death of his true, wise friend, Piggy, he weeps for all the human race. /117/

THE CORAL ISLAND REVISITED

CARL NIEMEYER

William Golding is the author of four novels, three of which have been published in the United States. They are *Lord of the Flies* (1954), which is the subject of this paper; *The Inheritors* (1955), which has not appeared in this country, the story of the death of the last Neanderthal men at the hands of human beings, who surpass them in ruthless cruelty and cunning; *The Two Deaths of Christopher Martin* (1956)—the English title is *Pincher Martin*—about an English naval officer who lives through a purgatorial and ultimately redemptive experience at the moment of drowning; and finally *Free Fall* (1959), which concerns an English artist in a Nazi prison camp, who at some time in his life made a wrong moral choice and who seeks in retrospect to find the moment at which he freely chose to fall. There is also an extended short story, "Envoy Extraordinary," which Golding has turned into a play called *The*

Carl Niemeyer, "The Coral Island Revisited," *College English*, XXII (January, 1961), 241-45. Reprinted with the permission of the National Council of Teachers of English and Carl Niemeyer.

Brass Butterfly. It is about an inventor who invents things at a period of history when the world is not ready for them.

Despite the wit of Golding's stories and the excellence of his writing, he has not always fared well at the hands of the critics, particularly the Americans. Anthony West in *The New Yorker* (April 30, 1960) does not make the grounds of his disapproval altogether clear, but the disapproval is evident. In England Golding is more highly regarded, as shown by John Bowen's article in *The Times Literary Supplement* for August 7, 1959, which discusses him along with Angus Wilson, Lawrence Durrell, and Iris Murdoch as artists seriously concerned with moral issues.

One interested in finding about Golding for oneself should probably begin with *Lord of the Flies,* now available in a paperback.[1] The story is simple. In a way not clearly explained, a group of children, all boys, presumably evacuees in a future war, are dropped from a plane just before it is destroyed, on to an uninhabited tropical island. The stage is thus set for a reworking of a favorite subject in children's literature: castaway children assuming adult responsibilities without adult supervision. Golding expects his readers to recall the classic example of such a book, R. M. Ballantyne's *The Coral Island* (1857), where the boys rise to the occasion and behave as admirably as would adults. But in *Lord of the Flies* everything goes wrong from the beginning. A few boys representing sanity and common sense, led by Ralph and Piggy, see the necessity for maintaining a signal fire to attract a rescue. But they are thwarted by the hunters, led by red-haired Jack, whose lust for blood is finally not to be satisfied by killing merely wild pigs. Only the timely arrival of a British cruiser saves us from an ending almost literally too horrible to think about. Since Golding is using a naive literary form to express sophisticated reflections on the nature of man and society, and since he refers obliquely to Ballantyne many times throughout the book, a glance at *The Coral Island* is appropriate. /241/

Ballantyne shipwrecks his three boys—Jack, eighteen; Ralph, the narrator, aged fifteen; and Peterkin Gay, a comic sort of boy, aged thirteen—somewhere in the South Seas on an uninhabited coral island. Jack is a natural leader, but both Ralph and Peterkin have abilities valuable for survival. Jack has the most common sense and foresight, but Peterkin turns out to be a skillful killer of pigs, and Ralph when later in the book he is temporarily separated from his

---

[1] Page references will be to this edition, which includes a critical discussion by E. L. Epstein, in Capricorn Books (Putnam's, 1959).

friends and alone on a schooner, coolly navigates it back to Coral
Island by dead reckoning, a feat sufficiently impressive, if not quite
equal to Captain Bligh's. The boys' life on the island is idyllic;
and they are themselves without malice or wickedness, though there
are a few curious episodes in which Ballantyne seems to hint at
something he himself understands as little as do his characters. One
is Peterkin's wanton killing of an old sow, useless as food, which the
boy rationalizes by saying he needs leather for shoes. This and one
or two other passages suggest that Ballantyne was aware of some
darker aspects of boyish nature, but for the most part he emphasizes the paradisiacal life of the happy castaways. Like Golding's,
however, Ballantyne's story raises the problem of evil, but whereas
Golding finds evil in the boys' own natures, it comes to Ballantyne's
boys not from within themselves but from the outside world. Tropical nature, to be sure, is kind, but the men of this non-Christian
world are bad. For example, the island is visited by savage cannibals, one canoeful pursuing another, who fight a cruel and bloody
battle, observed by the horrified boys, and then go away. A little
later the island is again visited, this time by pirates (i.e., white men
who have renounced or scorned their Christian heritage), who succeed in capturing Ralph. In due time the pirates are deservedly destroyed, and in the final episode of the book the natives undergo
an unmotivated conversion to Christianity, which effects a total
change in their nature just in time to rescue the boys from their
clutches.

Thus Ballantyne's view of man is seen to be optimistic, like his
view of English boys' pluck and resourcefulness, which subdues
tropical islands as triumphantly as England imposes empire and
religion on lawless breeds of men. Golding's naval officer, the *deus
ex machina* of *Lord of the Flies,* is only echoing Ballantyne when,
perceiving dimly that all has not gone well on the island, he says
(p. 248): "I should have thought that a pack of British boys—you're
all British aren't you?—would have been able to put up a better
show than that—I mean—"

This is not the only echo of the older book. Golding boldly calls
his two chief characters Jack and Ralph. He reproduces the comic
Peterkin in the person of Piggy. He has a wanton killing of a wild pig,
accomplished, as E. L. Epstein points out (p. 253), "in terms of sexual
intercourse." He uses a storm to avert a quarrel between Jack and
Ralph, as Ballantyne used a hurricane to rescue his boys from death
at the hands of cannibals. He emphasizes physical cruelty but inte-
grates it into his story, and by making it a real if deplorable part
of human, or at least boyish, nature improves on Ballantyne, whose

descriptions of brutality—never of course performed by the boys—
are usually introduced merely for their sensational effect. Finally,
on the last page Golding's officer calls Ralph mildly to task for not
having organized things better.

> "It was like that at first," said Ralph, "before things—"
> He stopped.
> "We were together then—"
> The officer nodded helpfully.
> "I know. Jolly good show. Like the Coral Island."

Golding invokes Ballantyne, so that the kind but uncomprehending adult, the instrument of salvation, may recall to /242/ the child
who has just gone through hell, the naïveté of the child's own early
innocence, now forever lost; but he suggests at the same time the
inadequacy of Ballantyne's picture of human nature in primitive
surroundings.

Golding, then, regards Ballantyne's book as a badly falsified map
of reality, yet the only map of this particular reality that many of
us have. Ralph has it and, through harrowing experiences, replaces
it with a more accurate one. The naval officer, though he should
know better, since he is on the scene and should not have to rely
on memories of his boyhood reading, has it, and it seems unlikely
that he is ever going to alter it, for his last recorded action is to
turn away from the boys and look at his "trim" cruiser, in other
words to turn away from a revelation of the untidy human heart to
look at something manufactured, manageable, and solidly useful.

Golding, who being a grammar-school teacher should know boys
well, gives a corrective of Ballantyne's optimism. As he has explained, the book is "an attempt to trace the defects of society back
to the defects of human nature" (p. 250). These defects turn out, on
close examination, to result from the evil of inadequacy and mis-
takenness. Evil is not the positive and readily identifiable force it
appears to be when embodied in Ballantyne's savages and pirates.
Golding's Ralph, for example, has real abilities, most conspicuous
among them the gift of leadership and a sense of responsibility
toward the "littluns." Yet both are incomplete. "By now," writes
Golding, "Ralph had no self-consciousness in public thinking but
would treat the day's decisions as though he were playing chess."
Such detachment is obviously an important and valuable quality in
a leader, but significantly the next sentence reads: "The only
trouble was that he would never be a very good chess player"
(p. 145). Piggy on the other hand no doubt would have been a good
chess player, for with a sense of responsibility still more acute than

Ralph's he combines brains and common sense. Physically, however, he is ludicrous—fat, asthmatic, and almost blind without his
specs. He is forever being betrayed by his body. At his first appearance he is suffering from diarrhoea; his last gesture is a literally
brainless twitch of the limbs, "like a pig's after it has been killed"
(p. 223). His further defect is that he is powerless, except as he
works through Ralph. Though Piggy is the first to recognize the
value of the conch and even shows Ralph how to blow it to summon
the first assembly, he cannot sound it himself. And he lacks imagination. Scientifically minded as he is, he scorns what is intangible
and he dismisses the possibility of ghosts or an imaginary beast.
"'Cos things wouldn't make sense. Houses an' streets, an'—TV—
they wouldn't work" (p. 115). Of course he is quite right, save that
he forgets he is now on an island where the artifacts of the civilization he has always known are meaningless.

It is another important character, Simon, who understands that
there may indeed be a beast, even if not a palpable one—"maybe
it's only us" (p. 111). The scientist Piggy has recognized it is possible
to be frightened of people (p. 105), but he finds this remark of
Simon's dangerous nonsense. Still Simon is right, as we see from his
interview with the sow's head on a stake, which is the lord of the
flies. He is right that the beast is in the boys themselves, and he
alone discovers that what has caused their terror is in reality a dead
parachutist ironically stifled in the elaborate clothing worn to
guarantee survival. But Simon's failure is the inevitable failure of
the mystic—what he knows is beyond words; he cannot impart his
insights to others. Having an early glimpse of the truth, he cannot
tell it. /243/

> Simon became inarticulate in his effort to express mankind's essential
> illness. Inspiration came to him.
> "What's the dirtiest thing there is?"
> As an answer Jack dropped into the uncomprehending silence that
> followed it the one crude expressive syllable. Release was like an or-
> gasm. Those littluns who had climbed back on the twister fell off again
> and did not mind. The hunters were screaming with delight.
> Simon's effort fell about him in ruins; the laughter beat him cruelly
> and he shrank away defenseless to his seat (p. 111).

Mockery also greets Simon later when he speaks to the lord of the
flies, though this time it is sophisticated, adult mockery:

> "Fancy thinking the Beast was something you could hunt and kill!"
> said the head. For a moment or two the forest and all the other dimly
> appreciated places echoed with the parody of laughter (p. 177).

Tragically, when Simon at length achieves a vision so clear that it is readily communicable he is killed by the pig hunters in their insane belief that he is the very evil which he alone has not only understood but actually exorcised. Like the martyr, he is killed for being precisely what he is not.

The inadequacy of Jack is the most serious of all, and here perhaps if anywhere in the novel we have a personification of absolute evil. Though he is the most mature of the boys (he alone of all the characters is given a last name), and though as head of the choir he is the only one with any experience of leadership, he is arrogant and lacking in Ralph's charm and warmth. Obsessed with the idea of hunting, he organizes his choir members into a band of killers. Ostensibly they are to kill pigs, but pigs alone do not satisfy them, and pigs are in any event not needed for food. The blood lust once aroused demands nothing less than human blood. If Ralph represents purely civil authority, backed only by his own good will, Piggy's wisdom, and the crowd's easy willingness to be ruled, Jack stands for naked ruthless power, the police force or the military force acting without restraint and gradually absorbing the whole state into itself and annihilating what it cannot absorb. Yet even Jack is inadequate. He is only a little boy after all, as we are sharply reminded in a brilliant scene at the end of the book, when we suddenly see him through the eyes of the officer instead of through Ralph's (pp. 247-48), and he is, like all sheer power, anarchic. When Ralph identifies himself to the officer as "boss," Jack, who has just all but murdered him, makes a move in dispute, but overawed at last by superior power, the power of civilization and the British Navy, implicit in the officer's mere presence, he says nothing. He is a villain (are his red hair and ugliness intended to suggest that he is a devil?), but in our world of inadequacies and imperfections even villainy does not fulfill itself completely. If not rescued, the hunters would have destroyed Ralph and made him, like the sow, an offering to the beast; but the inexorable logic of Ulysses makes us understand that they would have proceeded thence to self-destruction.

> Then everything includes itself in power,
> Power into will, will into appetite;
> And appetite, an universal wolf,
> So doubly seconded with will and power,
> Must make perforce an universal prey,
> And last eat up himself.

The distance we have travelled from Ballantyne's cheerful unrealities is both artistic and moral. Golding is admittedly symbolic;

Ballantyne professed to be telling a true story. Yet it is the symbolic tale that, at least for our times, carries conviction. Golding's boys, who choose to remember nothing of their past before the plane accident; who, as soon as Jack commands the choir to take off the robes marked with the cross of Christian- /244/ ity, have no trace of religion; who demand to be ruled and are incapable of being ruled properly; who though many of them were once choir boys (Jack could sing C sharp) never sing a note on the island; in whose minds the great tradition of Western culture has left the titles of a few books for children, a knowledge of the use of matches (but no matches), and hazy memories of planes and TV sets—these boys are more plausible than Ballantyne's. His was a world of blacks and whites: bad hurricanes, good islands; good pigs obligingly allowing themselves to be taken for human food, bad sharks disobligingly taking human beings for shark food; good Christians, bad natives; bad pirates, good boys. Of the beast within, which demands blood sacrifice, first a sow's head, then a boy's, Ballantyne has some vague notion, but he cannot take it seriously. Not only does Golding see the beast; he sees that to keep it at bay we have civilization; but when by some magic or accident civilization is abolished and the human animal is left on his own, dependent upon his mere humanity, then being human is not enough. The beast appears, though not necessarily spontaneously or inevitably, for it never rages in Ralph or Piggy or Simon as it does in Roger or Jack; but it is latent in all of them, in the significantly named Piggy, in Ralph, who sometimes envies the abandon of the hunters (p. 94) and who shares the desire to "get a handful" of Robert's "brown, vulnerable flesh" (p. 142), and even in Simon burrowing into his private hiding place. After Simon's death Jack attracts all the boys but Ralph and the loyal Piggy into his army. Then when Piggy is killed and Ralph is alone, only civilization can save him. The timely arrival of the British Navy is less theatrical than logically necessary to make Golding's point. For civilization defeats the beast. It slinks back into the jungle as the boys creep out to be rescued; but the beast is real. It is there, and it may return. /245/

TWO FABULISTS: GOLDING AND CAMUS
MARGARET WALTERS

To describe Camus and Golding as fabulists rather than novelists is not, of course, to posit any clear-cut distinction between two different forms. Nor is there much profit in trying to define the fable very strictly. We might call it a mode, rather than a separate kind, of fictional narrative—one possible direction fiction may take; it includes works that range from the schematized allegories of some eighteenth-century moralists, to the rich exploration of symbolic situations in some of Henry James's short stories. The term has to be elastic enough to suggest common elements in very diverse works by writers themselves as diverse as Swift and Orwell, Bunyan and Kafka, Hawthorne and Faulkner. And clearly, these form nothing like a developing tradition of any kind.

But if we cannot define the fable in any simple way, the term does serve to indicate certain qualities that tend to fall outside the critical expectations we bring to the novel. These qualities are not unlike those Richard Chase discovered in what he called the romance-novel: a formal clarity and coherence; a sharp patterning of experience in the light of some intuition of order; while situation and character are reduced to a kind of abstract representativeness as a way of establishing their universal import. At any rate, both Camus and Golding have been praised for qualities of just this kind; and the nature of their success, their moral intensity and immediate relevance, prompt at least a tentative definition of the conditions, the potentialities, and the limits of the mode in which they write.

The peculiar nature of the fable is usually thought to lie in the particular kind of relationship it establishes between generalized significance and the direct rendering of life. Thus Arnold Kettle in his *Introduction to the English Novel* (vol. 1), and John Peter in a recent article on Golding *(Kenyon Review, 19, 1957, 577-92)* both point to the way the fabulist's preconceived intentions seem to be directly translated into fictional terms and to control the whole fabric of the work. To Kettle, the fable "illustrates an idea about

Margaret Walters, "Two Fabulists: Golding and Camus," *Melbourne Critical Review*, IV (1961), 18-29. Reprinted by special permission.

life", though he adds the necessary proviso that "idea" may imply anything from a precept to a whole vision of experience. And as F. R. Leavis remarks in his analysis of *Hard Times,* this pervasive control means that "the representative significance of everything in the fable—character, episode, and so on—is immediately apparent as we read." This last point, incidentally, suggests the difference between the fable and the novel *à thèse,* which are sometimes confused—as when Kettle, for example, calls Graham Greene's *The Heart of the Matter* a fable because here too "the /18/ central discovery seems to have been made by the author prior to the conception of the book." The difference emerges, I think, if we compare this, or a novel like Koestler's *Darkness at Noon,* with *The Plague* by Camus. The distinction is not a sharp one, but it seems true to say that in the Greene and the Koestler, particular characters and events, though shaped by and illuminating a general idea about life, still remain individual examples of that idea in action, with vitality and meaning in their own right. With Camus, however, the whole action has significance and interest only in the light of the idea it embodies; the whole of it becomes a direct and universal image of the content of the idea.

But one danger of stressing the author's pre-verbal intention in discussing a fable, however necessary it may be to do so at times, is that it may easily blur the difference between the author's aim and his achievement, or between a paraphrase of the book and the book itself. Of course abstractions are obviously important in shaping a fable: the frequent summaries of Golding's *Lord of the Flies* in terms of the doctrine of Original Sin, or the interpretation of *The Plague* as a simple illustration of Camus' philosophy, are partly invited by the very nature of fable. Even at their finest, fables do tend to exploit a somewhat crude equivalence of image and idea, to shape the dramatic action by some more or less explicitly formulated pattern. And even though this pattern may be fully embodied in the action, and hence modified and enriched, it does obviously restrict the subtler possibilities of dramatic development and exploration. In the last resort this is probably the limitation of the mode. Nevertheless, it is a mistake to suppose that the only way we can discuss fables is by abstracting and then debating their controlling ideas, as if a paraphrase were the whole import of the book, or as if we exhausted the fable's imaginative meaning by reformulating the author's intention or thesis. We ought rather to look at what gives it its special kind of vitality (and its peculiar weaknesses) as literature: the interplay between its controlling design on the one hand, and its openness to life on the other.

In its element of design at least, fable is obviously akin to allegory, with its precise correspondences between different levels of meaning. In the latter, however, the cross-reference between literal narrative and a body of abstractions is usually specific, sustained at length, and rather arbitrary. And while, as various critics have rightly pointed out, most fables use some allegorical correspondences (this is true even of Kafka's shifting enigmas), the more important fact to notice is the way the fabulist always tries to make his dramatic situation serve as an *analogy* of the world at large. A fable really offers its individual story as an analogue, a metaphor, of an order to be found in a wider reality. /19/

Golding and Camus are interesting in that both illustrate the strengths and limits of the mode. The dangers to which the fable is open are obvious enough: the failure to translate abstractions into dramatic terms, which leads to explicit commentary or didacticism; the tendency to distort experience by schematizing it too rigidly; the claiming of a universal relevance that the particular situation fails to suggest; in short, the lapsing of the necessary interplay between its elements. And with both, we are also forced to consider the nature and adequacy of their central, analogical, situations. When Golding, for example, claims that his true business is with man *sub specie aeternitatis,* not with current affairs and everyday social living which are simply expressions of a continuing and basic human condition, we may well ask whether this deliberate narrowing of range really does enable him to concentrate, to distil the essence of a much broader range of experience; or whether, instead, his success depends on excluding most of the complexities of actual life. For the particular dangers to which the fabulist is prone are perhaps only aspects of a more insidious temptation. He can so easily dazzle us with the apparently flawless inner logic of his work that we barely realize its "universal" significance is not universal at all since it depends on leaving out so much of human reality.

Golding's first book, *Lord of the Flies,* seems to me decidedly more successful than any of his later work. The central situation is simple enough: a group of schoolboys, who have been evacuated from Britain during an atomic war, are stranded alone on an island somewhere in the Pacific. The children's activities on the island—the society they construct, their attempts to cooperate, their quarrels, their terror of the unknown, the rituals they develop—are obviously images of human acivities at large. And the analogy is given a further twist by the very reason for their isolation: their conflicts and descent into savagery are paralleled by constant rumours of a world destroying itself in war.

Even as a realistic narrative, the story is both convincing and absorbing; it develops, in fact, by a rigorous inversion of *Coral Island*. But its main interest lies in its force as an embodiment of a controlling idea. As one critic puts it, without undue distortion, "the story shows how intelligence (Piggy) and commonsense (Ralph) will always be overthrown in society by sadism (Roger) and the lure of totalitarianism (Jack)" (R. G. Cox, *The Critical Quarterly*, 2, 1960, 112-7). But as we grasp Golding's general thesis we must also ask how fully the story embodies it and how far it remains an abstract intention; and even whether it does not induce in Golding a too narrow, too selective, grasp of life. /20/

The characters and events, though representative in a fairly obvious way, do make us feel some real force in this overall pattern. Throughout the book, the children are seen as products of a particular society, reflecting its customs and values in their habits of thought and behaviour. At first, their old identities, and all that these imply, act as a restraining force—Jack hesitates to kill a pig "because of the enormity of the knife descending and cutting into living flesh", while Roger throws stones to frighten, but not injure, the small child:

> Round the squatting child was the protection of parents and school and policemen. Roger's arm was conditioned by a civilization that knew nothing of him and was in ruins. (ch. 4)

This is a good example of how the particular situation, given an ironic significance by its wider implications, both reflects and comments on the outside world. When the boys' inhibitions are undermined, and habit and good sense prove inadequate to calm their irrational terrors, Golding convinces us that their collapse is inevitable simply because they are human. Although a few of the boys—Ralph, the elected leader, Piggy, and Simon—do try to cling to the "rules", most find release and some kind of security behind Jack's painted masks and ritualistic tribal organization. First Simon, then Piggy are brutally killed, and Ralph—who has occasional lapses into savagery himself—is saved only by chance when a naval detachment suddenly arrives at the island and interrupts with adult authority the hunting of Ralph across the "burning wreckage" of the island.

The close, with its startling shift to the adults' point of view, has interesting implications. One critic (James Gindin, "Metaphor and Gimmick in the Novels of William Golding", *Modern Fiction Studies,* 6, 1960, 145-52) claims that like all Golding's endings it is simply a trick that "palliates the force of the original metaphor", and makes it less universally applicable. "If the adult world rescues the boys in *Lord of the Flies,*" he asks, "is the depravity and brutality of human nature so complete?"—though he also suggests that it may save the book from hardening into a rigid allegory. This last point does raise a very real problem, but leaving it aside for a moment, we ought to notice that the ending is less arbitrary than Gindin seems to think. For the boys' situation is constantly linked with the outside world. As well as unconsciously revealing common human traits and tendencies, they deliberately imitate what seemed to them adult good sense and sanity. Piggy constantly berates the others for behaving "like a pack of kids", for example, and Ralph contrasts the order and stability of adults with their own inadequacies. The action underlines the bitter inaccuracy of all this. When Ralph cries out for /21/ a sign from the adult world, the only answer is the corpse of the parachutist drifting down from a battle ten miles above the island. This incident in particular (tremendously effective in dramatic terms) illustrates the subtlety and range of suggestion the book can achieve: the fairly obvious intention takes on a richness that transcends predictable and abstract formulations. The body, caught in the rocks at the top of the mountain, terrifies the children who, seeing only a vague moving shape, identify it with the mysterious "Beast" which haunts their imaginations. The upsurge of terror precipitates their break-up; and only Simon has the courage to face the horror and discover the truth— that the evil they fear is only human, and that the "Beast" itself is a human being, a victim of the same chaos into which the children are descending. When he tries to bring the truth to the others, he stumbles into one of their frenzied ritualistic dances, is forced to act the part of the "Beast", and is killed.

Thus the last scenes of the book intensify a point made by the action as a whole—that the children bring ruin on themselves, and that their disintegration can't be dismissed on the grounds that they *are* only children. We have, in fact, almost forgotten this. That we now see them through the officer's eyes as "a semi-circle of little boys, their bodies streaked with clay, sharp sticks in their hands", suddenly illuminates the universality of the evil in them, and the horror of what they have done. The double irony of the analogy becomes explicit in the officer's failure to see this, and that he himself represents a more sophisticated form of the impulses that appal him in the boys. We accept the last generalized comment of the book because the action has convinced us of its universal application:

> . . . in the middle of them, with filthy body, matted hair, and unwiped nose, Ralph wept for the end of innocence, the darkness of man's heart, and the fall through the air of the true wise friend called Piggy.
>
> The officer, surrounded by these noises, was moved and a little embar-

rassed. He turned away to give them time to pull themselves together; and waited, allowing his eyes to rest on the trim cruiser in the distance.

For the most part, then, the story embodies very powerfully Golding's sense of evil forces at work in the human soul, against which reason and its constructs are finally powerless. But there are lapses. Golding does tend rather too often to exploit his style and even the overall pattern in order to obtrude an unnecessary comment on the action; or sometimes to slip into simple and explicit assertions of what it means. The former fault appears, for example, in Simon's repeated remarks about the evil being in themselves—he is used, needlessly, as a mouthpiece for something that emerges quite adequately from the story. The scene where he confronts the pig's head, left by the hunters to placate the "Beast", sums /22/ up both weaknesses. Golding seems to distort the story by forcing a crude and implausible symbolism upon it; the scene is dramatically unconvincing and obscure, and at the same time over-explicit. Simon has a strange conversation with the head, which becomes the "Lord of the Flies", a personification of evil and "the infinite cynicism of adult life":

> "Fancy thinking the Beast was something you could hunt and kill!" said the head. For a moment or two the forest and all the other dimly appreciated places echoed with the parody of laughter. "You knew, didn't you? I'm part of you? Close, close, close! I'm the reason why it's no go?" (ch. 8)

Indeed, the figure of Simon is constantly weakened by Golding's attempt to endow him with a mysterious authority and insight, and by his obtrusive stress on the boy's role as some kind of saviour— a stress necessary because the figure, on the dramatic level, is neither plausible nor representative. All this seems to spring from Golding's attempt to give the situation a universal relevance that it fails, at some points, to achieve in itself, an attempt to gloss over the places where the analogue is limited in scope and doesn't correspond to the varied possibilities of human experience. He convinces us of the inevitability of these particular events, but not that they form a complete and adequate image of the complexities of actual living.

The temptation to pass off a partial interpretation of experience as the whole truth is a perpetual danger for the fabulist. It is this, issuing in a rigid schematization of life, that weakens, say, the political satire of Orwell's *Animal Farm;* and it can easily degenerate, as in some eighteenth-century moralists, or in certain political fabulists in the nineteen-thirties, into the use of fable as a propagandist weapon, a moral or political bludgeon. Again, the fabulist may try to achieve a width of meaning by a purely rhetorical complication of style and structure, as Golding tends to do in the scene between Simon and the pig's head, though the tendency is far more pronounced in his later books. But an obvious example of a work drastically flawed in this way is Faulkner's *A Fable*. The retelling of the Christian story in terms of modern warfare neither illuminates the world of actual living, nor suggests the contemporary relevance of the Christian myth. The parallels remain quite arbitrary, while the deliberate mystifications, the involutions of sentence and plot, and the long didactic passages only reveal that the myth never becomes an adequate focus for the various meanings that Faulkner tries to suggest. And those meanings remain correspondingly abstract and remote. Again, so different a book as Hesse's *The Journey to the East* fails for similar reasons. The central metaphor of the journey, both communal and intensely private, in but not limited by time and space, remains rather obvious /23/ and static in its significance. The esoteric remoteness, and the surrealist fantasy of the trial scenes towards the end seem to be part of an attempt to complicate and enrich an analogy that remains basically abstract and inert. Like Faulkner's *A Fable*, it is weakened by a paradoxical combination of mystification and crude explicitness.

Golding's later books do, of course, as various critics have pointed out, avoid the trap of direct commentary and explicit assertion of meaning. All three are less obviously allegorical than *Lord of the Flies*, and the central metaphors work more obliquely, in many ways more subtly. But if the situation in, say, *The Inheritors* is a more complete translation of Golding's thesis than he achieved in *Lord of the Flies*, the remoteness of the situation suggests that his thesis involves a far more limited apprehension of life. The vision the book offers—Man seen through the eyes of a race of creatures preceding him on the earth whose qualities contrast sharply with the evil Man brings—seems to me merely an oversimplifying fantasy. At the other extreme, his latest book, *Free Fall*, is firmly rooted in a detailed social setting, and it does render one individual's experience very fully. It takes the form of a prolonged meditation by an artist named Sammy Mountjoy who searches through his past for "that decision made freely that cost me my freedom". The book claims, that is, to *discover* significant pattern in the flux of life. In fact, however, the terms in which the search is conducted are laid down very strictly; clearly, Golding knows all too well from the start what Mountjoy will "discover". The "exploration" seems a not very honest contrivance. It is hardly surprising, therefore, that much of the writing is so turgidly obscure; Golding has somehow to assert a universal significance in characters and events that remain irredeemably trivial. In neither book, that is, does the situation become an irresistibly illuminating image of "the human condition". In each, the preconceived and controlling idea is too obviously preconceived and too obviously controlling.

In a different way this is equally true of *Pincher Martin,* though the book has greater potentialities than any of the others. It has been hailed by many critics as Golding's most satisfactory fable; John Peter, for example, in the article mentioned earlier, claims that it quite transcends the earlier books, becoming "a configuration of symbols rather than an allegory". In fact, the undeniably forceful image of Pincher Martin's struggle for survival on a rock in mid-Atlantic, and its wider human implications, seem rather to work *against* the explicit meaning of the book, and to set up disturbing ambiguities within it.

One reason why the book has attracted so much attention is the surprise ending—the revelation, carefully prepared but sprung /24/ only in the last chapter, that physically Martin drowned before he reached the rock. Reviewers have pointed out the technical skill with which the effect is obtained. Martin's gradual crumbling, which seems at first evidence of his incipient madness, corresponds to our gradual awareness that his whole existence is illusory. We gradually see the significance of his fear of sleep, as a death into the "ultimate truth of things"; of his panic at unrealities in the physical world; and of his various self-dramatizations, which are merely fragments shored against an inevitable ruin. Finally he welcomes insanity and flings himself eagerly into the part of a madman, for "madness would explain everything".

As with *Lord of the Flies,* the close is integral to the meaning of the whole book. The whole point of the fable lies in Martin's assertion of his own will and intelligence and existence to the point where they seem to triumph over death itself. A series of flashbacks, to his life on board ship and in England, reveals the quality of his personality—the greed and ruthless egoism that make him cling to his own personality and reject any possibilities beyond himself, reject even the possibility of his own salvation. In short, he "lacks the technique of dying into heaven".

This is coherent enough; and yet the dominant imaginative impression the book makes upon us is neither the inadequacy of man's personal resources to achieve salvation, nor the ignobility of his preoccupation with his own small existence. We feel, rather, the resource and courage—the vitality—in Martin's fight for life, even as we recognize his egoism; in fact the egoism, which the book claims damns him, emerges as a necessary condition of that vitality. Such a struggle for life cannot, I think, serve as an image of damnation and spiritual death; it suggests possibilities and moral complexities that the author's thesis, the controlling pattern, fails to comprehend. The latter actually constricts and simplifies the dramatic material, preventing it from speaking its own meaning.

With Camus, on the other hand, the problems inherent in the fable-mode emerge in a rather different, though related way. At his finest, as in *The Plague,* Camus does reveal how deeply fable can engage the moral imagination; the situations he creates are informed by a passionate concern with the crises, moral and political, of contemporary living. Through his abstracted simplifications, he achieves an urgent concentration. But even he is limited by the apparent impossibility of any one image crystallizing all the variety and fluid ambiguity of reality. His fables raise a wide range of issues and possibilities, and the representative crises throw light on the world of actual choices, yet they still at least partially limit and oversimplify. This is particularly obvious in *The Plague,* /25/ perhaps the most ambitious in scope: the book raises questions that grow wider than, and almost independent of, the dramatic situation that embodies them. It is less noticeable, in fact, in the much slighter work, *The Outsider,* where situation and significance are more closely integrated (though here once again we feel the constricting effect of the author's abstract intent). Perhaps it is significant that the book is far more limited in its scope: it would seem that the fable is often most successful when it is least ambitious.

Nevertheless, *The Plague* is a very considerable achievement. Purely as a narrative, the epidemic, which isolates the town of Oran from the rest of the world for several months, disrupts all normal activities, and demands a complete concentration of individual and administrative resources to fight it, is vividly and specifically rendered through the eyes of an anonymous narrator (later revealed as Rieux, one of the main characters). His account deliberately suppresses all personal emotion; he consciously strives for objectivity through the accumulation of scientific detail, statistics, and eyewitness reports. We are made constantly aware of the stifling atmosphere of the ugly town "humped snailwise on its plateau and shut off almost everywhere from the sea" and of the grotesquely terrible physical ravages of the disease: the situation emerges all the more powerfully for the narrative detachment. But

this detachment, with the distancing of experience it implies, is
doubly important. In the first place, it means that our emotional
response is based upon, and given integrity by, a clear-sighted
awareness of all aspects of the situation. And secondly, it also extends that response from the particular situation to the wider one
of which it is an image. The scenes recounting the death of Othon's
son are a good example; the compassion for this one child is extended without strain to all causeless suffering, and all struggles
against death. His cries become, for the characters who hear them
as well as the reader, "the angry death-cry that has sounded through
the ages of mankind". Or we might recall the moving final paragraph, where Rieux's meditations on the epidemic, now past, retain
the same rich balance of particular and general significance:

> And indeed, as he listened to the cries of joy rising from the town,
> Rieux remembered that such joy is always imperilled. He knew what
> those jubilant crowds did not know but could have learned from books:
> that the plague bacillus never dies or disappears for good; that it can
> lie dormant for years and years in furniture and linen-chests; that it
> bides its time in bedrooms, cellars, trunks and bookshelves; and that
> perhaps the day would come when, for the bane and the enlightening of
> men, it roused up its rats again and sent them forth to die in a happy
> city.

The book moves between general analysis of the situation and
the description of various characters who represent different human
reactions to it. These characters are sharply individual, but their
/26/ individuality is defined only in relation to the plague. They
are differentiated by their responses to it, and any dramatic development springs from their growing awareness of its realities. As
Paneloux, the Jesuit priest, is reported to say in his second sermon,
"we were all up against the wall that plague had built around us,
and in its lethal shadow we must work out our salvation." In fact
they all try to do so, though the reactions and types of resistance are
placed side by side without comment, against the objective facts of
the situation. Even Cottard, who welcomes the epidemic because it
temporarily frees him of the fear of arrest, and who "in his heart
approved of something that killed off men, women, and children",
is not condemned until the final chapter. And even there, an austere
compassion dominates: he is described as a man with "an ignorant,
that is to say lonely, heart". With some, their original attitudes
change radically. This is so with the journalist Rambert, for example, who after devoting all his energies to finding a means of escaping to the woman he loves, decides on the very point of success to
remain and fight the plague. He still believes in the primary claims

of human happiness, but finds himself, unwillingly, involved in a situation with a prior demand on his humanity, and one which would prevent his happiness if he evaded it. Paneloux's attitudes, too, change very dramatically. His first sermon, for example, presents a fairly crude Christian response to suffering: the plague is simply the scourge of God. Only when he becomes more immediately aware of the realities of human suffering does he come, while still retaining his full faith, to face and comprehend those realities. Rieux and Tarrou on the other hand both reject his faith for themselves; as the former remarks,

> I've a very different idea of love. And until my dying day I shall refuse to love a scheme of things in which children are put to torture. . . . Salvation's much too big a word for me. . . . I'm concerned with man's health and for me his health comes first. (Part 4, ch. 3)

Rieux's dogged and disillusioned humanism is given the weight of the book's approval; but it is complemented by Paneloux's tortured Christianity, by Rambert's insistence on the importance of happiness in human love, by Grand's quiet heroism in carrying out routine jobs, and by Tarrou's search for peace of mind and sanctity without God. The varied questionings, and the attitudes the characters formulate, deepen our awareness of the objective situation from which they spring; the whole fable takes on a significance for the reader that is not summed up by any one reaction within the book, though each opens out further possibilities.

But in the last resort, the dramatic integrity of the book is slightly flawed. Even structurally, the abstract ideas tend to stand apart from the action. It is revealing that in order to discuss the book, /27/ we must concentrate on passages of explicit statement and conversations in which differing positions are formulated; and within the book itself, too many of the differing attitudes are represented dramatically only to the extent that the characters tell one another what those attitudes are. Again, the obvious meaning of the epidemic—an image of all kinds of evil, human as well as non-human—seems strained at times. This is particularly marked in Tarrou's statement of what the plague means to him. To him, it is a moral and social corruption of the same kind that manifests itself in the legalized murder which is the basis both of organized society and of the revolutionary movements seeking to amend society. Even those ostensibly fighting for life seem to be infected with plague, death-carriers, and no one is ever freed of responsibility or guilt. The only safeguard is an everlasting vigilance (never fully successful) against doing even unintentional evil and infecting others with "plague". But all this is more than the plague, as we see it, can bear. In itself the epidemic is hardly a fully satisfactory image of the evil caused by human activity, and the attempt to extend its meaning in this way is often, as here, obtrusive and unconvincing.

We feel this even more strongly in the deliberate parallels between the plague and the German Occupation of France: the isolation of the town, the reactions of its inhabitants, and the ruthless and monotonous efficiency of the hostile onslaught. Many critics claim that this is, in fact, one constant allegorical level, worked out fully at all points. The parallel exists, but only intermittently, used to give an added meaning to the struggle against suffering and all the forms of death; we might perhaps compare it with Kafka's harmony of political and psychological resonances. But even so, the political parallel also introduces (as some of the same critics go on to suggest) some unhappy ambiguities, just because "resistance" to the non-human visitation of the plague won't serve as a fully adequate metaphor for the more complex moral choices involved in the political Resistance. This is the kind of inadequacy that constantly leads to the separation in the book between concrete situation and abstract meaning, and that tends to oversimplify both situation and abstractions. Nor can the flaw be explained away by arguing, as some critics have done, that the book's interest is "ethical" rather than "aesthetic". It may be a truism to point out that the two are finally inseparable; it seems necessary to repeat it, however, when it is so frequently ignored in discussion of Camus. In so far as the ethical and aesthetic experiences remain disparate, we have to say that the book is oversimplified both morally and artistically. In the last analysis, and even taking into account the dramatic intensity with which /28/ the situation is rendered, we must conclude that though that situation raises many moral issues very suggestively, it fails to comprehend their actual complexity in its own terms.

And what seems to emerge from this rather scattered survey of a few fables is simply that their strengths and limits are inseparable, and perhaps too that their appeal springs as much from their necessary oversimplifications as from the force they gain by concentration. They can compel our attention by the clarity with which they represent life; by their universality of reference; and by their freedom from what Hawthorne called the "probable and ordinary" course of events. The fabulist's generalizations seem more immediately relevant, sharper and more comprehensible, than any tenuous pattern of meanings that might be culled from the bewildering particulars of everyday experience. But he achieves his intensity and coherence only at the risk, and often at the price, of a retreat from actuality and an oversimplified view of experience. The successful fable is never merely a personal assertion of meaning; it is, however, always something of a personal *tour de force*. /29/

University of Melbourne

THE NOVELS OF WILLIAM GOLDING

FRANK KERMODE

The critical reception of Mr. Golding's fourth novel, *Free Fall* (1959) was on the whole hostile; that of its predecessor *Pincher Martin*, (1956) uncomprehending. Not since his first, *Lord of the Flies* (1954), has he enjoyed general acclaim; yet the opinion that he is the most important practising novelist in English has, over this period of five or six years, become almost commonplace. One reason for this apparent paradox is that Golding's books do not (if only because each is extremely original in construction) yield themselves at one reading; *The Inheritors* (1955) and *Pincher Martin* have been better understood with the passing of time, and the same will be true of *Free Fall*. This suggests that Golding is a difficult writer; and it would not be strange if this were true. We have become accustomed, for intelligible historical reasons, to the idea that significant works of art are necessarily obscure.

It is, however, true only in a limited sense. We may note at once that despite the roar of baffled critics Mr. Golding's intentions are always simple. Of *Pincher Martin* he says 'I fell over backwards in making that novel explicit. I said to myself, "Now here is going to be a novel, it's going to be a blow on behalf of the ordinary universe, which I think on the whole likely to be the right one, and I'm going to write it so vividly and accurately and with such an exact programme that nobody can possibly mistake exactly what I

Frank Kermode, "The Novels of William Golding," *International Literary Annual*, III (1961), 11-29. Reprinted by special permission.

mean".'* But he /11/ goes on to admit that his handling of the story was 'unspecific'; he did not actually *tell* the reader that Martin drowns on page two; the evidence that he did so is oblique and is completed only by the last sentence of the book. Golding is unlike many modern writers in his willingness to state the 'programme' of his book (and also in denying the reader much liberty of interpretation); but he does not pretend that what seems to him simple must be so explicitly and directly set down that the reader will not have to work. In short, his simplicity is a quality best understood as an intellectual economy. His theme takes the simplest available way to full embodiment. But embodiment is not explanation; and all that can be guaranteed the reader is that there is no *unnecessary* difficulty, nothing to make the business of explaining and understanding more difficult than, in the nature of the case, it has to be.

The best course for sympathetic critics is to be a shade more explicit, to do what the novelist himself perhaps cannot do without injury to the books, which grow according to imaginative laws, and cannot be adjusted to the extravagant needs of readers. If critics have any reason for existence, this is it; to give assurances of value, and to provide, somehow—perhaps anyhow—the means by which readers may be put in possession of the valuable book.

It is worth noting that Golding is to a marked degree isolated from intellectual fashion: 'I think that my novels have very little genesis outside myself. That to a large extent I've cut myself off from contemporary literary life, and gained in one sense by it, though I may have lost in another.' (He is more interested in Greek than in modern literature.) Thus there are in his books preoccupations one would not expect in a high-brow modern novelist—that Ballantyne was wrong about the behaviour of English boys on a desert island, or H. G. Wells about the virtue of Neanderthal men are not points many would care to dispute, but few would find in them points of de- /12/ parture for passionate and involved fictions. In the same way Mr. Golding, though he is in some degree an allegorical writer, is entirely free of Kafka's influence, and this makes him very unlike Rex Warner, with whom he is sometimes implausibly compared. His technical equipment is as sophisticated as Conrad's; yet, like Conrad, he begins each new book as if it were his first, as if the germination of the new theme entailed the creation of its own incomparable form. (There are, however, some habitual devices—the sudden shift of viewpoint at the end of the first three novels, for instance). Perhaps the resemblance to Conrad could be developed: an isolated, indeed exiled sensibility, a pre-

---

* This, and several other remarks attributed to Mr. Golding in this article, are derived from a transcript of a B.B.C. discussion programme.

occupation with guilt, desperate technical resource. Sometimes this last power re-invents what others have done before, old devices labelled in text books: stream of consciousness, changing point of view, time-shifts. There was a time, according to the author himself, when he wrote novels intended to meet the requirements of the public, as far as he could guess them; but these novels failed, were never even published. Then, with *Lord of the Flies,* he saw that it was himself he had to satisfy; he planned it in very great detail, and wrote it, as if tracing over words already on the page. How, in pleasing his own isolated taste, and doing it in these essentially unmodish and rather private ways, has he come to so many to represent the best in modern writing?

The answer to this is necessarily involved, though the situation is in itself simple enough. One thinks of Mr. Golding's world: he sees it swinging through its space, its wet or rocky surfaces lifting under the pull of the moon; its inhabitants, locked on to it by gravity, walking upright, containing floating brains, peristaltic entrails, secreting seed at the base of the spine, somehow free and somehow guilty. Golding once called himself 'a propagandist for Neanderthal man'; his way of looking at the world has something of the candour of Lascaux. In *The Inheritors* Neanderthal man is superseded by *homo* /13/ *sapiens,* who has a better brain, and weapons; but it is the innocence of the doomed predecessor that we see enacted, for, until the last pages, we see the activities of the new man, intelligent and so capable of evil, through the bewildered eyes of the old. And Golding though he admits that we belong with the new man, supposes that we could not recapture that innocence, that natural veneration for Oa, the mother-goddess, had not something of it survived in us.

I am groping for an answer to the question, how such a writer can strike us as profoundly attuned to contemporary sensibility? It seems to be that in his own way, and short-circuiting a great deal of fashionable and sophisticated mythologizing, Golding gives remarkably full expression to a profound modern need, the need for reassurance in terms of the primitive; the longing to know somehow of a possible humanity that lived equably in the whole world; the need for myths of total and satisfactory explanation. Our developed consciousness, our accumulated knowledge are marks of guilt; the fragmentary nature of our experience is the theme of our artists. To discover again the undifferentiated myth, to return to Eden or to Neanderthal man—or indeed to the primary germ-cell the splitting of which is the beginning of guilt: that is to find innocence and wisdom.

Golding has been called a writer of 'fables'; 'what I would re-

gard as a tremendous compliment to myself,' he says, 'would be if
someone would substitute the word "myth" for "fable" . . . I do
feel fable as being an invented thing on the surface whereas myth is
something which comes out from the roots of things in the ancient
sense of being the key to existence, the whole meaning of life, and
experience as a whole.' And he accepted the description, 'myths of
total explanation' for his works. The genesis of these myths is
naturally obscure. They do not much resemble the myths of Joyce
or those of Mr. Eliot or Mr. David Jones; yet they are related to
the same Symbolist aspira- /14/ tions towards pre-logical primitive
images which animate all these authors.

The differences are attributable to Mr. Golding's relative isolation from any mainstream of speculation. To put it too simply: he
sees a world enormously altered by new knowledge. He understands
by the strong reaction against this new knowledge which is characteristic of modern art, an art in love with the primitive. And the
very patterns of human behaviour are now very generally explained
by reference to psychic residua or infantile guilt. It is a world you
can blame 'science' for if you like, a world in which the myth of
progress has failed; but the rival myth of necessary evil and universal guilt has come back without bringing God with it. He looks
at this world, understanding what it contains, as the painters at
Lascaux understood theirs. He thinks of the books of his childhood—*The Coral Island,* Wells's *Outline of History*—and observes
that they are wrong about the world, because they thought cannibals more wicked than white men and Neanderthal man less worthy
than his conqueror. These books have, in his own figure, rotted to
compost in his mind; and in that compost the new myth puts down
roots. When it grows it explains the ancient situation to which our
anxieties recall us: loss of innocence, the guilt and ignominy of
consciousness, the need for pardon. Mr. Golding owns that he is a
religious man. He believes that some people are saints: in *Lord of
the Flies* Simon is a saint, and this is why, he says, literary people
have found Simon incomprehensible; but 'he *is* comprehensible to
the illiterate person. . . . The illiterate person believes in saints and
sanctity.' (This is not the first time a modern artist has found his
allies among the illiterate—Yeats and Eliot have made similar declarations.) Golding believes in human guilt and the human sense of
paradise lost; he also believes in divine mercy.

The evidence for holiness lies scattered among the fragments /15/
of our world, and those fragments are represented in Golding's
books; they form part of the whole. But this whole is a world of
imagination, where everything is related, everything counts, and

truth is accessible; the world of myth. For Golding's own term
'myth' is the right one; out of the single small seed grows this instrument 'for controlling . . . ordering . . . giving a shape and
significance to the immense paradox of futility and anarchy which
is contemporary history.' These are Mr. Eliot's words on Joyce's
myth; but they will serve for Golding. Art, says Cassirer, requires a
step back into mythical thinking; perhaps this has always been so
since mythical thinking became obsolete, but never has the step
back been more consciously taken than in our times. And in the
contrast between our consciousness of this, and the momentary for-
getfulness of our Darwinian grandfathers, Golding found the theme
of his first novel.

   Lord of the Flies has 'a pretty big connection' with Ballantyne.
In *The Coral Island* Ralph, Jack and Peterkin are cast away on a
desert island, where they live active, civilised, and civilising lives.
Practical difficulties are easily surmounted; they light fires with
bowstrings and spyglasses, hunt pigs for food, and kill them with
much ease and a total absence of guilt—indeed of bloodshed. (They
are all Britons—a term they use to compliment each other—all brave,
obedient and honourable.) There is much useful information conveyed concerning tropical islands, including fieldworkers' reporting
of the conduct of cannibals: but anthropology is something nasty
that clears up on the arrival of a missionary, and Jack himself prevents an act of cannibalism by telling the flatnoses not to be such
blockheads and presenting them with six newly slaughtered pigs.
The parallel between the island and the Earthly Paradise causes a
trace of literary sophistication: 'Meat and drink on the same tree!
My dear boys, we're set up for life; it must be the ancient paradise
—hurrah! . . . We afterwards found, however, that /16/ these lovely
islands were very unlike Paradise in many things.' But these
'things' are non-Christian natives and, later, pirates; the boys themselves are cleanly (cold baths recommended) and godly—regenerate,
empire-building boys, who know by instinct how to turn paradise
into a British protectorate.
   The Coral Island (1858) could be used as a document in the history of ideas; it belongs inseparably to the period when boys were
sent out of Arnoldian schools certified free of Original Sin. Golding
takes Ralph, Jack and Peterkin (altering this name to Simon
'called Peter') and studies them against an altered moral landscape.
He is a schoolmaster, and knows boys well enough to make their
collapse into savagery plausible, to see *them* as the cannibals; the
authority of the grown-ups is all there is to prevent savagery. If you
dropped these boys into an Earthly Paradise 'they would not behave

like God-fearing English gentlemen' but 'as like as not . . . find
savages who were kindly and uncomplicated. . . . The devil would
rise out of the intellectual complications of the three white men.'
Golding leaves the noble savages out of *Lord of the Flies,* but this
remark is worth quoting because it states the intellectual position in
its basic simplicity. It is the civilised who are corrupt, out of phase
with natural rhythm. Their guilt is the price of evolutionary success; and our awareness of this fact can be understood by duplicat-
ing Ballantyne's situation, borrowing his island, and letting his
theme develop in this new and more substantial context. Once
more every prospect pleases; but the vileness proceeds, not from
cannibals, but from the boys, though Man is not so much vile as
'heroic and sick'. Unlike Ballantyne's boys, these are dirty and inefficient; they have some notion of order, symbolised by the beautiful
conch which heralds formal meetings; but when uncongenial effort
is required to maintain it, order disappears. The shelters are inadequate, the signal fire goes out at the very moment when Jack first
succeeds in killing a pig. Intelligence fades; irrational /17/ taboos
and blood rituals make hopeless the task of the practical but partial
intellect of Piggy; his glasses, the firemakers, are smashed and
stolen, and in the end he himself is broken to pieces as he holds
the conch. When civilised conditioning fades—how tedious Piggy's
appeal to what adults might do or think!—the children are capable
of neither savage nor civil gentleness. Always a little nearer to raw
humanity than adults, they slip into a condition of animality depraved by mind, into the cruelty of hunters with their devil-
liturgies and torture: they make an unnecessary, evil fortress, they
steal, they abandon all operations aimed at restoring them to
civility. Evil is the natural product of their consciousness. First the
smallest boys create a beastie, a snake—'as if it wasn't a good island'.
Then a beast is created in good earnest, and defined in a wonderful
narrative sequence. The emblem of this evil society is the head of a
dead pig, fixed, as a sacrifice, on the end of a stick and animated by
flies and by the imagination of the *voyant,* Simon.

Simon is Golding's first 'saint, and a most important figure.' He is
for the illiterate a proof of the existence of God because the illiterate
(to whom we are tacitly but unmistakably expected to attribute a
correct insight here) will say, 'well, a person like this cannot exist
without a good God'. For Simon 'voluntarily embraces the beast . . .
and tries to get rid of him'. What he understands—and this is wisdom Golding treats with awe—is that evil is 'only us'. He climbs up
to where the dead fire is dominated by the beast, a dead airman in
a parachute, discovers what this terrible thing really is, and rushes

off with the good news to the beach, where the maddened boys at their beast-slaying ritual mistake Simon himself for the beast and kill him. As Piggy, the dull practical intelligence, is reduced to blindness and futility, so Simon, the visionary, is murdered before he can communicate his comfortable knowledge. Finally, the whole Paradise is destroyed under the puzzled eyes of an adult observer. Boys will be boys. /18/

The difference of this world from Ballantyne's simpler construction from similar materials is not merely a matter of incomparability of the two talents at work; our minds have, in general, darker needs and obscurer comforts. It would be absurd to suppose that the change has impoverished us; but it has seemed to divide our world into 'two cultures'—the followers of Jack and the admirers of Simon, those who build fortresses and those who want to name the beast.

Lord of the Flies 'was worked out carefully in every possible way', and its author holds that the 'programme' of the book *is* its meaning. He rejects Lawrence's doctrine, 'Never trust the artist, trust the tale' and its consequence, 'the proper function of the critic is to save the tale from the artist'. He is wrong, I think; in so far as the book differs from its programme there is, as a matter of common sense, material over which the writer has no absolute authority. This means not only that there are possible readings which he cannot veto, but even that some of his own views on the book may be in a sense wrong. The interpretation of the dead parachutist is an example. This began in the 'programme', as straight allegory; Golding says that this dead man 'is' History. 'All that we can give our children' in their trouble is this monstrous dead adult, who's 'dead, but won't lie down'; an ugly emblem of war and decay that broods over the paradise and provides the only objective equivalent for the beasts the boys imagine. Now this limited allegory (I may even have expanded it in the telling) seems to me not to have got out of the 'programme' into the book; what does get in is more valuable because more like myth—capable, that is, of more various interpretation than the rigidity of Golding's scheme allows. And in writing of this kind all depends upon the author's mythopoeic power to transcend the 'programme'. Golding has this poetic power, and nowhere is it more impressively used than in his second book, *The Inheritors*.

Prefixed to *The Inheritors* is a passage from Wells's *Out-* /19/ *line of History,* and this serves the same purpose as Ballantyne's novel in the genesis of the earlier book; it sets off an antithetical argument. 'Wells's *Outline* played a great part in my life because my father was a rationalist, and the *Outline* was something he took neat. It is the rationalist gospel *in excelsis*. . . . By and by it seemed to me not to be large enough . . . too neat and too slick. And when I re-read it as an adult I came across his picture of Neanderthal man, our immediate predecessors, as being these gross brutal creatures who were possibly the basis of the mythological bad man . . . I thought to myself that this is just absurd. . . .' The difference between Golding and the Wells of the *Outline* is simple; to Wells the success of the high-foreheaded, weapon-bearing, carnivorous *homo sapiens* was progress, but to Golding it was the defeat of innocence, the sin of Adam seen in terms of a new kind of history.

Golding's real power, the true nature of his mythopoeic obsession, became evident only with the publication of this second book. This root-idea is, as I have suggested, a variant of the Fall, transplanted from theology. Golding is fascinated by the evidence—in the nature of the case ubiquitous—that human consciousness is a biological asset purchased at a price; the price is the knowledge of evil. This evil emanates from the human mind, a product of its action upon the environment. *The Inheritors* is about the accumulation of guilt that necessarily attended the historical success of *homo sapiens;* the intellectual superiority of Man over his simian victim is precisely measured by the cruelty and guilt which dominate his life and are relatively absent from his predecessor's. The creatures to be exterminated are almost innocent, as near it as we can imagine; they practise no deceit, have no obscure sense of life as a mystery, understand wickedness as killing, but their lives are controlled by the seasons, by inhibiting fears of water, above all by a physiological equipment excellent in its way but prohibiting intellect. They know the world with senses like an /20/ animal's; they depend much upon involuntary reflexes—keen scent, night vision, acuteness of ear; they are not men at all, and that is why they are innocent. Only after prolonged observation of the new men can Lok associate sex with cruelty, derange his senses with alcohol, offer violence to a friend; or even think of one thing or process as 'like' another. Not to know evil is, in a sense, to know nothing. The new men sail away, successful and guilty, leaving Lok with the doll-goddess which is his only image of the intelligent and creative mind. Clutching this toy, he who had known useful fear is now the prey of useless terror as well as of his animal enemies; they, the real creators, plan a bloody and intelligent future.

Technically *The Inheritors* attempts a little less than *Pincher Martin,* but has fewer flaws. The natural setting, of obvious importance, needed to be wonderfully done and is. Above all, the feat of recording observations of the activities of *homo sapiens* made with the sensory equipment of Lok is of astonishing virtuosity. We are constantly reminded of the involuntary powers that sustain him; his ears speak to him even if he will not listen, small areas of skin react with useful knowledge, the nose marvellously distinguishes and identifies. We can always see, too, that the extinction of this animal is *necessary,* as in the passage where he observes a new man aiming at him with a bow and can no more conceive of what the man is doing than he can impute enmity to so similar a being or explain his tall face—his senses simply report a series of inexplicable events. In the heart of the book there is a remarkable passage of some fifty pages in which Lok and the female Fa observe the communal activities of the new people from a vantage-point in a tree. This is carried out with a fierce imaginative power that is not in the least inconsistent with a very minute attention to the complicated effect to be communicated. What we have to be shown is that although we are experiencing these events innocently, by way of the passive, vegetarian, inhuman senses /21/ of Lok, we *belong* down below in the clearing, corrupt and intelligent. And at the end we abruptly leave Lok; suddenly, with a loss of sympathy, observe him with our normal sight, joining the new men, our own sort. With these anxious and responsible technicians we sail away, with only a last glimpse of superseded innocence stumbling about on the shore of a dead world. *The Inheritors* does not, like *Lord of the Flies,* qualify as a spanking good tale, and with its publication Golding met for the first time that mutter of baffled reviewers with which he is now so familiar. The book was written, presumably at white-heat, in a few weeks. It has not been surpassed.

Pincher Martin is, however, a bigger book. It is another imaginative 'forcing' of the same seminal ideal, but more densely written, with much interweaving of image and reference—more like a poem, in fact, for undoubtedly this kind of novel 'aspires' to the condition of poetry. It takes more reading than the others; it lacks the adventitious accessibility of *Lord of the Flies* and is less recognisably a story than *The Inheritors.* For all that, its wisp of narrative is handled with great skill, and after all the full import of the book depends upon a most ingenious narrative device. The talent remains clearly that which produced the earlier books, and some of the procedures, particularly those involving the extraction of significance from symbolic objects, are easy to recognise. And there is a continuity of theme. But it is, all the same, a book demanding unremitting attention.

Golding has himself provided 'a mental lifeline' to readers who find the book difficult; it appeared in *The Radio Times* and it might be useful to copy part of what he said.

> Christopher Hadly Martin had no belief in anything but the importance of his own life, no God. Because he was created in the image of God he had a freedom of choice which he used to centre the world on himself. He did not believe in purgatory and therefore when he died it was not presented to him in overtly /22/ theological terms. The greed for life which had been the mainspring of his nature forced him to refuse the selfless act of dying. He continued to exist separately in a world composed of his own murderous nature. His drowned body lies rolling in the Atlantic but the ravenous ego invents a rock for him to endure on. It is the memory of an aching tooth. Ostensibly and rationally he is a survivor from a torpedoed destroyer: but deep down he knows the truth. He is not fighting for bodily survival but for his continuing identity in face of what will smash it and sweep it away—the black lightning, the compassion of God. For Christopher, the Christ-bearer, has become Pincher Martin who is little but greed. Just to be Pincher is purgatory; to be Pincher for eternity is hell.

The man is called Martin so that his worldly name may be Pincher (a naval nickname for all Martins) and nobody calls him 'Christopher' until God does so at the end, out of the black lightning, as the resisting Martin shrinks to a mere pair of claws. Again the myth is worked out in fanatical detail; Martin calls his rock 'Rockall' not only because that is a real rock, but because he remembers a poor joke turning on a word which is a bad rhyme for Rockall, and which is an obscene word for 'nothing'. The geology and animal life of the rock he invents out of memories of childhood holidays. He is horribly aware of the self-deceit, the Promethean posing, the shrinking identity; he will do anything rather than accept the loss of himself, even in exchange for the mercy of God.

Martin is 'fallen man—fallen more than most'; a type of depravity. His human consciousness is an evolutionary specialisation, like a pig's snout, used to ensure handsome survival. He is hideously greedy, hence the recurrent metaphors from eating. 'He takes the best part (Martin had been an actor), the best seat, the most money, the best notice, the best woman. He was born with his mouth and his flies open and both hands out to grab. He's a cosmic case of the bugger who gets his penny and someone else's bun.' But this efficiency only makes his suffering more characteristic; he declares for madness /23/ rather than extinction, intellect rather than love, and makes his own most appropriate purgatory. Martin's boast is that he controls and imposes his will on the world: 'I can outwit you; you are a machine.' He is relieved to discover that the cause of apparently 'evil' manifestations lie entirely within himself; that his fear of the gull which makes him think of lizards originates in something he's read; that he can cure the world by curing his own disorder. There is a crucial and astonishing episode in which, with all the gestures of heroism, he undertakes to expel the poison from within him. He has eaten disgusting food, and it has made his mind sick as well as his body. 'I am in servitude to a coiled tube the length of a cricket pitch. All the terrors of hell can come down to nothing more than a stoppage. Why drag in good and evil when the serpent lies coiled in my own body?' His intelligent solution is a self-inflicted enema.

But although it is true that the evil proceeds from within him, it will not be dispersed by intelligence. That only preserves him alive for torture, and he creates his hell with the same effort that he puts forth to preserve his identity. Of the plenitude with which this and all the related paradoxes inherent in the theme are developed I have room to say virtually nothing. But one of them requires notice, since I argue for the totality of the imaginative act. Martin's acts are willed, but also necessary; and this is beautifully translated into narrative at the point where, as officer of the watch, he gives a helm-order a moment before the torpedo strikes. The order was freely willed and murderous; it was also necessary and proper in the circumstance. All that happened was 'because of what I did', but it could not have been otherwise. Only the best in fiction has invention of this order.

This is not quite the whole story. It would seem, as a hypothesis stemming from the situation described, that another heaven might be possible, a God to whom some other question than 'If I ate them, who gave me a mouth?' might be /24/ addressed. Golding's Nathaniel, whose natural goodness Martin recognises and resents, is there to say that only in the abandonment of the beloved self is there any way to this. Nathaniel is the second in what may be a band of Golding's elect, those who see and know. But Nathaniel is anything but a respectable saint; his religion has a seedy quality and it contributes to Martin's agony as well as shadowing it with some ecstatic alternative. It isn't a pill of doctrine but another part of the imaginative structure.

Pincher Martin is a wonderful achievement, the book of a drowned man soaked and battered by an actual sea, making substantial rock out of nightmare; it is as if one's own hands grew soft and swollen in the idiot water and bruised on the dripping stone. It is a horrible book too; because the man is shrunk so mercilessly into his minimal disgusting humanity, the fattest maggot of all; and because Golding's knowledge of human egotism and cruelty is horrible. What makes all this bearable and Golding a major novelist is the total technical control: nightmare, hysteria, every kind of beastliness and depravity are given the virtue of form. There is no distinguishing here between a compassion that might be called religious and the skill of an artist; they are the same thing. There are those who find Golding sadistic; it is a judgment that calls in question their ability to read any book whatsoever, because it betrays an insensitivity to the moral quality of form. Yeats spoke of an intellectual construct which enables him to 'hold in a single thought reality and justice'; *Pincher Martin* is such a thought.

Of *Free Fall,* Golding's fourth and perhaps his most ambitious book, I must say that although I do not feel that I have yet got to know it well I have no expectation that it can ever possess my mind as the others have done. It should be remembered that Golding asks a lot of his critics—this is a matter, I think, of emphasis, of his not saying 'The first page and the last page are crucial.' He does not say so because it /25/ seems to him self-evident.* It is not in such reticences that Mr. Golding fails (if he does fail); for in everything related to the shape of this myth his skill is all that it was in *Pincher Martin*. Technically *Free Fall* (which depends upon a system of 'time-shifts' devised to expose the religious significance of a man's experience) is at least as accomplished as any novel of Conrad's. It is a mark of Golding's integrity that in every book he employs technical devices of remarkable ingenuity but never indulges his skill; it is never a hair's-breadth in excess of what the moral occasion demands. One's coolness towards the book has other causes.

The myth of *Free Fall* is, basically, that of all Golding's books: the Fall of Man, the expulsion from Paradise, erected wit and infected will. It is a myth which has accumulated an enormous and various theology, which does not matter until the novelist turns theologian himself. Golding's hero is examining his life (made a typical life by many allegorical devices) with a view to discovering a pattern, some connexion between his two worlds of experience, one deterministic, the world of empirical observation, the other a world in which the burning bush is not consumed, a world of horror and glory, heaven and hell. Sammy's conclusion (which is not the conclusion of the novel) is that 'there is no bridge'. In his brooding over different episodes in his life, Sammy Mountjoy is necessarily theologising; in other words, there is within the book con-

---

* There is a perceptive study of the opening and the conclusion of *Free Fall* in an article by Ian Gregor and Martin Kinkead-Weekes called 'Mr. Golding and His Critics' (*Twentieth Century*, February, 1960). [See page 60—Ed.]

tinuous comment—admittedly not directly vouched for by the author—on the myth. I do not think that this works; there is un-
wonted hollowness in these passages, the shabbiness of a do-it-
yourself theology; and the book at moments lies open to the
Coleridgean charge of mental bombast—'thoughts and images too
great for the subject'—the subject being not the Fall but a *com-* /26/
mentary upon it. In Golding's earlier books—and this is unique in
modern fiction—guilt, unconscious innocence, the taste of isolation,
good and evil are made actual, like vomit in the mouth. It is this
actuality that is lacking in *Free Fall;* its absence takes the nature
out of Golding's prose, it takes the plasticity out of the narrative.
The crucial episode, a nightmare experience in a prison-cell, calls
for, and is not provided with, the savage compassion which went
into the writing of *Pincher Martin.* Yet it is in a way wonderfully
composed, passionate and cunning; there is no question of a failure
of power or of nerve, only—to be bold—of a flaw in the original
conception.

     This flaw is one to which Mr. Golding's gifts render him pe-
culiarly liable. Myths of total explanation are religious; comment
upon them is theology. *Free Fall,* like *Paradise Lost,* is about *everything;* the author knows this, devises his narrative and even names
his characters accordingly. Samuel Mountjoy at first misunder-
stands his vocation (like Samuel in the Bible) and is as a child in his
slum an inhabitant of Paradise (Mountjoy). As he writes, he lives on
Paradise Hill, 'thirty seconds from the shop and the local'. A central event of his life, as of Dante's, is the recognition of the beauty
of a girl called Beatrice; later, by a positive act of will, he rejects
the possibility of living by this vision, and subjects her to his lust.
The two worlds between which his life is suspended (in a condition of 'free fall' as understood in science fiction) are represented
by a religious schoolmistress and a science master called Nick. The
child does not have to choose; in childhood the two worlds inter-
lock. He chooses, as a young man, to desecrate Beatrice. The other
world he finds again in a prison-camp, where he is subjected by a
German officer named Halde* to an interrogation /27/ modelled
on that of Christ in the desert. Will he reject the 'world'? Is he a
a son of God? He does not know enough to betray his comrades,
and Halde sends him to a cell which he peoples with his own egotistical terrors; at the height of his agony he bursts out (or is let

---

* It has been pointed out that *Halde* means 'slope', and that this name is
also allegorical, since Halde is the agent by which Sammy moves into the
gravitational field of his spiritual work. Mr. Golding tells me he did not think
of this. It is allegorist's luck.

out) of the cell, forgiven. He walks into the world of vision: 'The power of gravity, dimension and space, the movement of the earth and sun and unseen stars, these made what might be called music and I heard it.' Beatrice has been reduced (and this passage is as fine as anything in Golding) to an incontinent idiot in an asylum; but Sammy still finds himself called to Paradise. He cannot reconcile the two worlds but the novelist, on the last page, builds a kind of bridge between them.

That it is mythologically substantial, this bridge, I do not doubt; but I do not understand it. The novel is about delivery from the body of this death; not only about the Fall but also about regeneration. This account of it is too scanty to be fair even to my imperfect understanding of the book, but it may be enough to help me make my point: that it is not the religious but the theological element that limits the imaginative scope, and brings into the writing a kind of dry heat, a brittleness, absent before. I ought to say that Messrs. Gregor and Kinkead-Weekes, in the intelligent article I have already quoted, find the theology satisfactory, and indeed orthodox. But Mr. Golding is not orthodox. He has done what writers in the Romantic tradition have done before—as Mallarmé discovered Nirvana without knowing Buddhism, or as Yeats dwelt, though heretically, on the Annunciation, he has found in experience and embodied in his own myths the truths that inform all others. But to provide accounts of mystical experience is one thing—admittedly a difficult thing, if only because of the qualitative differences between St. John of the Cross and a mescalin addict; to invent a mystical theology is another. The first is work for a genius, the second for a church. Not to see this is the /28/ flaw of all the Romantic and Symbolist writers who lapsed into the pseudo-theologies of occultism.

A final word on 'simplicity'. Golding's novels are simple in so far as they deal in the primordial patterns of human experience and in so far as they have skeletons of parable. On these simple bones the flesh of narrative can take extremely complex forms. This makes for difficulty, but of the most acceptable kind, the difficulty that attends the expression of what is profoundly simple. For all that I have said against *Free Fall* it is this kind of book, like the others a work of genius by a writer from whom we can hope for much more, since he is in superbly full possession of his great powers. /29/

MEN OF A SMALLER GROWTH:
A PSYCHOLOGICAL ANALYSIS OF
WILLIAM GOLDING'S LORD OF THE FLIES

CLAIRE ROSENFIELD

When an author consciously dramatizes Freudian theory—and dramatizes it successfully—only the imaginative re-creation of human behavior rather than the sustaining structure of ideas is apparent. In analyzing William Golding's *Lord of the Flies*, the critic must assume that Golding knows psychological literature and must then attempt to show how an author's knowledge of theory can vitalize his prose and characterization. The plot itself is uncomplicated, so simple, indeed, that one wonders how it so effortlessly absorbs the burden of meaning. During some unexplained man-made holocaust a plane, evacuating a group of children, crashes on the shore of a tropical island. All adults are conveniently killed. The narrative follows the children's gradual return to the amorality of childhood, and it is the very nature of that state of non-innocence which makes them small savages. Or we might make the analogy to the childhood of races and compare the child to the primitive. Denied the sustaining and repressing authority of parents, church, and state, they form a new culture the development of which reflects that of the genuine primitive society, evolving its gods and demons (its myths), its rituals and taboos (its social norms). On the level of pure narrative, the action proceeds from the gradual struggle between Ralph and Jack, the two oldest boys, for precedence. Ralph is the natural leader by virtue of his superior height, his superior strength, his superior beauty. His mild expression proclaims him "no devil." He possesses the symbol of authority, the conch, or sea shell, which the children use to assemble their miniature councils. Golding writes, "The being that had blown . . . [the conch] had sat waiting for them on the platform with the delicate thing balanced on his knees, was set apart." Jack, on the other hand, is described in completely antithetical terms; he is distinguished by his ugliness and his red hair, a traditional demonic attribute. He first

Claire Rosenfield, " 'Men of a Smaller Growth': A Psychological Analysis of William Golding's *Lord of the Flies*," *Literature and Psychology*, XI (Autumn, 1961), 93-96, 99-101. Reprinted by special permission of publisher and author.

appears as the leader of a church choir, which "creature-like" marches in two columns behind him. All members of the choir wear black; "their bodies, from throat to ankle, were hidden by black cloaks."¹ Ralph initially blows the conch to discover how many children have escaped death in the plane crash. As Jack approaches with his choir from the "darkness of the forest," he cannot see Ralph, whose back is to the sun. The former is, symbolically, sun-blinded. These two are very obviously intended to recall God and the Devil, whose confrontation, in the history of Western religions, establishes the moral basis for all actions. But, as Freud reminds us, "metaphysics" becomes "metapsychology"²; gods and devils are "nothing other than psychological processes projected into the outer world."³ If Ralph is a projection of man's good impulses from which we derive the authority figures—whether god, king, or father—who establish the necessity for our valid ethical and social action, then Jack becomes an externalization of the evil instinctual forces of the unconscious. Originally, as in the more primitive religions, gods and devils were one; even Hebraic-Christian tradition makes Satan a fallen angel.

The temptation is to regard the island on which the children are marooned as a kind of Eden, uncorrupted and Eveless. But the actions of the children negate any assumption about childhood innocence. Even though Golding himself momentarily becomes a victim of his Western culture and states that Ralph wept for the "end of innocence," events have simply supported Freud's conclusions that no child is innocent. On a third level, Ralph is every man—or every child—and his body becomes the battleground where reason and instinct struggle, each to assert itself. For to regard Ralph and Jack as Good and Evil is to ignore the role of the child Piggy, who in the child's world of make-believe is the outsider. Piggy's composite description not only manifests his dif- /93/ ference from the other boys; it also reminds the reader of the stereotype image of the old man who has more-than-human wisdom: he is fat, inactive because asthmatic, and generally reveals a disinclination for physical labor. Because he is extremely nearsighted, he wears thick glasses—a further mark of his difference. As time passes, the hair of the other boys grows with abandon. "He was the only boy on the island whose hair never seemed to grow. The rest were shock-headed, but Piggy's hair still lay in wisps over his head as though baldness were his natural state, and this imperfect covering would soon go, like the velvet on a young stag's antlers" (81). In these images of age and authority we have a figure reminiscent of the children's past—the father. Moreover, like the father he counsels common sense; he alone leavens with a reasonable gravity the constant exuberance of the others for play or for play at hunting. When they scamper off at every vague whim, he scornfully comments, " 'Like a pack of kids.' " Ungrammatically but logically, he tries to allay the "littluns" fear of a "beast." " 'Life is scientific, that's what it is. . . . I know there isn't no beast—not with claws and all that, I mean—but I know there isn't no fear, either' " (105). He has excessive regard for the forms of order: the conch must be held by a child before that child can speak at councils. When the others neglect responsibility, fail to build shelters, swim in the pools or play in the sand or hunt, allow the signal fire on the mountain to go out or to get out of hand and burn up half the island, he seconds Ralph by admonishing the others vigorously and becomes more and more of a spoil-sport who robs play of its illusions, the adult interrupting the game. Ralph alone recognizes his superior intelligence but wavers between what he knows to be wise and the group acceptance his egocentricity demands. Finally, Piggy's role—as man's reasoning faculties and as a father—derives some of its complexity from the fact that the fire which the children foster and guard on the mountain in the hope of communicating with the adult world is lighted with his glasses. In mythology, after all, the theft of fire brought civilization—and, hence, repression—to man. As the new community becomes more and more irrational, its irrationality is marked by Piggy's progressive blindness. An accident following an argument between Ralph and Jack breaks one of the lenses. When the final breach between the two occurs and Piggy supports Ralph, his remaining lens is stolen in a night raid by Jack. This is a parody of the traditional fire theft, which was to provide light and warmth for mankind. After this event Piggy must be led by Ralph. When he is making his final plea for his glasses—reasoned as always—he is struck on the head by a rock and falls. "Piggy fell forty feet and landed on his back on that square, red rock in the sea. His head opened and stuff came out and turned red. Piggy's arms and legs twitched a bit, like a pig's after it has been killed" (223).

The history of the child Piggy on the island dramatizes in terms of the individual the history of the entire group. When they first assemble to investigate their plight, they treat their island isolation as a temporary phenomenon; they want to play games until they are rescued—until their parents reassert the repressive actions of authority. This microcosm of the great world seems to them to be a fairy land.

A kind of glamour spread over them and the scene and they were conscious of the glamour and made happy by it (33).

> The coral was scribbled in the sea as though a giant had bent down to reproduce the shape of the island in a flowing, chalk line but tired before he had finished (38).

> "This is real exploring," said Jack. "I'll bet nobody's been here before" (35). /94/

> Echoes and birds flew, white and pink dust floated, the forest further down shook as with the passage of an enraged monster: and then the island was still (37).

They compare this reality to their reading experiences: it is Treasure Island or Coral Island or like pictures from their travel books. This initial reaction conforms to the pattern of play which Johan Huizinga establishes in *Homo Ludens*.[4] In its early stages their play has no cultural or moral function; it is simply a "stepping out of real life into a temporary sphere of activity."[5] Ironically, the child of *Lord of the Flies* who thinks he is "only pretending" or that this is "only for fun" does not realize that his play is the beginning of the formation of a new society which has regressed to a primitive state, with all its emphasis upon taboo and communal action. What begins by being like other games in having a distinct "locality and duration"[6] apart from ordinary life is—or becomes—reality. The spatial separation necessary for the make-believe of the game is represented first by the island. In this new world the playground is further narrowed: the gatherings of the children are described as a circle at several points, a circle from which Piggy is excluded:

> For the moment the boys were a closed circuit of sympathy with Piggy outside (29).

> They became a circle of boys round a camp fire and even Ralph and Piggy were half-drawn in (92).

Piggy approximates the spoil-sport who "robs the play of its illusion."[7]

The games of the beginning have a double function: they, first of all, reflect the child's attitude toward play as a temporary cessation from the activities imposed by the adult world; but like the games played before the formation of civilization, they anticipate the ritual which reveals a developing society. So the children move from voluntary play to ritual, from "only pretending" to reality, from representation to identification. The older strictures imposed by parents are soon forgotten—but every now and then a momentary remembrance of past prohibitions causes restraint. One older child hides in order to throw stones at a younger one.

Yet there was a space round Henry, perhaps six yards in diameter, into which he dare not throw. Here, invisible yet strong, was the taboo of the old life. Round the squatting child was the protection of parents and school and policemen and the law (78).

Jack hesitates when, searching for meat, he raises his knife to kill his first pig.

The pause was only long enough for them to understand what an enormity the downward stroke would be. Then the piglet tore loose from the creepers and scurried into the undergrowth. . . .
"Why didn't you——?"
They knew very well why he hadn't: because of the enormity of the knife descending and cutting into living flesh; because of the unbearable blood (40-41).

The younger children first, then gradually the older ones, like primitives in the childhood of races, begin to people the darkness of night and forest with spirits and demons which had previously appeared only in their dreams or fairy tales. Now there are no comforting mothers to dispel the terrors of the unknown. They externalize these fears into the figure of a "beast." Once the word "beast" is mentioned, the menace of the irrational becomes overt; name and thing become one. At one critical council when the first communal feeling begins to disintegrate, Ralph cries, " 'If only they could send us something grown-up . . . a sign or something' " (117). And a sign does come from the outside. /95/ That night, unknown to the children, a plane is shot down and its pilot parachutes dead to earth and is caught in the rocks on the mountain. It requires no more than the darkness of night together with the shadows of the forest vibrating in the signal fire to distort the hanging corpse with its expanding silk 'chute into a demon that must be appeased. Ironically, the fire of communication does touch this object of the grown-up world only to foster superstition. Security in this new situation can be achieved only by establishing new rules.

During the first days the children, led by Jack, play at hunting. But eventually the circle of the playground extends to the circle of the hunted and squealing pig seeking refuge—and it is significant that the first animal slain for food is a nursing sow—which itself anticipates the circle of consecrated ground where the children perform the new rites of the kill.

The first hunt accomplishes its purpose: the blood of the animals is spilled; the meat, used for food. But because Jack and his choir undertake this hunt, they desert the signal fire, which is dictated by the common-sense desire for rescue, and it goes out and a ship passes the island. Later the children reenact the killing with one boy, Maurice, assuming the role of the pig running its frenzied circle. The others chant in unison: " 'Kill the pig. Cut her throat. Bash her in.' " At this dramatic representation each child is still aware that this is a display, a performance. He is never "so beside himself that he loses consciousness of ordinary reality."[8] Each time they reenact the same event, however, their behavior becomes more frenized, more cruel, less like representation than identification. The chant then becomes, " 'K i l l the beast. C u t his throat. S p i l l his blood.' " It is as if the first event, the pig's death, is forgotten in the recesses of time; a new myth defines the primal act. Real pig becomes mythical beast.

Jack's ascendancy over the group begins when the children's fears distort the natural objects around them: twigs become creepers, shadows become demons. I have already discussed the visual imagery suggesting Jack's demonic function. He serves as a physical manifestation of irrational forces. After an indefinite passage of time, he appears almost dehumanized, his "nose only a few inches from the humid earth." He is "dog-like" and proceeds forward "on all fours" "into the semi-darkness of the undergrowth." His cloak and clothing have been shed. Indeed, except for a "pair of tattered shorts held up by his knife-belt, he was naked." His eyes seemed "bolting and nearly mad." He has lost his ability to communicate with Ralph as on the first day. "He tried to convey the compulsion to track down and kill that was swallowing him up" (65). "They walked along, two continents of experience and feeling, unable to communicate" (70). When Jack first explains to Ralph the necessity to disguise himself from the pigs he wants to hunt, he rubs his face with clay and charcoal. At this point he assumes a mask, begins to dance, is finally freed from all the repressions of his past. "He capered towards Bill, and the mask was a thing on its own, behind which Jack hid, liberated from shame and self-consciousness" (80). At the moment of the dance the mask and Jack are one. The first kill, as I have noted, follows the desertion of the signal fire and the passage of a possible rescue ship. Jack is still revelling in the knowledge that he has "outwitted a living thing, imposed their will upon it, taken away its life like a long and satisfying drink" (88). Already he has begun to obliterate the distinctions between animals and men, as do primitives; already he thinks in terms of the metaphor of a ritual drinking of blood, the efficacy of which depended on the drinker's assumption of his victim's strength and spirit. Ralph and Piggy confront him with his defection of duty.

The two boys faced each other. There was the brilliant world of hunting, tactics, fierce exhilaration, skill; and there was the world of longing and baffled common- /96/ sense. Jack transferred the knife to his left hand and smudged blood over his forehead as he pushed down the plastered hair (89).

Jack's unconscious gesture is a parody of the ritual of initiation in which the hunter's face is smeared with the blood of his first kill. In the subsequent struggle one of the lenses of Piggy's spectacles is broken. The dominance of reason is over; the voice of the old world is stilled. The primary images are no longer those of fire and light but those of darkness and blood. The link between Ralph and Jack "had snapped and fastened elsewhere."

The rest of the group, however, shifts its allegiance to Jack because he has given them meat rather than something useless like fire. Gradually, they begin to be described as "shadows" or "masks" or "savages" or "demoniac figures" and, like Jack, "hunt naked save for paint and a belt." Ralph now uses Jack's name with the recognition that "a taboo was evolving around that word too." Name and thing again become one; to use the word is to incite the bearer. But more significant, the taboo, according to Freud, is "a very primitive prohibition imposed from without (by an authority) and directed against the strongest desires of man."[9] In this new society it replaces the authority of the parents. Now every kill becomes a sexual act, is a metaphor for childhood sexuality.

The afternoon wore on, hazy and dreadful with damp heat; the sow staggered her way ahead of them, bleeding and mad, and the hunters followed, wedded to her in lust, excited by the long chase and dropped blood. . . . The sow collapsed under them and they were heavy and fulfilled upon her (167-168).

Every subsequent "need for ritual" fulfills not only the desire for communication and a substitute security to replace that of civilization, but also the need to liberate both the repressions of the past and those imposed by Ralph. Indeed, the projection of those impulses that they cannot accept in themselves into a beast is the beginning of a new mythology. The earlier dreams and nightmares can now be shared as the former subjectivity could not be.

When the imaginary demons become defined by the rotting corpse and floating 'chute on the mountain which their terror distorts into a beast, Jack wants to track the creature down. After the next kill, the head of the pig is placed upon a stake to placate it. Finally one of the children, Simon, after an epileptic fit, creeps out of the forest at twilight while the others are engaged in enthusiastic dancing following a hunt. Seized by the rapture of reenactment or perhaps terrorized by fear and night into believing that this little creature is a beast, they circle Simon, pounce on him, bite and tear his body to death. He becomes not a substitute for beast but beast itself; representation becomes absolute identification, "the mystic repetition of the initial event."[10] At the moment of Simon's death, nature speaks; a cloud bursts; rain and wind fill the parachute on the hill and the corpse of the pilot falls or is dragged among the screaming boys. Both Simon and the dead man, beast and beast, are washed into the sea and disappear. After this complete resurgence of savagery in accepted ritual, there is only a short interval before Piggy's remaining lens is stolen, he is intentionally killed as an enemy, and Ralph, the human being, becomes hunted like beast or pig.

Simon's mythic and psychological role has earlier been suggested. Undersized, subject to epileptic fits, bright-eyed, and introverted, he constantly creeps away from the others to meditate among the intricate vines of the forest. To him, as to the mystic, superior knowledge is given intuitively which he cannot communicate. When the first report of the beast-pilot reaches camp, /97/ Simon, we are told, can picture only "a human at once heroic and sick." During the day preceding his death, he walks vaguely away and stumbles upon the pig's head left in the sand in order to appease the demonic forces they imagine. Shaman-like, he holds a silent colloquy with it, a severed head covered with innumerable flies. It is itself the titled Lord of the Flies, a name applied to the Biblical demon Beelzebub and later used in Goethe's *Faust, Part I,* to describe Mephistopheles.[11] From it he learns that it is the Beast, and the Beast cannot be hunted because it is within. Simon feels the advent of one of his fits and imagines the head expanding, an anticipation or intuition of the discovery of the pilot's corpse. Suddenly Golding employs a startling image, "Simon was inside the mouth. He fell down and lost consciousness" (178). Literally, this image presents the hallucination of a sensitive child about to lose control of his rational faculties. Metaphorically, it suggests the ritual quest in which the hero is swallowed by a serpent or dragon or beast whose belly is the underworld, undergoes a symbolic death in order to gain the elixir to revitalize his stricken society, and returns with his knowledge to the timed world as a redeemer. Psychologically, this narrative pattern is a figure of speech connoting the annihilation of the ego, an internal journey necessary for self-understanding, a return to the timelessness of the unconscious. When Simon wakes, he realizes that he must confront the beast on the mountain because "what else is there to do?" He is relieved of "that dreadful feeling of the pressure of personality" which had oppressed him earlier. When he discovers the hanging corpse, he first frees it in compassion although it is rotting and surrounded by flies, and then staggers unevenly down to report to the others. Redeemer and scapegoat, he becomes the victim of the group he seeks to enlighten. In death—before he is pulled into the sea—his head is surrounded by flies in an ironic parody of the halo of saints and gods.

Piggy's death, soon to follow Simon's, is foreshadowed when the former proclaims at council that there is no beast. " 'What would a beast eat?' " " 'Pig.' " " 'We eat pig,' " he rationally answers. " 'Piggy!' " (104) is the next word. At Piggy's death his body twitches "like a pig's after it has been killed." Not only has his head been smashed, but also the conch, symbol of order, is simultaneously broken. A complex group of metaphors unite to form a total meta-phor involving Piggy and the pig, hunted and eaten by the children, and the pig's head which is at once left to appease the beast's hunger and is the beast itself. But the beast is within, and the chil-dren are defined by the very objects they seek to destroy.

In these associated images we have the whole idea of a communal and sacrificial feast and a symbolic cannibalism, all of which Freud discussed in *Totem and Taboo*. Here the psychology of the indi-vidual contributes the configurations for the development of re-ligion. Indeed, the events of *Lord of the Flies* imaginatively parallel the patterns which Freud detects in primitive mental processes.

Having populated the outside world with demons and spirits which are projections of their instinctual nature, these children—and primitive men—must then unconsciously evolve new forms of worship and laws, which manifest themselves in taboos, the oldest form of social repression. With the exception of the first kill—in which the children still imagine they are playing at hunting—the subsequent deaths assume a ritual form; the pig is eaten commu-nally by all and the head is left for the "beast," whose role consists in sharing the feast. This is much like the "public ceremony"[12] described by Freud in which the sacrifice of an animal provided food for the god and his worshippers. The complex relationships within the novel between the "beast," the pigs which are sacrificed, the children whose asocial impulses are externalized in the beast—this has already been discussed. So we see that, as Freud points out, the "sacrificing community, /98/ its god [the 'beast'], and the sacri-ficial animal are of the same blood,"[13] members of a clan. The pig, then, may be regarded as a totem animal, an "ancestor, a tutelary spirit and protector";[14] it is, in any case, a part of every child. The taboo or prohibition against eating particular parts of the totem animal coincides with the children's failure to eat the head of the pig. It is that portion which is set aside for the "beast." Just as Freud describes the primitive feast, so the children's festive meal is accompanied by a frenzied ritual in which they temporarily release their forbidden impulses and represent the kill. To consume the pig and to reenact the event is not only to assert a "common identity"[15] but also to share a "common responsibility" for the deed. None of the boys is excluded from the feast. The later ritual, in which Simon, as a human substitute identified with the totem, is killed, is in this novel less an unconscious attempt to share the responsibility for the killing of a primal father in prehistoric times, than it is a social act in which the participants celebrate their new society by commemorating their severance from the authority of the civilized state. Because of the juxtaposition of Piggy and pig, the eating of pig at the communal feast might be regarded as the symbolic cannibalism by which the children physically partake of the qualities of the slain and share responsibility for their crime. (It must be remembered that, although Piggy on a symbolic level represents the light of reason and the authority of the father, on the psychological and literal level of the story he shares that bestiality and irrationality which to Golding dominate all men, even the most rational or civilized.)

In the final action, Ralph is outlawed by the children and hunted like an animal. Roger sharpens a stick at both ends so that it will be ready to receive the severed head of the boy as if he were a pig. Jack keeps his society together because it, like the brother horde of Robertson Smith[16] and Freud, "is based on complicity in the common crimes."[17] In his flight Ralph, seeing the grinning skull of a pig, thinks of it as a toy and remembers the early days on the island when all were united in play. In the play world, the world of day, he has become a "spoil-sport" like Piggy; in the world based upon primitive rites and taboos, the night world where fears become demons and sleep is like death, he is the heretic or outcast. This final hunt, after the conch is broken, is the pursuit of the figure representing law and order, the king or the god. Finally, Jack, through misuse of the dead Piggy's glasses, accidentally sets the island on fire. A passing cruiser, seeing the fire, lands to find only a dirty group of sobbing little boys. " 'Fun and games,' said the officer. . . . 'What have you been doing? Having a war or something?' " (246-47).

But are all the meanings of the novel as clear as they seem? To restrict it to an imaginative re-creation of Freud's theory that children are little savages, that no child is innocent whatever Christian theology would have us believe, is to limit its significance for the adult world. To say that the "beasts" we fear are within, that man is essentially irrational—or, to place a moral judgment on the irrational, that man is evil—that, again, is too easy. In this forced isolation of a group of children, Golding is making a statement about the world they have left—a world, we are told, "in ruins." According to Huizinga's theory of play, war is a game, a contest for prestige which, like the games of primitives or of classical athletes, may be fatal. It, too, has its rules, although the modern concept of total war tends to obscure both its ritualistic and its ennobling character. It, too, has its spatial and temporal limitations, as the new rash of "limited" wars makes very clear. More than once the children's acts are compared to those of the outside world. When Jack first blackens his face like a savage, he gives his explanation: " 'For hunting. Like in war. You know—dazzle paint. Like things trying to look like something else' " (79). Appalled by one of the ritual dances, Piggy and Ralph discuss the authority and ration- /99/ ality of the apparently secure world they have left:

"Grown-ups know things," said Piggy. "They ain't afraid of the dark. They'd meet and have tea and discuss. Then things 'ud be all right—"
"They wouldn't set fire to the island. Or lose—"
"They'd build a ship—"
The three boys stood in the darkness, striving unsuccessfully to convey the majesty of adult life.
"They wouldn't quarrel—"
"Or break my specs—"
"Or talk about a beast—"
"If only they could get a message to us," cried Ralph desperately. "If only they could send us some thing grown-up . . . a sign or something" (117).

The sign does come that night, unknown to them, in the form of the parachute and its attached corpse. The pilot is the analogue in the adult world to the ritual killing of the child Simon on the island; he, like Simon, is the victim and scapegoat of his society, which has unleased its instincts in war. Both he and Simon are associated by a cluster of visual images. Both are identified with beasts by the children, who do see the truth—that all men are bestial—but do not understand it. Both he and Simon attract the flies from the Lord of the Flies, the pig's head symbolic of the demonic; both he and Simon are washed away by a cleansing but not reviving sea. His position on the mountain recalls the Hanged or Sacrificed god of Frazer; here, however, we have a parody of fertility. He is dead proof that Piggy's exaggerated respect for adults is itself irrational. When the officer at the rescue jokingly says, " 'What have you been doing? Having a war or something?' " this representative of the grown-up world does not understand that the games of the children, which result in two deaths, are a moral commentary upon the primitive nature of his own culture. The ultimate irrationality is war. Paradoxically, the children not only return to a primitive and infantile morality, but they also degenerate into adults. They prove that, indeed, "children are but men of a smaller growth."

NOTES

[1] William Golding, *Lord of the Flies* (London, 1958), p. 25. Subsequent references to this work will be noted parenthetically by page numbers in the text.
[2] Sigmund Freud, *The Psychopathology of Everyday Life*, as quoted by Ernest Jones, *The Life and Work of Sigmund Freud* (New York, 1957), III, 53.
[3] *Ibid.*
[4] Johan Huizinga, *Homo Ludens* (Boston, 1955).
[5] *Ibid.*, p. 8.
[6] *Ibid.*, p. 9.
[7] *Ibid.*, p. 7.
[8] *Ibid.*, p. 14.
[9] Sigmund Freud, "Totem and Taboo," in *The Basic Writings of Sigmund Freud*, trans. A. A. Brill (New York, 1938), p. 834.
[10] *Ibid.*, p. 834.
[11] *Ibid.* /100/
[12] There are further affinities to Sartre's *Les Mouches*.
[13] *Totem and Taboo*, p. 878.
[14] *Ibid.*, p. 808.
[15] *Ibid.*, p. 914.
[16] William Robertson Smith, *Lectures on the Religion of the Semites*, 3rd ed., with introduction by Stanley A. Cook (New York, 1927).
[17] *Totem and Taboo*, p. 916. /101/

"GIMMICK" AND METAPHOR IN THE NOVELS OF WILLIAM GOLDING

JAMES GINDIN

William Golding has written four novels. *Lord of the Flies* (1954); *The Inheritors* (1955); *Pincher Martin* (1956); *Free Fall* (1959). Each of the first three demonstrates the use of unusual and striking

James Gindin, *Postwar British Fiction* (Berkeley, California: University of California Press, 1962), pp. 196-206. Reprinted by special permission.

literary devices. Each is governed by a massive metaphorical structure—a man clinging for survival to a rock in the Atlantic Ocean or an excursion into the mind of man's evolutionary antecedent—designed to assert something permanent and significant about human nature. The metaphors are intensive, far-reaching; they permeate all the details and events of the novels. Yet at the end of each novel the metaphors, unique and striking as they are, turn into "gimmicks," into clever tricks that shift the focus or the emphasis of the novel as a whole. And, in each instance, the "gimmick" seems to work against the novel, to contradict or to limit the range of reference and meaning that Golding has already established metaphorically. The turn from metaphor to "gimmick" (and "gimmick" is the word that Golding himself has applied to his own endings) raises questions concerning the unity and, perhaps more important, the meaning of the novels.

Golding's first novel, *Lord of the Flies,* tells the story of a /196/ group of English schoolboys, between the ages of six and twelve, who survive a plane crash on a tropical island. The boys were apparently evacuated during a destructive atomic war and are left, with no adult control anywhere about, to build their own society on the island. The chance to create a new paradise is clear enough, but Golding quickly indicates that the boys are products of and intrinsically parts of current human society. Even on the very first page: "The fair boy stopped and jerked his stockings with an automatic gesture that made the jungle seem for a moment like the Home Counties." The island provides food, plenty of opportunity for swimming, and "fun." But a conflict quickly develops between the boys, led by Ralph, who would keep a fire going (they cherish some hope of rescue) and build adequate shelters, and those, led by Jack, originally members of a choir, who would hunt wild pigs and give full reign to their predatory and savage instincts. In the first, democratic meeting Ralph wins most of the boys' votes and is elected the leader of the island. But the rational democracy is not able to cope very well with the fears of the younger boys, the occasional tendency to rash mob action, the terror of the unexplained "beast" which fills the night. Gradually Jack gains more followers. He paints himself in savage colors, neglects to tend the fire because he is mercilessly tracking down a wild pig, establishes a wild and ritualistic dance that fascinates the boys. When one of the boys, having discovered the rational truth of the "beast" at the top of the mountain (the "beast" is a dead man in his parachute, dropped from a battle ten miles above the island), stumbles into the ritualistic dance, he is forced by Jack to enact the role of the pig. The boy is never given the time or the opportunity to make the rational truth clear, for the dancers, cloaked in frenzy and darkness, kill him. Ralph is unable to stop the others, and even, to his shame, recognizes some of the same dark frenzy at the center of his own being. And Piggy, Ralph's "brain trust" though always unattractive and unpopular, the boy whose glasses got the fire going in the first place, is killed by Jack's principal lieutenant. Jack is victorious. His dogmatic authority, his cruelty, /197/ and his barbaric frenzy have a deeper hold on the nature of man than do Ralph's sensible regulations. The forces of light and reason fail to alleviate the predatory brutality and the dark, primeval fear at the center of man.

But the metaphor of the society the boys construct is not left to do its work alone. Just when the savage forces led by Jack are tracking down Ralph and burning the whole island to find him, a British naval officer arrives to rescue the boys. Ironically, the smoke of barbaric fury, not the smoke of conscious effort, has led to rescue. Throughout the novel, frequent references to possible rescue and to the sanity of the adult world seemed the delusions of the rational innocent. Ralph and Piggy often appealed to adult sanity in their futile attempt to control their world, but, suddenly and inconsistently at the end of the novel, adult sanity really exists. The horror of the boys' experience on the island was, after all, really a childish game, though a particularly vicious one. The British officer turns into a public school master: "I should have thought that a pack of British boys—you're all British aren't you?— would have been able to put up a better show than that" (p. 248). The officer's density is apparent, but the range of the whole metaphor has been severely limited. Certainly the whole issue, the whole statement about man, is not contradicted by the ending, for, as Golding directly points out, Ralph has learned from the experience: "And in the middle of them, with filthy body, matted hair, and unwiped nose, Ralph wept for the end of innocence, the darkness of man's heart, and the fall though the air of the true, wise friend called Piggy" (p. 248). But the rescue is ultimately a "gimmick," a trick, a means of cutting down or softening the implications built up within the structure of the boys' society on the island.

Golding's second novel, *The Inheritors,* relates the story of the last family of man's ancestors, conquered and supplanted by man. The family of "'people" (Golding's word for the heavy, hairy, apelike forerunners of man) migrate to their spring home and slowly realize that things have changed, slowly discover the encroachments of a tribe of "others" (men). The "people" are /198/ not capable of thinking, of abstraction, or of forming rational connections. They simply act by instinct and "have pictures," many of which they do not understand. Yet, for all their perceptual and intellectual limitations, the "people" have a code of ethics (they will not kill other animals, though they do eat the meat of animals already killed), a deep and humble sense of their own limitations, and a faith in the divine power and goodness of the earth. In addition, the "people" enjoy a family life free from fighting, guilt, and emotional squabbling. Each has his function, carefully defined and limited, each his respect for the other members of the family. The novel is the process of man conquering the "people," capturing or killing them one by one. The last of the "people" is able to watch man, to understand dimly man's power and victory. But this last survivor of the "people" is also able to sense in what ways man is a creature different from the "people." He watches man brawl and fight, steal other men's mates, suffer guilt and anxiety, tear himself apart between his real ability and his failure to exceed his limitations. The novel carries the implication that man's unique power to reason and think carries with it his propensity toward pride and sin and guilt, toward those qualities that cause him pain and misery.

Most of the novel is told from the point of view of the last of the "people," a humble creature who depicts the issues without fully understanding them. The last chapter, however, provides a switch in point of view, for it is seen through the eyes of one of the men after the "people," the "devils" in human terminology, have been wiped out. The theme does not change: man sees himself as a being tortured by pride and guilt, one who has faith in his power but continually runs into conflict with other men and with his own limitations. Here, the "gimmick" does not change or vitiate the point of the novel. Rather, the "gimmick," the switch in point of view, merely repeats what the rest of the novel has already demonstrated. Awareness and rational intelligence are still inextricably connected with human sin, and the "gimmick" at the end of the novel breaks the unity /199/ without adding relevant perspective. The contrast between the "people" and men is more effectively detailed, made more sharply applicable and relevant, when dimly apprehended by the last of the "people."

Man's capacity to reason is again ineffectual in Golding's third novel, *Pincher Martin*. Christopher Martin ("Pincher" because he has presumably stolen almost everything he's ever had), a naval officer, is blown into the North Atlantic when a submarine attacks his ship. Fighting the water and shrieking for rescue, he eventually finds a rock in the middle of the ocean. He laboriously makes his way to the surface of the rock. Convinced of his health, his education, and his intelligence, he consciously sets about organizing his routine, naming places, gathering food, doing all that rational man can do to insure his survival and rescue, his ultimate salvation. But time and weather, forces stronger than he, in addition to his guilty consciousness of past sins (brought up through his memory of his past as actor, seducer, pincher of whatever his friends had), wear down the rational man. All his rational efforts fail and he is pushed by nature, both external and internal, toward death and damnation.

The conflict between survival and extinction is extended by a consistent use of microcosmic imagery. When Martin first sees the rock, Golding writes: "A single point of rock, peak of a mountain range, one tooth set in the ancient jaw of a sunken world, projecting through the inconceivable vastness of the whole ocean" (p. 30). The rock is constantly compared with a tooth of the world; the struggles taking place on the rock are a mirror of the struggles taking place all over the world. Martin's battle for survival is imagistically made the battle of all men for salvation, a battle in which reason, sanity, and careful order are not enough. As the rock is imagistically linked to the larger world, so is Martin himself made a kind of universal focus. His head is frequently a "globe," his own teeth are linked to the shape of the rock:

> His tongue was remembering. It pried into the gap between the teeth and re-created the old, aching shape. It touched the rough /200/ edge of the cliff, traced the slope down, trench after aching trench . . . understood what was so hauntingly familiar and painful about an isolated and decaying rock in the middle of the sea.   [P. 174.]

Similarly, the issues of Martin's salvation or damnation are presented within his own body. He sometimes feels his "center" in conflict with the memory of his loins. His eyes are "windows." The forces of nature that defeat him are linked to forces within himself. Ocean currents are tongues; the mind is a "stirred pudding":

> . . . how can the stirred pudding keep constant? Tugged at by the pull of the earth, infected by the white stroke that engraved the book, furrowed, lines burned through it by hardship and torment and terror-unbalanced, brain-sick, at your last gasp on a rock in the sea, the pudding has boiled over and you are no worse than raving mad.
>
> [Pp. 190-191.]

The microcosmic imagery, connecting the man to the rock to the

universe, becomes a vast metaphor to convey the futility of man's
sanity, of man's careful and calculated attempts to achieve salvation.

The "gimmick" in *Pincher Martin* occurs in the final chapter.
His body is washed ashore and the naval officer who comes to
identify him points out that Martin couldn't have suffered long
because he didn't even have time to kick off his sea boots. Sup-
posedly, in the narrative itself, the first thing Martin did, before
he even sighted the rock, was to kick his sea boots off. In other
words, the final scene shows that the whole drama on the rock
was but a momentary flash in Martin's mind. The dimension of
time has been removed and all the microcosmic metaphor is but
an instantaneous, apocalyptic vision. In the ultimate sense this
revelation enhances the microcosm, compresses all the issues into
a single instant in time. But the revelation, in fact, makes the
situation too complete, too contrived, seems to carry the development of the microcosm to the point of parodying itself. One can
accept the struggle of forces on the rock as emblematic of a constant human struggle, but, when the dimension of time is /201/
removed, when the struggle is distilled to an instantaneous flash,
one immediately thinks of parody in which the stuggle was not
significant at all. Here the "gimmick" extends the technique, but
so magnifies and exaggerates the extension that the novel ends by
supplying its own parody.

In his most recent novel, *Free Fall,* Golding also deals with the
limitation and the folly of the assumption that man can control
his universe rationally, but here the futility of rationalism is not
the central issue of the novel. The novel, anchored in social probability more securely than is any of the others, tells the story of
Sammy Mountjoy who rose from the slums of Rotten Row to become a successful artist. Sammy, telling his own story, searches for
the moment at which he lost his freedom, at which he made a
crucial decision that inescapably hardened his natural propensity
toward sin. The metaphor is Faustian: at what point and for what
reason was this soul given over to Satan? Sammy, guilt-ridden,
traces his career looking for the point and the reason. He quickly
dismisses the poverty of his background, his illegitimate birth, his
youthful blasphemy against the Church, his early membership in
the Communist party—most of these were external and Sammy
was essentially innocent then. He waves aside his seduction and
subsequent desertion of the dependent Beatrice, his willingness
to betray his comrades when a prisoner of war in Germany, his
dishonesty—these were not causes, but effects, the patterns established by a man already irrevocably fallen. He examines his attrac-

tion to the rationalism preached by an early science teacher, but decides that this was not the cause, for, though the doctrine was shoddy and incomplete, the teacher himself was a man of principles deeper than those he avowed, and Sammy had always preferred the man to the doctrine. Finally, Sammy localizes his loss of freedom in his early decision to pursue Beatrice at whatever cost. He had, while at school, drawn a picture of her and given it to one of his less talented friends to hand in as his own. The picture was highly praised; none of Sammy's other drawings received the recognition that this one did, and this one was publicly credited to /202/ someone else. Sammy kept trying, unsuccessfully, to draw Beatrice again. She then became an obsession for him; he had to track her down, pursue her, possess her, sacrifice everything in order to gain her. And this decision, taken as he left school, marks Sammy's loss of freedom. The decision, the willingness to sacrifice everything to achieve his aim, is an indication of human pride and egoism, the conscious human impulse to abandon concern for others, freedom of action, salvation itself, for the satisfaction of one's own end. Sammy relentlessly pursues and possesses Beatrice, overcoming her apathy and gentility by sheer energy and force. She does not satisfy him, for the appetite of human pride is endless, and he deserts her. Like Faust, Sammy loses his freedom when he is willing to stake everything on the satisfaction of his human pride.

At the end of the novel, when Sammy has discovered his sin, the reader suddenly learns that Beatrice has been in a mental institution ever since Sammy deserted her seven years earlier. Sammy visits her, but she will not speak to him and she urinates, in fright, on the floor when he tries to force her to acknowledge his existence. The doctor later tells him that Beatrice is incurable. When Sammy seeks to pin down just how guilty he is, the doctor replies:

> "You probably tipped her over. But perhaps she would have tipped over anyway. Perhaps she would have tipped over a year earlier if you hadn't been there to give her something to think about. You may have given her an extra year of sanity and—whatever you did give her. You may have taken a lifetime of happiness away from her. Now you know the chances as accurately as a specialist."   [Pp. 248-249.]

Here the "gimmick," the final scene at the mental institution, both exaggerates and palliates the metaphorical structure of the novel. The fact that Beatrice is in an institution at all magnifies the external consequences of Sammy's sin and becomes, in Beatrice's unfortunate behavior, almost a parody of the damage caused by human pride. The novel shifts from Sammy's self- /203/ examination to the disastrous effect of his pride on others. After Sammy's sin is externalized, the doctor's sensible comment questions the possibility of directly charging one person with the responsibility for another and, to some measure, cuts down Sammy's guilt. But the novel was originally concerned with Sammy's loss of freedom, with this individual and interior issue, reflected by implication inside other human beings. By making the issue exterior, the ending both exaggerates and simplifies the description of the nature of man involved, both softens and hedges concerning man's guilt. The Faust legend loses much of its power if Faust is to be charged with preaching sedition to his students or if Faust is to wonder about his share of guilt when his students break church windows. The final "gimmick" in *Free Fall*, in making interior issues exterior, changes some of the meaning, dissipates some of the force and relevance, of the novel.

In each novel the final "gimmick" provides a twist that, in one way or another, palliates the force and the unity of the original metaphor. In each instance Golding seems to be backing down from the implications of the metaphor itself, never really contradicting the metaphor, but adding a twist that makes the metaphor less sure, less permanently applicable. The metaphors are steered away from what would seem to be their relentless and inevitable conclusions, prevented, at the very last moment, from hardening into the complete form of allegory. In one sense, each "gimmick" seems to widen the area of the artist's perception as it undoubtedly lessens the force of the imaginative concept. The "gimmicks" supply a wider perspective that makes each of the following questions relevant: If the adult world rescues the boys in *Lord of the Flies*, are the depravity and the brutality of human nature so complete? How adequate is *Pincher Martin's* microcosmic synthesis, if it all flashes by in a microsecond? Can Sammy Mountjoy, living in a world that includes others, talking to them, sleeping with them, helped by them, keep his guilt and the problem of his freedom all to himself? Is the Faust legend an adequate expression of the problems of contemporary man? All these relevant questions are implicit /204/ in the "gimmicks" Golding uses, "gimmicks" that qualify the universality of the metaphors, question the pretense that the metaphors contain complete truth. But this qualification is achieved at the expense of artistic form, for the "gimmicks" also palliate and trick, force the reader to regard the issue somewhat more superficially even though they widen the range of suggestion. The "gimmicks" are ultimately unsatisfactory modifiers, for, in the kind of qualification they provide, they reduce the issues of the novels to a simpler and trickier plane of experience.

Golding's metaphors can all be read as orthodox and traditional Christian statements about the nature of man. Each metaphor underlines man's depravity, pride, the futility of his reason. The novels are permeated with the sense of man's sin and guilt, and the images depict these qualities in conventional Christian terms. The "gimmicks," however, back down from the finality of the theologically orthodox statements. In an age when many other writers view man's experience as disparate, impossible to codify, existential, Golding's metaphors are at least sufficiently unique to suggest the reality, the permanence of the traditional Christian explanation of the nature of man. But, then, the "gimmicks" seem to provide some concession to contemporary man's fear of generalized absolutes, to his existential attitude. This is not to suggest that Golding reverses his metaphors with these slender "gimmicks," that the novels ultimately demonstrate the failure of the orthodox explanations. Rather, the metaphors still stand; the orthodox Christian versions of man's depravity and limitations, in Golding's world, still convey a great deal that is relevant and permanent. But they do not convey everything. The "gimmicks" suggest that the orthodox Christian explanations are not quite adequate for contemporary man, although they are too tricky and slender to do more than suggest. The "gimmicks," precisely because they are "gimmicks," fail to define or to articulate fully just how Golding's metaphors are to be qualified, directed, shaped in contemporary and meaningful terms. The "gimmicks" tend to simplify and to palliate, rather than to /205/ enrich and intensify the experience of the novels. For all his unique brilliance and his striking metaphors, Golding has not yet worked out a novelistic form adequate for the full tonal and doctrinal range of his perception. /206/

LORD OF THE CAMPUS
TIME

Back in England last week after a year in the U.S., British Author William Golding recalled his interrogation by American college students. "The question most asked was, 'Is there any hope for humanity?' I very dutifully said 'Yes.'" Golding's credentials for being asked such a monumental query—and for answering it—rest on one accomplishment: his *Lord of the Flies,* a grim parable that holds out precious little hope for humanity, and is the most influential novel among U.S. undergraduates since Salinger's *Catcher in the Rye.*

When *Lord of the Flies* was first published in the U.S. in 1955, it sold only 2,383 copies, and quickly went out of print. But British enthusiasm for it has been gradually exported to Ivy League English departments, and demand for the book is now high. The paperback edition, published in 1959, has already sold more than 65,000 copies. At the Columbia University bookstore, it outsells Salinger.

Lord of the Flies is required reading at a hundred U.S. colleges, is on the list of suggested summer reading for freshmen entering colleges from Occidental to Williams. At Harvard it is recommended for a social-relations course on "interpersonal behavior."

An M.I.T. minister uses it for a discussion group on original sin. At Yale and Princeton—where Salinger, like the three-button suit, has lost some of his mystique as he becomes adopted by the outlanders—the in-group popularity of Golding's book is creeping up. At Smith, where *Lord of the Flies* runs a close second in sales to Salinger's *Franny and Zooey,* 1,000 girls turned out for a lecture by Golding. The reception was the same at the thirty campuses Golding visited during his year as a rarely resident writer-in-residence at Virginia's Hollins College.

Creating Their Own Misery. The British schoolboys in *Lord of The Flies* are a few years younger than Salinger's Holden Caulfield—they are six to twelve—but they are not self-pitying innocents in a world made miserable by adults. They create their own world,

"Lord of the Campus," *Time,* DXXIX (June 22, 1962), 64. Reprinted by permission from *Time* The Weekly Newsmagazine; copyright © Time Inc., 1962.

their own misery. Deposited unhurt on a deserted coral island by a plane during an atomic war, they form the responsible vacationland democracy that their heritage calls for, and it gradually degenerates into anarchy, barbarism and murder. When adult rescue finally comes, they are a tribe of screaming painted savages hunting down their elected leader to tear him apart. The British naval officer who finds them says, "I should have thought that a pack of British boys would have been able to put up a better show than that." Then he goes back to his own war.

Says Golding: "The theme is an attempt to trace the defects of society back to the defects of human nature. Before the war, most Europeans believed that man could be perfected by perfecting his society. We all saw a hell of a lot in the war that can't be accounted for except on the basis of original evil."

"People I Knew in Camp." What accounts for the appeal? Part of it is, of course, pure identification. A Harvard undergraduate says the book "rounds up all the people I knew in camp when I was a counselor." On another level, Golding believes students "seem to have it in for the whole world of organization. They're very cynical. And here was someone who was not making excuses for society. It was new to find someone who believes in original sin." The prickly belief in original sin is not Golding's only unfashionable stance. Under questioning by undergraduates, he cheerfully admitted he has read "absolutely no Freud" (he prefers Greek plays in the original) and said there are no girls on the island because he does not believe that "sex has anything to do with humanity at this level."

At 51, bearded, scholarly William Golding claims to have been writing for 44 years—through childhood in Cornwall, Oxford, wartime duty as a naval officer, and 19 years as a schoolmaster. Golding claims to be an optimist—emotionally if not intellectually —and has a humor that belies the gloomy themes of his allegories. One critical appraisal of *Lord of the Flies* that impressed him came from an English schoolboy who went to an island near Puerto Rico last year to make a movie based on the book. Wrote the little boy from the idyllic island, surrounded by his happy peers and pampered by his producer: "I think *Lord of the Flies* stinks. I can't imagine what I'm doing on this filthy island, and it's all your fault." In Golding's view, a perfectly cast savage. /64/

BEHIND THE VOGUE, A RIGOROUS UNDERSTANDING

EDMUND FULLER

The literary conversation piece of the last year has been the eruption in American schools and colleges of a vogue for William
Golding on a scale matched only by that for J. D. Salinger. Though
the enthusiasm for the two men is comparable, it does not spring
from similarity in the work. Golding and Salinger are unlike in
method, manner, material, and in the vision which they bring to
bear on life. They appeal to youth on different grounds. It is
gratifying to see this interest in both, for it is a response to good
writing that touches in differing ways the nerve roots of modern
man. But I regard the taste for Golding as more discriminating,
more demanding, and thus more heartening than that for Salinger.

Holden Caulfield and assorted members of the American family
Glass all are special, but with a neurotic unity in their diversity.
They are infinitely "sensitive" in the current cliché. Notwithstanding their pronounced peculiarities, they so reflect certain patterns
of contemporary personality, emotional problems, and pressures
that young people at least recognize and often identify with them.
Salinger speaks with a vocabulary and a tone that induce sympathetic resonances in youthful ears. In a student paper I have read:
". . . he writes about us; he writes about urban prep school life
in contemporary, northeastern America."

These are subjective resonances. Some of this recognition is self-
indulgent and some of the identification is self-pitying. I think
the core of Salinger is soft, and part of the reader response is soft.
The pictures he draws are intensely real in their small frames. I
don't think there is in him the kind of depth and insight to draw
us toward a more rigorous and objective understanding of ourselves and our kind. It is this latter rare and valuable ability that
Golding has, which makes the enthusiasm for him potentially
more significant. Salinger implicitly traces the defects of individuals
back to the defects of society. Golding in his own words is attempt-

Edmund Fuller, "Behind the Vogue, a Rigorous Understanding," New York
Herald Tribune Weekly Book Review, XXXIX (November 4, 1962), 3. Reprinted by permission of New York *Herald Tribune.*

ing "to trace the defects of society back to the defects of human nature." This is the more honest, responsible way.

I have had many conversations with secondary school students about Golding—chiefly about *Lord of the Flies* which is the book principally responsible for his vogue. Whether the enthusiasm for Golding is a flash flood or—as I hope and think—a phenomenon that will last and deepen, will be tested by whether or not the other three novels are able to consolidate the attention *Lord of the Flies* aroused.

Recurrent words from school students about this book are that it terrifies, fascinates, shocks, depresses. Not so commonly articulated but widely and clearly implied is that it illuminates something about the nature of man—which is to say, something about themselves. It strikes home to students because it is about very young people on their own resources. Much bitter or "sensitive" writing of the day harps on the notion that the old are worse than the young. This view underlies Salinger's peculiar 20th-century innocents. Golding is saying that the young are no better than the old. The seeds of our general behavior are in them already.

Those who have heard of "original sin" (all too few) recognize the operation of it here. Those who have heard of the id (even fewer) see it in action. In his notes on *Lord of the Flies,* E. L. Epstein's emphasis on the id leaves gaps that the concept of original sin more fully fills. With or without those interesting terms, young readers see in this novel the powerful thrust of aggressive, destructive, irrational forces. They recognize that in spite of circumstances environmental and psychological, there are surrenders, yieldings, choices—in short, responsibilities—for all the dark acts involved. They see also a brave resistance to deterioration by a few. Many of the castaway lads fall in readily with the demonic Jack who is dragging the island band down to savagery. But Ralph and the sad-valiant Piggy resist to the extremity. They cannot win alone— they need rescue and help. What comes is the dubious rescue by warring adults. In Golding's own penetrating question about the story's end: ". . . who will rescue the adult and his cruiser?"

A theological reading of *Lord of the Flies* is possible. Students equipped for it respond to it strongly. I have read a paper by a secondary schoolgirl so interpreting it that would grace any literary journal. But it does not have to be consciously interpreted in theological terms: its message simply *is* in its self-contained frame of events. *The Inheritors* and *Pincher Martin,* each a remarkable fable in its own way, work also by metaphor and implication. The probing student will find Golding's questions and conjectural answers about existence more overtly intellectualized in *Free Fall* which bears the stamp of individuality, yet is the most conventional of the novels in terms of social realism, the least a "fable" as he calls most of his works.

Its repeated, driving, motivating questions are: "When did I lose my freedom?" "How did I lose my freedom?" Seeking answers, his narrator says, "I have hung all systems on the wall like a row of useless hats. They do not fit." Most subtle and penetrating thought of all: "What men believe is a function of what they are; and what they are is in part what has happened to them."

Free Fall cannot have for young people the direct narrative impact and the intimate identification that *Lord of the Flies* offers. Though this book is about boys only, girls identify themselves with it in terms of human nature and the roots of behavior. But *Free Fall* can carry forward in intellectual awareness and definition what the other book establishes through intuitions. In all his work, Golding the sometime schoolmaster is teaching strongly and well. The youthful are drawn to Salinger chiefly to look for mirror images, to feel, and to lament. They are drawn to Golding to question reflectively, to try to answer and to know. /3/

GOLDING'S VIEW OF MAN

JOHN M. EGAN, O. P.

When William Golding's *Lord of the Flies* was first published in this country in 1955, it sold only 2,383 copies and quickly went out of print. Imperceptibly, however, the book took hold of the undergraduate imagination, and the paperback edition published in 1959 has already sold well over 65,000 copies. *Time* magazine earlier this year estimated that the book has become the most influential novel among U. S. undergraduates since Salinger's *Catcher in the Rye*, and that it is on the required reading list of a hundred colleges. The present article is offered in the hope that it may prompt

John M. Egan, "Golding's View of Man," *America*, CVIII (January 26, 1963), 140-41. Reprinted with permission from *America*, The National Catholic Weekly Review, 920 Broadway, New York 10, N.Y.

further discussion of a novel which offers a world view far removed from the Christian.

The book is an allegory. The boys are presented as typical of human nature as it is essentially. Their isolation on an island is a device whereby the author is able to transcend what he would consider the façade of civilization in order to reach man as he truly is. The book prescinds entirely from anything of the supernatural and, even more so, from anything derived from revelation.

The theme of the book is that the human condition is irrational. Man has no nature, but rather is an excrescence from chaotic, cruel and blind forces which are violent and yet meaningless. Man springs forth from these forces and regresses into them. The violence which develops on the island only reflects in microcosm the violence of the rest of the world: the boys appear on the island as the result of some atomic catastrophe, the sole intruder on the island is the dead pilot who is shot down from the firmament overhead, and the boys leave the island in the company of armed men traveling in a warship. When all is said and done, man's condition is represented as something hateful. Thus the novel is representative of the spirit of much of modern thought and art.

Ralph's obsession with maintaining a fire is symbolic of man's illusion that civilization will bring salvation. The usage of fire to symbolize the arts and sciences of civilization was canonized in the Prometheus legend, and a reflection of that myth is found in the book when the forces of chaos plan to steal back the fire. Civilization, however, is merely a momentary veneer which ill conceals man's essential nature. Under pressure, even Ralph, the protagonist of civilization, begins to revert to his primal condition, forgetting the importance of the fire.

Almost immediately after the boys' arrival on the island, the forces of violence, blind power and cruelty, typified by Jack, Roger and their associates, begin to struggle to attain ascendency over the values of civilization and traditional authority, represented by the fire and Ralph with his conch. These boys hanker for violence and a return to the primordial chaos, typified by the hunt. Soon their antagonism becomes hostility, as the hunt and blood-lust become responsible for the fire dying out and the chance for a return to civilization being missed. It is at this time, significantly, that the specter of some mysterious beast begins to loom up before the boys. The beast becomes a source of terror and division among them as fear grows of some unchained and superior force in their midst.

What is the beast? It is man himself. Piggy intimates this. "I know

there isn't no beast—not with claws and all that, I mean. But I
know it isn't fear either—unless we get frightened of people." But
it is Simon, the seer, who spells out the truth explicitly. " 'Maybe
there is a beast. . . . What I mean is—maybe it's only us. We could
be sort of. . . .' Simon became inarticulate in his effort to express
mankind's essential illness. Inspiration came to him. 'What's the
dirtiest thing there is?' As an answer, Jack dropped into the uncomprehending silence that followed it the one crude, expressive
syllable'."

This paragraph is critical. The vilest of human things is used
as a symbol of man himself. This is not a random remark, for an
underlying concern with human excrement runs throughout the
book. Any doubt as to the correctness of this interpretation is dissi-
pated when the beast appears to Simon and confirms Simon's insight. "Fancy thinking that the Beast was something you could
hunt and kill! You knew, didn't you? I'm part of you? Close, close,
close! I'm the reason why it's no go? Why things are what they are?"
And what name is given to this beast? He is the "lord of the flies."
This is a cryptogram for the reader because the Aramaic word in
question, "beelzebub," is not always translated thus. Another meaning given for this word is "lord of dung." The beast then is human
nature itself /140/ —vile and hateful, worthy to be symbolized by
human excrement. It is this hateful power which Jack apotheosizes
and begins to worship.

Man, however, is merely part of a larger chaos from which he
has come and toward which he regresses. The murder of Simon
takes place when the boys are in an orgy of frenzied dancing, a
frenzy which reflects in microcosm the tearing wind, jagged lightning and powerful rain of the universe. And where do the dead
return? Simon, the aviator and Piggy, the book explicitly states,
all are carried out to sea, to the sea which in its ineluctable movement reflects the vast and meaningless movement of the universe.
This is the significance of the last paragraph of chapter nine.
"Only two dead," Ralph later informs his rescuers, and then he
adds significantly, "and they've gone."

The book, then, presents man and the universe as a cruel and
irrational chaos. This artistic vision, typical of modern art, induces
a sense of despair and even hatred of what is human. One joins
with Satan himself in the devil's loathing of man. This is why certain critics have termed some aspects of modern art diabolic. There
is supreme irony in the title of the book itself. The term "lord of
the flies" is, as has been mentioned, a translation of the word
"beelzebub." And Beelzebub is Satan. /141/

SALINGER AND GOLDING:
CONFLICT ON THE CAMPUS

FRANCIS E. KEARNS

In bookstores and newsstands surrounding college campuses a promi-
nent display place is consistently given to William Golding's *Lord
of the Flies*. Probably no other post-World War II novel has so
seriously threatened to dislodge J. D. Salinger's *Catcher in the Rye*
as the most influential work in the literary initiation of the American undergraduate.

The popularity of Golding's novel is not limited to the student
body. At an increasing number of American colleges the book is
being adopted for classroom study, and its central themes are discussed with as much vigor in the faculty dining room as in the
student snack bar. That *Catcher in the Rye* and *Lord of the Flies*
should both enjoy such high regard in the same academic climate
appears at first paradoxical, for it would be hard to conceive of
two other books rooted in such diametrically opposed ideological
traditions. Indeed, though neither novel is intended as a philosophical dissertation or political tract, the conflicting attitudes implicit in the two books on such questions as the nature of good
and evil and the relationship of man to society underscore a long-
standing antagonism in Western thought, one which has existed in
America since Anne Hutchinson was banished from the Massachu-
setts Bay Colony.

Salinger's novel is rooted in the tradition of liberal humanitarianism. Beginning in this country with the rebellion against the
heavy hand of Calvinist orthodoxy and its doctrine of predestination by such nonconformists as Anne Hutchinson and Roger Williams, the humanitarian tradition was gradually secularized as religious enthusiasm gave way, throughout the 18th century, to the
lucid rationality of the Enlightenment. The fundamental theories
of the tradition received, perhaps, their most cogent and literate
expression in the writings of Shaftesbury and Rousseau. Later, the
tradition was readily adopted by the romantic poets of the early

Francis E. Kearns, "Salinger and Golding: Conflict on the Campus," *America*,
CVIII (January 26, 1963), 136-39. Reprinted with permission from *America*,
The National Catholic Weekly Review, 920 Broadway, New York 10, N.Y.

19th century. At the same time, it became allied with liberal politics and, in this country, manifested itself in the proliferation of reforms ranging from abolition to the agrarian communism of Brook Farm.

Having weathered the ethnic diversity produced by waves of immigration during the late 19th and early 20th centuries, and having encountered what Will Herberg, in *Protestant-Catholic-Jew*, regards as the present-day realignment of power among the three chief religious establishments in this country, the humanitarian tradition is today neither a coherent political force nor a recognizable philosophy. Indeed, the very difficulty involved in labeling the "humanitarian tradition"—a variety of adjectives could have preceded the term, including "idealistic," "liberal" and "romantic"— indicates its fundamental eclecticism and compositeness. Nevertheless, the spirit of this tradition played an important part in the humane reforms of Franklin D. Roosevelt. Today, its influence may still be found in the writings of such Presidential advisers as Kenneth Galbraith and Arthur Schlesinger Jr.

A fundamental tenet of the humanitarian tradition is perfectabilitarianism—the belief in progress, the belief in man's innate capacity to better his social order through the exercise of good will and reason. Concurrent with this tenet is a belief in man's natural goodness and a distrust of social institutions. Thus Rousseau believed that the American Indian was noble because the more primitive the institutions of a society, the more noble would its citizens be. Men are naturally good; when they are evil, it is because their society is evil.

In *Catcher in the Rye* Holden Caulfield, an innocent and painfully sensitive teen-ager, cracks up against the obduracy of a depraved society. Fleeing the preparatory school, an institution designed to facilitate the passage of youth from innocence to that state of sophisticated corruption necessary for success in society, Holden enters a cheap New York hotel and finds himself in a contemporary Sodom and Gomorrah. Unable to endure even the lesser artificialities of society—whether expressed in the banal pageants of Radio City Music Hall or in the pose of casualness demanded in the teen-age courtship ritual—he steadily disintegrates. By the end of the novel, he is in a West Coast mental hospital.

In New York, the city of his birth, Holden had hoped /136/ to recapture the innocence of childhood. He finds temporary relief against the inevitable progression from childhood to adult corruption in the seeming permanence of the displays at the Field Museum of Natural History. Here, behind the glass case, the Eskimo is still poised above his fishing hole, and there is no passage of time. Similarly, on the carrousel in Central Park, a child moves (for the time being) in a permanent circle and not toward decadent maturity. Like Huck Finn—a character with whom he is frequently compared—Holden considers escaping adult society by fleeing to the West. There he hopes to find an isolated mountain cabin where he can pretend to be a deaf mute. But, in the 20th century, there is no Western frontier to offer refuge from civilization; and Holden cannot, like Salinger, afford to buy a secluded and fenced-in home in New Hampshire.

Despite Holden's revulsion from the "phony" values of the adult world, the adults who inhabit Salinger's novel are not basically evil. Their cruelty and artificiality result, not from willed malice, but from fear and ignorance. Unaware of their own potentialities as persons, they have fallen into the habit of judging themselves according to the materialistic standards imposed by their society. They have come to believe in their own poses.

It is Holden's painful state to be aware of his personhood, and he constantly frustrates himself in dealing with others by trying to reach behind the mask and touch the real person. Thus, when he is trapped by his own bravado into ordering a prostitute sent to his hotel room, he is unable to employ her services because he can't feel "personal" about it. And when he is beaten and robbed by the elevator boy and pimp, Maurice, he thinks himself a coward because he can't bear to see his opponent's face.

Holden is torn between his desire to flee society and his desire to be responsible for the innocent and downtrodden—to be, in other words, a "catcher in the rye." In the end, his sense of responsibility wins out, for he is unable to desert his little sister Phoebe. But Holden's concept of responsibility has been tempered by his experiences in the city, experiences which relentlessly prod him into adulthood. He comes to realize that the child on the carrousel must be allowed to reach for the gold ring, even though this aspiration involves the danger of a fall. Innocence cannot be permanently protected from a confrontation with temptation.

Yet, there is no dynamic force of evil in Holden's world. At the novel's conclusion, writing from the sanitarium, he expresses an almost Whitmanesque, all-embracing love of mankind. He misses everyone, even Maurice. And, though Holden is inevitably a committed person, it is appropriate that the book ends with the analyst's couch, the center of moral neutrality in the modern world.

The setting of *Lord of the Flies* is anything but the lurid city in which Holden's adventures take place. In Golding's novel, the youthful characters, a group of English schoolboys being evacuated from their homeland during World War III, find themselves abandoned on an idyllic Pacific island. Their refuge offers unlimited food and natural beauty. It is, in short, a neatly Edenic situation where innocence may be tested.

Alone on the island, and without adult supervision, the boys are faced with the problem of erecting a government. Their choice of a democratic, parliamentarian form of government indicates the influence still exerted over them by Western civilization. The chief mover in bringing about a coherent form of self-government is Piggy, who throughout the book stands for reasonableness and decency. But Piggy, fat, bespectacled and suffering from asthma, is physically incapable of the role of leader. At Piggy's prompting, that role is given, through democratic election, to Ralph. It's from Ralph's point of view that most of the story is told. He is a type of representative man, only of the better sort. Possessed of instinctively decent feelings, Ralph is not as intelligent as Piggy, but he has sense enough to perceive in Piggy a wise adviser, though at first he is contemptuous of Piggy's weakness.

Opposed to fair-haired Ralph is dark-haired Jack, leader of a boys' choir included among the evacuees abandoned on the island. Jack is used to administering severe discipline to the choristers, and he resents Ralph's election as chief. Just as Piggy and Ralph stand for reasonableness and social order, Jack stands for irrationality and anarchy. Clad in his school's military cap and cape, Jack is a leader of another sort. He possesses that charismatic attraction so frequently found in the 20th-century dictator. Combined with this are his lust for power, worship of physical prowess and contempt for the ineffectual speechmaking of Ralph's parliamentarian assembly.

Rounding out the group of central characters is Simon, the young mystic. Simon has the deepest insight into the social and moral dilemma which develops on the island, but he is prevented from communicating his thoughts by overpowering timorousness and insecurity.

Little is accomplished at the meetings of the island's parliament, for, although all agree on the necessity of building shelters and maintaining a signal fire to guide would-be rescuers, few are willing to carry out the physical labor involved. A crucial blow to responsibility and order in the boys' society occurs when a dead parachutist lands on a mountain commanding the island. His body, flapped about by the winds, comes to be regarded as a threatening beast. The rational /137/ arguments of Ralph and Piggy are thus defeated by animal fear. Jack, followed by his choristers, is now able to set up a separate tribe, and he wins over almost all the boys through his promise of protection from the beast.

Only Simon, the mystic, has courage enough to seek out the beast and discover its nature. But before he can ascend the mountain, he comes face to face with the Lord of the Flies. Here is the novel's central symbol. The "Lord of the Flies" (a translation of the word *Beelzebub,* or "devil") is the head of a pig slain by Jack's hunter-choristers. The head, now covered with ravenous flies, had been impaled on a stick and erected in a jungle clearing by Jack as a tribute to the beast on the mountain.

Simon enters into a delirious "conversation" with the symbolic head, the head staring at him all the time "with the infinite cynicism of adult life." The pig's head tells him that "everything is a bad business," that "I'm part of you . . . I'm the reason why it's no go. . . ." In short, the Lord of the Flies represents that depravity which is inevitable in mankind and which makes futile all human attempts at justice or order. Nevertheless, Simon struggles against this recognition and continues his journey to the mountain. There he discovers the parachutist. The mystic then comes down from the mountain bearing the truth, but he is slain by those he intended to save before he can deliver the truth. Thus the pronouncement on human nature by the Lord of the Flies is validated.

Soon only Ralph and Piggy are left as representatives of sanity and order on the island. The two friends go to confer with Jack in an attempt to settle their dispute reasonably, but Jack and his followers murder Piggy and pursue Ralph into the jungle. In a consummate act of irrationality, Jack then decides to set fire to the bush in order to smoke out Ralph. Fruit, flowers and pigs all are swept away by flames. Thus fire—which throughout the novel has functioned, in the form of the signal fire, as a hope of salvation— now is used to destroy the paradise. But just as Ralph is about to be cornered and killed, he is rescued by a British naval party. Nevertheless, Ralph's good fortune is not the gratuitous rescue of melodrama, for the reader realizes that the cruiser which saves Ralph is itself involved in the same evil that exists in the lives of the children and will soon return to its own deadly manhunt at sea.

Lord of the Flies is permeated by the conviction that man is naturally depraved. In Golding's universe there is a dynamic force of evil, centered in man himself, which triumphs over all human attempts at goodness and order. In this respect, the Englishman's novel stands close to a tradition that Leslie Fiedler, in *Love and*

Death in the American Novel, has seen as an abiding force in American fiction. It is this same tradition that Denis de Rougemont, in *Love in the Western World,* has traced back through medieval courtly love poetry to its roots in the Albigensian heresy and that heresy's brooding sense of evil and the depravity of human flesh.

In America, the most confident spokesmen for the view that man is naturally depraved were, of course, the Calvinist-oriented magistrates and ministers of the early Puritan establishment—men such as Thomas Hooker and the various members of the Mather dynasty. The beliefs of these Puritans have not only had a lasting effect on American literature and thought, but have also been a formative influence on our economic system. As Max Weber pointed out in his classic study, *The Protestant Ethic,* the Calvinist ethos, with its emphasis on the pursuit of material gain as a barometer of God's pleasure, was a necessary precondition for the establishment of a capitalist economic system.

The Calvinist ethic remains an important influence in American politics today. According to Richard Hofstadter's *Social Darwinism in American Thought,* American conservatives in the late 19th century adopted a philosophy which was an amalgam of Calvanist and Darwinian thought. The Calvinist emphasis on man's depravity and the difficulty of his relation to God grooved smoothly with the Darwinian view of man's relation to nature as hard and demanding. There resulted a type of "naturalistic Calvinism" which emphasized hard work and hard saving as cardinal virtues, and looked with distrust on leisure and waste. Thus was introduced into American thought "an inherited conception of economic life, even today fairly widespread among conservatives . . . under which economic activity was considered to be above all a field for the development and encouragement of personal character." Moreover, the Calvinist view of predestination (the view that man could not change his nature or destiny, that he was rooted in the past), /138/ when combined with the Darwinian idea of development over aeons, brought new force to the conservatives' belief that all sound social development must be slow and unhurried.

It is against this background of the historical development of American conservatism and its adoption of the Calvinist ethic that the impact on the American college campus of Englishman Golding's novel must be viewed. It would be interesting, in this respect, to consider whether the campus success of Golding's book, with its pessimistic views of both human nature and the ideal of progress, is in part due to the recent revival of conservative thought in college dormitories. One wonders whether some day the members of such rightist student groups as Young Americans for Freedom may come to consider the novel as a testament equal in importance to *Conscience of a Conservative* or *God and Man at Yale*. Unfortunately, the novel is such a recent arrival on the campus that it is difficult to obtain a consensus.

To categorize *Lord of the Flies* and *Catcher in the Rye* as belonging to two different traditions—the Calvinist-conservative on the one hand, the liberal-humanitarian on the other—is not to deny that the two novels bear certain important similarities. Among the most important of such similarities is the fact that both books hesitate to view evil in a religious framework, to deal with it as something connected to a meaningful world order. In spite of their disagreement on the ultimate source of evil, each tends to define evil as a type of irrationality and fear.

There is in Salinger, of course, a certain religious impulse which appears to be expressed with increasing coherence as the saga of the Glass family works itself out in the pages of the *New Yorker*. But, though Salinger is equally at home with the Koran, the Bhagavad-Gita or the New Testament, there is about his view of religion the noncommittal air of the comparative-religion textbook or the Ethical Culture lecture. Moreover, he avoids a direct confrontation with the idea of evil as willed choice for which man is ultimately responsible. Thus, when Franny becomes obsessed with the Jesus Prayer—"Lord Jesus Christ, have mercy on me, a miserable sinner"—Zooey remarks that ". . . none of the adepts . . . put any emphasis—thank *God*—on the miserable-sinner part." And, in spite of the many phonies and degenerates who inhabit the pages of *Catcher,* the reader senses that Salinger's ultimate judgment on human nature is summed up in the inherent innocence and decency of the children appearing in the same novel. In the end, his religious view is liberal and humanitarian; it eschews metaphysical subtleties and focuses not so much on God as on the fat lady of *Franny and Zooey*.

Golding can deal comfortably with Beelzebub, or the Lord of the Flies, as an artistic symbol. But, as in the case of Salinger, his view of evil is not primarily a religious one. Indeed, the irrelevance of such a religious view is marked when Jack, much in the style of Freud's *Future of an Illusion* or Frazer's *Golden Bough,* attempts to assuage the threat of the unknown beast by initiating a ritual dance in its honor and by offering the head of the pig as a sacrificial tribute. Moreover, the very familiarity of Golding's evil—its localization in the psychotic figure of Jack, a totalitarian and a militarist—tends to mitigate its impact on the modern reader.

Golding is content to picture evil and then stand back. In the end, what is missing from his novel is a sense of personal desperation in the face of evil. All is too neatly symbolic, too patently artistic. And this absence of desperation results, I believe, from Golding's deterministic view of man's capacity for evil, from his belief that "everything is a bad business, everything is no go." In short, it results from the fact that in the world of *Lord of the Flies* free will is meaningless.

Seventy years before the writing of Golding's novel, Herman Melville's *Billy Budd* dealt with the same theme—the inevitable destruction of youthful innocence in a world where the evil side of man's nature is dominant. But Melville's book is marked by a terrifying awareness of the consequences of free decisions that must be made in the half-light of man's ethical perceptions and, at the same time, by faith in a meaningful universe in which innocence transcends worldly defeat. Perhaps, though, one can hardly expect the contemporary novelist, living in a post-Buchenwald, post-Hiroshima era, to view evil as meaningful.

In the end, the problems that the two novels encounter in dealing with the idea of evil reflect the attitudes toward evil of their separate intellectual traditions. Salinger demonstrates the liberal's healthy acceptance of the challenge of freedom and possibility. But, at the same time, his inability to come to grips with the problem of evil reflects what Lionel Trilling's *Liberal Imagination* has termed the liberal's failure "to perceive complexity and difficulty." On the other hand, Golding manifests the conservative's profound insight into the limitations of human nature. Yet his acceptance of the inevitable triumph of the dark side of man's nature vitiates the possibility of meaningful reform and manifests the Calvinist's inevitable gravitation toward determinism or antinomianism.

Perhaps from the clash of ideologies in the two books there will result on the college campus a more enlightened grasp of the concomitant wisdom and danger embodied in both the liberal and conservative traditions. /139/

THE APPEAL OF GOLDING
LUKE M. GRANDE

Despite its dismissal by one reviewer as a "well-written but completely unpleasant story," William Golding's *Lord of the Flies,* published with little fanfare back in 1954, has since that time become a much-heralded best-seller. Its great popularity may be attributed largely to the tremendous and unforeseen interest in it on the part of college and high school students throughout the country.

College campuses in the late fifties and early sixties have been stirred by discussions over it in much the same way that they were stimulated in the early fifties by J. D. Salinger's *Catcher in the Rye* —and perhaps for the same reasons. Undoubtedly there is an aspect of modishness about the book's success, but the students' involvement with it actually goes much deeper.

In fact, the adoption of Golding's book by today's youth may be an implicit judgment on much of what has passed in the last ten or twenty years for significant literature. The crop of novels that appeared after World War II was characterized by a type of pessimism and spiritual fatigue that, upon rereading, seems strangely dated.

To students, some of whom were not yet born when the war ended, the themes of the war are for the most part dead, living only in American History courses and on television shows like *Twentieth Century.* They are a bit incredulous (even bored by the fact, perhaps) that we who were living during World War II could be torn by anxieties centered around a German paper-hanger or could take the goose-step seriously. Their reading of the literature of the period is simply not colored, sharpened, and enriched by personal memories, as is their elders'.

Then, when battle memoirs and novels about civilian adjustment had actually reached a dead end, the new wave of the European anti-novel came into its own. Conceived in a depersonalizing milieu, the anti-novel necessarily substituted a rather sterile super-cerebral literary exercise for the formerly action-packed studies in realism.

Although these later experiments frequently proved to be fascinating, often brilliant, *tours de force* that pleased readers intellectually, when compared with the great literature of the past they yielded,

Luke M. Grande, "The Appeal of Golding," *Commonweal,* LXXVII (January 25, 1963), 457-59. Reprinted by permission of *Commonweal,* the weekly journal of opinion edited by Catholic laymen.

for many, rather meager insights into the human condition. In them, form as an end in itself tended either to obscure totally the communication of experience or to provide shabby and inconsequential material with a mere penumbra of importance. /457/

The anti-novel may indeed continue to evoke from professional critics and litterateurs esoteric monographs on the anti-novelists' contribution to literature. But it has failed to touch the vital center of the student, who, with a naive but surprisingly trustworthy instinct, seems to sense the vacuum behind such fiction and turns rather to the more traditional humanistic concerns of a William Golding.

In a world that tends to equate evil with unfavorable environment, Golding sees instead man's inner responsibility for choosing between good and evil; in a world that defines personality as a functional phenomenon, Golding emphasizes the substantive reality and absolute value of each human being. Finally, in a world that can affirm at one and the same time a belief in human perfectibility and in instinctive and natural depravity, Golding projects the timeless predicament of man who, despite his moral weakness, struggles to attain heroic ideals.

In a sense, Golding's method is, like his subject matter, atavistic. He returns to the story-teller's technique in anatomizing human springs of action. He avoids the pitfalls of non-communicating stream-of-consciousness techniques and the superficial flashiness of "existential" narrative. Investigating the *way* and the *why* men act, an investigation that he carries on in common with all of Western Civilization's greatest creators of imaginative literature, Golding goes back to the fable, to the apparently straightforward story that is actually multi-radiant in meaning. All the best writers tell a crashing good story; but, without resorting to impenetrable obscurities, they also admit an indefinite number and variety of subtle themes.

Perrault's fairy tale about the Frog Prince, for instance, has been enjoyed for centuries by children who knew nothing about its Freudian or Hegelian under- and overtones. *Gulliver's Travels* is still considered a child's book by many readers, while the *cognoscenti* interpret it as literary satire, economic analysis, political history, and theological didacticism. Like Perrault and Swift, Golding is a born story-teller, whether he is talking about the extinction of Neanderthal men (in *The Inheritors,* his latest book), about the "remembrance of things past" of a Nazi torture victim (in *Free Fall*), about a castaway naval officer (in *Pincher Martin*), or about castaway children (in *Lord of the Flies*).

But all of Golding's work is much more than just good story-telling. For the reader can not go far without becoming aware of the parabolic direction of his writing, the presence in his story of a symbolic level. And it is Golding's understanding of man's nature and the moral problem symbolically underlying the fable to which the student responds—particularly in *Lord of the Flies:* not to the possible and even valid id-ego-superego interpretation of the characters Jack-Ralph-Piggy, nor to the democracy-versus-totalitarianism allegory, but to the fundamental battle between good and evil that goes on in the youth as well as in the adult. In a word, Golding takes the young seriously, recognizing their part in an ancient spiritual struggle.

The story of *Lord of the Flies,* to restate it, concerns a group of English schoolboys marooned on an island and their discovery (along with that of political, social, and religious organization) of the reality of evil in the world through its existence in themselves. In this best of all possible worlds—a pink-rocked, flower-laden paradise, where food is abundant and leisure for playing games is possible—all should be right and happiness assured.

To outline the essential symbolism of the story in rather simplistic terms, Ralph (the philosopher-king, who "had no devil"), with the help of Piggy ("right reason," symbolized by his spectacles) and Jack (the "hunter" and provider of meat and the "onions of Egypt") establish order (symbolized by a "conch shell") over the island. But in a short time an undefinable fear of evil—first vaguely alluded to as a "snake-thing," then, in ascendingly concrete images, as a "beastie," an "animal," a "pig" and finally as Simon/Ralph—makes its appearance.

But only Simon seems to grasp the truth ("However Simon thought of the beast, there arose before his inward sight the picture of a human at once heroic and sick"), an intuition verified in the climactic and mystic confrontation between Simon and the impaled head of a sow, killed savagely by the children. (In worshipping the head, the "Lord of the Flies," they thus satanically enthrone their own power of blackness.) While the others hide from the truth behind masks, Simon hears the words of the "Lord": "Fancy thinking the Beast was something you could hunt and kill! You knew, didn't you? I'm part of you? Close, close, close! I'm the reason why it's no go? Why things are what they are?"

The symbols work as all good symbols should; they crystallize the intangible, they clarify the obscure; they function both in plot development and in the parabolic movement of the story.

Each character, although larger than life—an age-old /458/ convention in any artistic medium—is distinctly individual and is realistically drawn. Ralph, who begins as a more or less irresponsible child (who, for example, stands on his head to exorcise his high spirits), gradually sobers up with the help of experience, to the point where he bitterly questions, "What was a face? What was anything?" and agonizes in confusion, "Things are breaking up. I don't understand why. We began well; we were happy. And then—." And then the bat-like shadow of evil that flaws every creature covered Eden and made an Inferno out of it.

In the midst of some horrifying scenes, the ultimate irony, the myth of adult omniscience and indefectibility, resounds like a diabolic laugh behind the pathetic hopes of the children:

" 'Grown-ups know things. They ain't afraid of the dark. They'd meet and have tea and discuss. Then things 'ud be all right—'

'They wouldn't set fire to the island. Or lose—'

'They'd build a ship—'

'They wouldn't quarrel—'

'Or talk about a beast—'

'If only they could get a message to us,' cried Ralph."

The children *do* receive a message from the adult world: a corpse from an air battle, parachuted to the mountain where the children's pathetic "fire" of hope is burning!

A generation of school children today have looked at Golding's world and recognized it as their own. With a response, at which the adults are unnecessarily surprised, the child also weeps with Ralph "for the end of innocence, the darkness of man's heart."

Yet there is hope in his world: there are the Ralph's who are still able to weep; there are the Piggy's who hold onto the "conch of order" and the "spectacles" of right reason.

Golding has struck the note to which the strings of the twentieth-century youth are attuned. A student in his teens or twenties has not known at first-hand the horrors of war, but he has seen international hatred and the unbridled tyranny of totalitarianism. He has seen a loss of values and of faith; he has seen the twisted faces of hatred in metropolitan ghettoes and on green campuses. In sum, he has seen the frightening possibilities of his own nature.

It is no wonder that Golding's treatment of a perennial problem has called forth such a response and has become almost a minor masterpiece, while more sophisticated and ambitious works drop back into the limbo of literary obscurity.

An inevitable touch of the fashionable, it is true, is present in the new evaluations of Golding and his work. He is not yet a modern Chaucer, or a Dostoievski of the sixties. Yet he has in common with these writers the qualities of the genuine artist. And the "children" were among the first to recognize him. /459/

AN EXCHANGE OF VIEWS:
"THE APPEAL OF GOLDING"

FRANCIS E. KEARNS AND
LUKE M. GRANDE

Washington, D.C.

To THE EDITORS: I find it difficult to accept Brother Luke Grande's view ["The Appeal of Golding," Jan. 25] that there is hope in the world of William Golding's *Lord of the Flies*. Brother Luke argues that "there are the Ralph's who are still able to weep; there are the Piggy's who hold onto 'the conch of order' and the 'spectacles' of right reason." But in actuality, by the novel's conclusion Piggy and the conch have been smashed, the spectacles have been used to destroy the island paradise, and Ralph is saved at the last minute only by the somewhat awkward device of having the adult world intrude upon the island's. That Ralph can weep only underlines the darkness of Golding's world view: man realizes not only his innate depravity but also his inability to control that depravity within a workable social order. In short, man's free will, if it exists at all, is ineffectual. This point is further underlined by the fact that Ralph's rescuers must return to their own adult war and seek out their prey.

It is difficult, moreover, to resolve Brother Luke's enthusiasm for Golding's understanding of man's nature and moral problem with his acceptance at face value of the scene in which Simon, the young mystic, confronts the "Lord of the Flies." In this scene the "Lord" tells Simon that "Everything is a bad business," that "I'm part of you . . . I'm the reason why it's no go. . . ." In other words, the "Lord of the Flies" holds that man lives in insuperable darkness, that there is a depravity in man which makes all his attempts at justice and order futile. (It is, of course, possible that "The Lord of the Flies," or "Beelzebub," is lying, but Simon's death and the other depraved actions which take place on the island would indicate that Golding intends the "Lord's" words as an accurate pronouncement on human nature.) Now it is one thing to reject a

Francis E. Kearns and Luke M. Grande, "An Exchange of Views," *Commonweal*, LXXVII (February 22, 1963), 569-71. Reprinted by permission of *Commonweal*, the weekly journal of opinion edited by Catholic laymen.

Rousseauistic view that evil derives from social institutions, but it is quite another to regard man as incapable of overcoming his own proclivity to evil.

What I regard as Brother Luke's misreading of the novel derives largely, I think, from his enthusiasm for Golding's symbolic technique: "The symbols work as /569/ all good symbols should; they crystallize the intangible, they clarify the obscure. . . ." On the contrary, I believe that Golding's lavish array of symbols tends to make the novel too patently "artistic" and to mitigate the possibility of genuine human anguish in many scenes. As Henry James said of Hawthorne's symbolic approach in *The Scarlet Letter:* "there is a great deal of symbolism; there is, I think, too much. It is overdone at times, and becomes mechanical . . . in such a process discretion is everything, and when the image becomes importunate it is in danger of seeming to stand for nothing more serious than itself."

Moreover, rather than making the tale clearer, Golding's symbols tend to obscure certain of the book's inconsistencies. Thus, on the moral level, the symbols contribute little to our understanding of Golding's attitude toward free will. Nor do they clarify the level of social criticism. Jack "symbolizes" the mentality of the twentieth-century totalitarian militarist and functions as villain in destroying the island's democracy. Yet what would be the point of resisting Jack if the "Lord" is right and man is insuperably depraved? After all, Calvin's Geneva was a totalitarian state.

I thoroughly agree with Brother Luke's point that the book's popularity is directly attributable to its large school-age audience. But this fact is hardly a compliment to the schools. Rather, it reflects a divorce between the English classroom and social and political realities; it reflects the "find-the-symbol-pick-your-Christ-figure" approach which has dominated American literary criticism since the end of World War II. In this respect it is interesting to note that Golding is himself a teacher, that his novel has achieved its popularity largely as a textbook and student discussion piece, and that the novelist has even attained a type of academic Valhalla in being catalogued in the "*PMLA* Annual Bibliography."

Brother Luke hails student enthusiasm for *Lord of the Flies* as an instinct toward the reassertion of moral responsibility by the young, a reassertion which involves a rejection of the perfectibilitarians and their belief that evil is the product of unfavorable environment. It is interesting to note, however, that at the heart of Golding's view of man are two key concepts which social historians such as Richard Hofstadter have seen as cornerstones of American conservative political theory: the Darwinian view of life as a jungle struggle and the Calvinist view of man as innately depraved. I wonder whether this instinct toward moral responsibility on the part of our youth is the same instinct which keeps Georgetown students indifferent toward the plight of the Negro in southeast Washington or which prompts Fordham students to remain unresponsive to the problems of Spanish Harlem. I wonder whether this is the same instinct which motivates the current campus popularity of such spokesmen for moral responsibility as William F. Buckley.

FRANCIS E. KEARNS

THE AUTHOR REPLIES

Memphis, Tenn.

TO THE EDITORS: I am afraid that the prospect of a critical quarrel between Francis Kearns and me, despite the possibly exciting charges and counter-charges that might have taken place over the absolute meaning or significance of Golding's *Lord of the Flies,* is doomed not to take place. Such controversies depend largely upon the intransigence of two parties in maintaining positions that are respectively black and white or easily simplistic—and I long ago learned to distrust sweeping generalizations and easy labels. In fact, I had thought such neat categories as *Rousseauvian/Hobbesian, liberal/conservative*—although adaptable to nicely balanced sentences with rhetorical feeling and rhythmic antitheses—had gone out with the "liberal imagination" of a couple of decades ago.

And what seems crucial in Mr. Kearns' objection to my treatment of Golding is my failure to tag and pigeonhole him as a philosophical pessimist, whole and complete, in the congregation of Calvin. Mr. Kearns, of course, has his own thesis (in *America,* Jan. 26) that *Lord of the Flies* is a conservative-Calvinist allegory—a very stimulating interpretation that makes for symmetrical contrast with the liberal-Rousseauistic tradition /570/ which he proposes as the literary ethos of Salinger's *Catcher in the Rye.* But, while interesting, such a schema should be proposed tentatively, since the method can become a kind of literary game where "you pays your money and you takes your chances."

For example, in his own evaluation of *The Catcher* (which he ultimately pegs as "liberal" and "Rousseauistic"), Mr. Kearns says that Holden Caulfield cracks up against "the obduracy of a depraved society," against the "inevitable progression from childhood to adult corruption." He is eventually a victim of this society—which sounds strangely like a "Calvinistic" one. While I would be the first to grant a measure of plausibility to the liberal-Rousseauistic characterization, why cannot Holden's world (on the basis of Mr. Kearns' own text just quoted) be considered conservative-Calvinistic rather than liberal-Rousseauistic? My purpose in using Mr. Kearns' own text is not to "get out from under" my own analysis, which, after all, is the interpretation under discussion here, but to illustrate the alarming ease with which the game of picking your quotes and proving your thesis can be played. Nor am I suggesting that Mr. Kearns is guilty of critical chicanery so much as that he may be a victim of a slight case of oversimplification.

I am wary, as a result of frequent and painful disillusionment, of any thesis quite so pat. Swift is still erroneously judged by some to be a misanthrope, despite the reams of defense stemming from Quintana-days, and the error is again one of attempting to reduce a complex statement to a simple one: the simple statement, the valid examination of one facet of a work, should not be taken as a summary of the whole. There is a measure of truth to Mr. Kearns' thesis, but it is a measure and not an epitome of the book's truth.

Mr. Kearns assumes that *Lord of the Flies* holds that "man lives in insuperable darkness, that there is a depravity in man which makes all his attempts at justice and order futile"; on this assumption he attacks the efficacy of Golding's symbolism (for example, "Jack" as symbol): Mr. Kearns says, "Yet what would be the point of resisting Jack if the 'Lord' is right and man is insuperably depraved? After all, Calvin's Geneva was a totalitarian state." The "if" clause is not completely acceptable, nor is this perhaps unconscious "straw-man" technique; for while Golding's mood is "somber" it is not unmitigated pessimism, while his metaphysic is "gloomy" it is not uncontrasted black. True, "Piggy" is killed. But, by analogy, is Marlowe a pessimist simply because "Faustus" goes to hell? Must one assume that there will never be another "Faustus" in whom the branch might grow full straight rather than crooked or a "Piggy" that might win the struggle of right reason? Furthermore, "Ralph" *is* saved, a fact that cannot be ignored or dismissed as an "awkward device" merely because it does not fit one's thesis. One cannot have it both ways.

Essentially the difference in our reading of the book concerns Mr. Kearns' assumption that the book is a throwback to the "Calvinistic doctrine of natural depravity." But one need not be a Calvinistic pessimist to believe that evil exists in man—whether it is "natural Calvinistic depravity" or the old belief that "In Adam's fall/We sinnéd all." Evil *does* occur in the world because man fails to use his free will for what is right and just; evil is no longer evil if it is the result of unwilled fate (even Montaigne in his "infamous" *Apology for Raymond Sebond* was aware of this). And it is difficult to see *Lord of the Flies* as neutral naturalism; in it there is at least implicit judgment against evil in the world resulting from abuse of freedom, resulting from aberration from right reason.

The tenor of much philosophy in the last century, despite the vogue of existential pessimism, has been largely optimistic, basing its rosy outlook upon scientific progress and, as Mr. Kearns has pointed out so well in his article on Salinger, upon a Rousseauistic, prelapsarian conception of man. If Golding has rejected such euphoric prepossessions, he need not be listed necessarily as a Calvinistic pessimist.

I refuse, of course, to be trapped into a position of defending Golding as a happy primitivist, but just as certainly do I refuse to deny him the title of at least "humanist"—which, in my definition, would include the admission of willed human struggle between good and evil rather than the determinism of degeneration. "Simon," after all, who has the "mystic-vision" of evil, *does* see man not only as "sick," but as "heroic"—and in the game of picking quotes one can hardly underscore the word *sick* and ignore the word *heroic*.

Finally, in continuing the game of picking through the pile for convenient either/or evidence, Mr. Kearns, citing specific examples of student-indifference to social injustices, doubts, apparently, that the student's instinct for moral responsibility really exists; however, for every case of student indifference, a believer in twentieth-century youth's generous commitment could cite cases of mature social awareness—let's say, in sympathetic sit-ins in the South, in C.C.D. work throughout the United States, in Catholic Action in New York City (I refer you to Monsignor Rea), and in the Peace Corps.

Perhaps I am an incorrigible optimist in sensing a light in Golding's gloom—but, in literature, it has always taken great optimists, who expect so much of struggling human nature, to project the most bitter contrasts with the ideal. May Golding not be such an idealist? I will make no categorical answer. But, if I am wrong, a vast number of readers have been hoodwinked, and the book is either a muddle-headed hoax or a herald of another Calvinistic "Great Awakening." *I* see it as a persistence of the perennial humanist vision in the twentieth century.   LUKE M. GRANDE, F.S.C. /571/

GOLDING REVISITED

FRANCIS E. KEARNS

I am afraid that Brother Luke Grande's use of such terms as "critical chicanery" and "straw-man technique" has done little to clarify the grounds of our exchange of views over William Golding's *Lord of the Flies*. And, though he implies on at least three occasions that I have quoted out of context, it is interesting to note that he never cites a specific example of such improper quotation.

Moreover, I am not quite convinced that it is a reasonable procedure for Brother Luke to answer a criticism I have made of his *Commonweal* article on Golding by attacking a point made in my discussion of Salinger in *America*. But, since this new issue has been raised, let me answer it. Brother Luke claims that I am guilty of oversimplification in "pegging" the ethical outlook of *Catcher in the Rye* as "liberal" and "Rousseauistic." He contends, further, that since I regard the society in which Holden finds himself as "depraved" and corrupted, this society might easily be termed "conservative-Calvinist" rather than "liberal-Rousseauistic." One difficulty with Brother Luke's argument here is the fact that in my *America* article I never apply the term "Rousseauistic" to *Catcher*. The term I use is "liberal-humanitarian." But, even ignoring Brother Luke's doubtless unintentional lapse in dealing with the facts, I think he overlooks a major distinction between the Calvinist and Rousseauistic ethical schemes. For the Calvinist, social institutions reflect that universal order instituted by God, and depravity is centered in man. For the follower of Rousseau, on the other hand, depravity is centered in social institutions, and man becomes more innocent in so far as he is removed from society. Thus, a novelist who describes society as depraved and deals with the attempt of an inherently innocent youth to escape that society could hardly be regarded as having adopted a Calvinist point of view.

Several of the points mentioned by Brother Luke in his defense of *Lord of the Flies* as an optimistic work are, I believe, equally unconvincing. First there is his insistence on the significance of

A rejoinder to the comments of Mr. Luke Grande; published here for the first time. Ed. Copyright © 1963 by Francis E. Kearns.

Ralph's rescue: " 'Ralph' *is* saved, a fact that cannot be ignored or dismissed as an 'awkward device' merely because it does not fit one's thesis." In reply I would ask merely what is Ralph saved for? Remember that the naval cruiser which has saved Ralph from being cornered and murdered is engaged in a nuclear war and has just interrupted the stalking of its own prey. Thus in taking the children aboard, the naval party is returning them to the sane adult world of seahunts and nuclear bombs. As Golding himself asks, in a critical note prepared for the Capricorn edition of his novel, "And who will rescue the adult and his cruiser?" Furthermore, it seems to me that if one stresses the *deus ex machina* through which Ralph is rescued and ignores the bitter irony implicit in such a rescue, then one tends to reduce Golding's complicated novel to sheer melodrama.

When Brother Luke asks "Must one assume that there will never be another . . . 'Piggy' that might win the struggle of right reason?" I am afraid he goes beyond the critical framework of the novel under discussion. Such a conjecture destroys what Wellek and Warren, in *Theory of Literature,* have described as the "aesthetic distance" which must be maintained between the reader and the work of fiction. This critical principle was used in the movie "Never on Sunday," wherein the prostitute is unable to accept the *Medea* as tragedy because the slain actors reappear after the play's conclusion to receive the applause of the audience. Moreover, I am afraid that I find speculation about what might happen to another Piggy in another novel no more sensible than I do conjectures about what might happen to another Hamlet in a possible sixth act.

A more telling point in Brother Luke's argument for an optimistic interpretation of *Lord of the Flies* is his reference to Simon's view of man: " 'Simon,' after all, who has the 'mystic-vision' of evil, *does* see man not only as 'sick,' but as 'heroic'—and in the game of picking quotes one can hardly underscore the word *sick* and ignore the word *heroic.*" To begin with, let me dispel the doubtless unintentional impression created by Brother Luke that I am guilty of misquoting. In neither my *America* article nor my letter to *The Commonweal* do I either refer to this opinion by Simon or use the word "sick." As for Simon's opinion, it is important to note that Brother Luke has, again doubtless unintentionally, reversed the novel's chronology—that is, Simon offers the opinion that man is both sick and heroic some fifty pages *before* he encounters the "Lord of the Flies" and achieves a "mystic-vision" of evil. Moreover, I think Simon's view of man as "heroic" cannot be read without a certain sense of irony when one considers that he is later cruelly murdered by the very human beings whom he regards as "heroic" and that even Ralph and the noble Piggy participate in the murder.

One of the key questions raised in my letter to *The Commonweal* remains, I believe, unanswered by Brother Luke's reply. I would still like to know how Brother Luke can accept at face value the confrontation scene shared by Simon and the "Lord of the Flies" (the scene in which the "Lord" declares that "Everything is a bad business. . . . I'm the reason why it's no go") and yet maintain that the novel offers an optimistic view of man. How can the words of the "Lord" here be interpreted as anything but a pronouncement on man's innate depravity? How else can the series of depraved actions which take place on the island—the killing of Simon, the destruction of the conch, the murder of Piggy, the burning of the paradise—be viewed except as confirmations of the Lord's pronouncement?

Much of the debate over the question of whether there is hope in Golding's universe revolves, I think, around the problem of whether one chooses to stress the "Lord of the Flies" scene, the scene in which the "Lord" pronounces his dark view of human existence, or the concluding scene, the scene in which Ralph is rescued and then weeps for "the end of innocence, the darkness of man's heart, and the fall through the air of the true, wise friend called Piggy." It seems to me that there are two ways of interpreting this concluding scene. On the one hand, it could be a thoroughly bitter scene: man not only fails to achieve a workable social order, but he is not even allowed sufficient blindness to remain ignorant of his failure and is even further tortured by a keen awareness of the value of that which has been lost. On the other hand, the passage could be viewed optimistically: despite all the evil which has taken place on the island, Ralph, in weeping for the death of Piggy, has achieved a sense of compassion and this sense may prove effectual in bringing about a new social order.

Unfortunately, if this optimistic view of the scene is adopted we are faced with several critical problems. First of all, what is optimistic about the fact of Ralph's compassion when one considers the general darkness of Golding's universe, the series of depraved actions which have taken place on the island, and the nuclear war to which Ralph returns? We have seen compassion in Piggy and Simon, yet they have both been destroyed. What is there about Ralph's sense of compassion which would indicate that he will be effective in bringing about a new social order? It may be argued that Ralph's attainment of compassion is an end in itself and a sufficient grounds for viewing the book as hopeful. However, such a view is, I believe, untenable, for to stress Ralph's compassion as the turning point of the novel implies that there is at the background of the book a whole system of order outside of man which makes man's inner disposition meaningful and which compensates for his wordly defeats. Yet no such system of order is delineated or implied by Golding in *Lord of the Flies*. The only pronouncement on the meaning of life we have here consists of the negative view of the "Lord" that "Everything is a bad business," everything is "no go." Indeed, the irrelevance of a religious sense of order in Golding's universe is further stressed when Jack, much in the style of Freud's *Future of an Illusion* or Frazer's *Golden Bough,* attempts to assuage the threat of the unknown beast by initiating a ritual dance in its honor and by offering a pig's head as a sacrificial tribute. Moreover, from the very outset of the novel we are faced with the problems of what type of society the boys will erect on their island and whether that society will work. And as Golding himself has written, "The theme is an attempt to trace the defects of society back to the defects of human nature." Clearly, then, the characters' achievement of insight is not an ultimate concern in this novel. Any such insight must finally be measured in terms of its effect on the novel's society.

A further problem involved in regarding Ralph's compassion as an expression of Golding's optimism is the fact that such a view renders violence to the novel's structure. If Ralph's achievement of compassion is stressed as a climactic event rather than as a further ironic twist, then it is obviously the turning point of the book. But what is there in Ralph's background to motivate such a change? What is there in the series of events on the island to lay the groundwork for such an abrupt change from gloom to hope? As I have suggested earlier, Ralph's last-minute rescue is undeniably a *deus ex machina,* but what saves the novel's ending from the shabbiness of the gratuitous happy ending of melodrama is the bitter irony inherent in the fact of our understanding that Ralph has been rescued only to endure the further darkness of a nuclear war. If, on the other hand, one chooses to regard Ralph's rescue as an optimistic, "uplift" ending, then I am afraid he does Golding the disservice of viewing his novel as not only melodrama but sheer sentimentality.

To return to Brother Luke's reply, though, he is to be commended for his firm refusal to accept such labels as "happy primitivist" and "neutral naturalism" in regard to Golding and *Lord of the Flies*. His refusal is none the less commendable for the fact that

I have used neither label. Indeed, if two can play, I am willing to take an equally firm stand against the application to Golding of such terms as "depressed dadaist" or "manic Marxist."

In the end, I suspect that what is far more important than our differing interpretations of *Lord of the Flies* is the fact that Brother Luke and I disagree over the reasons for the great popularity of the book with contemporary youth. In his original article on "The Appeal of Golding," Brother Luke hails youth's enthusiasm for the book as an expression of a sense of personal moral responsibility "in a world that tends to equate evil with unfavorable environment. . . ." I, on the other hand, fear that the book's popularity stems largely from the general conservatism on our college campuses. I fear that our college students acclaim *Lord of the Flies* for the same reason that they acclaim the novels of Ayn Rand— because Golding's dismissal of the idea of progress and his inherent view of man as predatory reassure the average student in his assumption that the chief use of a college education is as a means to a good income and a comfortable suburban existence. I make no claim that Golding intended his novel as a conservative tract, but, as I indicated in my original criticism, it is interesting to note that at the heart of Golding's novel are two key concepts which Richard Hofstadter, in *Social Darwinism in America,* has seen as cornerstones of American conservative political theory: the Darwinian view of life as a jungle struggle and the Calvinist view of man as innately depraved.

I am disturbed by the fact that Brother Luke so closely relates the acceptance of personal moral responsibility to the rejection of environmental or sociological causes of evil. He is unquestionably correct in claiming that "Evil *does* occur in the world because man fails to use his free will for what is right and just. . . ." But I feel he must also admit that man's perception of the grounds of moral decision is tremendously influenced by the circumstances of his environment. Moreover, I detect a certain irony in the fact that as an example of youth's sense of personal moral responsibility he cites its participation "in sympathetic sit-ins in the South, in C.C.D. work throughout the United States, in Catholic Action in New York City . . . and in the Peace Corps"—all projects involved in improving the environment of the underprivileged.

THE WORLD OF WILLIAM GOLDING
PETER   GREEN

Today, a century and a half after it first began to gather momen-
tum, the Industrial Revolution remains the largest, most far-reaching, and least appreciated influence on all our lives. The physical
effects it produced, and continues to produce, carry moral, social,
and spiritual implications which only now are we beginning to
understand, and most of which we are powerless to alter. Essentially, what the Machine Age has meant in human terms is the by-
passing of man's irrational, non-logical element. This is a vast
over-simplification, but it contains a basic truth.

Most of the changes that have taken place during the last hundred years or so are, however improbably, inter-related; they share
a common causality. The growth of an urban industrial society,
the decay of traditional religious fundamentalism, the dissemina-
tion of scientific method; moral uncertainty, technological advance,
the artificial retreat to primitivism, the flourishing neuroses which
facilitated the development of psychology and psychiatry; automa-
tion, logical positivism, thermo-nuclear deterrents, Admass, political propaganda, Billy Graham, horror comics, science fiction, rock
'n roll, angst, the death-wish, sexual frustration or hysteria: one
pattern binds them all together.

This needs further explanation in historical terms. The more
obvious by-products of the Industrial Revolution have become
textbook truisms; but historians are seldom interested in following up their conclusions in terms of the individual. We know that
our society has become urbanized, that labour is constantly drain-
ing from the country to the town. We are by no means so certain
what this means in its overall context. We are not sure how *we*
are affected by the breakdown of rural culture; we cannot judge
the long-term effects of city life. Things have moved too fast for
us. Man's metabolism changes slowly by nature; and in a century
it has had to adapt itself more than in the previous thirty thousand
years. /37/

Several factors have combined to offer us a comforting, but ulti-

Peter Green, "The World of William Golding," *Transactions and Proceedings
of the Royal Society of Literature*, 32 (1963), 37-57. Presented before the Royal
Society of Literature 25 February 1960, C. Day Lewis in the Chair. Reread by
the author, 1963.

mately dangerous protection. Foremost among these has been the notion that science could, in some mysterious way, be made a substitute for religion. It is no coincidence that such a large proportion of scientists are, or used to be, Marxists. Man is a creature for whom patterns are essential; and when Huxley and his successors destroyed the absolute sanctity of traditional Christianity, what was more natural than that the iconoclasts should themselves set up a new (if secular) Church? Reason was their sovereign god; reason could solve all the problems of the universe. The soul was a fiction, emotions could be rationalized in terms of hormones. God (to revive the old Voltairean gibe) was a Job's Comforter created by man in his own narcissistic image.

The consequences of this strangely unilateral creed were grave in the extreme: but then, most human attempts to upset the balance of nature tend to be calamitous. What happened, in effect, was that half of human nature—the emotional, instinctive, irrational element, the back rather than the front of the mind—was treated simply as if it did not exist. There is a popular delusion among scientists, which they share, incidentally with primitive witch-doctors, that by naming a thing they render it harmless. Logic stuck its labels on the universe, and analogies from the natural sciences multiplied thick and fast. Natural selection was used to justify racial persecution; the notion of evolution became transformed into Wellsian social progressivism. The smug religious superiority of the early Victorians gave place to the smug scientific superiority of the early anthropologist. The universe was as tidy and as comprehensible, for a few years, as the Crystal Palace.

For a few years, but no longer. Violent suppression tends to breed violent reaction; and soon the air was thick with cries of 'back to the Land', while urban radicals preached a new urban egalitarianism. Neuroses grew and proliferated alarmingly. It was the functional scientific attitude to sex no less than Puritan repression or industrial materialism which produced the mere casual concupiscence which both D. H. Lawrence and Mr. Eliot attacked. Reason could stick new labels on the emotions; but it could neither argue nor legislate them out of existence. It could rationalize God by discussing religion in terms of personal psychology; but God (under whatever name) remained. And of course, above all, reason could rationalize its own motives; it seldom occurs to any scientist to admit that /38/ his tenets are no less dogmatic than those of Christianity, and that his logical inferences normally rest on a solid bedrock of emotional prejudice. He has a name and a label for everything.

This may seem a long, perhaps an irrelevant introduction to

William Golding's work: but it is, I think, indispensable if we are
to understand that work fully. 'His job', Golding once wrote of
the novelist, 'is to scrape the labels off things, to take nothing for
granted, to show the irrational where it exists.' The novels he has
so far published demonstrate this process in action. Man, Golding
is saying, has grown away both from nature and himself. He is
protected from reality not only by city life, labour-saving devices,
canned food, electric light, running water, daily papers, and indifference to the seasons, but also by the spiritual blindness which
such conditions breed. He is cushioned in smugness; he has become
his own God. Nothing can touch him. Golding has made it his
task to break down these false illusions: his creed is that of the
Delphic Oracle, *Know Yourself*. He has put it on record that he 'is
making statements all the time about John Smith, Twentieth Century citizen. Writing about schoolboys, Neanderthalers and dead
sailors appears to him to be a simple means of turning a light on
contemporary human nature. He believes the only hope for humanity is self-knowledge, attained and practised by the individual.' In
an interview for *Books and Art*[1] he also made it clear that the basic
problem of modern humanity, in his view, was that of learning
to live fearlessly with the natural chaos of existence, without forcing artificial patterns on it. To his interviewer he asserted: 'The
difference between being alive and being an inorganic substance
is just this proliferation of experience, this absence of pattern.'

In an earlier article[2] he had also clarified his position as a novelist
with regard to political 'involvement' and modern scientific discoveries:

> Current affairs [he wrote] are only expressions of the basic human
> condition where his [the novelist's] true business lies. If he has a
> serious, an Aeschylean, preoccupation with the human tragedy, that is
> only to say that he is committed to looking for the root of the disease
> instead of describing the symptoms. I can't help feeling that critics of
> this Aeschylean outlook are those who think they have an easy answer
> to all problems simply because they have never looked /39/ further
> than the rash appearing on the skin. They want Gulliver to declare
> himself for one end or other of the egg.
>
> As for awareness of recent discoveries in biology, astronomy and psy-
> chology, it is a necessary part of any mind's equipment. . . . [But] to
> be aware of discoveries need not mean that we over-rate their import-
> ance—need not mean that we should picture our flesh under the electron
> microscope when our real job is to show it *sub specie aeternitatis*. . . .

[2] *The London Magazine*, vol. iv, no. 5 [May 1957], pp. 45-46.

Golding, in fact, is, primarily, a religious novelist: his central theme
is not the relationship of man to man (which I suspect he considers
of secondary importance) but the relationship of man, the individual, to the universe; and through the universe, to God. He is
going back behind our distracting modern clutter of physical im-
pedimenta to search for basic truths that have been obscured by
material progress. He is a spiritual cosmologist.

Any attentive reader of his three published novels will perceive
at once that their symbolism is, in essence, theological. Both *Lord
of the Flies* and *The Inheritors* are concerned with the primal loss
of innocence. *The Inheritors,* indeed, can be read as an anthropological allegory of the Fall, with Lok and Fa as a prelapsarian
Adam and Eve. *Pincher Martin,* as the last chapter proves, explicitly concerns the sufferings of a dead man who has created his own
Purgatory. It is a moral axiom of Golding's that Man, and Man
alone, introduced evil into the world: a view which is hardly sepa-
rable from the doctrine of Original Sin. This is suggestive. To a
critic who suggested that good was equally an exclusive human concept, he replied: 'Good can look after itself. Evil is the problem.'
This attitude suggests both the emotional strength of his work and
the intellectual paradox underlying it. He wants to scrape off the
labels, to destroy artificial patterns. He represents himself, theologically, as what used to be loosely termed a Deist; and yet the whole
moral framework of his novels is conceived in terms of traditional
Christian symbolism.

Nevertheless, the paradox, on closer thought, can be resolved.
In the first place, a novelist with a fundamental moral problem
to communicate must be understood by his audience; and to be
understood he must use symbols which are familiar and can be
readily apprehended, preferably those that have sunk into the
archetypal consciousness of European readers. Secondly, Golding
is a man in search of cosmological truth; and it might well be
argued that—as he himself has often proclaimed in a slightly different context—the names, the labels, do not matter. It is /40/ only
the ultimate reality that counts, and must at all costs be communicated.

Having established the background, let us now consider the four
novels separately, in the order of their appearance.

Lord of the Flies was published in 1954, and acclaimed, though
somewhat uneasily, by English critics. The main outline of the
plot is by now well known. Somewhere an atomic war is raging
(the novel is, ironically, set in the future), and a plane-load of
schoolboys crashes on a deserted tropical island in the Pacific.

There are palm-trees, sandy beaches, a lagoon to swim in, plentiful ripe fruit; the setting is perfect for the re-enactment of that perennial and highly charged boyhood myth, which found its most famous expression in R. M. Ballantyne's *The Coral Island*—life, primitive life, unhampered by pettifogging, over-civilized, authoritarian adults.

Since Golding's explicit purpose is to stand the Ballantyne myth on its head—in ways *Lord of the Flies* deliberately parodies the earlier book—it is instructive to re-read *The Coral Island* with this in mind. It was published exactly a century ago, in 1858, at the high tide of Victorian self-confidence, and is permeated with smug national complacency, synthetic missionary fervour, and a kind of paralysing condescension which could only blossom in a safe, stable, unreflecting society. The boys are pint-sized adults, whose priggish conversation is spattered with semi-colons. The social and moral scale of things is clearly delineated: Britons come at the top of it, savages and pigs at the bottom. The boys kill pigs with the same unthinking self-assurance they employ to bully the natives into Christianity, or read them a moral lecture on the sin of cannibalism. The book ends with the burning of the false gods of Mango, and then hurrah for dear old England. Nothing, moreover, is allowed to disrupt the emotional unity of the three boys, Jack, Ralph, and Peterkin. 'There was, indeed,' Ballantyne wrote, in a particularly mawkish moment, 'no note of discord whatever in the symphony we played together on that sweet Coral Island; and I am now persuaded that this was owing to our having been all tuned to the same key, namely, that of *love!*'[1]

Now it is easy enough to see how a novelist armed with the findings of Frazer, Freud and Piaget could turn this rubbishy myth inside out. *A High Wind in Jamaica* pointed the way; a century of social change lies between Ballantyne's and Golding's position. Mr. V. S. Pritchett, writing in *The New Statesman*, /41/ both summarized this development and hinted at its further implications:

> In *Coral Island* [he wrote] we see the safe community. . . . In Richard Hughes's book, we saw the first sign of disintegration: the psychologists have discovered that children are not small fanciful adults, but are a cut-off savage race. In *Lord of the Flies* we understand that the children are not cut-off; anthropology, the science of how people live together, not separately, reflects the concern of the modern world which has seen its communities destroyed.

Golding's children, then, are isolated on their desert island for a spe-

[1] 1st edition, p. 165.

cific spiritual experiment, much as a scientist might isolate a culture
in a Petri dish; and their behaviour must be considered in the light
of their author's known convictions.

At one level—and this is the aspect of the book which most critics
have emphasized—*Lord of the Flies* portrays a gradual reversion
to the most primitive and bloodthirsty savagery. To begin with
the children impose 'civilized' standards of conduct on their small
community. As Jack observes, in a recognizable parody of Ballantyne: 'We've got to have rules and obey them. After all, we're not
savages. We're English; and the English are best at everything. So
we've got to do the right things.' They elect a leader, Ralph. They
have a meeting-place for discussion, and a conch-shell to summon
them. This conch also becomes a symbol of rational behaviour; no
one may speak unless he is holding it. And here, already, the per-
cipient reader gets his first twinge of uneasiness, remembering that
a similar habit prevailed among Homer's heroes. Just as the embryo in the womb recapitulates evolutionary development, so these
young boys are slipping back on the path that leads to primitivism.

And so it turns out. Gradually, conditions being right for it,
the shibboleths of twentieth-century civilization are erased with
appalling ease from these middle-class boys' minds. First come
irrational fears: of imaginary monsters and the numinous unknown.
There is a feeling of 'something behind you all the time in the
jungle'. Then the boys split into two groups: the hunters, and those
struggling to retain their civilized standards. The hunters, their
initial squeamishness lost, revel in the blood-lust induced by pig-
sticking. They daub their faces with coloured clay: Jack, their
leader, is 'safe from shame or self-consciousness behind the mask
of his paint'. Then comes the inevitable ritual *mimesis: 'Kill the
pig!'* they howl, dancing round its reeking, /42/ dismembered
corpse. *'Cut his throat! Kill the pig! Bash him in!'* It is only a
matter of time before their collective anger turns against a human
victim.

'Which is better?' cries Ralph in desperation: 'law and rescue,
or hunting and breaking things up?' There is no doubt which Jack
will choose: not 'the world of longing and baffled commonsense',
but 'the brilliant world of hunting, tactics, fierce exhilaration, skill'.
It is characteristic of the hunters that they loathe and despise those
who will not join them. Two of these, Piggy and Simon, are murdered; the third, Ralph himself, is hunted across the island, and
only saved by the opportune arrival of a Royal Navy landing-party.
(The last episode, incidentally, allows the author to bang his point
home with superb irony. 'I should have thought,' remarks the

hearty officer who stumbles on the survivors, 'I should have thought that a pack of British boys—you're all British aren't you?—would have been able to put up a better show than that—I mean—' and trails away into incoherence, only rallying to add, with hopeful optimism: 'Jolly good show. Like the Coral Island.')

But behind this main narrative structure, as always in Golding's work, we find more universal moral implications. What Ralph weeps for, on the last page, is 'the end of innocence, the darkness of man's heart'. Piggy is more than a fat, asthmatic, coddled, myopic, stubbornly sensible Cockney: he is the voice of sanity personified, a Promethean symbol. It is his thick-lensed spectacles which are used to light the vital signal-fire, and are later stolen by the hunters. He will have no truck with the group-consciousness, but remains embarrassingly individual; and because of this he is killed. Seen in this sense the book reveals a terrifying microcosm of political totalitarianism. The experiment acquires unexpected relevance to the whole human condition.

With Simon we are at a deeper level still. Simon—we have Golding's own word for it—is a saint, mystic and clairvoyant. It is Simon, and Simon alone, who sees the others' fear and superstition for what they are. This point is made by the use of two very explicit symbols: the Beast, and the Lord of the Flies himself.

The Beast, to begin with, is nothing more than a focal point for the boys' vague, inarticulate, archaic fears. 'What I mean is,' stammers Simon (and is shouted down for his pains), 'maybe it's only us': he is, as Golding puts it, 'inarticulate in his effort to express mankind's essential illness'. Later the Beast is given /43/ a spurious reality: the corpse of an airman, still harnessed to its parachute, drifts down from some aerial battle on to the beacon hill at the top of the island. Two children see it in the dark, and instantly the myth of terror is established. But Simon, again, is incredulous: 'however Simon thought of the beast, there rose before his inward sight the picture of a human at once heroic and sick.'

Meanwhile Jack, whose instinct tells him the Beast must be placated, erects a pole in the forest with a pig's head stuck on top of it as an offering. Simon, walking alone, stumbles on this totemic emblem, buzzing with flies, and instantly, instinctively, knows it for what it is. The more sophisticated reader quickly works out the equation. Baalzebub was the Philistine Lord of Flies; the Jews transmuted his name to mean Lord of Dung or Filth; by the time of the New Testament he was Lord of the Devils, a generalized Satan. It is this potent deity with whom Simon has his strange conversation in the jungle:

Simon's head was tilted slightly up. His eyes could not break away and the Lord of the Flies hung in space before him.

'What are you doing out here all alone? Aren't you afraid of me?' Simon shook.

'There isn't anyone to help you. Only me. And I'm the Beast.' Simon's mouth laboured, brought forth audible words.

'Pig's head on a stick.'

'Fancy thinking the Beast was something you could hunt and kill!' said the head. For a moment or two the forest and all the other dimly appreciated places echoed with the parody of laughter. 'You knew, didn't you? I'm part of you. Close, close, close! I'm the reason why it's no go? Why things are what they are?'

In other words, it is man who creates his own hell, his own devils; the evil is in him. As John Peter put it:[1] Beelzebub, Lord of the Flies, is Roger and Jack and you and I, ready to declare himself as soon as we permit him to.'

Armed with this self-knowledge, Simon climbs the hill and sees the rotting corpse for what it is; he cuts it adrift and lets the wind carry it, still in its parachute, out to sea. Then, eager to tell the healing truth, he starts off down to the shore: 'the beast was harmless and horrible; and the news must reach the others as soon as possible.' But the frenzied hunters will not listen to him: they tear him limb from limb in a ritual orgy, while he is still shrieking about a dead man up on the hill. Man, Golding seems to be saying, cherishes his guilt, his fears, his taboos, and /44/ will crucify any saint or redeemer who offers to relieve him of his burden by telling the simple truth. There is a horrible symbolic appropriateness about the corpse itself: the nameless devil and its victims are identical. Evil is ineradicable: the Earthly Paradise is a delusion. Man's heart is dark, and no innocence lives beneath the sun: or if it does, it must, inevitably, suffer and die as Piggy and Simon died, their wisdom and virtue destroyed by the Beast's devotees.

Now from the reviews which *Lord of the Flies* received on publication it is plain that few critics or readers worked out its deeper implications consciously. All recognized its power; but it reached them in the same way as a good poem, through direct emotional apprehension. Like any good propagandist, Mr. Golding slipped a fast one on his audience: he got beneath their rational guard. At the same time, there was a general question in the air: what in the world (or out of it) would he do next? Had he landed himself in a creative cul-de-sac? A year later all such doubts were dispelled by the publication of *The Inheritors*. Indeed, it almost looked as

[1] *Kenyon Review*, vol. xix, no. 4 [1957], p. 583.

though this unpredictable author had deliberately set himself an impossible task. A novel about Neanderthal Man? It would either be incomprehensible or a joke. But it was not: it was a more brilliant *tour de force* than *Lord of the Flies,* and demonstrated with even greater clarity Golding's extraordinary gift for identifying himself, in an empathic sense, with beings totally beyond the normal range of human creative awareness.

Once again, Golding set himself the task of standing a traditional *idée reçue* on its head. This time he moved on a little, from an old complacency to a new one. In *Lord of the Flies* he attacked the moral self-satisfaction of Victorian society. In *The Inheritors* he challenged its direct successor, the smugly superior progressivism of evolutionary science. No one single man is more closely associated with this movement in the popular mind than H. G. Wells; and it was from Wells's *Outline of History,* accordingly, that Golding took his epigraph, where Neanderthal Man is patronizingly described as an inferior creature who probably suggested the cannibalistic ogre of folk-tale. There is little doubt that he also had in mind Wells's own story of the meeting of Neanderthal Man and *homo sapiens, The Grisly Folk.*[1] In this tale all Wells's sympathies, as we might expect, are with *homo sapiens,* humanity, achievement, discovery, progress. The Neanderthalers are huge, half-witted, cruel monsters: one of them /45/ steals a human child, and Wells exults in their hunting down and ultimate destruction.

Golding exactly reverses this concept. Here it is the Neanderthalers who are creatures of primal innocence: it is the new men, and they alone, who introduce guilt, crime, suffering, and conscious ambition into the world. Professor Kermode[1] has summed up the major theme admirably: 'The price of human consciousness, of technical and linguistic power', he writes, 'is guilt. . . . The intellectual superiority which enables this victory is precisely measured by the cruelty and guilt invented in the process. Man, who cooks, makes drawings, alcohol and love, can think; he replaces with language that picture-dialect, guiltless of all abstracting, which the victim used, and which is found in *homo sapiens* only in certain pathological conditions.' It at once becomes clear that there is a close thematic connexion between *The Inheritors* and *Lord of the Flies*: Mr. Golding has simply set up a different working model to illustrate the eternal human verities from a new angle. Again it is humanity, and humanity alone, that generates evil; and when

[1] *Collected Short Stories,* pp. 607-21. /45/
[1] *The Spectator,* 22 August 1958, p. 257.

the new men triumph, Lok, the Neanderthaler, weeps as Ralph wept, for the corruption and end of innocence.

But what most immediately astonishes and impresses any reader of *The Inheritors* is its incredible atmosphere of immediacy and realism. 'The grisly folk,' Wells wrote—and what better illustrates his entrenched progressivist dogma?—'we cannot begin to understand. We cannot conceive in our different minds the strange ideas that chased one another through those queerly shaped brains. As well might we try to dream and feel as a gorilla dreams and feels.' *The Inheritors* gives this statement the lie direct. Striking a superb technical balance between external comment (which permits intellectual glossing) and internal impressionism, Mr. Golding projects a wholly convincing recreation of the Neanderthaler's cloudy, static, non-abstract awareness of life. This is a world where past and future are both little more than extensions of the present; where ideas and communication are a series of separate 'pictures', like a lantern-lecture; where neither action nor its corollary, speech, contains any subordinate clauses.

Coupled with Golding's intense awareness of the natural world, organic or inorganic (he seems to see each separate rock, tree, beast, or fish as Aldous Huxley saw jewels under the influence of mescalin), this insight into his Neanderthalers' /46/ minds enables him to sustain the sense of actuality throughout *The Inheritors*. Skilfully he introduces his essential clues: the first whiff of the unknown creature on the wind; the sense of kinship with earth; the primal cosmogony, the badness of killing earth's children; at last the contact with the new men.

Till the last chapter we see *homo sapiens* entirely from the viewpoint of the Neanderthaler. We share Lok's puzzlement at their incomprehensible appearance and habits: 'they were people,' he decides, 'without pictures in their heads.' When one of them shoots a poisoned arrow at him, Lok 'had a confused idea that someone was trying to give him a present.' By this method Golding jolts us out of our unthinking assumptions, forces us to re-examine what hitherto we had taken for granted. All primary human activities are filtered through the polarized lens of Lok's unfamiliarity: sympathetic hunting magic, ritual mimesis (the magician in a stag's head), the use of artefacts such as dug-out canoes; murder; religious heave-offerings, intoxication, the conscious and deliberate pursuit of pleasure in the act of love. Gradually, as he and Fa spy on these strange, alien creatures, they too are corrupted. Experience breeds awareness. They drink the alcoholic mead and feel identification with the new folk, only to wake and vomit afterwards. Lok looks at Fa with new eyes; and he also, in a brilliantly suggested passage, stumbles on the notion of 'likeness': dimly we sense him reaching forward to the simile, the metaphor, the first stirrings of poetry, the magic neutralization by naming: 'Likeness could grasp the white-faced hunters with a hand, could put them into the world where they were thinkable and not a random and unrelated irruption'.

Again the identification with *Lord of the Flies* becomes apparent. These new, bony-faced creatures, Tuami and the rest, hunting, performing magic, placating their devils—what are they but Jack and Roger reincarnate in the backwardness of time? 'They have gone over us like a hollow log,' cries Lok in his agony. 'They are like a winter.' From the beginning their triumph is inevitable; with a last flick of malice at Wells, Golding ends his story by making the New Men abduct a Neanderthal baby. Nothing is solved; corruption is complete; evil and knowledge have triumphed.

As I suggested earlier, *The Inheritors* can be read as an allegory, at one level, of the Fall; and since Golding himself insists that Lok is a prelapsarian, this is almost certainly how he intended it. Lok and Fa thus become anthropological analogues /47/ of Adam and Eve; but it is Man himself whom Golding identifies with the Serpent, and who tempts Lok to eat of the Tree of Knowledge. This blazingly heretical version of the Paradisal legend, again, does not seem to have been consciously appreciated by most critics; but its latent effect, I fancy, was considerable. One extremely intelligent Catholic novelist flatly refused to review the book; it is not hard to see why.

The Inheritors, like all successful works of art, is self-contained: it stands or falls without reference to its historical validity. On the other hand, since Golding knows a great deal about anthropology, and has been a life-long amateur archaeologist, it is interesting to see whether or not he has reshaped Neanderthal Man to suit his particular moral purpose. In fact he has: no mention is made of their undoubted cannibalism, or primitive tool-making, or glimmerings of magic; and consequently their primal innocence is clearly over-emphasized.[1] Recently, too, the discovery of a human skeleton *twelve million years old* in an Italian lignite mine has meant the total revision of anthropological prehistory. Neanderthal Man is no longer *homo sapiens'* precursor, but over many thousands of years his contemporary; perhaps an aberrant mutation. While this new

[1] See Jacquetta Hawkes, *Man on Earth* [1954], pp. 98 ff.

evidence does not in any way impair the creative achievement of *The Inheritors,* it does give an unexpected and unfortunate twist to its underlying symbolism.

Between *The Inheritors* and his next novel, *Pincher Martin,* Golding wrote, unexpectedly, a short satirical *novella, Envoy Extraordinary,* later dramatized as *The Brass Butterfly.* To most readers this was merely a welcome proof that the author, after all, had a sense of humour. The plot has close affinities with 'The Rewards of Industry', a story in Richard Garnett's *The Twilight of the Gods:* it concerns a Greek inventor, Phanocles, who comes to the court of an unspecified but highly decadent Roman Emperor with five premature inventions: the steamship, gunpowder, printing, the compass, and the pressure cooker. After a demonstration of the disastrous effects which steam and explosives can have on human society, Phanocles is hurried off to China, out of the way, leaving the Emperor with the pressure cooker—the most Promethean discovery of them all'.

Both the *novella* and the play (which differ in significant details) are an attack on the scientific temperament and the abuse of scientific knowledge. 'Confused, illogical, and ex- /48/ tremely hubristic', the Emperor remarks of Phanocles' pretensions, and goes on: 'I said you are hubristic. You are also selfish. You are alone in your universe with natural law and people are an interruption, an intrusion. . . . Your single-minded and devoted selfishness, your royal preoccupation with the only thing that can interest you could go near to wiping life off the earth as I wipe the bloom from this grape'. Once again, Golding has indissolubly linked the concepts of human knowledge and human evil. But now we understand, retrospectively, that an additional element has been present throughout his work: the Prometheus myth. Man the maker, the inventor, the builder must suffer for his knowledge. Like Piggy, he has stolen fire from heaven. Like Lok, he has eaten the forbidden fruit. Expulsion from Paradise is only the beginning; it leads by slow degrees to the purgatorial Caucasian rock, the eagle tearing endlessly at his vitals. So the scene is set for the third, Aeschylean novel, *Pincher Martin.*

It is essential, right from the beginning, to make it quite clear what *Pincher Martin* is about. Most critics, with a few honourable exceptions, though they lauded the book to the skies, completely missed its point. In particular, they objected to what was generally described as the 'trick ending'. The entire novel, you will remember, has concerned a naval lieutenant's desperate efforts, after being torpedoed, to survive, alone, on Rockall.[1] In the first chapter he kicks off his sea-boots to avoid drowning. On the last page, when his corpse is washed ashore, it is made clear that he was drowned *before* he had time to kick them off. What is the explanation? /49/

'The essential point', John Peters wrote in *Kenyon Review*, 'is that this is a story about a dead man. . . .'[1] The existence he enjoys is a figment of his own will only, and in the most secret recesses of his being he remains horrifiedly aware of its unreality. Mr. W. J. Harvey, echoing this interpretation,[2] adds that 'the whole action of the novel takes place in the few seconds of his actual drowning or perhaps in some after-death state in which he is given the chance to choose salvation or damnation'.[3] Golding himself is even more

---

[1] Source-hunting in literature is an unprofitable study, but it does seem at least probable that the setting, as well as the central theme, of *Pincher Martin* may have been suggested by the late Michael Roberts's poem, 'Rockall' (*Collected Poems* [1958], p. 148):

> Comforting is sleep, but the comfort fails:
> The waves break on the bare rock; the traveller remembers
> Shipwreck, the struggle with the waters, the wild climb,
> Cries of the wind; and then nothing.

> Rockall, two hundred miles west of Benbecula.
> Bare rock, eighty-three feet wide, seventy feet high.
> First seen by Captain Hall, 1810, reported inaccessible
> The last spur on the Great Atlantic Shelf.

> .   .   .   .   .

> How shall the mind think beyond the last abandoned islands?
> The gulls cry, as they cry in the isles of despair,
> The waves break, as they break on Tiree or Foula;
> Man is alone, and death is certain. /49/

[1] The American publishers, anxious to avoid any repetition in the U.S.A. of English critical obtuseness, carefully retitled the book *The Two Deaths of Christopher Martin*. The guy was dead already: get it?

[2] *Essays in Criticism*, vol. viii, no 2 [April 1958], pp. 184-5.

[3] This particular device is not new to fiction, which makes its misunderstanding all the more inexplicable. The most exact parallel I know is Ambrose Bierce's story 'An Occurrence at Owl Creek' (*In the Midst of Life* [1892], pp. 25-39). This concerns the hanging of a Southerner during the American Civil War. He is to be hanged from Owl Creek Bridge; and when he drops—so we are led to believe—the rope breaks, and he swims down-river to safety, bullets scattering around him. It is only when he is reaching home, and his wife is stretching out her arms to welcome him, that the vision abruptly ends; in the very last sentence we are made to realize that the whole episode has taken place in the split second between Peyton Farquhar's fall and the breaking of his neck. Like Golding, Bierce hints at the illusory nature of Farquhar's experience by heightening his faculties to an extraordinary degree: his physical senses, we are told, 'were . . . preternaturally keen and alert. Something in the awful disturbance of his physical system had so exalted and refined them that they made record of things never before perceived. . . . He . . . saw the individual trees, the leaves and the veining of each leaf. . . . He noted the prismatic colours in all the dewdrops upon a million blades of grass. . . . He dug his fingers into the sand, threw it

explicit: 'Pincher', he writes, 'is simply in hell. The whole of
Pincher Martin is Pincher's *post mortem* experience of himself
("Nothing burns in hell but the self").' 'Myself am Hell': 'Why,
this is Hell, nor am I out of it.' From Marlowe to Blake, from
Milton to Sartre, echoes of Pincher's self-inflicted purgatory come
crowding to the mind.

Now Mr. Golding makes it quite clear that Pincher's struggle
for survival is not intended to be seen as heroic, but rather as egotistical, in the Hobbesian sense. He is clinging with fierce desperation to his own small, mean pattern of existence. He refuses to
acknowledge the cosmic chaos of death. Yet, paradoxically enough,
it is just at this point that Pincher—like Milton's Satan—breaks
away from his creator's original intention. However despicable
his character—and Mr. Golding, as we shall see in a moment, makes
him out a classic four-letter man—he nevertheless compels our ad-
miring respect for his epic, unyielding struggle in the face of overwhelming odds. He feeds off limpets and sea-anemones. He im-
provises shelter, /50/ builds a cairn to attract ships, makes a huge
S.O.S. sign out of seaweed in the hope that a passing aircraft will
spot it. He pits three thousand years of human knowledge, intelligence, and will-power against the blind forces of nature. 'I am busy
surviving', he remarks to himself. 'I am netting down this rock
with names and taming it. Some people would be incapable of
understanding the importance of that. What is given a name is
given a seal, a chain. If this rock tries to adapt me to its ways I will
refuse and adapt it to mine. I will impose my routine on it, my
geography. I will tie it down with names.'

Indeed, Christopher Martin is more than an individual sailor,
suffering on a specific rock: he is a mythic symbol of man's steadfast endurance. He is the much-travelled, long-enduring, crafty
Odysseus, spewing the salt water from his lungs, battered yet surviving. He is Ajax defying the lightning. 'Why drag in good and
evil', he cries, 'when the serpent lies coiled in my own body? . . . I
am Atlas. I am Prometheus.' He is Lear in his madness and defiant
to the end. He sums up every quality that distinguishes man from
the beasts.

To offset this Mr. Golding presents Pincher, in a series of flashbacks, as one of the nastiest characters ever to appear in fiction. Like
Phlebas the Egyptian, he passes 'the stages of his age and youth
entering the whirlpool', and reveals himself as an adulterer, a homo-

---

over himself in handfuls and audibly blessed it. It looked like gold, like dia-
monds, rubies, emeralds; he could think of nothing beautiful which it did not
resemble.' /50/

sexual, a thief, a rapist, and a would-be murderer. Here is how one of his peacetime friends, an actor like himself, describes him: 'This painted bastard here takes anything he can lay his hands on. . . . He takes the best part, the best seat, the most money, the best notice, the best woman. He was born with his mouth and his flies open and both hands out to grab. He's a cosmic case of the bugger who gets his penny and someone else's bun.' For the purposes of Mr. Golding's allegory he has to be: if he were a good man, or even *l'homme moyen sensuel,* he would never have created this hell for himself in the first place.

'Like a dead man!' he exclaims at one point; and of course he *is* dead. Occasionally his imagination makes a mistake. He sees a red lobster swimming, scales a cliff by using limpets as suckers, forgets that guano is insoluble in water. The clue to his purgatorial experience is to be found in his exchanges with Nathaniel, again the innocent, saintly fool, who is simply Simon grown up. "Take us as we are now', Nathaniel tells him, 'and heaven would be sheer negation, . . . a sort of black lightning destroying everything that we call life.' What Pincher lacks is /51/ 'the technique of dying into heaven'; he adamantly refuses to admit the validity of spiritual experience, which Golding himself treats always 'as factual, not illusion'. When God appears to Pincher at the novel's apocalyptic climax, in the guise of the Old Man of the Sea, Pincher cries out: 'You are a projection of my mind. . . . I have created you and I can create my own heaven.' 'You have created it', the Old Man replies, with sombre irony. But even then Pincher stands fast. 'I spit on your comparison', he shrieks, as the black lightning plays about him; and his last words are: 'I shit on your heaven.'

This novel suggests the limitations as well as the possibilities of Golding's creative method. Nathaniel, as Professor Kermode pointed out, tells Prometheus-Pincher 'that evil is human' (which we know) 'and would vanish if the mind could alter its theme'— both of which premises seem highly arguable. *Au fond,* Golding is a religious mystic, for whom the bulk of mankind is fiercely repellent, and in whose eyes only the saint or the prelapsarian— Simon, Lok, Nathaniel—can justify human existence. (Golding never, we may note—except in the doubtful case of Nathaniel and Mary—portrays a full emotional relationship between a man and a woman. It is no accident, one feels, that the mysterious, glamorous Euphrosyne of *Envoy Extraordinary* turns out in the end to have a hare-lip. This touch seems to have been too much for the producer of *The Brass Butterfly,* who removed the hare-lip and substituted a romantic affair with the Emperor's grandson.) This has some curious consequences. In the first place, it virtually excludes the normal range of human relationships which the novel covers. As Mr. Harvey observed, Golding's imagination has always worked at a fair remove from the full body of human life. Only in *Pincher Martin*—and then only by means of flashbacks—is this rule broken; and here, so loathsome is the glimpse given of man's social behaviour, one returns to the bare wind-swept rock with a sigh of relief.

After the publication of *Pincher Martin*, Golding was asked, in an interview, what he now aimed to achieve. 'This time', he stated in reply, 'I want to show the patternlessness of life before we impose our patterns on it.' This was a local last step for him to contemplate, and one which hinted broadly at the creative impasse with which he was confronted. It was becoming increasingly difficult for him either to come to terms with humanity, or to ignore it. In the event, however, his new novel, *Free Fall*, avoids the amoebic paradox suggested by his own /52/ prophecy, and falls into a more normal pattern of development: normal, that is, for Golding. In the title itself we can at once recognize his two overriding themes, the perennial conflict. Man is doomed by Original Sin, and Fall is a reality. Yet the will remains free: self-destruction is a matter of choice. Once again Golding is exploring the two counterpoised worlds of human awareness—the physical universe and the metaphysical, the worlds of Science and God.

This universal moral conflict is crystallized internally, in the mind of one man, Sammy Mountjoy, an English artist. For the first time Golding is presenting us with first-person narrative; and in Sammy we have exactly the type of *l'homme moyen sensuel* which we missed in Pincher. Structurally the two novels must be bracketed together: both use the same system of flashbacks to unite and give depth to the perspective of a single vision, and both depend on the use of delayed shock-treatment. Only on the last line do we realize fully that Pincher is dead; only half-way through *Free Fall* do we become aware that Sammy's present predicament—at the time of thinking, as it were—is that of a P.O.W. officer under interrogation in a Nazi concentration camp during the war. His interrogator, a coldly clever academic psychologist, is applying various pressures in order to make him betray his comrades' escape-plans. What we are hearing is Sammy's *apologia pro vita sua*, his frantic autobiographical search for the incidents which, in the past, made him take one moral decision rather than another, his corrosive fear of spiritual bankruptcy. Has he, in fact, the inner resources necessary to hold out against his tormentor?

The web of memory shuttles to and fro: where was the failure, the wrong turning? Was it in the Kentish slum-tenement where he lived with his huge, boozy, warm-hearted slattern of a mother? Or later, at school, fumbling through the thickset, glimmering hedges of adolescence? Not here, he cries silently, not here. Did Miss Pringle, the frustrated religious puritan, turn me against her God because she was mean and cruel, just as old Nick Shales, that devoted teacher and scientist, drew me with the paradoxical love that irradiated his material world? When did I lose my freedom? By what act, what choice, what suffering?

It is Beatrice who offers the clue, and hints at the Dantean symbolism underlying so much of Golding's work. Sammy's own name, Mountjoy, suggests the Paradisal Mountain: if *Pincher Martin* is Golding's *Purgatorio, Free Fall* is his tragically /53/ marred *Paradiso*. Beatrice was the child whom Sammy tried to draw, the girl with the light of Paradise round her brow. Golding himself says of her:

> But where Dante, presented with a coherent cosmos, was able to fit her into it, Sammy's confused cosmos ended by putting her through the whole mill of seduction—a scientific, rationalistic approach, so to speak, so that Beatrice who took Dante up to the vision of God becomes a clog to Sammy and a skeleton in his cupboard.

Sammy is responding, as he must, to the muddled, broken cosmos which is his inheritance; and Beatrice, abandoned, an ugly, incontinent, mindless wreck, is the cross he must bear. It is in solitary prison confinement, alone in a dark room, that he comes through to the truth—the same truth which Simon discovered in *Lord of the Flies*—that all terror, fear, despair are born of the human mind, and the human mind alone. The horrible Poe-like cell is revealed as an ordinary broom-cupboard; the fragment of cold, dead flesh is an abandoned floor cloth; the diabolical psychologist who investigated Sammy's past 'does not', the Camp Commandant apologetically explains, 'know about peoples'. And on this ironic note, with Sammy's burden of guilt clarified if not alleviated, the novel ends.

Or rather, as with all Golding's novels, begins. *In my end is my beginning.* From the cell Sammy cried *de profundis,* to the God in whom he could not completely believe; and the cell door opened, the drab prison camp outside was transmuted in Traherne-like splendour, Sammy had the Pentecostal vision and saw his companions walking in their glory like Kings of Egypt. And this tremendous experience at once swings us back to the opening pages of the book: indeed, to its opening paragraph:

I have walked by stalls in the market place where books, dog-eared and faded from their purple, have burst with a white hosanna. I have seen people crowned with a double crown, holding in either hand the crook and flail, the power and the glory. I have understood how the scar becomes a star, I have felt the flake of fire fall, miraculous and pentecostal. My yesterdays walk with me. They keep step, they are grey faces that peer over my shoulder. I live on Paradise Hill, ten minutes from the station, thirty seconds from the shops and the local. Yet I am a burning amateur, torn by the irrational and incoherent, violently searching and self-condemned.

This, as Ian Gregor and Mark Kinkead-Weekes have pointed out, in a penetrating though perhaps too wholly defensive article,[1] contains the whole subsequent essence of the novel in /54/ miniature. Here are the torn and conflicting halves of Sammy's world and self: body and spirit, faith and pragmatism, Paradise Hill and the Mount of Venus. But it is only *after* the transfiguring experience in his prison cell that Sammy as narrator, and we as readers, can look back and fit the pieces of the puzzle together. (Yet Mr. Golding always plays fair: there are plenty of 'hints and guesses, hints followed by guesses' for those who care to see them. A whole article could be written on his symbolic names, with their wealth of associative allusiveness: Christopher Martin, Christopher the Christ-bearer who becomes 'Pincher', the grasping egotist; or Sammy Mountjoy, who is not only an inhabitant of the Paradisal Mountain, but the Infant Samuel and, in another sense, the sex-obsessed devotee of the Mons Veneris.) Finally and most important, it is only in this new novel that Mr. Golding's perennial Everyman, astride the ages, at last brings himself to accept. Pincher died blaspheming; Sammy cries for help out of the depths of his uncertainty.

William Golding demands—insistently demands—to be judged by the very highest standards, both aesthetic and moral. On this level his new novel is a flawed masterpiece, the inordinately ambitious work of an indisputable genius just missing the centre of the target. Technically, *Free Fall* buckles a little here and there beneath its cumulative weight of symbolism and flashback, the latter occasionally achieving a probably unintentional ambiguity. For example: does the terrible asylum reunion with Beatrice take place in fact, after the war, or is it merely the creation of Sammy's imprisoned mind, the flash of tortured self-knowledge? Here and there, too, the writing, normally so objective and crystalline, blurs a little, as though from sheer intensity of desire to express the inexpressible.

[1] *Twentieth Century*, vol. clxvii, no. 996, February 1960, pp. 115-25.

The twin problem of loneliness and communication dogs Sammy, as it has always dogged his creator:

> It is the unnameable, unfathomable and invisible darkness that sits at the centre of him, always awake, always different from what you believe it to be, always thinking and feeling what you can never know it thinks and feels, that hopes hopelessly to understand and to be understood. Our loneliness is the loneliness not of the cell or the castaway; it is the loneliness of that dark thing that sees as at the atom furnace by reflection, feels by remote control and hears only words phoned out to it in a foreign tongue. To communicate is our passion and our despair.

But for moral sincerity and cosmic splendour of vision this novel towers above most contemporary fiction. /55/

It is no accident that the term of praise most often used to describe Golding's work is 'a *tour de force*'. In each novel he has created special conditions—a desert island, a prehistoric wilderness, a lonely rock, a prison cell—where he could experiment in isolation, without external influence. In each, again, he has chosen his characters so as to exclude the exploration of full adult relationships: pre-adolescent boys, inarticulate Neanderthalers, a shipwrecked sailor who is dead into the bargain and therefore doubly *hors concours*. With Sammy Mountjoy we see him beginning, with immense effort, to struggle free of this isolating tendency. Sammy speaks for himself, and therefore, inevitably, with a degree of self-justification as well as guilty self-reproach. He is asking questions, not imposing patterns; shaking the bars of his cage, challenging his own inner convictions. Sammy, the contemporary, fumbling, destructive, yet essentially well-meaning hedonist—Sammy the visionary, the artist, who loves his coarse Welsh wife with a ferocious tenderness, however he may ruin the Beatrices of this world—Sammy is the character through whom Mr. Golding, one suspects, is beginning to be reconciled to the loss of his primal Eden.

It has been suggested by an American scholar (and the irony of the labelling must appeal to Golding) that he does not write novels, but fables. There is some truth in this, but it is not the whole truth. Where most fables and allegories and satires fail is in their lack of individual reality. The idea is more important than the figure which gives it life. But Golding has never fallen into this trap. He is intensely, blindingly aware of physical immediacy. Whatever they may symbolize, his schoolboys (for instance) exist as sharply differentiated individuals. Most important of all, he has an intimate, concrete, cosmic awareness of nature in the raw, and a poet's gift of words for describing it. His characters, as Professor Kermode memorably wrote, live in a world of rock and sea and amoebae heaving in the pull of the moon, refusing to be locked fast by human imaginings of good or evil, obstinately talking its own language of sucking, plopping and roaring, against the human language which gives it another kind of life.

Though in *Free Fall,* with its re-affirmation of human spiritual potential, the symbolic emphasis has shifted to the microcosm, it remains true that this narrowing of focus in one sense is Golding's strength: it releases him into cosmic awareness. /56/ Despite all his self-imposed limitations, he remains the most powerful writer, the most original, the most profoundly imaginative, to have turned his hand to fiction in this country since the war; and if he never wrote another word his place in English letters would be secure. /57/

WILLIAM GOLDING

VINETA COLBY

Probably the most sensational literary sleeper of the past decade is William Golding's *Lord of the Flies.* Published with little fanfare in England in 1954 and in the United States by Coward-McCann the following year, it received generally favorable reviews and an approving nod from E. M. Forster, who chose it as the "outstanding novel of the year." It was not until 1959, however, when Capricorn issued a paperback edition, that the public—and the younger generation in particular—discovered William Golding. *Lord of the Flies* is now a best seller. College bookstores can scarcely keep enough copies in stock to meet the demand, and it is required reading in many college and high school courses. A grim fable of a group of English schoolboys stranded on a Pacific island during an atomic war, it has caught the horrified imaginations of young

Vineta Colby, "William Golding," *Wilson Library Bulletin,* XXXVII (February, 1963), 505. Reprinted by courtesy of the H. W. Wilson Company, New York City.

readers and old alike. But for the young particularly, Golding's solemnly stated theme—"an attempt to trace the defects of society back to the defects of human nature"—has a disturbing urgency.

Literary success has not come early to Mr. Golding. Just past fifty, he is now somewhat dizzyingly experiencing its rewards, most of them in America—television interviews, lectures, guest-stints at writers' conferences, a year (1961-62) as writer-in-residence at Hollins College in Virginia. But in his quiet old thatched cottage in Wiltshire, Golding continues to go about the serious business of reading, thinking, and writing.

The son of Alec and Mildred Golding, William (Gerald) Golding was born in Cornwall, September 19, 1911. He was educated at Marlborough Grammar School and Brasenose College, Oxford, taking his B.A. in 1935. Although he claims to have had literary ambitions since the age of seven, his career bloomed very slowly. His only published work before *Lord of the Flies* was a slim and ephemeral volume of *Poems* in 1934. In the twenty years between these books he wrote, acted, and produced in what has been described as "the London equivalent of very, very far-off-Broadway theatre," taught school, and in World War II served with the Royal Navy as a commander of a rocket ship. He returned to teaching and to writing after the war, completing three novels that never were published, before *Lord of the Flies* finally appeared.

Part of the fascination of *Lord of the Flies* is its evocation of the past: the civilized children who revert to barbarism turn back the course of history swiftly and violently. But Golding's preoccupation with the past is more profound than this book alone would indicate. As a student at Oxford he had been especially interested in Anglo-Saxon. During the war years at sea he found in Homer a sense of the continuity of man's history. Thus in *The Inheritors* (1955; published in the U.S. in 1962 by Harcourt), he made the daring if not completely successful attempt to reconstruct out of the darkness of the unknown the life of Neanderthal man. This novel treats of the eight last surviving members of a tribe of ape-men who are destroyed by the coming of a new, advanced breed, the *homo sapiens*. Because his characters are almost inarticulate, their fate, while pathetic, is never rendered dramatic, nor are the deeper implications of his theme made sufficiently concrete. Nevertheless his imagination and technical skill impressed many readers.

From exploring man's link with his dark past Golding moved, perhaps inevitably, to exploring man's link with his inner self. In *Lord of the Flies* he had already acknowledged the fundamental beast in man, what E. L. Epstein calls his "ravenous, unreasoning and eternally insatiable nature." *Pincher Martin* (1956; published 1957 in U.S. by Harcourt as *The Two Deaths of Christopher Martin*) is the story of a naval officer lost at sea and, just before he dies, reliving his life and seeing its horror. *Free Fall* (1959; 1960, by Harcourt, in U.S.), less dramatically but far more profoundly, deals with the quest of a successful painter for the source of his terrible sense of isolation, his inability to make moral choices, to find meaning in life. His tragic dilemma, Golding makes it clear, is symptomatic of the universal condition of man.

In the treatment of such themes, Golding echoes the modern masters—Conrad, James, Faulkner, Malraux, Camus, Graham Greene; and his affinity with them, R. W. B. Lewis suggests, "extends to the genuine beauty, the harmony and movement, of his novel's structure" (*New York Herald Tribune*). No serious critic has yet suggested that Golding has the stature of these writers. His novels are brilliant virtuoso exercises, but they share certain failings—a contrived quality, the literary "gimmick," over-explicitness. John Peter (*Kenyon Review*, Autumn 1957) describes his novels as "fables," where the thesis is not completely translated into the story and tends therefore to stand out glaringly and inartistically. There is no denying, however, the promise of his talent, or the generalization of John W. Aldridge that Golding "is on his way to being very widely recognized . . . as one of the truly original and gifted writers of the present time" (*New York Times*).

Lord of the Flies has been made into a motion picture, not yet released; and a play by Golding, *Brass Butterfly*, which was produced in London in 1958, has been announced for an off-Broadway production in New York in the spring of 1963. Golding is married to the former Ann Brookfield, and they have one son and one daughter. A bearded, heavy-set man whom Aldridge describes as looking "rather like an astute, well-feasted Viking," he cites his favorite recreation, not surprisingly, as sailing. /505/

RELATED READINGS

from THE CORAL ISLAND

ROBERT MICHAEL BALLANTYNE

It was a bright, beautiful, warm day, when our ship spread her canvas to the breeze, and sailed for the regions of the south. Oh, how my heart bounded with delight as I listened to the merry chorus of the sailors, while they hauled at the ropes and got in the anchor! The captain shouted; the men ran to obey; the noble ship bent over to the breeze, and the shore gradually faded from my view, while I stood looking on with a kind of feeling that the whole was a delightful dream.

The first thing that struck me as being different from anything I had yet seen during my short career on the sea, was the hoisting of the anchor on deck, and lashing it firmly down with ropes, as if we had now bid adieu to the land forever, and would require its services no more.

"There, lass," cried a broad-shouldered jack-tar, giving the fluke of the anchor a hearty slap with his hand after the housing was completed, "there, lass, take a good nap now, for we shan't ask you to kiss the mud again for many a long day to come!"

And so it was. That anchor did not 'kiss the mud' for many a long day afterwards; and when at last it did, it was for the last time!

There were a number of boys in the ship, but two of them were my special favourites. Jack Martin was a tall, strapping, broad-shouldered youth of eighteen, with a handsome, good-humoured, firm face. He had had a good education, was clever and hearty and lion-like in his actions, but mild and quiet in disposition. Jack was a general favourite, and had a peculiar fondness for me. My other companion was Peterkin Gay. He was little, quick, /25/ funny, decidedly mischievous, and about fourteen years old. But Peterkin's mischief was almost always harmless, else he could not have been so much beloved as he was. /26/

*　　　*　　　*

R. M. Ballantyne, *The Coral Island* (London and Glasgow: Collins, Ltd.; New York: W. W. Norton) pp. 25-26, 27-28, 31, 41-43, 81-82, 94, 97, 101-102, 131, 133, 168, 170-177, 269-271, 309-311. Reprinted by special permission.

One night, soon after we entered the tropics, an awful storm burst upon our ship. The first squall of wind carried away two of our masts, and left only the foremast standing. Even this, however, was more than enough, for we did not dare to hoist a rag of sail on it. For five days the tempest raged in all its fury. Everything was swept off the decks except one small boat. The steersman was lashed to the wheel, lest he should be washed away, and we all gave ourselves up for lost. The captain said that he had no idea where we were, as we had been blown far out of our course; and we feared much that we might get among the dangerous coral reefs which are so numerous in the Pacific. At daybreak on the sixth morning of the gale we saw land ahead. It was an island encircled by a reef of coral on which the waves broke in fury. There was calm water within this reef, but we could only see one narrow opening into it. For this opening we steered, but ere we reached it a tremendous wave broke on our stern, tore the rudder completely off, and left us at the mercy of the winds and waves.

"It's all over with us now, lads!" said the captain to the /27/ men. "Get the boat ready to launch; we shall be on the rocks in less than half an hour."

The men obeyed in gloomy silence, for they felt that there was little hope of their boat living in such a sea.

"Come, boys," said Jack Martin, in a grave tone, to me and Peterkin, as we stood on the quarter-deck awaiting our fate, "come, boys, we three shall stick together. You see it is impossible that the little boat can reach the shore, crowded with men. It will be sure to upset, so I mean rather to trust myself to a large oar. I see through the telescope that the ship will strike at the tail of the reef, where the waves break into the quiet water inside; so, if we manage to cling to the oar till it is driven over the breakers, we may perhaps gain the shore. What say you; will you join me?"

We gladly agreed to follow Jack, for he inspired us with confidence, although I could perceive, by the sad tone of his voice, that he had little hope; and, indeed, when I looked at the white waves that lashed the reef and boiled against the rocks as if in fury, I felt that there was but a step between us and death. My heart sank within me; but at that moment my thoughts turned to my beloved mother, and I remembered those words, which were among the last that she said to me: "Ralph, my dearest child, always remember in the hour of danger to look to your Lord and Saviour Jesus Christ. He alone is both able and willing to save your body and your soul." So I felt much comforted when I thought thereon.

The ship was now very near the rocks. The men were ready with the boat, and the captain beside them giving orders, when a tremendous wave came towards us. We three ran towards the bow to lay hold of our oar, and had barely reached it when the wave fell on the deck with a crash like thunder. At the same moment the ship struck, the foremast broke off close to the deck and went over the side, carrying the boat and men along with it. Our oar got entangled with the wreck, and Jack seized an axe to cut it free, but, owing to the motion of the ship, he missed the cordage and struck the axe deep into the oar. Another /28/ wave, however, washed it clear of the wreck. We all seized hold of it, and the next instant we were struggling in the wild sea, The last thing I saw was the boat whirling in the surf, and all the sailors tossed into the foaming waves. Then I became insensible.

On recovering from my swoon, I found myself lying on a bank of soft grass, under the shelter of an overhanging rock, with Peterkin on his knees by my side, tenderly bathing my temples with water, and endeavouring to stop the blood that flowed from a wound in my forehead. /31/

[The boys get ashore with a few simple tools.]

"Now, lads," said Jack, . . . "I propose that we should go to the tail of the island, where the ship struck, which is only a quarter of a mile off, and see if anything else has been thrown ashore. I don't expect anything, but it is well to see. When we get back here it will be time to have our supper and prepare our beds."

"Agreed!" cried Peterkin and I together, as, indeed, we could have agreed to any proposal that Jack made; for, besides his being older, and much stronger and taller than /41/ either of us, he was a very clever fellow, and I think would have induced people much older than himself to choose him for their leader, especially if they required to be led on a bold enterprise.

Now, as we hastened along the white beach, which shone so brightly in the rays of the setting sun that our eyes were quite dazzled by its glare, it suddenly came into Peterkin's head that we had nothing to eat, except the wild berries which grew in profusion at our feet.

"What shall we do, Jack?" said he, with a rueful look; "perhaps they may be poisonous!"

"No fear," replied Jack confidently; "I have observed that a few of them are not unlike some of the berries that grow wild on our own native hills. Besides, I saw one or two strange birds eating them just a few minutes ago, and what won't kill the birds won't kill us. But, look up there, Peterkin," continued Jack, pointing to the branched head of a cocoanut palm. "There are nuts for us in all stages."

"So there are!" cried Peterkin, who, being of a very unobservant nature, had been too much taken up with other things to notice anything so high above his head as the fruit of a palm-tree. But, whatever faults my young comrade had, he could not be blamed for want of activity or animal spirits. Indeed, the nuts had been scarcely pointed out to him when he bounded up the tall stem of the tree like a squirrel, and in a few minutes returned with three nuts, each larger than a man's fist.

"You had better keep them till we return," said Jack. "Let us finish our work before eating."

"So be it, captain; go ahead," cried Peterkin, thrusting the nuts into his trousers pocket. "In fact, I don't want to eat just now, but I would give a good deal for a drink. Oh, that I could find a spring! but I don't see the smallest sign of one hereabouts. I say, Jack, how does it happen that you seem to be up to everything? You have told us the names of half a dozen trees already, and yet you say that you were never in the South Seas before."

"I'm not up to *everything*, Peterkin, as you'll find out ere long," replied Jack, with a smile; "but I have been /42/ a great reader of books of travel and adventure all my life, and that has put me up to a good many things that you are, perhaps, not acquainted with."

"Oh, Jack, that's all humbug. If you begin to lay everything to the credit of books, I'll quite lose my opinion of you," cried Peterkin, with a look of contempt. "I've seen a lot o' fellows that were *always* poring over books, and when they came to try to *do* anything, they were no better than baboons!"

"You are quite right," retorted Jack; "and I have seen a lot of fellows who never looked into books at all, who knew nothing about anything except the things they had actually seen, and very little they knew even about these. Indeed, some were so ignorant that they did not know that cocoanuts grew on cocoanut-trees!"

I could not refrain from laughing at this rebuke, for there was much truth in it, as to Peterkin's ignorance.

"Humph! maybe you're right," answered Peterkin; "but I would not give *tuppence* for a man of books, if he had nothing else in him."

"Neither would I," said Jack; "but that's no reason why you should run books down, or think less of me for having read them." /43/

[The boys explore the island and its resources.]

While we were thus engaged, we were startled by a distant but most strange and horrible cry. It seemed to come from the sea, but was so far away that we could not clearly distinguish its precise direction. Rushing out of our bower, we hastened down to the beach and stayed to listen. Again it came, quite loud and distinct on the night air—a prolonged, hideous cry, something like the braying of an ass. The moon had risen, and we could see the islands in and beyond the lagoon quite plainly, but there was no object visible to account for such a cry. A strong gust of wind was blowing from the point whence the sound came, but this died away while we were gazing out to sea.

"What can it be?" asked Peterkin, in a low whisper, while we all involuntarily crept closer to each other.

"Do you know," said Jack, "I have heard that mysterious sound twice before, but never so loud as to-night. Indeed, it was so faint that I thought I must have merely fancied it, so, as I did not wish to alarm you, I said nothing about it."

We listened for a long time for the sound again, but as it did not come, we returned to the bower and resumed our work.

"Very strange," said Peterkin, quite gravely. "Do you believe in ghosts, Ralph?"

"No," I answered, "I do not. Nevertheless, I must confess that strange, unaccountable sound, such as we have just heard, makes me feel a little uneasy."

"What say you to it, Jack?"

"I neither believe in ghosts nor feel uneasy," he replied. "I never saw a ghost myself, and I have never met with any one who had; and I have generally found that strange and unaccountable things have almost always been accounted for, and found to be quite simple, on close examination. I certainly can't imagine what *that* sound is; but I'm quite sure I shall find out before long, and if it's a ghost I'll—I'll——"

"Eat it," cried Peterkin. /81/

"Yes, I'll eat it! Now, then, my bow and two arrows are finished; so, if you're ready, we had better turn in." /82/

*　　　*　　　*

Just in front of us, at the distance of about ten yards, grew a superb tree, which certainly was the largest we had yet seen on the island. Its trunk was at least five feet in diameter, with a smooth grey bark; above this the spreading branches were clothed with light green leaves, amid which were clusters of bright yellow fruit, so numerous as to weigh down the boughs with their great weight. This fruit seemed to be of the plum species, of an oblong form, and a good deal larger than the magnum bonum plum. The ground at the foot of this tree was thickly strewn with fallen fruit, in the midst of which lay sleeping, in every possible attitude, at least twenty hogs of all ages and sizes, apparently quite surfeited with a recent banquet.

Jack and I could scarce restrain our laughter as we gazed at these coarse, fat, ill-looking animals, while they lay groaning and snoring heavily amid the remains of their supper.

"Now, Ralph," said Jack, in a low whisper, "put a stone in your sling—a good big one—and let fly at that fat fellow with his back towards you. I'll try to put an arrow into yon little pig."

"Don't you think we had better put them up first?" I whispered; "it seems cruel to kill them while asleep."

"If I wanted *sport*, Ralph, I would certainly set them up; but as we only want *pork*, we'll let them lie. Besides, we're not sure of killing them; so, fire away."

Thus admonished, I slung my stone with so good aim that it went bang against the hog's flank as if against the head of a drum; but it had no other effect than that of causing the animal to start to its feet, with a frightful yell of surprise, and scamper away. At the same instant Jack's bow twanged and the arrow pinned the little pig to the ground by the ear.

"I've missed, after all," cried Jack, darting forward with uplifted axe, while the little pig uttered a loud squeal, tore the arrow from the ground, and ran away with it, along with the whole drove, into the bushes and dis- /94/ appeared, though we heard them screaming long afterwards in the distance.

"That's very provoking, now," said Jack, rubbing the point of his nose.

"Very," I replied, stroking my chin.

"Well, we must make haste and rejoin Peterkin," said Jack. "It's getting late." And without further remark we threaded our way quickly through the woods towards the shore.

When we reached it, we found wood laid out, the fire lighted and beginning to kindle up, with other signs of preparation for our encampment, but Peterkin was nowhere to be found. We wondered very much at this; but Jack suggested that he might have gone to fetch water; so he gave a shout to let him know that we had arrived, and sat down upon a rock, while I threw off my jacket, and seized the axe, intending to split up one or two billets of wood. But I had scarce moved from the spot when, in the distance, we heard a most appalling shriek, which was followed up by a chorus of yells from the hogs, and a loud hurrah.

"I do believe," said I, "that Peterkin has met with the hogs."

"When Greek meets Greek," said Jack, soliloquizing, "then comes the tug of——"

"Hurrah!" shouted Peterkin in the distance.

We turned hastily towards the direction whence the sound came, and soon descried Peterkin walking along the beach towards us with a little pig transfixed on the end of his long spear!

"Well done, my boy!" exclaimed Jack, slapping him on the shoulder when he came up, "you're the best shot amongst us." /97/

*   *   *

We had not advanced on our journey much above a mile or so, and were just beginning to feel the pleasant glow that usually accompanies vigorous exercise, when, on turning a point that revealed to us a new and beautiful cluster of islands, we were suddenly arrested by the appalling cry which had so alarmed us a few nights before. But this time, we were by no means so much alarmed as on the previous occasion, because, whereas at that time it was night, now it was day; and I have always found, though I am unable to account for it, that daylight banishes many of the fears that are apt to assail us in the dark.

On hearing the sound, Peterkin instantly threw forward his spear.

"Now, what can it be?" said he, looking round at Jack. "I tell you what it is: if we are to go on being pulled up in a constant state of horror and astonishment, as we have been for the last week, the sooner we're out o' this island the better, notwithstanding the yams and lemonade, and pork and plums!"

Peterkin's remark was followed by a repetition of the cry, louder than before.

"It comes from one of these islands," said Jack.

"It must be the ghost of a jackass, then," said Peterkin, "for I never heard anything so like."

We all turned our eyes towards the cluster of islands, /101/ where, on the largest, we observed curious objects moving on the shore.

"Soldiers they are—that's flat!" cried Peterkin, gazing at them in the utmost amazement.

And, in truth, Peterkin's remark seemed to me to be correct; for, at the distance from which we saw them, they appeared to be an army of soldiers. There they stood, rank and file, in lines and in squares, marching and countermarching, with blue coats and white trousers. While we were looking at them, the dreadful cry came again over the water, and Peterkin suggested that it must be a regiment sent out to massacre the natives in cold blood. At this remark Jack laughed and said,—

"Why, Peterkin, they are penguins!"

"Penguins?" repeated Peterkin.

"Ay, penguins, Peterkin, penguins—nothing more or less than big sea-birds, as you shall see one of these days, when we pay them a visit in our boat, which I mean to set about building the moment we return to our bower."

"So, then, our dreadful yelling ghosts and our murdering army of soldiers," remarked Peterkin, "have dwindled down to penguins —big sea-birds! Very good." /102/

*   *   *

. . . After having told all we could to Peterkin about the Diamond Cave under Spouting Cliff, as we named the locality, we were wending our way rapidly homewards, when a grunt and a squeal were borne down by the land-breeze to our ears.

"That's the ticket!" was Peterkin's remarkable exclamation, as he started convulsively, and levelled his spear.

"Hist!" cried Jack; "these are your friends, Peterkin. They must have come over expressly to pay you a friendly visit, for it is the first time we have seen them on this side of the island."

"Come along!" cried Peterkin, hurrying towards the wood, while Jack and I followed, smiling at his impatience.

Another grunt, and half a dozen squeals, much louder than before, came down the valley. At this time, we were just opposite the small vale which lay between the Valley of the Wreck and Spouting Cliff.

"I say, Peterkin," cried Jack, in a hoarse whisper.

"Well, what is't?"

"Stay a bit, man. These grunters are just up there on the hill-side. If you go and stand with Ralph in the lee of yon cliff, I'll cut round behind, and drive them through the gorge, so that you'll have a better chance of picking out a good one. Now, mind you pitch into that fat young pig, Peterkin," added Jack as he sprang into the bushes.

"Won't I, just!" said Peterkin, licking his lips, as we took our station beside the cliff. "I feel quite a tender affection for young pigs in my heart. Perhaps it would be more correct to say in my s——"

"There they come!" cried I, as a terrific yell from Jack sent the whole herd screaming down the hill. Now, Peterkin, being unable to hold back, crept a short way up a very steep grassy mound, in order to get a better view of the hogs before they came up; and, just as he raised his head above the summit, two little pigs, which had outrun their companions, rushed over the top with the utmost precipitation. One of these brushed close past Peterkin's ear; the other, unable to arrest its headlong flight, went, as Peterkin himself afterwards expressed it, "bash" into his arms with a sudden squeal, which was caused more by the force of the blow than the will of the animal, and both of them rolled violently down to the foot of the mound. No sooner was this reached than the little pig recovered its feet, tossed up its tail, and fled shrieking from the spot. /131/ But I slung a large stone after it, which, being fortunately well aimed, hit it behind the ear, and felled it to the earth.

"Capital, Ralph! that's your sort!" cried Peterkin, who, to my surprise, and great relief, had risen to his feet, apparently unhurt, though much dishevelled. He rushed frantically towards the gorge, which the yells of the hogs told us they were now approaching. I had made up my mind that I would abstain from killing another, as, if Peterkin should be successful, two were more than sufficient for our wants at the present time. Suddenly they all burst forth— two or three little round ones in advance, and an enormous old sow with a drove of hogs at her heels.

"Now Peterkin," said I, "there's a nice little fat one; just spear it."

But Peterkin did not move; he allowed it to pass unharmed. I looked at him in surprise, and saw that his lips were compressed and his eyebrows knitted, as if he were about to fight with some awful enemy.

"What is it?" I inquired, with some trepidation.

Suddenly, he levelled his spear, darted forward, and, with a yell that nearly froze the blood in my veins, stabbed the old sow to the heart. Nay, so vigorously was it done that the spear went in at one side and came out at the other!

"Oh, Peterkin!" said I, going up to him, "what have you done?"

"Done? I've killed their great-great-grandmother, that's all," said he, looking with a somewhat awestruck expression at the transfixed animal.

"Hallo! what's this?" said Jack, as he came up. "Why, Peterkin, you must be fond of a tough chop. If you mean to eat this old hog, she'll try your jaws, I warrant. What possessed you to stick *her*, Peterkin?

"Why, the fact is I want a pair of shoes."

"What have your old shoes to do with the old hog?" said I, smiling.

"My present shoes have certainly nothing to do with her," replied Peterkin; "nevertheless she will have a good deal to do with my future shoes. The fact is, when I saw you floor that pig so neatly, Ralph, it struck me that there was little use in killing another. Then I remembered all at once that I had long wanted some leather or tough substance to make shoes of, and this old grandmother seemed so tough that I just made up my mind to stick her, and you see I've done it!"

"That you certainly have, Peterkin," said Jack, as he was examining the transfixed animal. /133/

[They build a boat and explore the nearby islands. A storm keeps them on "Penquin Island." They return to Coral Island and find their home has not been destroyed by the storm.]

For many months after this we continued to live on our island in uninterrupted harmony and happiness. Sometimes we went out a-fishing in the lagoon, and sometimes went a-hunting in the woods, or ascended to the mountain-top, by way of variety, although Peterkin always asserted that we went for the purpose of hailing any ship that might chance to heave in sight. But I am certain that none of us wished to be delivered from our captivity, for we were extremely happy, and Peterkin used to say that as we were young we should not feel the loss of a year or two. Peterkin, as I have said before, was thirteen years of age, Jack eighteen, and I fifteen. But Jack was very tall, strong, and manly for his age, and might easily have been mistaken for twenty.

The climate was so beautiful that it seemed to be a perpetual summer, and as many of the fruit-trees continued to bear fruit and blossom all the year round, we never wanted for a plentiful supply of food. The hogs, too, seemed rather to increase than diminish, although Peterkin was very frequent in his attacks on them with his spear. If at any time we failed in finding a drove, we had only to pay a visit to the plum-tree before mentioned, where we always found a large family of them asleep under its branches. /168/

*   *   *

Now, while we were engaged with these occupations and amusements, an event occurred one day which was as unexpected as it was exceedingly alarming and very horrible.

Jack and I were sitting, as we were often wont to do, on the rocks at Spouting Cliff, and Peterkin was wringing the water from his garments, having recently fallen by accident into the sea—a thing he was constantly doing—when our attention was suddenly arrested by two objects which appeared on the horizon.

"What are yon, think you?" I said, addressing Jack.

"I can't imagine," answered he, "I've noticed them for some time, and fancied they were black sea-gulls, but the more I look at them the more I feel convinced they are much larger than gulls."

"They seem to be coming towards us," said I.

"Hallo! what's wrong?" inquired Peterkin, coming up.

"Look there," said Jack.

"Whales!" cried Peterkin, shading his eyes with his hands. "No—eh—*can* they be boats, Jack?"

Our hearts beat with excitement at the very thought of seeing human faces again.

"I think you are about right, Peterkin; but they seem to me to move strangely for boats," said Jack, in a low tone, as if he were talking to himself.

I noticed that a shade of anxiety crossed Jack's countenance as he gazed long and intently at the two objects, which were now nearing us fast. At last he sprang to his feet. "They are canoes, Ralph! whether war canoes or not I cannot tell; but this I know, that all the natives of the South Sea Islands are fierce cannibals, and they have little respect for strangers. We must hide if they land here, which I earnestly hope they will not do." /170/

I was greatly alarmed at Jack's speech, but I confess I thought less of what he said than of the earnest, anxious manner in which he said it, and it was with very uncomfortable feelings that Peterkin and I followed him quickly into the woods.

"How unfortunate," said I, as we gained the shelter of the bushes, "that we have forgotten our arms."

"It matters not," said Jack; "here are clubs enough and to spare." As he spoke he laid his hand on a bundle of stout poles of various sizes, which Peterkin's ever busy hands had formed during our frequent visits to the cliff, for no other purpose, apparently, than that of having something to do.

We each selected a stout club according to our several tastes, and lay down behind a rock, whence we could see the canoes approach, without ourselves being seen. At first we made an occasional remark on their appearance, but after they entered the lagoon and drew near the beach, we ceased to speak, and gazed with intense interest at the scene before us.

We now observed that the foremost canoe was being chased by the other, and that it contained a few women and children as well as men—perhaps forty souls altogether; while the canoe which pursued it contained only men. They seemed to be about the same in number, but were better armed, and had the appearance of being a war-party. Both crews were paddling with all their might, and it seemed as if the pursuers exerted themselves to overtake the fugitives ere they could land. In this, however, they failed. The foremost canoe made for the beach close beneath the rocks behind which we were concealed. Their short paddles flashed like meteors in the water, and sent up a constant shower of spray. The foam curled from the prow, and the eyes of the rowers glistened in their black faces as they strained every muscle of their naked bodies; nor did they relax their efforts till the canoe struck the beach with a violent shock; then, with a shout of defiance the whole party sprang, as if by magic, from the canoe to the shore. Three women, two of whom /171/ carried infants in their arms, rushed into the woods; and the men crowded the water's edge, with stones in their hands, spears levelled, and clubs brandished, to resist the landing of their enemies.

The distance between the two canoes had been about half a mile, and, at the great speed they were going, this was soon passed. As the pursuers neared the shore, no sign of fear or hesitation was noticeable. On they came like a wild charger—received but recked not of a shower of stones. The canoe struck, and, with a yell that seemed to issue from the throats of incarnate fiends, they leaped into the water, and drove their enemies up the beach.

The battle that immediately ensued was frightful to behold. Most of the men wielded clubs of enormous size and curious shapes, with which they dashed out each other's brains. As they were almost entirely naked, and had to bound, stoop, leap, and run in their terrible hand-to-hand encounters, they looked more like demons than human beings. I felt my heart grow sick at the sight of this bloody battle, and would fain have turned away, but a species of fascination seemed to hold me down and glue my eyes upon the combatants. I observed that the attacking party was led by a most extraordinary being, who, from his size and peculiarity, I concluded was a chief. His hair was frizzed out to an enormous extent, so that it resembled a large turban. It was of a light-yellow hue, which surprised me much, for the man's body was as black as coal, and I felt convinced that the hair must have been dyed. He was tattooed from head to foot; and his face, besides being tattooed, was besmeared with red paint, and streaked with white. Altogether, with his yellow turban-like hair, his Herculean black frame, his glittering eyes, and white teeth, he seemed the most terrible monster I ever beheld. He was very active in the fight, and had already killed four men.

Suddenly the yellow-haired chief was attacked by a man quite as strong and large as himself. He flourished a heavy club something like an eagle's beak at the point. For a second or two these giants eyed each other warily, /172/ moving round and round, as if to catch each other at a disadvantage; but seeing that nothing was to be gained by this caution, and that the loss of time might effectually turn the tide of the battle either way, they apparently made up their minds to attack at the same instant, for, with a wild shout, and simultaneous spring, they swung their heavy clubs, which met with a loud report. Suddenly the yellow-haired savage tripped, his enemy sprang forward, the ponderous club was swung, but it did not descend, for at that moment the savage was felled to the ground by a stone from the hand of one who had witnessed his chief's danger. This was the turning-point in the battle. The savages who landed first turned and fled towards the bush, on seeing the fall of their chief. But not one escaped. They were all overtaken and felled to the earth. I saw, however, that they were not all killed. Indeed, their enemies, now that they were conquered, seemed anxious to take them alive; and they succeeded in securing fifteen, whom they bound hand and foot with cords, and, carrying them up into the woods, laid them down among the bushes. Here they left them, for what purpose I knew not, and returned to the scene of the late battle, where the remnant of the party were bathing their wounds.

Out of the forty blacks that composed the attacking party, only twenty-eight remained alive, two of whom were sent into the bush to hunt for the women and children. Of the other party, as I have said, only fifteen survived, and these were lying bound and helpless on the grass.

Jack and Peterkin and I looked at each other, and whispered our fears that the savages might clamber up the rocks to search for fresh water, and so discover our place of concealment; but we were so much interested in watching their movements that we agreed to remain where we were; and, indeed, we could not easily have risen without exposing ourselves to detection. One of the savages now went up to the wood and soon returned with a bundle of firewood, and we were not a little surprised /173/ to see him set fire to it by the very same means used by Jack the time we made our first fire—namely, with the bow and drill. When the fire was kindled, two of the party went again to the woods and returned with one of the bound men. A dreadful feeling of horror crept over my heart as the thought flashed upon me that they were going to burn their enemies. As they bore him to the fire my feelings almost overpowered me. I gasped for breath, and seizing my club, endeavoured to spring to my feet; but Jack's powerful arm pinned me to the earth. Next moment one of the savages raised his club, and fractured the wretched creature's skull. He must have died instantly; and strange though it may seem, I confess to a feeling of relief when the deed was done, because I now knew that the poor savage could not be burned alive. Scarcely had his limbs ceased to quiver when the monsters cut slices of flesh from his body, and, after roasting them slightly over the fire, devoured them.

Suddenly there arose a cry from the woods, and, in a few seconds, the two savages hastened towards the fire dragging the three women and their two infants along with them. One of those women was much younger than her companions, and we were struck with the modesty of her demeanour and the gentle expression of her face, which, although she had a flattish nose and the thick lips of the others, was of a light-brown colour, and we conjectured that she must be of a different race. She and her companions wore short petticoats and a kind of tippet on their shoulders. Their hair was jet black, but instead of being long, was short and curly—though not woolly—somewhat like the hair of a young boy. While we gazed with interest and some anxiety at these poor creatures, the big chief advanced to one of the elder females and laid his hand upon the child. But the mother shrank from him, and clasping the little one to her bosom, uttered a wail of fear. With a savage laugh, the chief tore the child from her arms and tossed it into the sea. A low groan burst from Jack's lips as we witnessed this atrocious act and heard the mother's shrieks, as she fell insensible on the sand. /174/ The rippling waves rolled the child on the beach, as if they refused to be a party in such a foul murder, and we could observe that the little one still lived.

The young girl was now brought forward, and the chief addressed her; but although we heard his voice and even the words distinctly, of course we could not understand what he said. The girl made no answer to his fierce questions, and we saw by the way in which he pointed to the fire that he threatened her life.

"Peterkin," said Jack, in a hoarse whisper, "have you got your knife?"

"Yes," replied Peterkin, whose face was pale as death.

"That will do. Listen to me, and do my bidding quick. Here is the small knife, Ralph. Fly both of you through the bush, cut the cords that bind the prisoners, and set them free. There! quick ere it be too late." Jack sprang up and seized a heavy but short bludgeon, while his strong frame trembled with emotion, and large drops rolled down his forehead.

At this moment the man who had butchered the savage a few minutes before advanced towards the girl with his heavy club. Jack uttered a yell that rang like a death-shriek among the rocks. With one bound he leaped over a precipice full fifteen feet high, and, before the savages had recovered from thir surprise, was in the midst of them; while Peterkin and I dashed through the bushes towards the prisoners. With one blow of his staff Jack felled the man with the club, then turning round with a look of fury, he rushed upon the big chief with the yellow hair. Had the blow which Jack aimed at his head taken effect, the huge savage would have needed no second stroke; but he was as agile as a cat, and avoided it by springing to one side, while, at the same time, he swung his ponderous club at the head of his foe. It was now Jack's turn to leap aside, and well was it for him that the first outburst of his blind fury was over, else he had become an easy prey to his gigantic antagonist; but Jack was cool now. He darted his blows rapidly and well, and the superiority of his light weapon was strikingly proved in this combat, for while /175/ he could easily evade the blows of the chief's heavy club, the chief could not so easily evade those of his light one. Nevertheless, so quick was he, and so frightfully did he fling about the mighty weapon, that although Jack struck him almost every blow, the strokes had to be delivered so quickly that they wanted force to be very effectual.

It was lucky for Jack that the other savages considered the success of their chief in this encounter to be so certain that they refrained from interfering. Had they doubted it, they would have probably ended the matter at once by felling him. But they contented themselves with awaiting the issue.

The force which the chief expended in wielding his club now began to be apparent. His movements became slower, his breath hissed through his clenched teeth, and the surprised savages drew nearer in order to render assistance. Jack observed this movement. He felt that his fate was sealed, and resolved to cast his life upon the next blow. The chief's club was again about to descend on his head. He might have evaded it easily, but instead of doing so, he suddenly shortened his grasp of his own club, rushed in under the blow, struck his adversary right between the eyes with all his force, and fell to the earth, crushed beneath the senseless body of the chief. A dozen clubs flew high in air ready to descend on the head of Jack, but they hesitated a moment, for the massive body of the chief completely covered him. That moment saved his life. Ere the savages could tear the chief's body away, seven of their number fell prostrate beneath the clubs of the prisoners whom Peterkin and I had set free, and two others fell under our own hand. We could never have accomplished this had not our enemies been so engrossed with the fight between Jack and their chief that they had failed to observe us until we were upon them. They still outnumbered our party by three; but we were flushed with victory, while they were taken by surprise and dispirited by the fall of their chief. Moreover, they were awe-struck by the sweeping fury of Jack, who seemed to have lost his senses altogether, and had no sooner shaken /176/ himself free of the chief's body than he rushed into the midst of them, and in three blows equalised our numbers. Peterkin and I flew to the rescue, the savages followed us, and in less than ten minutes the whole of our opponents were knocked down or made prisoners, bound hand and foot, and extended side by side upon the seashore. /177/

[After the departure of the natives and their chief, Tararo, the English boys continue life on the island. A pirate ship arrives and Ralph is captured and carried away. The pirate ship visits a cannibal island and Ralph is made aware of the evils of "civilized" men as well as of the savages. After several adventures, Ralph captures the pirate ship and sails back to Coral Island alone. All three boys then decide to return to the "cannibal" island to rescue a native girl.]

. . . But I will not drag my reader through the details of this voyage. Suffice it to say, that, after an agreeable sail of about three weeks, we arrived off the island of Mango, which I recognised at once from the description that the pirate Bill had given me of it during one of our conversations.

As soon as we came within sight of it we hove the ship to and held a council of war. /269/

"Now, boys," said Jack, as we seated ourselves beside him on the cabin skylight, "before we go further in this business, we must go over the pros and cons of it; for, although you have so generously consented to stick by me through thick and thin, it would be unfair did I not see that you thoroughly understand the danger of what we are about to attempt."

"Oh, bother the danger!" cried Peterkin. "I wonder to hear *you*, Jack, talk of danger. When a fellow begins to talk about it, he'll soon come to magnify it to such a degree that he'll not be fit to face it when it comes, no more than a suckin' baby."

"Nay, Peterkin," replied Jack, gravely, "I won't be jested out of it. I grant you that when we've once resolved to act, and have made up our minds what to do, we should think no more of danger. But before we have so resolved, it behoves us to look at it straight in the face, and examine into it, and walk round it; for if we flinch at a distant view, we're sure to run away when the danger is near. Now, I understand from you, Ralph, that the island is inhabited by thorough-going, out-and-out cannibals, whose principal law is, "Might is right, and the weakest goes to the wall?"

"Yes," said I; "so Bill gave me to understand. He told me, however, that at the southern side of it the missionaries had obtained a footing amongst an insignificant tribe. A native teacher had been sent there by the Wesleyans, who had succeeded in persuading the chief at that part to embrace Christianity. But instead of that being of any advantage to our enterprise, it seems the very reverse; for the Chief Tararo is a determined heathen, and persecutes the Christians—who are far too weak in numbers to offer any resistance—and looks with dislike upon all white men, whom he regards as propagators of the new faith."

" 'Tis a pity," said Jack, "that the Christian tribe is so small, for we shall scarcely be safe under their protection, I fear. If Tararo takes it into his head to wish for our vessel, or to kill ourselves, he could take us from them by force. You say that the native missionary talks English?" /270/

"So I believe."

"Then, what I propose is this," said Jack. "We will run round to the south side of the island, and cast anchor off the Christian village. We are too far away just now to have been descried by any of the savages, so we shall get there unobserved, and have time to arrange our plans before the heathen tribes know of our presence. But in doing this we run the risk of being captured by the ill-disposed tribes, and being very ill-used, if not—a—"

"Roasted alive and eaten," cried Peterkin. "Come out with it,

Jack; according to your own showing, it's well to look the danger straight in the face!"

"Well, that *is* the worst of it, certainly. Are you prepared, then, to take your chance of that?"

"I've been prepared and had my mind made up long ago," cried Peterkin, swaggering about the deck with his hands thrust into his breeches pockets. "The fact is, Jack, I don't believe that Tararo will be so ungrateful as to eat us; and I'm quite sure that he'll be too happy to grant us whatever we ask: so the sooner we go in and win the better."

Peterkin was wrong, however, in his estimate of savage gratitude, as the sequel will show. /271/

[They rescue the native girl and flee the island with her in a canoe, but are overtaken and returned. They are imprisoned by the cannibals.]

For a long, long month we remained in our dark and dreary prison, during which dismal time we did not see the face of a human being, except that of the silent savage who brought us our daily food.

There have been one or two seasons in my life during which I have felt as if the darkness of sorrow and desolation that crushed my inmost heart could never pass away until death should make me cease to feel. The present was such a season.

During the first part of our confinement we felt a cold chill at our hearts every time we heard a footfall near the cave—dreading lest it should prove to be that of our executioner. But as time dragged heavily on we ceased to feel this alarm, and began to experience such a deep, irrepressible longing for freedom, that we chafed and fretted in our confinement like tigers. Then a feeling of despair came over us, and we actually longed for the time when the savages would take us forth to die! But these changes took place very gradually, and were mingled sometimes with brighter thoughts; for there were times when we sat in that dark cavern on our ledge of rock and conversed almost pleasantly about the past, until we well-nigh forgot the dreary present. But we seldom ventured to touch upon the future.

A few decayed leaves and boughs formed our bed; and a scanty supply of yams and taro, brought to us once a day, constituted our food.

"Well, Ralph, how have you slept?" said Jack, in a listless tone, on rising one morning from his humble couch. "Were you much disturbed by the wind last night?"

"No," said I; "I dreamed of home all night, and I thought that my mother smiled upon me, and beckoned me to go to her; but I could not, for I was chained." /309/

"And I dreamed too," said Peterkin; "but it was of our happy home on the Coral Island. I thought we were swimming in the Water Garden; then the savages gave a yell, and we were immediately in the cave at Spouting Cliff, which, somehow or other, changed into this gloomy cavern; and I awoke to find it true."

Peterkin's tone was so much altered by the depressing influence of his long imprisonment, that, had I not known it was he who spoke, I should scarcely have recognised it, so sad was it, and so unlike to the merry, cheerful voice we had been accustomed to hear. I pondered this much, and thought of the terrible decline of happiness that may come on human beings in so short a time; how bright the sunshine in the sky at one time, and in a short space how dark the overshadowing cloud! I have no doubt that the Bible would have given me much light and comfort on this subject, if I had possessed one, and I once more had occasion to regret deeply having neglected to store my memory with its consoling truths.

While I meditated thus, Peterkin again broke the silence of the cave, by saying, in a melancholy tone, "Oh, I wonder if we shall ever see our dear island more."

His voice trembled, and, covering his face with both hands, he bent down his head and wept. It was an unusual sight for me to see our once joyous companion in tears, and I felt a burning desire to comfort him; but, alas, what could I say? I could hold out no hope; and although I essayed twice to speak, the words refused to pass my lips. While I hesitated, Jack sat down beside him, and whispered a few words in his ear; while Peterkin threw himself on his friend's breast, and rested his head on his shoulder.

Thus we sat for some time in deep silence. Soon after, we heard footsteps at the entrance of the cave, and immediately our jailer entered. We were so much accustomed to his regular visits, however, that we paid little attention to him, expecting that he would set down our meagre fare, as usual, and depart. But, to our surprise, instead of doing so, he advanced towards us with a knife in his hand, and going up to Jack, he cut the thongs that bound his wrists; /310/ then he did the same to Peterkin and me! For fully five minutes we stood in speechless amazement, with our freed hands hanging idly by our sides. The first thought that rushed into my mind was, that the time had come to put us to death; and although, as I have said before, we actually wished for death in the strength of our despair, now that we thought it drew really near I felt all the natural love of life revive in my heart, mingled with a chill of horror at the suddenness of our call.

But I was mistaken. After cutting our bonds, the savage pointed to the cave's mouth, and we marched, almost mechanically, into the open air. Here, to our surprise, we found the teacher, standing under a tree, with his hands clasped before him, and the tears trickling down his dark cheeks. On seeing Jack, who came out first, he sprang towards him, and clasping him in his arms, exclaimed:

"O! my dear young friend, through the great goodness of God you are free!"

"Free!" cried Jack.

"Ay, free," repeated the teacher, shaking us warmly by the hands again and again, "free to go and come as you will. The Lord has unloosed the bands of the captive and set the prisoners free. A missionary has been sent to us, and Tararo has embraced the Christian religion! The people are even now burning their gods of wood! Come, my dear friends, and see the glorious sight." /311/

from *LEVIATHAN*

THOMAS HOBBES

OF THE NATURAL CONDITION OF MANKIND AS CONCERNING THEIR FELICITY, AND MISERY

Men by nature equal. Nature hath made men so equal, in the faculties of the body, and mind; as that though there be found one man sometimes manifestly stronger in body, or of quicker mind than another; yet when all is reckoned together, the difference between man, and man, is not so considerable, as that one man can thereupon claim to himself any benefit, to which another may not pretend, as well as he. For as to the strength of body, the weakest has strength enough to kill the strongest, either by secret machination, or by confederacy with others, that are in the same danger with himself.

And as to the faculties of the mind, setting aside the arts grounded upon words, and especially that skill of proceeding upon general, and infallible rules, called science; which very few have, and but in few things; as being not a native faculty, born with us; nor attained, as prudence, while we look after somewhat else, I find yet a greater equality amongst men, than that of strength. For prudence, is but experience; which equal time, equally bestows on all men, in those things they equally apply themselves unto. That which may perhaps make such equality incredible, is but a vain conceit of one's own wisdom, which almost all men think they have in a greater degree, than the vulgar; that is, than all men but themselves, and a few others, whom by fame, or for concurring with themselves, they approve. For such is the nature of men, that howsoever they may acknowledge many others to be more witty, or more eloquent, or more learned; yet they will hardly believe there be many so wise as themselves; for they see their own wit at hand, and other men's at a distance. But this proveth rather that men are in that point equal, than unequal. For there is not ordinarily a greater sign of the equal distribution of any thing, than that every man is contented with his share. /80/

Thomas Hobbes, *Leviathan* (Oxford: Basil Blackwell, [1947]), Part I, chap. xiii, pp. 80-84. Reprinted by special permission.

From equality proceeds diffidence. From this equality of ability, ariseth equality of hope in the attaining of our ends. And therefore if any two men desire the same thing, which nevertheless they cannot both enjoy, they become enemies; and in the way to their end, which is principally their own conservation, and sometimes their delectation only, endeavour to destroy, or subdue one another. And from hence it comes to pass, that where an invader hath no more to fear, than another man's single power; if one plant, sow, build, or possess a convenient seat, others may probably be expected to come prepared with forces united, to dispossess, and deprive him, not only of the fruit of his labour, but also of his life, or liberty. And the invader again is in the like danger of another.

From diffidence war. And from this diffidence of one another, there is no way for any man to secure himself, so reasonable, as anticipation; that is, by force, or wiles, to master the persons of all men he can, so long, till he see no other power great enough to endanger him: and this is no more than his own conservation requireth, and is generally allowed. Also because there be some, that taking pleasure in contemplating their own power in the acts of conquest, which they pursue farther than their security requires; if others, that otherwise would be glad to be at ease within modest bounds, should not by invasion increase their power, they would not be able, long time, by standing only on their defence, to subsist. And by consequence, such augmentation of dominion over men being necessary to a man's conservation, it ought to be allowed him.

Again, men have no pleasure, but on the contrary a great deal of grief, in keeping company, where there is no power able to overawe them all. For every man looketh that his companion should value him, at the same rate he sets upon himself: and upon all signs of contempt, or undervaluing, naturally endeavours, as far as he dares, (which amongst them that have no common power to keep them in quiet, is far enough to make them destroy each other), to extort a greater value from his contemners, by damage; and from others, by the example.

So that in the nature of man, we find three principal causes of quarrel. First, competition; secondly, diffidence; thirdly, glory.

The first, maketh men invade for gain; the second, for safety; and the third, for reputation. The first use violence, to make themselves masters of other men's persons, wives, children, and cattle; the second, to defend them; the third, for trifles, as a word, a smile, a different /81/ opinion, and any other sign of undervalue, either direct in their persons, or by reflection in their kindred, their friends, their nation, their profession, or their name.

Out of civil states, there is always war of every one against every one. Hereby it is manifest, that during the time men live without a common power to keep them all in awe, they are in that condition which is called war; and such a war, as is of every man, against every man. For WAR, consisteth not in battle only, or the act of fighting; but in a tract of time, wherein the will to contend by battle is sufficiently known: and therefore the notion of *time,* is to be considered in the nature of war; as it is in the nature of weather. For as the nature of foul weather, lieth not in a shower or two of rain; but in an inclination thereto of many days together: so the nature of war, consisteth not in actual fighting; but in the known disposition thereto, during all the time there is no assurance to the contrary. All other time is PEACE.

The incommodities of such a war. Whatsoever therefore is consequent to a time of war, where every man is enemy to every man; the same is consequent to the time, wherein men live without other security, than what their own strength, and their own invention shall furnish them withal. In such condition, there is no place for industry; because the fruit thereof is uncertain: and consequently no culture of the earth; no navigation, nor use of the commodities that may be imported by sea; no commodious building; no instruments of moving, and removing, such things as require much force; no knowledge of the face of the earth; no account of time; no arts; no letters; no society; and which is worst of all, continual fear, and danger of violent death; and the life of man, solitary, poor, nasty, brutish, and short.

It may seem strange to some man, that has not well weighed these things; that nature should thus dissociate, and render men apt to invade, and destroy one another: and he may therefore, not trusting to this inference, made from the passions, desire perhaps to have the same confirmed by experience. Let him therefore consider with himself, when taking a journey, he arms himself, and seeks to go well accompanied; when going to sleep, he locks his doors; when even in his house he locks his chests; and this when he knows there be laws, and public officers, armed, to revenge all injuiries shall be done him; what opinion he has of his fellow-subjects, when he rides armed; of his fellow citizens, when he locks his doors; and of his children, and servants, when he /82/ locks his chests. Does he not there as much accuse mankind by his actions, as I do by my words? But neither of us accuse man's nature in it. The desires, and other passions of man, are in themselves no sin. No more are the actions, that proceed from those passions, till they know a law that forbids them: which till laws be made they cannot know: nor can any law be made, till they have agreed upon the person that shall make it.

It may peradventure be thought, there was never such a time, nor condition of war as this; and I believe it was never generally so, over all the world: but there are many places, where they live so now. For the savage people in many places of America, except the government of small families, the concord whereof dependeth on natural lust, have no government at all; and live at this day in that brutish manner, as I said before. Howsoever, it may be perceived what manner of life there would be, where there were no common power to fear, by the manner of life, which men that have formerly lived under a peaceful government, use to degenerate into, in a civil war.

But though there had never been any time, wherein particular men were in a condition of war one against another; yet in all times, kings, and persons of sovereign authority, because of their independency, are in continual jealousies, and in the state and posture of gladiators; having their weapons pointing, and their eyes fixed on one another; that is, their forts, garrisons, and guns upon the frontiers of their kingdoms; and continual spies upon their neighbours; which is a posture of war. But because they uphold thereby, the industry of their subjects; there does not follow from it, that misery, which accompanies the liberty of particular men.

In such a war nothing is unjust.   To this war of every man, against every man, this also is consequent; that nothing can be unjust. The notions of right and wrong, justice and injustice have there no place. Where there is no common power, there is no law: where no law, no injustice. Force, and fraud, are in war the two cardinal virtues. Justice, and injustice are none of the faculties neither of the body, nor mind. If they were, they might be in a man that were alone in the world, as well as his senses, and passions. They are qualities, that relate to men in society, not in solitude. It is consequent also to the same condition, that there be no propriety, no dominion, no *mine* and *thine* distinct; but only that to be every man's, that he can get: and for so long as he can keep it. And thus much for the ill condition, which man by mere nature is actually placed in; /83/ though with a possibility to come out of it, consisting partly in the passions, partly in his reason.

The passions that incline men to peace.   The passions that incline men to peace, are fear of death; desire of such things as are necessary to commodious living; and a hope by their industry to obtain them. And reason suggesteth convenient articles of peace, upon which men may be drawn to agreement. These articles, are they, which otherwise are called the Laws of Nature: whereof I shall speak more particularly, in the two following chapters. /84/

from *A DISCOURSE ON THE ORIGIN OF INEQUALITY*

JEAN JACQUES ROUSSEAU

THE FIRST PART

Important as it may be, in order to judge rightly of the natural state of man, to consider him from his origin, and to examine him, as it were, in the embryo of his species, I shall not follow his organization through its successive developments, nor shall I stay to inquire what his animal system must have been at the beginning, in order to become at length what it actually is. I shall not ask whether his long nails were at first, as Aristotle supposes, only crooked talons; whether his whole body, like that of a bear, was covered with hair; or whether the fact that he walked upon all fours, with his looks directed toward the earth, confined to a horizon of a few paces, did not at once point out the nature and limits of his ideas. On this subject I could form none but vague and almost imaginary conjectures. Comparative anatomy has as yet made too little progress, and the observations /199/ of naturalists are too uncertain, to afford an adequate basis for any solid reasoning. So that, without having recourse to the supernatural information given us on this head, or paying any regard to the changes which must have taken place in the internal, as well as the external, conformation of man, as he applied his limbs to new uses, and fed himself on new kinds of food, I shall suppose his conformation to have been at all times what it appears to us at this day; that he always walked on two legs, made use of his hands as we do, directed his looks over all nature, and measured with his eyes the vast expanse of Heaven.

If we strip this being, thus constituted, of all the supernatural gifts he may have received, and all the artificial faculties he can have acquired only by a long process; if we consider him, in a word, just as he must have come from the hands of nature, we behold in him an animal weaker than some, and less agile than others; but, taking him all round, the most advantageously organized of any. I see him

Jean Jacques Rousseau, *The Social Contract and Discourses,* Everyman's Library (New York: E. P. Dutton, 1950), pp. 199-210, 221-27, 273-82. Reprinted by special permission of the publisher.

satisfying his hunger at the first oak, and slaking his thirst at the first brook; finding his bed at the foot of the tree which afforded him a repast; and, with that, all his wants supplied.

While the earth was left to its natural fertility and covered with immense forests, whose trees were never mutilated by the axe, it would present on every side both sustenance and shelter for every species of animal. Men, dispersed up and down among the rest, would observe and imitate their industry, and thus attain even to the instinct of the beasts, with the advantage that, whereas every species of brutes was confined to one particular instinct, man, who perhaps has not any one peculiar to himself, would appropriate them all, and live upon most of those different foods, which other animals shared among themselves; and thus would find his subsistence much more easily than any of the rest. /200/

Accustomed from their infancy to the inclemencies of the weather and the rigour of the seasons, inured to fatigue, and forced, naked and unarmed, to defend themselves and their prey from other ferocious animals, or to escape them by flight, men would acquire a robust and almost unalterable constitution. The children, bringing with them into the world the excellent constitution of their parents, and fortifying it by the very exercises which first produced it, would thus acquire all the vigour of which the human frame is capable. Nature in this case treats them exactly as Sparta treated the children of her citizens: those who come well formed into the world she renders strong and robust, and all the rest she destroys; differing in this respect from our modern communities, in which the State, by making children a burden to their parents, kills them indiscriminately before they are born.

The body of a savage man being the only instrument he understands, he uses it for various purposes, of which ours, for want of practice, are incapable: for our industry deprives us of that force and agility which necessity obliges him to acquire. If he had had an axe, would he have been able with his naked arm to break so large a branch from a tree? If he had had a sling, would he have been able to throw a stone with so great velocity? If he had had a ladder, would he have been so nimble in climbing a tree? If he had had a horse, would he have been himself so swift of foot? Give civilized man time to gather all his machines about him, and he will no doubt easily beat the savage; but if you would see a still more unequal contest, set them together naked and unarmed, and you will soon see the advantage of having all our forces constantly at our disposal, of being always prepared for every event, and of carrying one's self, as it were, perpetually whole and entire about one.

Hobbes contends that man is naturally intrepid, and is intent only upon attacking and fighting. Another illus- /201/ trious philosopher holds the opposite, and Cumberland and Puffendorf also affirm that nothing is more timid and fearful than man in the state of nature; that he is always in a tremble, and ready to fly at the least noise or the slightest movement. This may be true of things he does not know; and I do not doubt his being terrified by every novelty that presents itself, when he neither knows the physical good or evil he may expect from it, nor can make a comparison between his own strength and the dangers he is about to encounter. Such circumstances, however, rarely occur in a state of nature, in which all things proceed in a uniform manner, and the face of the earth is not subject to those sudden and continual changes which arise from the passions and caprices of bodies of men living together. But savage man, living dispersed among other animals, and finding himself betimes in a situation to measure his strength with theirs, soon comes to compare himself with them; and, perceiving that he surpasses them more in adroitness than they surpass him in strength, learns to be no longer afraid of them. Set a bear, or a wolf, against a robust, agile, and resolute savage, as they all are, armed with stones and a good cudgel, and you will see that the danger will be at least on both sides, and that, after a few trials of this kind, wild beasts, which are not fond of attacking each other, will not be at all ready to attack man, whom they will have found to be as wild and ferocious as themselves. With regard to such animals as have really more strength than man has adroitness, he is in the same situation as all weaker animals, which notwithstanding are still able to subsist; except indeed that he has the advantage that, being equally swift of foot, and finding an almost certain place of refuge in every tree, he is at liberty to take or leave it at every encounter, and thus to fight or fly, as he chooses. Add to this that it does not appear that any animal naturally makes war on man, except in case of self-defence /202/ or excessive hunger, or betrays any of those violent antipathies, which seem to indicate that one species is intended by nature for the food of another.

This is doubtless why negroes and savages are so little afraid of the wild beasts they may meet in the woods. The Caribs of Venezuela among others live in this respect in absolute security and without the smallest inconvenience. Though they are almost naked, Francis Corréal tells us, they expose themselves freely in the woods, armed only with bows and arrows; but no one has ever heard of one of them being devoured by wild beasts.

But man has other enemies more formidable, against which he is not provided with such means of defence: these are the natural infirmities of infancy, old age, and illness of every kind, melancholy proofs of our weakness, of which the two first are common to all animals, and the last belongs chiefly to man in a state of society. With regard to infancy, it is observable that the mother, carrying her child always with her, can nurse it with much greater ease than the females of many other animals, which are forced to be perpetually going and coming, with great fatigue, one way to find subsistence, and another to suckle or feed their young. It is true that if the woman happens to perish, the infant is in great danger of perishing with her; but this risk is common to many other species of animals, whose young take a long time before they are able to provide for themselves. And if our infancy is longer than theirs, our lives are longer in proportion; so that all things are in this respect fairly equal; though there are other rules to be considered regarding the duration of the first period of life, and the number of young, which do not affect the present subject. In old age, when men are less active and perspire little, the need for food diminishes with the ability to provide it. As the savage state also protects them from gout and rheumatism, and old age is, of all ills, that which human aid can least alleviate, /203/ they cease to be, without others perceiving that they are no more, and almost without perceiving it themselves.

With respect to sickness, I shall not repeat the vain and false declamations which most healthy people pronounce against medicine; but I shall ask if any solid observations have been made from which it may be justly concluded that, in the countries where the art of medicine is most neglected, the mean duration of man's life is less than in those where it is most cultivated. How indeed can this be the case, if we bring on ourselves more diseases than medicine can furnish remedies? The great inequality in manner of living, the extreme idleness of some, and the excessive labour of others, the easiness of exciting and gratifying our sensual appetites, the too exquisite foods of the wealthy which overheat and fill them with indigestion, and, on the other hand, the unwholesome food of the poor, often, bad as it is, insufficient for their needs, which induces them, when opportunity offers, to eat voraciously and overcharge their stomachs; all these, together with sitting up late, and excesses of every kind, immoderate transports of every passion, fatigue, mental exhaustion, the innumerable pains and anxieties inseparable from every condition of life, by which the mind of man is incessantly tormented; these are too fatal proofs that the greater part of our ills are of our own making, and that we might have avoided them nearly all by adhering to that simple, uniform, and solitary manner of life which nature prescribed. If she destined man to be healthy, I venture to declare that a state of reflection is a state contrary to nature, and that a thinking man is a depraved animal. When we think of the good constitution of the savages, at least of those whom we have not ruined with our spirituous liquors, and reflect that they are troubled with hardly any disorders, save wounds and old age, we are tempted to believe that, in following the history of civil society, we shall be telling also that of human sickness. /204/ Such, at least, was the opinion of Plato, who inferred from certain remedies prescribed, or approved, by Podalirius and Machaon at the siege of Troy, that several sicknesses which these remedies gave rise to in his time, were not then known to mankind: and Celsus tells us that diet, which is now so necessary, was first invented by Hippocrates.

Being subject therefore to so few causes of sickness, man, in the state of nature, can have no need of remedies, and still less of physicians: nor is the human race in this respect worse off than other animals, and it is easy to learn from hunters whether they meet with many infirm animals in the course of the chase. It is certain they frequently meet with such as carry the marks of having been considerably wounded, with many that have had bones or even limbs broken, yet have been healed without any other surgical assistance than that of time, or any other regimen than that of their ordinary life. At the same time their cures seem not to have been less perfect, for their not having been tortured by incisions, poisoned with drugs, or wasted by fasting. In short, however useful medicine, properly administered, may be among us, it is certain that, if the savage, when he is sick and left to himself, has nothing to hope but from nature, he has, on the other hand, nothing to fear but from his disease; which renders his situation often preferable to our own.

We should beware, therefore, of confounding the savage man with the men we have daily before our eyes. Nature treats all the animals left to her care with a predilection that seems to show how jealous she is of that right. The horse, the cat, the bull, and even the ass are generally of greater stature, and always more robust, and have more vigour, strength, and courage, when they run wild in the forests than when bred in the stall. By becoming domesticated, they lose half these advantages; and it seems as if all our care to feed and treat them well serves only to de- /205/ prave them. It is thus with man also: as he becomes sociable and a slave, he grows weak, timid, and servile; his effeminate way of life totally enervates his strength and courage. To this it may be added that there is still a greater difference between savage and civilized man than between wild and tame beasts: for men and brutes having been treated alike by nature, the several conveniences in which men indulge themselves still more than they do their beasts, are so many additional causes of their deeper degeneracy.

It is not therefore so great a misfortune to these primitive men, nor so great an obstacle to their preservation, that they go naked, have no dwellings, and lack all the superfluities which we think so necessary. If their skins are not covered with hair, they have no need of such covering in warm climates; and, in cold countries, they soon learn to appropriate the skins of the beasts they have overcome. If they have but two legs to run with, they have two arms to defend themselves with, and provide for their wants. Their children are slowly and with difficulty taught to walk; but their mothers are able to carry them with ease; an advantage which other animals lack, as the mother, if pursued, is forced either to abandon her young, or to regulate her pace by theirs. Unless, in short, we suppose a singular and fortuitous concurrence of circumstances of which I shall speak later, and which would be unlikely to exist, it is plain in every state of the case, that the man who first made himself clothes or a dwelling was furnishing himself with things not at all necesasry; for he had till then done without them, and there is no reason why he should not have been able to put up in manhood with the same kind of life as had been his in infancy.

Solitary, indolent, and perpetually accompanied by danger, the savage cannot but be fond of sleep; his sleep too must be light, like that of the animals, which think but /206/ little and may be said to slumber all the time they do not think. Self-preservation being his chief and almost sole concern, he must exercise most those faculties which are most concerned with attack or defence, either for overcoming his prey, or for preventing him from becoming the prey of other animals. On the other hand, those organs which are perfected only by softness and sensuality will remain in a gross and imperfect state, incompatible with any sort of delicacy; so that, his senses being divided on this head, his touch and taste will be extremely coarse, his sight, hearing, and smell exceedingly fine and subtle. Such in general is the animal condition, and such, according to the narratives of travellers, is that of most savage nations. It is therefore no matter for surprise that the Hottentots of the Cape of Good Hope distinguish ships at sea, with the naked eye, at as great a distance as the Dutch can do with their telescopes; or that the savages of America should trace the Spaniards, by their smell, as well as the best dogs could have done; or that these barbarous peoples feel no pain in going naked, or that they use large quantities of pimento with their food, and drink the strongest European liquors like water.

Hitherto I have considered merely the physical man; let us now take a view of him on his metaphysical and moral side.

I see nothing in any animal but an ingenious machine, to which nature hath given senses to wind itself up, and to guard itself, to a certain degree, against anything that might tend to disorder or destroy it. I perceive exactly the same things in the human machine, with this difference, that in the operations of the brute, nature is the sole agent, whereas man has some share in his own operations, in his character as a free agent. The one chooses and refuses by instinct, the other from an act of free will: hence the brute cannot deviate from the rule prescribed to it, even when it would be advantageous for it to do /207/ so; and, on the contrary, man frequently deviates from such rules to his own prejudice. Thus a pigeon would be starved to death by the side of a dish of the choicest meats, and a cat on a heap of fruit or grain; though it is certain that either might find nourishment in the foods which it thus rejects with disdain, did it think of trying them. Hence it is that dissolute men run into excesses which bring on fevers and death; because the mind depraves the senses, and the will continues to speak when nature is silent.

Every animal has ideas, since it has senses; it even combines those ideas in a certain degree; and it is only in degree that man differs, in this respect, from the brute. Some philosophers have even maintained that there is a greater difference between one man and another than between some men and some beasts. It is not, therefore, so much the understanding that constitutes the specific difference between the man and the brute, as the human quality of free agency. Nature lays her commands on every animal, and the brute obeys her voice. Man receives the same impulsion, but at the same time knows himself at liberty to acquiesce or resist: and it is particularly in his consciousness of this liberty that the spirituality of his soul is displayed. For physics may explain, in some measure, the mechanism of the senses and the formation of ideas; but in the power of willing or rather of choosing, and in the feeling of this power, nothing is to be found but acts which are purely spiritual and wholly inexplicable by the laws of mechanism.

However, even if the difficulties attending all these questions should still leave room for difference in this respect between men and brutes, there is another very specific quality which distinguishes them, and which will admit of no dispute. This is the faculty of self-improvement, which, by the help of circumstances, gradually de- /208/ velops all the rest of our faculties, and is inherent in the species as in the individual: whereas a brute is, at the end of a few months, all he will ever be during his whole life, and his species, at the end of a thousand years, exactly what it was the first year of that thousand. Why is man alone liable to grow into a dotard? It is not because he returns, in this, to his primitive state; and that, while the brute, which has acquired nothing and has therefore nothing to lose, still retains the force of instinct, man, who loses, by age or accident, all that his *perfectibility* had enabled him to gain, falls by this means lower than the brutes themselves? It would be melancholy, were we forced to admit that this distinctive and almost unlimited faculty is the source of all human misfortunes; that it is this which, in time, draws man out of his original state, in which he would have spent his days insensibly in peace and inno- cence; that it is this faculty, which, successively producing in dif- ferent ages his discoveries and his errors, his vices and his virtues, makes him at length a tyrant both over himself and over nature. It would be shocking to be obliged to regard as a benefactor the man who first suggested to the Oroonoko Indians the use of the boards they apply to the temples of their children, which secure to them some part at least of their imbecility and original happiness.

Savage man, left by nature solely to the direction of instinct, or rather indemnified for what he may lack by faculties capable at first of supplying its place, and afterwards of raising him much above it, must accordingly begin with purely animal functions: thus seeing and feeling must be his first condition, which would be common to him and all other animals. To will, and not to will, to desire and to fear, must be the first, and almost /209/ the only operations of his soul, till new circumstances occasion new developments of his faculties. /210/

*   *   *

It appears, at first view, that men in a state of nature, having no moral relations or determinate obligations one with another, could not be either good or bad, virtuous or vicious; unless we take these terms in a physical sense, and call, in an individual, those qualities vices which may be injurious to his preservation, and those virtues which contribute to it; in which case, he would have to be ac- counted most virtuous, who put least check on the pure impulses of nature. But without deviating from the ordinary sense of the words, it will be proper to suspend the judgment we might be led to form on such a state, and be on our guard against our prejudices, till we have weighed the matter in the scales of impartiality, and seen whether virtues or vices preponderate among civilized men: and whether their virtues do them more good than their vices do harm; till we have discovered whether the progress of the sciences sufficiently indemnifies them for the mischiefs they do one another, in proportion as they are better informed of the good they ought to do; or whether they would /221/ not be, on the whole, in a much happier condition if they had nothing to fear or to hope from any one, than as they are, subjected to universal dependence, and obliged to take everything from those who engage to give them nothing in return.

Above all, let us not conclude, with Hobbes, that because man has no idea of goodness, he must be naturally wicked; that he is vicious because he does not know virtue; that he always refuses to do his fellow-creatures services which he does not think they have a right to demand; or that by virtue of the right he truly claims everything he needs, he foolishly imagines himself the sole proprietor of the whole universe. Hobbes had seen clearly the defects of all the modern definitions of natural right: but the consequences which he deduces from his own show that he understands it in an equally false sense. In reasoning on the principles he lays down, he ought to have said that the state of nature, being that in which the care for our own preservation is the least prejudicial to that of others, was consequently the best calculated to promote peace, and the most suitable for mankind. He does say the exact opposite, in consequence of having improperly admitted, as a part of savage man's care for self-preservation, the gratification of a multitude of passions which are the work of society, and have made laws necessary. A bad man, he says, is a robust child. But it remains to be proved whether man in a state of nature is this robust child: and, should we grant that he is, what would he infer? Why truly, that if this man, when robust and strong, were dependent on others as he is when feeble, there is no extravagance he would not be guilty of; that he would beat his mother when she was too slow in giving him her breast; that he would strangle one of his younger brothers, if he should be troublesome to him, or bite the arm of another, if he put him to any inconvenience. But that man in the /222/ state of nature is both strong and dependent involves two contrary suppositions. Man is weak when he is dependent, and is his own master before he comes to be strong. Hobbes did not reflect that the same cause, which prevents a savage from making use of his reason, as our jurists hold, prevents him also from abusing his faculties, as Hobbes himself allows: so that it may be justly said that savages are not bad merely because they do not know what it is to be good: for it is neither the development of the understanding nor the restraint of law that hinders them from doing ill; but the peacefulness of their passions, and their ignorance of vice: *tanto plus in illis proficit vitiorum ignoratio, quam in his cognitio virtutis.*[1] There is another principle which has escaped Hobbes; which, having been bestowed on mankind, to moderate, on certain occasions, the impetuosity of egoism, or, before its birth, the desire of self-preservation, tempers the ardour with which he pursues his own welfare, by an innate repugnance at seeing a fellow-creature suffer.[2] I think I need not fear contradiction in holding man to be possessed of the only natural virtue, which /223/ could not be denied him by the most violent detractor of human virtue. I am speaking of compassion, which is a disposition suitable to creatures so weak and subject to so many evils as we certainly are: by so much the more universal and useful to mankind, as it comes before any kind of reflection; and at the same time so natural, that the very brutes themselves sometimes give evident proofs of it. Not to mention the tenderness of mothers for their offspring and the perils they encounter to save them from danger, it is well known that horses show a reluctance to trample on living bodies. One animal never passes by the dead body of another of its species: there are even some which give their fellows a sort of burial; while the mournfull lowings of the cattle when they enter the slaughter-house show the impression made on them by the horrible spectacle which meets them. We find, with

---

[1] [Justin. *Hist.* ii, 2. So much more does the ignorance of vice profit the one sort than the knowledge of virtue the other.]

[2] Egoism must not be confused with self-respect: for they differ both in themselves and in their effects. Self-respect is a natural feeling which leads every animal to look to its own preservation, and which, guided in man by reason and modified by compassion, creates humanity and virtue. Egoism is a purely relative and factitious feeling, which arises in the state of society, leads each individual to make more of himself than of any other, causes all the mutual damage men inflict one on another, and is the real source of the "sense of honour." This being understood, I maintain that, in our primitive condition, in the true state of nature, egoism did not exist; for as each man regarded himself as the only observer of his actions, the only being in the universe who took any interest in him, and the sole judge of his deserts, no feeling arising from comparisons he could not be led to make could take root in his soul; and for the same reason, he could know neither hatred nor the desire for revenge, since these passions can spring only from a sense of injury: and as it is the contempt or the intention to hurt and not the harm done which constitutes the /223/ injury, men who neither valued nor compared themselves could do one another much violence, when it suited them, without feeling any sense of injury. In a word, each man, regarding his fellows almost as he regarded animals of different species, might seize the prey of a weaker or yield up his own to a stronger, and yet consider these acts of violence as mere natural occurrences, without the slightest emotion of insolence or despite, or any other feeling than the joy or grief of success or failure. /224/

pleasure, the author of *The Fable of the Bees* obliged to own that man is a compassionate and sensible being, and laying aside his cold subtlety of style, in the example he gives, to present us with the pathetic description of a man who, from a place of confinement, is compelled to behold a wild beast tear a child from the arms of its mother, grinding its tender limbs with its murderous teeth, and tearing its palpitating entrails with its claws. What horrid agitation must not the eye-witness of such a scene experience, although he would not be personally concerned! What anxiety would he not suffer at not being able to give any assistance to the fainting mother and the dying infant!

Such is the pure emotion of nature, prior to all kinds /224/ of reflection! Such is the force of natural compassion, which the greatest depravity of morals has as yet hardly been able to destroy! for we daily find at our theatres men affected, nay, shedding tears at the sufferings of a wretch who, were he in the tyrant's place, would probably even add to the torments of his enemies; like the bloodthirsty Sulla, who was so sensitive to ills he had not caused, or that Alexander of Pheros who did not dare to go and see any tragedy acted, for fear of being seen weeping with Andromache and Priam, though he could listen without emotion to the cries of all the citizens who were daily strangled at his command.

> *Mollissima corda*
> *Humano generi dare se natura fatetur,*
> *Quae lacrimas dedit.*
>   JUVENAL, *Satires,* xv. 131.[1]

Mandeville well knew that, in spite of all their morality, men would have never been better than monsters, had not nature bestowed on them a sense of compassion, to aid their reason: but he did not see that from this quality alone flow all those social virtues, of which he denied man the possession. But what is generosity, clemency, or humanity but compassion applied to the weak, to the guilty, or to mankind in general? Even benevolence and friendship are, if we judge rightly, only the effects of compassion, constantly set upon a particular object: for how is it different to wish that another person may not suffer pain and uneasiness and to wish him happy? Were it even true that pity is no more than a feeling, which puts us in the place of the sufferer, a feeling, obscure yet lively in a savage, developed yet feeble in civilized man; this truth would have no other consequence than to confirm my argument. Compas-

---

[1] [Nature avows she gave the human race the softest hearts, who gave them tears.]

sion must, in fact, be the stronger, the more the animal beholding any kind of /225/ distress identifies himself with the animal that suffers. Now, it is plain that such identification must have been much more perfect in a state of nature than it is in a state of reason. It is reason that engenders self-respect, and reflection that confirms it: it is reason which turns man's mind back upon itself, and divides him from everything that could disturb or afflict him. It is philosophy that isolates him, and bids him say, at sight of the misfortunes of others: "Perish if you will, I am secure." Nothing but such general evils as threaten the whole community can disturb the tranquil sleep of the philosopher, or tear him from his bed. A murder may with impunity be committed under his window; he has only to put his hands to his ears and argue a little with himself, to prevent nature, which is shocked within him, from identifying itself with the unfortunate sufferer. Uncivilized man has not this admirable talent; and for want of reason and wisdom, is always foolishly ready to obey the first promptings of humanity. It is the populace that flocks together at riots and street brawls, while the wise man prudently makes off. It is the mob and the market-women, who part the combatants, and hinder gentlefolks from cutting one another's throats.

It is then certain that compassion is a natural feeling, which, by moderating the violence of love of self in each individual, contributes to the preservation of the whole species. It is this compassion that hurries us without reflection to the relief of those who are in distress: it is this which in a state of nature supplies the place of laws, morals, and virtues, with the advantage that none are tempted to disobey its gentle voice: it is this which will always prevent a sturdy savage from robbing a weak child or a feeble old man of the sustenance they may have with pain and difficulty acquired, if he sees a possibility of providing for himself by other means: it is this which, instead of inculcating that sublime maxim of rational justice, /226/ *Do to others as you would have them do unto you,* inspires all men with that other maxim of natural goodness, much less perfect indeed, but perhaps more useful; *Do good to yourself with as little evil as possible to others.* In a word, it is rather in this natural feeling than in any subtle arguments that we must look for the cause of that repugnance, which every man would experience in doing evil, even independently of the maxims of education. Although it might belong to Socrates and other minds of the like craft to acquire virtue by reason, the human race would long since have ceased to be, had its preservation depended only on the reasonings of the individuals composing it. /227/

*   *   *

APPENDIX

A famous author, reckoning up the good and evil of human life, and comparing the aggregates, finds that our pains greatly exceed our pleasures: so that, all things considered, human life is not at all a valuable gift. This conclusion does not surprise me; for the writer drew all his arguments from man in civilization. Had he gone back to the state of nature, his inquiries would clearly have had a different result, and man would have been seen to be subject to very few evils not of his own creation. It has indeed cost us not a little trouble to make ourselves as wretched as we are. When we consider, on the one hand, the immense labours of mankind, the many sciences brought to perfection, the arts invented, the powers employed, the deeps filled up, the mountains levelled, the rocks shattered, the rivers made navigable, the tracts of land cleared, the lakes emptied, the marshes drained, the enormous structures erected on land, and the teeming vessels that cover the sea; and, on the other hand, estimate with ever so little thought, the real advantages that have accrued from all these works to mankind, we cannot help being amazed at the vast disproportion there is between these things, and deploring the infatuation of man, which, to gratify his silly pride and vain self-admiration, induces him eagerly to pursue all the miseries he is capable of feeling, though beneficent nature had kindly placed them out of his way.

That men are actually wicked, a sad and continual experience of them proves beyond doubt: but, all the same, I think I have shown that man is naturally good. /273/ What then can have depraved him to such an extent, except the changes that have happened in his constitution, the advances he has made, and the knowledge he has acquired? We may admire human society as much as we please; it will be none the less true that it necessarily leads men to hate each other in proportion as their interests clash, and to do one another apparent services, while they are really doing every imaginable mischief. What can be thought of a relation, in which the interest of every individual dictates rules directly opposite to those the public reason dictates to the community in general—in which every man finds his profit in the misfortunes of his neighbour? There is not perhaps any man in a comfortable position who has not greedy heirs, and perhaps even children, secretly wishing for his death; not a ship at sea, of which the loss would not be good news to some merchant or other; not a house, which some debtor of bad faith would not be glad to see reduced to ashes with all the papers it contains; not a nation which does not rejoice at the disasters that befall its neighbours. Thus it is that we find our ad-

vantage in the misfortunes of our fellow-creatures, and that the loss
of one man almost always constitutes the prosperity of another.
But it is still more pernicious that public calamities are the objects of the hopes and expectations of innumerable individuals.
Some desire sickness, some mortality, some war, and some famine.
I have seen men wicked enough to weep for sorrow at the prospect
of a plentiful season; and the great and fatal fire of London, which
cost so many unhappy persons their lives or their fortunes, made
the fortunes of perhaps ten thousands others. I know that Montaigne censures Demades the Athenian for having caused to be
punished a workman who, by selling his coffins very dear, was a
great gainer by the deaths of his fellow-citizens; but, the reason
alleged by Montaigne being that everybody ought to be punished,
my point is /274/ clearly confirmed by it. Let us penetrate, therefore, the superficial appearances of benevolence, and survey what
passes in the inmost recesses of the heart. Let us reflect what must
be the state of things, when men are forced to caress and destroy
one another at the same time: when they are born enemies by duty,
and knaves by interest. It will perhaps be said that society is so
formed that every man gains by serving the rest. That would be all
very well, if he did not gain still more by injuring them. There
is no legitimate profit so great, that it cannot be greatly exceeded
by what may be made illegitimately; we always gain more by hurting our neighbours than by doing them good. Nothing is required
but to know how to act with impunity; and to this end the powerful employ all their strength, and the weak all their cunning.

Savage man, when he has dined, is at peace with all nature, and
the friend of all his fellow-creatures. If a dispute arises about a
meal, he rarely comes to blows, without having first compared the
difficulty of conquering his antagonist with the trouble of finding
subsistence elsewhere: and, as pride does not come in, it all ends in
a few blows; the victor eats, and the vanquished seeks provision
somewhere else, and all is at peace. The case is quite different with
man in the state of society, for whom first necessaries have to be
provided, and then superfluities; delicacies follow next, then immense wealth, then subjects, and then slaves. He enjoys not a
moment's relaxation; and what is yet stranger, the less natural and
pressing his wants, the more headstrong are his passions, and, still
worse, the more he has it in his power to gratify them; so that after
a long course of prosperity, after having swallowed up treasures
and ruined multitudes the hero ends up by cutting every throat

till he finds himself, at last, sole master of the world. Such is in miniature the moral picture if not of human life, at /275/ least of the secret pretensions of the heart of civilized man.

Compare without partiality the state of the citizen with that of the savage, and trace out, if you can, how many inlets the former has opened to pain and death, besides those of his vices, his wants, and his misfortunes. If you reflect on the mental afflictions that prey on us, the violent passions that waste and exhaust us, the excessive labour with which the poor are burdened, the still more dangerous indolence to which the wealthy give themselves up, so that the poor perish of want, and the rich of surfeit; if you reflect but a moment on the heterogeneous mixtures and pernicious seasonings of food; the corrupt state in which they are frequently eaten; on the adulteration of medicines, the wiles of those who sell them, the mistakes of those who administer them, and the poisonous vessels in which they are prepared; on the epidemics bred by foul air in consequence of great numbers of men being crowded together, or those which are caused by our delicate way of living, by our passing from our houses into the open air and back again, by the putting on or throwing off our clothes with too little care, and by all the precautions which sensuality has converted into necessary habits, and the neglect of which sometimes costs us our life or health; if you take into account the conflagrations and earthquakes, which, devouring or overwhelming whole cities, destroy the inhabitants by thousands; in a word, if you add together all the dangers with which these causes are always threatening us, you will see how dearly nature makes us pay for the contempt with which we have treated her lessons.

I shall not here repeat, what I have elsewhere said of the calamities of war; but wish that those, who have sufficient knowledge, were willing or bold enough to make public the details of the villainies committed in armies by the contractors for commissariat and hospitals: we /276/ should see plainly that their monstrous frauds, already none too well concealed, which cripple the finest armies in less than no time, occasion greater destruction among the soldiers than the swords of the enemy.

The number of people who perish annually at sea, by famine, the scurvy, pirates, fire, and shipwrecks, affords matter for another shocking calculation. We must also place to the credit of the establishment of property, and consequently to the institution of society, assassinations, poisonings, highway robberies, and even the punishments inflicted on the wretches guilty of these crimes; which, though expedient to prevent greater evils, yet by making the murder of one man cost the lives of two or more, double the loss to the human race.

What shameful methods are sometimes practised to prevent the birth of men, and cheat nature; either by brutal and depraved appetites which insult her most beautiful work—appetites unknown to savages or mere animals, which can spring only from the corrupt imagination of mankind in civilized countries; or by secret abortions, the fitting effects of debauchery and vitiated notions of honour; or by the exposure or murder of multitudes of infants, who fall victims to the poverty of their parents, or the cruel shame of their mothers; or, finally, by the mutilation of unhappy wretches, part of whose life, with their hope of posterity, is given up to vain singing, or, still worse, the brutal jealousy of other men: a mutilation which, in the last case, becomes a double outrage against nature from the treatment of those who suffer it, and from the use to which they are destined. But is it not a thousand times more common and more dangerous for paternal rights openly to offend against humanity? How many talents have not been thrown away, and inclinations forced, by the unwise constraint of fathers? How many men, who would have distinguished themselves in a fitting estate, have died dishonoured and /277/ wretched in another for which they had no taste! How many happy, but unequal, marriages have been broken or disturbed, and how many chaste wives have been dishonoured, by an order of things continually in contradiction with that of nature! How many good and virtuous husbands and wives are reciprocally punished for having been ill-assorted! How many young and unhappy victims of their parents' avarice plunge into vice, or pass their melancholy days in tears, groaning in the indissoluble bonds which their hearts repudiate and gold alone has formed! Fortunate sometimes are those whose courage and virtue remove them from life before inhuman violence makes them spend it in crime or in despair. Forgive me, father and mother, whom I shall ever regret: my complaint embitters your griefs; but would they might be an eternal and terrible example to every one who dares, in the name of nature, to violate her most sacred right.

If I have spoken only of those ill-starred unions which are the result of our system, is it to be thought that those over which love and sympathy preside are free from disadvantages? What if I should undertake to show humanity attacked in its very source, and even in the most sacred of all ties, in which fortune is consulted before nature, and, the disorders of society confounding all virtue and vice, continence becomes a criminal precaution, and a refusal to give life to a fellow-creature, an act of humanity? But, without drawing aside the veil which hides all these horrors, let us content ourselves with pointing out the evil which others will have to remedy.

To all this add the multiplicity of unhealthy trades, which shorten men's lives or destroy their bodies, such as working in the mines, and the preparing of metals and minerals, particularly lead, copper, mercury, cobalt, and arsenic: add those other dangerous trades which are daily fatal to many tilers, carpenters, masons, and miners; put /278/ all these together and we can see, in the establishment and perfection of societies, the reasons for that diminution of our species, which has been noticed by many philosophers.

Luxury, which cannot be prevented among men who are tenacious of their own convenience and of the respect paid them by others, soon completes the evil society had begun, and, under the pretence of giving bread to the poor, whom it should never have made such, impoverishes all the rest, and sooner or later depopulates the State. Luxury is a remedy much worse than the disease it sets up to cure; or rather it is in itself the greatest of all evils, for every State, great or small: for, in order to maintain all the servants and vagabonds it creates, it brings oppression and ruin on the citizen and the labourer; it is like those scorching winds, which, covering the trees and plants with devouring insects, deprive useful animals of their subsistence and spread famine and death wherever they blow.

From society and the luxury to which it gives birth arise the liberal and mechanical arts, commerce, letters, and all those superfluities which make industry flourish, and enrich and ruin nations. The reason for such destruction is plain. It is easy to see, from the very nature of agriculture, that it must be the least lucrative of all the arts; for, its produce being the most universally necessary, the price must be proportionate to the abilities of the very poorest of mankind.

From the same principle may be deduced this rule, that the arts in general are more lucrative in proportion as they are less useful; and that, in the end, the most useful becomes the most neglected. From this we may learn what to think of the real advantages of industry and the actual effects of its progress.

Such are the sensible causes of all the miseries, into which opulence at length plunges the most celebrated /279/ nations. In proportion as arts and industry flourish, the despised husbandman, burdened with the taxes necessary for the support of luxury, and condemned to pass his days between labour and hunger, forsakes his native field, to seek in town the bread he ought to carry thither. The more capital cities strike the vulgar eye with admiration, the greater reason is there to lament the sight of the abandoned countryside, the large tracts of land that lie uncultivated, the roads crowded with unfortunate citizens turned beggars or highwaymen, and doomed to end their wretched lives either on a dunghill or on the gallows. Thus the State grows rich on the one hand, and feeble and depopulated on the other; the mightiest monarchies, after having taken immense pains to enrich and depopulate themselves, fall at last a prey to some poor nation, which has yielded to the fatal temptation of invading them, and then, growing opulent and weak in its turn, is itself invaded and ruined by some other.

Let any one inform us what produced the swarms of barbarians, who overran Europe, Asia, and Africa for so many ages. Was their prodigious increase due to their industry and arts, to the wisdom of their laws, or to the excellence of their political system? Let the learned tell us why, instead of multiplying to such a degree, these fierce and brutal men, without sense or science, without education, without restraint, did not destroy each other hourly in quarrelling over the productions of their fields and woods. Let them tell us how these wretches could have the presumption to oppose such clever people as we were, so well trained in military discipline, and possessed of such excellent laws and institutions: and why, since society has been brought to perfection in northern countries, and so much pains taken to instruct their inhabitants in their social duties and in the art of living happily and peaceably together, we see them no longer produce such numberless hosts as they used once /280/ to send forth to be the plague and terror of other nations. I fear someone may at last answer me by saying, that all these fine things, arts, sciences, and laws, were wisely invented by men, as a salutary plague, to prevent the too great multiplication of mankind, lest the world, which was given us for a habitation, should in time be too small for its inhabitants.

What, then, is to be done? Must societies be totally abolished? Must *meum* and *tuum* be annihilated, and must we return again to the forests to live among bears? This is a deduction in the manner of my adversaries, which I would as soon anticipate as let them have the shame of drawing. O you, who have never heard the voice of heaven, who think man destined only to live this little life and die in peace; you, who can resign in the midst of populous cities your fatal acquisitions, your restless spirits, your corrupt hearts and endless desires; resume, since it depends entirely on yourselves, your ancient and primitive innocence: retire to the woods, there to lose the sight and remembrance of the crimes of your contemporaries; and be not apprehensive of degrading your species, by renouncing its advances in order to renounce its vices. As for men like me, whose passions have destroyed their original simplicity, who can no longer subsist on plants or acorns, or live without laws and magistrates; those who were honoured in their first father with supernatural instructions; those who discover, in the design of giving human actions at the start of morality which they must otherwise have been so long in acquiring, the reason for a precept in itself indifferent and inexplicable on every other system; those, in short, who are persuaded that the Divine Being has called all mankind to be partakers in the happiness and perfection of celestial intelligences, all these will endeavour to merit the eternal prize they are to expect from the practice of those virtues, which they make them- /281/ selves follow in learning to know them. They will respect the sacred bonds of their respective communities; they will love their fellow-citizens, and serve them with all their might: they will scrupulously obey the laws, and all those who make or administer them; they will particularly honour those wise and good princes, who find means of preventing, curing, or even palliating all these evils and abuses, by which we are constantly threatened; they will animate the zeal of their deserving rulers, by showing them, without flattery or fear, the importance of their office and the severity of their duty. But they will not therefore have less contempt for a constitution that cannot support itself without the aid of so many splendid characters, much oftener wished for than found; and from which, notwithstanding all their pains and solicitude, there always arise more real calamities than even apparent advantages. /282/

from *THE GOLDEN BOUGH*

SIR JAMES GEORGE FRAZER

THE PROPITIATION OF WILD ANIMALS BY HUNTERS

The explanation of life by the theory of an indwelling and practically immortal soul is one which the savage does not confine to human beings but extends to the animate creation in general. In so doing he is more liberal and perhaps more logical than the civilised man, who commonly denies to animals that privilege of immortality which he claims for himself. The savage is not so proud; he commonly believes that animals are endowed with feelings and intelligence like those of men, and that, like men, they possess souls which survive the death of their bodies either to wander about as disembodied spirits or to be born again in animal form.

Thus to the savage, who regards all living creatures as practically on a footing of equality with man, the act of killing and eating an animal must wear a very different aspect from that which the same act presents to us, who regard the intelligence of animals as far inferior to our own and deny them the possession of immortal souls. Hence on the principles of his rude philosophy the primitive hunter who slays an animal believes himself exposed to the vengeance either of its disembodied spirit or of all the other animals of the same species, whom he considers as knit together, like men, by the ties of kin and the obligations of the blood feud, and therefore as bound to resent the injury done to one of their number. Accordingly the savage makes it a rule to spare the life of those animals which he has no pressing motive for killing, at least such fierce and dangerous animals as are likely to exact a bloody vengeance for the slaughter of one of their kind. Crocodiles are animals of this sort. They are only found in hot countries, where, as a rule, food is abundant and primitive man has therefore little reason to kill them for the sake of their tough and unpalatable flesh. Hence it is a custom with some savages to spare crocodiles, or rather only to kill them in obedience to the law of blood feud, that is, as a retaliation for the slaughter of men by crocodiles. For example, the Dyaks of Borneo will not kill a crocodile unless a crocodile has first killed a man. "For why, say they, should they commit an act of aggression, when he and his kindred can so easily repay them? But should the alligator take a human life, revenge becomes a sacred duty of the living relatives, who will trap the man- /518/ eater in the spirit of an officer of justice pursuing a criminal. Others, even then, hang back, reluctant to embroil themselves in a quarrel which does not concern them. The man-eating alligator is supposed to be pursued by a righteous Nemesis; and whenever one is caught they have a profound conviction that it must be the guilty one, or his accomplice."

Like the Dyaks, the natives of Madagascar never kill a crocodile "except in retaliation for one of their friends who has been destroyed by a crocodile. They believe that the wanton destruction of one of these reptiles will be followed by the loss of human life, in accordance with the principle of *lex talionis*." The people who live near the lake Itasy in Madagascar make a yearly proclamation to the crocodiles, announcing that they will revenge the death of some of their friends by killing as many crocodiles in return, and warning all well-disposed crocodiles to keep out of the way, as they have no quarrel with them, but only with their evil-minded relations who have taken human life. Various tribes of Madagascar believe themselves to be descended from crocodiles, and accordingly they view the scaly reptile as, to all intents and purposes, a man and a brother. If one of the animals should so far forget himself as to devour one of his human kinsfolk, the chief of the tribe, or in his absence an old man familiar with the tribal customs, repairs at the head of the people to the edge of the water, and summons the family of the culprit to deliver him up to the arm of justice. A hook is then baited and cast into the river or lake. Next day the guilty brother, or one of his family, is dragged ashore, and after his crime has been clearly brought home to him by a strict interrogation, he is sentenced to death and executed. The claims of justice being thus satisfied and the majesty of the law fully vindicated, the deceased crocodile is lamented and buried like a kinsman; a mound is raised over his relics and a stone marks the place of his head.

Again, the tiger is another of those dangerous beasts whom the savage prefers to leave alone, lest by killing one of the species he should excite the hostility of the rest. No consideration will induce a Sumatran to catch or wound a tiger except in self-defence or immediately after a tiger has destroyed a friend or relation. When a

European has set traps for tigers, the people of the neighbourhood have been known to go by night to the place and explain to the animals that the traps are not set by them nor with their consent. The inhabitants of the hills near Rajamahall, in Bengal, are very averse to killing a tiger, unless one of their kinsfolk has been carried off by one of the beasts. In that case they go out for the purpose of hunting and slaying a tiger; and when they have succeeded they lay their bows and arrows on the carcase and invoke God, declaring that they slew the animal in retaliation for the loss of a kinsman. Vengeance having been thus taken, they swear not to attack another tiger except under similar provocation.

The Indians of Carolina would not molest snakes when they came /519/ upon them, but would pass by on the other side of the path, believing that if they were to kill a serpent, the reptile's kindred would destroy some of their brethren, friends, or relations in return. So the Seminole Indians spared the rattlesnake, because they feared that the soul of the dead rattlesnake would incite its kinsfolk to take vengeance. The Cherokee regard the rattlesnake as the chief of the snake tribe and fear and respect him accordingly. Few Cherokee will venture to kill a rattlesnake, unless they cannot help it, and even then they must atone for the crime by craving pardon of the snake's ghost either in their own person or through the mediation of a priest, according to a set formula. If these precautions are neglected, the kinsfolk of the dead snake will send one of their number as an avenger of blood, who will track down the murderer and sting him to death. No ordinary Cherokee dares to kill a wolf, if he can possibly help it; for he believes that the kindred of the slain beast would surely avenge its death, and that the weapon with which the deed had been done would be quite useless for the future, unless it were cleaned and exorcised by a medicine-man. However, certain persons who know the proper rites of atonement for such a crime can kill wolves with impunity, and they are sometimes hired to do so by people who have suffered from the raids of the wolves on their cattle or fish-traps. In Jebel-Nuba, a district of the Eastern Sudan, it is forbidden to touch the nests or remove the young of a species of black birds, resembling our blackbirds, because the people believe that the parent birds would avenge the wrong by causing a stormy wind to blow, which would destroy the harvest.

But the savage clearly cannot afford to spare all animals. He must either eat some of them or starve, and when the question thus comes to be whether he or the animal must perish, he is forced to overcome his superstitious scruples and take the life of the beast.

At the same time he does all he can to appease his victims and their kinsfolk. Even in the act of killing them he testifies his respect for them, endeavours to excuse or even conceal his share in procuring their death, and promises that their remains will be honourably treated. By thus robbing death of its terrors, he hopes to reconcile his victims to their fate and to induce their fellows to come and be killed also. For example, it was a principle with the Kamtchatkans never to kill a land or sea animal without first making excuses to it and begging that the animal would not take it ill. Also they offered it cedar-nuts and so forth, to make it think it was not a victim but a guest at a feast. They believed that this hindered other animals of the same species from growing shy. For instance, after they had killed a bear and feasted on its flesh, the host would bring the bear's head before the company, wrap it in grass, and present it with a variety of trifles. Then he would lay the blame of the bear's death on the Russians, and bid the beast wreak his wrath upon them. Also he would ask the bear to inform the other bears how well he had been treated, that they too might come without fear. Seals, sea-lions, /520/ and other animals were treated by the Kamtchatkans with the same ceremonious respect. Moreover, they used to insert sprigs of a plant resembling bear's wort in the mouths of the animals they killed; after which they would exhort the grinning skulls to have no fear but to go and tell it to their fellows, that they also might come and be caught and so partake of this splendid hospitality. When the Ostiaks have hunted and killed a bear, they cut off its head and hang it on a tree. Then they gather round in a circle and pay it divine honours. Next they run towards the carcase uttering lamentations and saying, "Who killed you? It was the Russians. Who cut off your head? It was a Russian axe. Who skinned you? It was a knife made by a Russian." They explain, too, that the feathers which sped the arrow on its flight came from the wing of a strange bird, and that they did nothing but let the arrow go. They do all this because they believe that the wandering ghost of the slain bear would attack them on the first opportunity, if they did not thus appease it. Or they stuff the skin of the slain bear with hay; and after celebrating their victory with songs of mockery and insult, after spitting on and kicking it, they set it up on its hind legs, "and then, for a considerable time, they bestow on it all the veneration due to a guardian god." When a party of Koryak have killed a bear or a wolf, they skin the beast and dress one of themselves in the skin. Then they dance round the skin-clad man, saying that it was not they who killed the animal, but some one else, generally a Russian. When they kill a fox they skin it, wrap the body in grass, and bid him go tell his companions how hospitably he has been received, and how he has received a new cloak instead of his old one. A fuller account of the Koryak ceremonies is given by a more recent writer. He tells us that when a dead bear is brought to the house, the women come out to meet it, dancing with firebrands. The bear-skin is taken off along with the head; and one of the women puts on the skin, dances in it, and entreats the bear not to be angry, but to be kind to the people. At the same time they offer meat on a wooden platter to the dead beast, saying, "Eat, friend." Afterwards a ceremony is performed for the purpose of sending the dead bear, or rather his spirit, away back to his home. He is provided with provisions for the journey in the shape of puddings or reindeer-flesh packed in a grass bag. His skin is stuffed with grass and carried round the house, after which he is supposed to depart towards the rising sun. The intention of the ceremonies is to protect the people from the wrath of the slain bear and his kinsfolk, and so to ensure success in future bear-hunts. The Finns used to try to persuade a slain bear that he had not been killed by them, but had fallen from a tree, or met his death in some other way; moreover, they held a funeral festival in his honour, at the close of which bards expatiated on the homage that had been paid to him, urging him to report to the other bears the high consideration with which he had been treated, in order that they also, following his example, might come and be slain. When the Lapps /521/ had succeeded in killing a bear with impunity, they thanked him for not hurting them and for not breaking the clubs and spears which had given him his death wounds; and they prayed that he would not visit his death upon them by sending storms or in any other way. His flesh then furnished a feast.

The reverence of hunters for the bear whom they regularly kill and eat may thus be traced all along the northern region of the Old World from Bering's Straits to Lappland. It reappears in similar forms in North America. With the American Indians a bear hunt was an important event for which they prepared by long fasts and purgations. Before setting out they offered expiatory sacrifices to the souls of bears slain in previous hunts, and besought them to be favourable to the hunters. When a bear was killed the hunter lit his pipe, and putting the mouth of it between the bear's lips, blew into the bowl, filling the beast's mouth with smoke. Then he begged the bear not to be angry at having been killed, and not to thwart him afterwards in the chase. The carcase was roasted whole and eaten; not a morsel of the flesh might be left over. The head, painted red and blue, was hung on a post and addressed by orators, who heaped praise on the dead beast. When men of the Bear clan in the Ottawa tribe killed a bear, they made him a feast of his own flesh, and addressed him thus: "Cherish us no grudge because we have killed you. You have sense; you see that our children are hungry. They love you and wish to take you into their bodies. Is it not glorious to be eaten by the children of a chief?" Amongst the Nootka Indians of British Columbia, when a bear had been killed, it was brought in and seated before the head chief in an upright posture, with a chief's bonnet, wrought in figures, on its head, and its fur powdered over with white down. A tray of provisions was then set before it, and it was invited by words and gestures to eat. After that the animal was skinned, boiled, and eaten.

A like respect is testified for other dangerous creatures by the hunters who regularly trap and kill them. When Caffre hunters are in the act of showering spears on an elephant, they call out, "Don't kill us, great captain; don't strike or tread upon us, mighty chief." When he is dead they make their excuses to him, pretending that his death was a pure accident. As a mark of respect they bury his trunk with much solemn ceremony; for they say that "the elephant is a great lord; his trunk is his hand." Before the Amaxosa Caffres attack an elephant they shout to the animal and beg him to pardon them for the slaughter they are about to perpetrate, professing great submission to his person and explaining clearly the need they have of his tusks to enable them to procure beads and supply their wants. When they have killed him they bury in the ground, along with the end of his trunk, a few of the articles they have obtained for the ivory, thus hoping to avert some mishap that would otherwise befall them. Amongst some tribes of Eastern Africa, when a lion is killed, the carcase is brought before the king, who does homage to it by prostrating himself on the /522/ ground and rubbing his face on the muzzle of the beast. In some parts of Western Africa if a negro kills a leopard he is bound fast and brought before the chiefs for having killed one of their peers. The man defends himself on the plea that the leopard is chief of the forest and therefore a stranger. He is then set at liberty and rewarded. But the dead leopard, adorned with a chief's bonnet, is set up in the village, where nightly dances are held in its honour. The Baganda greatly fear the ghosts of buffaloes which they have killed, and they always appease these dangerous spirits. On no account will they bring the head of a slain buffalo into a village or into a garden of plantains; they always eat the flesh of the head in the open country. Afterwards they place the skull in a small hut built for the purpose,

where they pour out beer as an offering and pray to the ghost to
stay where he is and not to harm them.

Another formidable beast whose life the savage hunter takes with
joy, yet with fear and trembling, is the whale. After the slaughter
of a whale the maritime Koryak of North-eastern Siberia hold a
communal festival, the essential part of which "is based on the
conception that the whale killed has come on a visit to the village;
that it is staying for some time, during which it is treated with
great respect; that it then returns to the sea to repeat its visit the
following year; that it will induce its relatives to come along, telling them of the hospitable reception that has been accorded to it.
According to the Koryak ideas, the whales, like all other animals,
constitute one tribe, or rather family, of related individuals, who
live in villages like the Koryak. They avenge the murder of one
of their number, and are grateful for kindnesses that they may have
received." When the inhabitants of the Isle of St. Mary, to the
north of Madagascar, go a-whaling, they single out the young
whales for attack and "humbly beg the mother's pardon, stating
the necessity that drives them to kill her progeny, and requesting
that she will be pleased to go below while the deed is doing, that
her maternal feelings may not be outraged by witnessing what
must cause her so much uneasiness." An Ajumba hunter having
killed a female hippopotamus on Lake Azyingo in West Africa,
the animal was decapitated and its quarters and bowels removed.
Then the hunter, naked, stepped into the hollow of the ribs, and
kneeling down in the bloody pool washed his whole body with the
blood and excretions of the animal, while he prayed to the soul of
the hippopotamus not to bear him a grudge for having killed her
and so blighted her hopes of future maternity; and he further en-
treated the ghost not to stir up other hippopotamuses to avenge
her death by butting at and capsizing his canoe.

The ounce, a leopard-like creature, is dreaded for its depreda-
tions by the Indians of Brazil. When they have caught one of
these animals in a snare, they kill it and carry the body home to
the village. There the women deck the carcase with feathers of
many colours, put bracelets on its legs, and weep over it, saying,
"I pray thee not to take vengeance on our little ones for having
been caught and killed through /523/ thine own ignorance. For
it was not we who deceived thee, it was thyself. Our husbands only
set the trap to catch animals that are good to eat; they never
thought to take thee in it. Therefore, let not thy soul counsel thy
fellows to avenge thy death on our little ones!" When a Blackfoot
Indian has caught eagles in a trap and killed them, he takes them

home to a special lodge, called the eagles' lodge, which has been prepared for their reception outside of the camp. Here he sets the birds in a row on the ground, and propping up their heads on a stick, puts a piece of dried meat in each of their mouths in order that the spirits of the dead eagles may go and tell the other eagles how well they are being treated by the Indians. So when Indian hunters of the Orinoco region have killed an animal, they open its mouth and pour into it a few drops of the liquor they generally carry with them, in order that the soul of the dead beast may inform its fellows of the welcome it has met with, and that they too, cheered by the prospect of the same kind reception, may come with alacrity to be killed. When a Teton Indian is on a journey, and he meets a grey spider or a spider with yellow legs, he kills it, because some evil would befall him if he did not. But he is very careful not to let the spider know that he kills it, for if the spider knew, his soul would go and tell the other spiders, and one of them would be sure to avenge the death of his relation. So in crushing the insect, the Indian says, "O Grandfather Spider, the Thunder-beings kill you." And the spider is crushed at once and believes what is told him. His soul probably runs and tells the other spiders that the Thunder-beings have killed him; but no harm comes of that. For what can grey or yellow-legged spiders do to the Thunder-beings? /524/

from *TOTEM AND TABOO*

SIGMUND FREUD

Let us call up the spectacle of a totem meal of the kind we have been discussing, amplified by a few probable features which we have not yet been able to consider. The clan is celebrating the ceremonial occasion by the cruel slaughter of its totem animal and is devouring it raw—blood, flesh and bones. The clansmen are there, dressed in the likeness of the totem and imitating it in sound and movement, as though they are seeking to stress their identity with it. Each man is conscious that he is performing an act forbidden to the individual and justifiable only through the participation of the whole clan; nor may anyone absent himself from the killing and the meal. When the deed is done, the slaughtered animal is lamented and bewailed. The mourning is obligatory, imposed by dread of a threatened retribution. As Robertson Smith (1894, 412) remarks of an analogous occasion, its chief purpose is to disclaim responsibility for the killing.

But the mourning is followed by demonstrations of festive rejoicing: every instinct is unfettered and there is license for every kind of gratification. Here we have easy access to an understanding of the nature of festivals in general. A festival is a permitted, or rather an obligatory excess, a solemn breach of a prohibition. It is not that men commit the excesses because they are feeling happy as a result of some injunction they have received. It is rather that excess is of the essence of a festival; the festive feeling is produced by the liberty to do what is as a rule prohibited.

What are we to make, though, of the prelude to this festive joy— the mourning over the death of the animal? If the clansmen rejoice over the killing of the totem—a normally forbidden act—why do they mourn over it as well?

As we have seen, the clansmen acquire sanctity by consuming the totem: they reinforce their identification with it and with one

Sigmund Freud, *The Standard Edition of the Complete Psychological Works*, Vol. XIII, *Totem and Taboo*, Trans. by James Strachey (London: The Hogarth Press, 1955), pp. 140-43.

another. Their festive feelings and all that follows from them might well be explained by the fact that they have /140/ taken into themselves the sacred life of which the substance of the totem is the vehicle.

Psycho-analysis has revealed that the totem animal is in reality a substitute for the father; and this tallies with the contradictory fact that, though the killing of the animal is as a rule forbidden, yet its killing is a festive occasion—with the fact that it is killed and yet mourned. The ambivalent emotional attitude, which to this day characterizes the father-complex in our children and which often persists into adult life, seems to extend to the totem animal in its capacity as substitute for the father.

If, now, we bring together the psycho-analytic translation of the totem with the fact of the totem meal and with Darwin's theories of the earliest state of human society, the possibility of a deeper understanding emerges—a glimpse of a hypothesis which may seem fantastic but which offers the advantage of establishing in unsuspected correlation between groups of phenomena that have hitherto been disconnected.

There is, of course, no place for the beginnings of totemism in Darwin's primal horde. All that we find there is a violent and jealous father who keeps all the females for himself and drives away his sons as they grow up. This earliest state of society has never been an object of observation. The most primitive kind of organization that we actually come across—and one that is in force to this day in certain tribes—consists of bands of males; these bands are composed of members with equal rights and are subject to the restrictions of the totemic system, including inheritance through the mother. Can this form of organization have developed out of the other one? and if so along what lines?

If we call the celebration of the totem meal to our help, we shall be able to find an answer. One day[1] the brothers who had been driven out came together, killed and devoured their father and so made an end of the patriarchal horde. United, they had the courage to do and succeeded in doing what would have been impossible for them individually. (Some cultural advance, perhaps, command over some new weapon, had given them a sense /141/ of superior strength.) Cannibal savages as they were, it goes without saying that they devoured their victim as well as killing him. The violent

---

[1] To avoid possible misunderstanding, I must ask the reader to take into account the final sentences of the following footnote as a corrective to this description.

primal father had doubtless been the feared and envied model of each one of the company of brothers: and in the act of devouring him they accomplished their identification with him, and each one of them acquired a portion of his strength. The totem meal, which is perhaps mankind's earliest festival, would thus be a repetition and a commemoration of this memorable and criminal deed, which was the beginning of so many things—of social organization, of moral restrictions and of religion.[1] /142/

In order that these latter consequences may seem plausible, leaving their premises on one side, we need only suppose that the tumultuous mob of brothers were filled with the same contradictory feelings which we can see at work in the ambivalent father-complexes of our children and of our neurotic patients. They hated their father, who presented such a formidable obstacle to their craving for power and their sexual desires; but they loved and admired him too. After they had got rid of him, had satisfied their hatred and had put into effect their wish to identify themselves with him, the affection which had all this time been pushed under

---

[1] This hypothesis, which has such a monstrous air, of the tyrannical father being overwhelmed and killed by a combination of his exiled sons, was also arrived at by Atkinson (1903, 220 f.) as a direct implication of the state of affairs in Darwin's primal horde: 'The patriarch had only one enemy whom he should dread . . . a youthful band of brothers living together in forced celibacy, or at most in polyandrous relation with some single female captive. A horde as yet weak in their impubescence they are, but they would, when strength was gained with time, inevitably wrench by combined attacks, renewed again and again, both wife and life from the paternal tyrant.' Atkinson, who incidentally passed his whole life in New Caledonia and had unusual opportunities for studying the natives, also pointed out that the conditions which Darwin assumed to prevail in the primal horde may easily be observed in herds of wild oxen and horses and regularly lead to the killing of the father of the herd. [Ibid., 222 f.] He further supposed that, after the father had been disposed of, the horde would be disintegrated by a bitter struggle between the victorious sons. Thus any new organization of society would be precluded: there would be 'an ever-recurring violent succession to the solitary paternal tyrant, by sons whose parricidal hands were so soon again clenched in fratricidal strife.' (Ibid., 228.) Atkinson, who had no psycho-analytic hints to help him and who was ignorant of Robertson Smith's studies, found a less violent transition from the primal horde to the next social stage, at which numbers of males live together in a peaceable community. He believed that through the intervention of maternal love the sons—to begin with only the youngest, but later others as well—were allowed to remain with the horde, and that in return for this toleration the sons acknowledged their father's sexual privilege by renouncing all claim to their mother and sisters. [Ibid., 231 ff.]

Such is the highly remarkable theory put forward by Atkinson. In its essential feature it is in agreement with my own; but its divergence results in its failing to effect a correlation with many other issues.

The lack of precision in what I have written in the text above, its abbreviation of the time factor and its compression of the whole subject- /142/ matter, may be attributed to the reserve necessitated by the nature of the topic. It would be as foolish to aim at exactitude in such questions as it would be unfair to insist upon certainty.

was bound to make itself felt.¹ It did so in the form of remorse. A sense of guilt made its appearance, which in this instance coincided with the remorse felt by the whole group. The dead father became stronger than the living one had been—for events took the course we so often see them follow in human affairs to this day. What had up to then been prevented by his actual existence was thenceforward prohibited by the sons themselves, in accordance with the psychological procedure so familiar to us in psycho-analyses under the name of 'deferred obedience'. They revoked their deed by forbidding the killing of the totem, the substitute for their father; and they renounced its fruits by resigning their claim to the women who had now been set free. They thus created out of their filial sense of guilt the two fundamental taboos of totemism, which for that very reason inevitably corresponded to the two repressed wishes of the Oedipus complex. Whoever contravened those taboos became guilty of the only two crimes with which primitive society concerned itself.² /143/

¹ This fresh emotional attitude must also have been assisted by the fact that the deed cannot have given complete satisfaction to those who did it. From one point of view it had been done in vain. Not one of the sons had in fact been able to put his original wish—of taking his father's place—into effect. And, as we know, failure is far more propitious for a moral reaction than satisfaction.

² Murder and incest, or offences of a like kind against the sacred laws of blood, are in primitive society the only crimes of which the community as such takes cognizance.' (Smith, 1894, 419.) /143/

from ON THE NATURE OF THE PSYCHE

C. G. JUNG

PATTERNS OF BEHAVIOR AND ARCHETYPES

We have stated that the lower reaches of the psyche begin when the function emancipates itself from the compulsive force of instinct and becomes amenable to the will, and we have defined the will as disposable energy. But that, as said, presupposes a disposing subject, capable of judgment and endowed with consciousness. In this way we arrived at the position of proving, as it were, the very thing that we started by rejecting, namely the identification of psyche with consciousness. This dilemma resolves itself once we realize how very relative consciousness is, since its contents are conscious and unconscious at the same time, i.e., conscious under one aspect and unconscious under another. As is the way of paradoxes, this statement is not immediately comprehensible.[70] We must, however, accustom ourselves to the thought that conscious and unconscious have no clear demarcations, the one beginning where the other leaves off. It is rather the case that the psyche is a conscious-unconscious whole. As to the no man's land which I have called the "personal unconscious," it is fairly easy to prove that its contents correspond exactly to our definition of the psychic. But—as we define "psychic"—is there a psychic unconscious that is not a "fringe of consciousness" and not personal?

I have already mentioned that Freud established the existence of /70/ archaic vestiges and primitive modes of functioning in the unconscious. Subsequent investigations have confirmed this result and brought together a wealth of observational material. In view of the

C. G. Jung, *The Basic Writings of C. G. Jung,* Ed. by Violet Staub de Laszlo (New York: The Modern Library, [1959]), pp. 70-76. Reprinted by permission of the Bollingen Foundation, New York City.

[70] Freud also arrived at similar paradoxical conclusions. Thus, in his article "The Unconscious" (Standard Edn., Vol. XIV, p. 177), he says: "An instinct can never become an object of consciousness—only the idea that represents the instinct can." *"Even in the unconscious, moreover, an instinct cannot be represented otherwise than by an idea."* (My italics.) As in my above account we were left asking, "Who is the subject of the unconscious will?" so we must ask here, "Exactly *who* has the idea of the instinct in the unconscious state?" For "unconscious" ideation is a *contradictio in adjecto.* /70/

structure of the body it would be astonishing if the psyche were the only biological phenomenon not to show clear traces of its evolutionary history, and it is altogether probable that these marks are closely connected with the instinctual base. Instinct and the archaic mode meet in the biological conception of the "pattern of behavior." There are in fact no amorphous instincts, as every instinct bears in itself the pattern of its situation. Always it fulfills an image, and the image has fixed qualities. The instinct of the leaf-cutting ant fulfills the image of ant, tree, leaf, cutting, transport, and the little ant garden of fungi.[71] If any of these conditions is lacking, the instinct does not function, because it cannot exist without its total pattern, without its image. Such an image is an a priori type. It is inborn in the ant prior to any activity, for there can be no activity at all unless an instinct of corresponding pattern initiates and makes it possible. This schema holds true of all instincts and is found in identical form in all individuals of the same species. The same is true also of man: he has in him these a priori instinct types which provide the occasion and the pattern for his activities, in so far as he functions instinctively. As a biological being he has no choice but to act in a specifically human way and fulfill his pattern of behavior. This sets narrow limits to his possible range of volition, the more narrow the more primitive he is, and the more his consciousness is dependent upon the instinctual sphere. Although from one point of view it is quite correct to speak of the pattern of behavior as a still existing archaic vestige, as Nietzsche did in respect of the function of dreams, such an attitude does scant justice to the biological and psychological meaning of these types. They are not just relics or vestiges of earlier modes of functioning; they are the ever-present and biologically necessary regulators of the instinctual sphere, whose range of action covers the whole realm of the psyche and only loses its absoluteness when limited by the relative freedom of the will. We may say that the image represents the *meaning* of the instinct.

/71/ Although the existence of an instinctual pattern in human biology is probable, it seems very difficult to prove the existence of distinct types empirically. For the organ with which we might apprehend them—consciousness—is not only itself a transformation of the original instinctual image, but also its transformer. It is therefore not surprising that the human mind finds it impossible to classify man into precise types similar to those we know in the animal kingdom. I must confess that I can see no direct way to

---

[71] For details see C. Lloyd Morgan, *Habit and Instinct* (London and New York, 1896).

solve this problem. And yet I have succeeded, or so I believe, in finding at least an indirect way of approach to the instinctual image.

In what follows I would like to give a brief description of how this discovery took place. I had often observed patients whose dreams pointed to a rich store of fantasy material. Equally, from the patients themselves, I got the impression that they were stuffed full of fantasies, without their being able to tell me just where the inner pressure lay. I therefore took up a dream image or an association of the patient's, and, with this as a point of departure, set him the task of elaborating or developing his theme by giving free rein to his fantasy. This, according to individual taste and talent, could be done in any number of ways, dramatic, dialectic, visual, acoustic, or in the form of dancing, painting, drawing, or modeling. The result of this technique was a vast number of complicated designs whose diversity puzzled me for years, until I was able to recognize that in this method I was witnessing the spontaneous manifestation of an unconscious process which was merely assisted by the technical ability of the patient, and to which I later gave the name "individuation process." But long before this recognition dawned upon me I had made the discovery that this method often diminished, to a considerable degree, the frequency and intensity of the dreams, thus reducing the inexplicable pressure exerted by the unconscious. In many cases this brought a large measure of therapeutic success, which encouraged both myself and the patient to press forward despite the baffling nature of the results.[72] I felt bound to insist that they were baffling, if only to stop myself from framing, on the basis of certain theoretical assumptions, interpretations which I felt were not only inadequate but liable to /72/ prejudice the ingenuous productions of the patient. The more I suspected these configurations of harboring a certain purposefulness, the less inclined I was to risk any theories about them. This reticence was not made easy for me, since in many cases I was dealing with patients who needed an intellectual *point d'appui* if they were not to get totally lost in the darkness. I had to try to give provisional interpretations at least, so far as I was able, interspersing them with innumerable "perhapses" and "ifs" and "buts" and never stepping beyond the bounds of the picture lying before me. I always took good care to let the interpretation of each image tail

[72] Cf. "Aims of Modern Psychotherapy" in *The Practice of Psychotherapy, Coll. Works*, Vol. 16, pars. 101 ff.; and *Two Essays on Analytical Psychology, Coll. Works*, Vol. 7, pars. 343 ff.

off into a question whose answer was left to the free fantasy activity of the patient.

The chaotic assortment of images that at first confronted me reduced itself in the course of the work to certain well-defined themes and formal elements which repeated themselves in identical or analogous form with the most varied individuals. I mention, as the most salient characteristics, chaotic multiplicity and order; duality; the opposition of light and dark, upper and lower, right and left; the union of opposites in a third, the quaternity (square, cross), rotation (circle, sphere), and finally the centering process and a radial arrangement that usually followed some quaternary system. Triadic formations, apart from the *complexio oppositorum* in a third, were relatively rare and formed notable exceptions which could be explained by special conditions.[73] The centering process is, in my experience, the never-to-be-surpassed climax of the whole development,[74] and is characterized as such by the fact that it brings with it the greatest possible therapeutic effect. The typical features listed above go to the limits of abstraction, yet at the same time they are the simplest expressions of the formative principles here at work. In actual reality the patterns are infinitely more variegated and far more concrete than this would suggest. Their variety defies description. I can only say that there is probably no motif in any known mythology that does not at some time appear in these configurations. If there was any conscious knowledge of mythological motifs worth mentioning in my patients, it is left far behind by the ingenuities of creative fantasy. /73/

These facts show in an unmistakable manner how fantasies guided by unconscious regulators coincide with the records of man's mental activity as known to us from tradition and ethnological research. All the abstract features I have mentioned are in a certain sense conscious: everyone can count up to four and knows what a circle is and a square; but, as formative principles, these are unconscious and by the same token their psychological meaning is not conscious either. My most fundamental views and ideas derive from these experiences. First I made the observations, and only then did I hammer out my views. And so it is with the hand that guides the crayon or brush, the foot that executes the dance step, with the eye and the ear, with the word and the thought: a dark impulse is the ultimate arbiter of the pattern, an unconscious a priori precipitates itself into plastic form, and one has no inkling that another

[73] The same applies to the pentadic figures.
[74] So far as the development can be ascertained from the objective material.

person's consciousness is being guided by these same principles at the very point where one feels utterly exposed to the boundless subjective vagaries of chance. Over the whole procedure there seems to reign a dim foreknowledge not only of the pattern, but of its meaning.[75] Image and meaning are identical; and as the first takes shape, so the latter becomes clear. Actually the pattern needs no interpretation: it portrays its own meaning. There are cases where I can let interpretation go as a therapeutic requirement. Scientific knowledge, of course, is another matter. Here we have to elicit from the sum total of our experience certain concepts of the greatest possible general validity, which are not given a priori. This particular work entails a translation of the timeless, ever-present operative archetype into the scientific language of the present.

These experiences and reflections lead me to believe that there are certain collective unconscious conditions which act as regulators and stimulators of creative fantasy activity and call forth corresponding formations by availing themselves of the existing conscious material. They behave exactly like the motive forces of dreams, for which reason active imagination, as I have called this method, to some extent takes the place of dreams. The existence of these unconscious regulators—I sometimes refer to them as "dominants"[76] because of their mode of functioning—seemed to /74/ me so important that I based upon it my hypothesis of an impersonal collective unconscious. The most remarkable thing about this method, I felt, was that it did not involve a *reductio in primam figuram,* but rather a synthesis—supported by an attitude voluntarily adopted, though for the rest wholly natural—of passive conscious material and unconscious influences, hence a kind of spontaneous amplification of the archetypes. The images are not to be thought of as a reduction of conscious contents to their simplest denominator, as this would be the direct road to the primordial images which I said previously was unimaginable; they only make their appearance in the course of amplification.

On this natural amplification process I also base my method of eliciting the meaning of dreams, for dreams behave in exactly the same way as active imagination, only the support of conscious contents is lacking. To the extent that the archetypes intervene in the shaping of conscious contents by regulating, modifying, and motivating them, they act like the instincts. It is therefore very natural to suppose that these factors are connected with the instincts and to inquire whether the typical situational patterns which these

[75] Cf. *Psychology and Alchemy,* pp. 211 f.
[76] Cf. *Two Essays on Analytical Psychology,* par 151.

collective form-principles apparently represent are not in the end identical with the instinctual patterns, namely, with the patterns of behavior. I must admit that up to the present I have not got hold of any argument that would finally refute this possibility.

Before I pursue my reflections further, I must stress one aspect of the archetypes which will be obvious to anybody who has practical experience of these matters. That is, the archetypes have, when they appear, a distinctly numinous character which can only be described as "spiritual," if "magical" is too strong a word. Consequently this phenomenon is of the utmost significance for the psychology of religion. In its effects it is anything but unambiguous. It can be healing or destructive, but never indifferent, provided of course that it has attained a certain degree of clarity.[77] /75/ This aspect deserves the epithet "spiritual" above all else. It not infrequently happens that the archetype appears in the form of a *spirit* in dreams or fantasy products, or even comports itself like a ghost. There is a mystical aura about its numinosity, and it has a corresponding effect upon the emotions. It mobilizes philosophical and religious convictions in the very people who deemed themselves miles above any such fits of weakness. Often it drives with unexampled passion and remorseless logic towards its goal and draws the subject under its spell, from which despite the most desperate resistance he is unable, and finally no longer even willing, to break free, because the experience brings with it a depth and fullness of meaning that was unthinkable before. I fully appreciate the resistance that all rooted convictions are bound to put up against psychological discoveries of this kind. With more foreboding than real knowledge most people feel afraid of the menacing power that lies fettered in each of us, only waiting for the magic word to release it from the spell. This magic word, which always ends in "ism," works most successfully with those who have the least access to their interior selves and have strayed the furthest from their instinctual roots into the truly chaotic world of *collective consciousness*. /76/

---

[77] Occasionally it is associated with synchronistic or parapsychic effects. I mean by synchronicity, as I have explained elsewhere, the not uncommonly observed "coincidence" of subjective and objective happenings, which just cannot be explained causally, at least in the present state of our knowledge. On this premise astrology is based. These observations, like the astrological findings, are not generally accepted, though as we know this has never hurt the facts. I mention these special effects solely for the sake of completeness and solely for the benefit of those readers who have had occasion to convince themselves of the reality of parapsychic phenomena. /75/

from *THE HERO WITH A THOUSAND FACES*

JOSEPH CAMPBELL

THE HERO TODAY

All of which is far indeed from the contemporary view; for the democratic ideal of the self-determining individual, the invention of the power-driven machine, and the development of the scientific method of research, have so transformed human life that the long-inherited, timeless universe of symbols has collapsed. In the fateful, epoch-announcing words of Nietzsche's Zarathustra: "Dead are all the gods."[3] One knows the tale; it has been told a thousand ways. It is the hero-cycle of the modern age, the wonder-story of mankind's coming to maturity. The spell of the past, the bondage of tradition, was shattered with sure and mighty strokes. The dream-web of myth fell away; the mind opened to full waking consciousness; and modern man emerged from ancient ignorance, like a butterfly from its cocoon, or like the sun at dawn from the womb of mother night.

It is not only that there is no hiding place for the gods from the searching telescope and microscope; there is no such society any more as the gods once supported. The social unit is not a carrier of religious content, but an economic-political organization. Its ideals are not those of the hieratic pantomime, making visible on earth the forms of heaven, but of the secular state, in hard and unremitting competition for material supremacy and resources. Isolated societies, dream-bounded within a mythologically charged horizon, no longer exist except as areas to be exploited. And within the progressive societies themselves, every last vestige of /387/ the ancient human heritage of ritual, morality, and art is in full decay.

The problem of mankind today, therefore, is precisely the opposite to that of men in the comparatively stable periods of those great co-ordinating mythologies which now are known as lies. Then all meaning was in the group, in the great anonymous forms, none

Joseph Campbell, *The Hero With A Thousand Faces,* The Bollingen Series XVII (New York: Pantheon Books, 1949), 387-91. By permission of Bollingen Foundation, New York.

[3] Nietzsche, *Thus Spake Zarathustra,* 1. 22. 3.

in the self-expressive individual; today no meaning is in the group—none in the world: all is in the individual. But there the meaning is absolutely unconscious. One does not know toward what one moves. One does not know by what one is propelled. The lines of communication between the conscious and the unconscious zones of the human psyche have all been cut, and we have been split in two.

The hero-deed to be wrought is not today what it was in the century of Galileo. Where then there was darkness, now there is light; but also, where light was, there now is darkness. The modern hero-deed must be that of questing to bring to light again the lost Atlantis of the co-ordinated soul.

Obviously, this work cannot be wrought by turning back, or away, from what has been accomplished by the modern revolution; for the problem is nothing if not that of rendering the modern world spiritually significant—or rather (phrasing the same principle the other way round) nothing if not that of making it possible for men and women to come to full human maturity through the conditions of contemporary life. Indeed, these conditions themselves are what have rendered the ancient formulae ineffective, misleading, and even pernicious. The community today is the planet, not the bounded nation; hence the patterns of projected aggression which formerly served to co-ordinate the in-group now can only break it into factions. The national idea, with the flag as totem, is today an aggrandizer of the nursery ego, not the annihilator of an infantile situation. Its parody-rituals of the parade ground serve the ends of Holdfast, the tyrant dragon, not the God in whom self-interest is annihilate. And the numerous /388/ saints of this anticult—namely the patriots whose ubiquitous photographs, draped with flags, serve as official icons—are precisely the local threshold guardians (our demon Sticky-hair) whom it is the first problem of the hero to surpass.

Nor can the great world religions, as at present understood, meet the requirement. For they have become associated with the causes of the factions, as instruments of propaganda and self-congratulation. (Even Buddhism has lately suffered this degradation, in reaction to the lessons of the West.) The universal triumph of the secular state has thrown all religious organizations into such a definitely secondary, and finally ineffectual, position that religious pantomime is hardly more today than a sanctimonious exercise for Sunday morning, whereas business ethics and patriotism stand for the remainder of the week. Such a monkey-holiness is not what the functioning world requires; rather, a transmutation of the whole social order is necessary, so that through every detail and act of secular life the vitalizing image of the universal god-man who is actually immanent and effective in all of us may be somehow made known to consciousness.

And this is not a work that consciousness itself can achieve. Consciousness can no more invent, or even predict, an effective symbol than foretell or control tonight's dream. The whole thing is being worked out on another level, through what is bound to be a long and very frightening process, not only in the depths of every living psyche in the modern world, but also on those titanic battlefields into which the whole planet has lately been converted. We are watching the terrible clash of the Symplegades, through which the soul must pass—identified with neither side.

But there is one thing we may know, namely, that as the new symbols become visible, they will not be identical in the various parts of the globe; the circumstances of local life, race, and tradition must all be compounded in the effective forms. Therefore, it is necessary for men to understand, and be able to see, that through various symbols the same redemption is revealed. "Truth /389/ is one," we read in the Vedas; "the sages call it by many names." A single song is being inflected through all the colorations of the human choir. General propaganda for one or another of the local solutions, therefore, is superfluous—or much rather, a menace. The way to become human is to learn to recognize the lineaments of God in all of the wonderful modulations of the face of man.

With this we come to the final hint of what the specific orientation of the modern hero-task must be, and discover the real cause for the disintegration of all of our inherited religious formulae. The center of gravity, that is to say, of the realm of mystery and danger has definitely shifted. For the primitive hunting peoples of those remotest human millenniums when the sabertooth tiger, the mammoth, and the lesser presences of the animal kingdom were the primary manifestations of what was alien—the source at once of danger, and of sustenance—the great human problem was to become linked psychologically to the task of sharing the wilderness with these beings. An unconscious identification took place, and this was finally rendered conscious in the half-human, half-animal, figures of the mythological totem-ancestors. The animals became the tutors of humanity. Through acts of literal imitation—such as today appear only on the children's playground (or in the madhouse)—an effective annihilation of the human ego was accomplished and society achieved a cohesive organization. Similarly, the tribes supporting themselves on plant-food became cathected to the plant; the life-rituals of planting and reaping were identified with those of human procreation, birth, and progress to maturity. Both the plant and the animal worlds, however, were in the end brought under social control. Whereupon the great field of instructive wonder shifted—to the skies—and mankind enacted the great pantomime of the sacred moon-king, the sacred sun-king, the hieratic, planetary state, and the symbolic festivals of the world-regulating spheres.

Today all of these mysteries have lost their force; their symbols no longer interest our psyche. The notion of a cosmic law, which /390/ all existence serves and to which man himself must bend, has long since passed through the preliminary mystical stages represented in the old astrology, and is now simply accepted in mechanical terms as a matter of course. The descent of the Occidental sciences from the heavens to the earth (from seventeenth-century astronomy to nineteenth-century biology), and their concentration today, at last, on man himself (in twentieth-century anthropology and psychology), mark the path of a prodigious transfer of the focal point of human wonder. Not the animal world, not the plant world, not the miracle of the spheres, but man himself is now the crucial mystery. Man is that alien presence with whom the forces of egoism must come to terms, through whom the ego is to be crucified and resurrected, and in whose image society is to be reformed. Man, understood however not as "I" but as "Thou": for the ideals and temporal institutions of no tribe, race, continent, social class, or century, can be the measure of the inexhaustible and multifariously wonderful divine existence that is the life in all of us.

The modern hero, the modern individual who dares to heed the call and seek the mansion of that presence with whom it is our whole destiny to be atoned, cannot, indeed must not, wait for his community to cast off its slough of pride, fear, rationalized avarice, and sanctified misunderstanding. "Live," Nietzsche says, "as though the day were here." It is not society that is to guide and save the creative hero, but precisely the reverse. And so every one of us shares the supreme ordeal—carries the cross of the redeemer—not in the bright moments of his tribe's great victories, but in the silences of his personal despair. /391/

from THE MASKS OF GOD: PRIMITIVE MYTHOLOGY

JOSEPH CAMPBELL

THE ENIGMA OF THE INHERITED IMAGE

I. *The Innate Releasing Mechanism*

A number of popular moving-picture films have shown the amazing phenomenon of the laying and hatching of the eggs of the sea turtle. The female leaves the water and crawls to a point on the beach safely above the tide line, where she digs a hole, deposits hundreds of eggs, covers the nest, and turns back to the sea. After eighteen days a multitude of tiny turtles come flipping up through the sand and, like a field of sprinters at the crack of the gun, make for the heavily crashing waves as fast as they can, while gulls drop screaming from overhead to pick them off.

No more vivid representation could be desired of spontaneity and the quest for the not-yet-seen. There is no question here of learning, trial-and-error; nor are the tiny things afraid of the great waves. They know that they must hurry, know how to do it, and know precisely where they are going. And finally, when they enter the sea, they know immediately both how to swim and that swim they must.

Students of animal behavior have coined the term "innate releasing mechanism" (IRM) to designate the inherited structure in the nervous system that enables an animal to respond thus to a circumstance never experienced before, and the factor triggering the response they term a "sign stimulus" or "releaser." It is obvious that the living entity responding to such a sign cannot be said to be the individual, since the individual has had no previous /30/ knowledge of the object to which it is reacting. The recognizing and responding subject is, rather, some sort of trans- or super-individual, inhabiting and moving the living creature. Let us not speculate here about the metaphysics of this mystery; for, as Schopenhauer sagely remarks in his paper on *The Will in Nature,* "we are sunk in a sea of riddles and inscrutables, knowing and understanding neither what is around us nor ourselves."

Chicks with their eggshells still adhering to their tails dart for cover when a hawk flies overhead, but not when the bird is a gull or duck, heron or pigeon. Furthermore, if the wooden model of a hawk is drawn over their coop on a wire, they react as though it were alive—unless it be drawn backward, when there is no response.

Here we have an extremely precise image—never seen before, yet recognized with reference not merely to its form but to its form in motion, and linked, furthermore, to an immediate, unplanned, unlearned, and even unintended system of appropriate action: flight, to cover. The image of the inherited enemy is already sleeping in the nervous system, and along with it the well-proven reaction. Furthermore, even if all the hawks in the world were to vanish, their image would still sleep in the soul of the chick—never to be roused, however, unless by some accident of art; for example, a repetition of the clever experiment of the wooden hawk on a wire. With that (for a certain number of generations, at any rate) the obsolete reaction of the flight to cover would recur; and, unless we knew about the earlier danger of hawks to chicks, we should find the sudden eruption difficult to explain. "Whence," we might ask, "this abrupt seizure by an image to which there is no counterpart in the chicken's world? Living gulls and ducks, herons and pigeons, leave it cold; but the work of art strikes some very deep chord!"

Have we here a clue to the problem of the image of the witch in the nervous system of the child? Some psychologists would say so. C. G. Jung, for example, identifies two fundamentally different systems of unconsciously motivated response in the human being. One he terms the personal unconscious. It is based on a context of forgotten, neglected, or suppressed memory images derived from /31/ personal experience (infantile impressions, shocks, frustrations, satisfactions, etc.), such as Sigmund Freud recognized and analyzed in his therapy. The other he names the collective unconscious. Its contents—which he calls archetypes—are just such images as that of the hawk in the nervous system of the chick. No one has yet been able to tell us how it got there; but there it is!

"A personal image," he writes, "has neither archaic character nor collective significance, but expresses unconscious contents of a personal nature and a personally conditioned conscious inclination.

"The primary image (*urtümliches Bild*), which I have termed 'archetype,' is always collective, i.e. common to at least whole peoples or periods of history. The chief mythological motifs of all times and races are very probably of this order; for example, in the dreams and fantasies of neurotics of pure Negro stock I have been able to identify a series of motifs of Greek mythology.

"The primary image," he then suggests, "is a memory deposit, an engram, derived from a condensation of innumerable similar experiences . . . the psychic expression of an anatomically, physiologically determined natural tendency."

Jung's idea of the "archetypes" is one of the leading theories, today, in the field of our subject. It is a development of the earlier theory of Adolf Bastian (1826–1905), who recognized, in the course of his extensive travels, the uniformity of what he termed the "elementary ideas" (*Elementargedanke*) of mankind. Remarking also, however, that in the various provinces of human culture these ideas are differently articulated and elaborated, he coined the term "ethnic ideas" (*Völkergedanke*) for the actual, local manifestations of the universal forms. Nowhere, he noted, are the "elementary ideas" to be found in a pure state, abstracted from the locally conditioned "ethnic ideas" through which they are substantialized; but rather, like the image of man himself, they are to be known only by way of the rich variety of their extremely interesting, frequently startling, yet always finally recognizable inflections in the panorama of human life.

Two possibilities of emphasis are implicit in this observation of Bastian. The first we may term the psychological and the second /32/ the ethnological; and these can be taken to represent, broadly, the two contrasting points of view from which scientists, scholars, and philosophers have approached our subject.

"First," wrote Bastian, "the idea as such must be studied . . . and as second factor, the influence of climatic-geological conditions." Only after that, as a third factor, according to his view, could the influence upon one another of the various ethnic traditions throughout the course of history be profitably surveyed. Bastian, that is to say, stressed the psychological, spontaneous aspect of culture as primary; and this approach has been the usual one of biologists, medical men, and psychologists to the present day. Briefly stated, it assumes that there is in the structure and functioning of the psyche a certain degree of spontaneity and consequent uniformity throughout the history and domain of the human species—an order of psychological laws inhering in the structure of the body, which has not radically altered since the period of the Aurignacian caves and can be as readily identified in the jungles of Brazil as in the cafés of

Paris, as readily in the igloos of Baffin Land as in the harems of Marrakech.

But on the other hand, if climate, geography, and massive social forces are to be regarded as of more moment in the shaping of the ideas, ideals, fantasies, and emotions by which men live than the innate structures and capacities of the psyche, then a diametrically contrary philosophical position must be assumed. Psychology in this case becomes a function of ethnology; or, to quote one representative authority, A. R. Radcliffe-Brown, in his work on *The Andaman Islanders:*

> A society depends for its existence on the presence in the minds of its members of a certain system of sentiments by which the conduct of the individual is regulated in conformity with the needs of the society. Every feature of the social system itself and every event or object that in any way affects the well-being or the cohesion of the society becomes an object of this system of sentiments. *In human society the sentiments in question are not innate but are developed in the individual by the action of the society upon him* [italics mine]. The ceremonial customs of a society are a means by which the sentiments in question are given collective expression on appropri-/33/ate occasions. The ceremonial (i.e. collective) expression of any sentiment serves both to maintain it at the requisite degree of intensity in the mind of the individual and to transmit it from one generation to another. Without such expression the sentiments involved could not exist.*

It will be readily seen that in such a view the ceremonials and mythologies of the differing societies are in no sense manifestations of psychologically grounded "elementary ideas," common to the human race, but of interests locally conditioned; and the fundamental contrast of the two approaches is surely clear.

Was the little girl's reaction to the idea of the witch that she had conjured into her mind comparable to the chick's reaction to the fashioned image of a hawk? Or should we say, rather, that because she had been brought up on the fairy tales collected by the Brothers Grimm, she had learned to associate certain imagined dangers with a German fictional character and these alone were the cause of her fright?

Before being satisfied that we know the answer, we must consider seriously the now well-proven fact that the human nervous system was the governor, guide and controller of a nomadic hunter, foraging for his food and protecting himself and his family from becom-

* A. R. Radcliffe-Brown, *The Andaman Islanders* (New York: Cambridge University Press). Reprinted by permission of the publisher.—Ed.

ing food in a very dangerous world of animals, for the first 600,000 years of its development; whereas it has been serving comparatively safe and sane farmers, merchants, professors, and their children for scarcely 8000 years (a segment of less than 1½ per cent of the known arc). Who will claim to know what sign stimuli smote our releasing mechanisms when our names were not Homo sapiens but Pithecanthropus and Plesianthropus, or perhaps even—millenniums earlier—Dryopithecus? And who that has knowledge of the numerous vestigial structures of our anatomy, surviving from the days when we were beasts (for example, the muscles of the caudal vertebrae that once wagged our tail), would doubt that in the central nervous system comparable vestiges must remain: images sleeping, whose releasers no longer appear in nature—but might occur in art? /34/

from *BASIC CHRISTIAN BELIEFS*

W. BURNET EASTON, JR.

3. ORIGINAL SIN

The understanding of man's fundamental nature as a Self in an intolerable isolation which he tries to overcome also illuminates the Christian doctrine of original sin. Unfortunately there is considerable confusion in the minds of many people today about what Christianity means by sin. Partly because of the ecclesiastical legalism of the Roman Catholic Church, and partly because of the moralistic legalism of much of Protestantism, the average man tends to think of "sins" (in the plural) and usually in terms of the moralities: drinking, swearing, stealing, adultery, lying, murder, and so forth. Emphatically these are not sins in the Christian sense, although they may be, and usually are, external expressions of the deeper sin. The fundamental sin according to the Bible is pride, egocentricity, self-deification, and the insistence that each of us is the final arbiter of what is good for him, an insistence that reveals a lack of trust in and submission to God. It is evidenced in the fact that, in seeking an answer to the perennial question, "What is going to happen to me?", we seek the good in terms which we, in the privacy of our own selfish judgment, have decided to be good. If I steal from a man, it is because I have decided in the privacy of my own judgment that my interests are more important than his interests. To make such a judgment is to assume, blasphemously, the divine right to judge between him and me. God alone has that right; for me to assume it is either actually to deny God, or to deny his goodness and trustworthiness. Thus sin is a form of self-deification.

This theme runs all through the Bible from beginning to end /89/ but it is most explicitly stated in the second Creation story. In this story Adam and Eve are condemned not because they stole some fruit and ate an apple. The temptation of the serpent was: "You will not die. For God knows that when you eat of it your eyes

W. Burnet Easton, Jr., *Basic Christian Beliefs* (Philadelphia: The Westminster Press, 1957), pp. 89-91. Reprinted by special permission of the author.

will be opened, and *you will be like God,* knowing good and evil."
(Gen. 3:4, 5.) The temptation to which Adam and Eve succumbed
was the temptation to a pride and a self-deification which refuses to
submit to God. It is a revolt of the creature against the Creator.
Such a revolt cannot be successful in the long run if God is God;
it is blasphemy which must be punished. And the punishment that
followed, according to the story, is that Adam and Eve were driven
from Paradise where they had an "original-we" relationship and
security with both God and all the rest of the created order. Now
they have to struggle to live in opposition to the world. It is highly
significant that it was not until Adam and Eve had eaten of the
fruit, that is, had defied God, that "they knew that they were
naked; and . . . hid themselves" (Gen. 3:7, 8). In other words the
"original-we" was broken and they became conscious of themselves
as individuals and of their aloneness.

The Biblical understanding of man as revealed in the story of
the Fall fits the analysis of man we have already made. As we have
seen, man is a Self, conscious of himself, because he belongs to a
world to which he is opposed at the same time and, therefore, he is
in an intolerable state of aloneness which he tries to overcome by
establishing we-relationships. But because of man's given situation
there are, in every we-relationship that man tries to establish, elements of self-concern, of selfishness, and of self-assertive pride. At
the heart of every altruistic and community-creating act there is a
corrupting seed of selfishness and will-to-power. To admit this is not
to deny the importance of altruistic and community-creating acts;
if it were not for them, life would be intolerable. To love our
neighbor as ourselves is the second commandment and the fact that
we can satisfy our own self-concern only by community-creating
(neighbor-loving) acts is seen, with the eyes of faith, as part of God's
grace making human life possible. Nevertheless, in every act of
community and brotherhood there is a /90/ selfish motive. It is
revealed in all areas of life. It is obvious in the bully or the dictator,
whether he is in government, or in the shop, or in the home. It is
equally the motive of the Uriah Heep and the clinging vine who
cultivate their weakness in order to get protection. It appears in the
family and in all love-relationships. In his book *Sexual Tensions in
Marriage,* Th. van de Velt points out that in every healthy home
there is a continual war for domination, which, if completely won
by one party, will cause a breakup of the home because the winner
loses respect for the loser, and the loser loses respect for himself or
herself. It appears even in religion. At the highest religious level it
involves self-sacrifice in order to win the approval of God (which is

legitimate). At lower levels it involves performing specified acts of ritual, or doing works in order to try to manipulate God to fulfill our selfish desires (which is both illegitimate and impossible). None of us ever completely escapes this element of self-concern and will-to-power, for it arises from the givens in human nature. It is what is meant by original sin.

Original sin is *original* not because long ago one historical man and woman, Adam and Eve, the historical original parents of all subsequent mankind, first committed a sin and then, by a process of biological inheritance, passed it on to their descendants forever. Such a conception makes God a fiend. Rather, it is that Adam and Eve are the prototypes of all men and women, symbolically describing the eternal human situation. We all go through the Adam and Eve experience of breaking the innocence and security of the "original-we" and of becoming self-conscious by discovering we are Selves belonging to a world to which we are opposed at the same time. And the first act in that discovery is the Adam and Eve act of self-assertion. Original sin is original because it arises from an original given nature without which man would not be man. /91/

from *GODS AND MEN: THE ORIGINS OF WESTERN CULTURE*

HENRY BAMFORD PARKES

In some of his writings, especially in the letter to the Romans, which was apparently planned as a formal statement of his beliefs, /406/ Paul went on to sketch the outlines of a cosmology. The enjoyment of the kingdom of heaven and of eternal life was man's proper destiny, according to the purposes of God and the nature of the world he had created. But the first man had abused the power of choice which God had given him by preferring his own selfish wishes to the will of God, and hence he and his descendants had forfeited their freedom and come under the domination of their own carnal passions, incurring death as the penalty of their sins. The God of Paul was the God of the Jewish prophets, the ruler of all mankind, but at the same time the especial deity of the Jews, whom he had chosen as the recipients of revelation; and the Mosaic law, now abrogated, was of divine origin. But God had also revealed himself to the gentiles indirectly through his works, and in the end both Jews and gentiles came under the same condemnation: all alike had failed to live in conformity with the divine order. Finally Jesus Christ, who was both the Messiah promised by the Jewish prophets and "the image of the invisible God, the firstborn of every creature,"[7] had canceled the sin of Adam, paid the penalty of human guilt by his death on the cross, and made it possible for men to regain their primal perfection and the immortality associated with it. Paul's expectations for the future seem to have been largely derived from the traditional Jewish eschatology, though dissociated from Jewish nationalism. Unlike some other early theologians, especially the author of the gospel of John, he declared that Christ would physically return and establish a terrestrial millennium. Membership in his kingdom, having been forfeited by the Jews, would be the privilege of Christians. This would be followed at a

Reprinted from *Gods and Men: The Origins of Western Culture* (pp. 406-410), by permission of Alfred A. Knopf, Inc. Copyright © 1959 by Henry Bamford Parkes.

[7] Colossians, i, 15.

later date by the end of the world, the resurrection of all men, and the day of judgment. A curious passage in the second letter to the Thessalonians suggests that Christ's second coming would be immediately preceded by a time of troubles in which the forces of evil would no longer be restrained by the beneficent authority of the Roman Empire.[8]

The Pauline vision of human destiny has been one of the decisive factors in the shaping of the Western mind. It was the principal medium by which the Messianic myth of the Jewish prophets was transmitted to the non-Jewish world and transformed /407/ from a nationalistic aspiration into a promise for all humanity. Paul was a faithful follower of Jesus, and the core of his religion was his acceptance of the gospel ethic; but it is probable that Jesus' teachings would quickly have been forgotten if Paul had not given the gospel experience a cosmological foundation. Yet Paul's theology was replete with problems, and during the nineteen centuries that have elapsed since he wrote his letters, Christians have rarely ceased to argue about what he really meant. Armies of learned divines have compiled libraries of commentaries, and during the age of Luther and Calvin the peoples of the Western world actually became divided into hostile armed camps separated by variant interpretations. If salvation came by faith, then why should the Christian perform good works? If only those whom God had elected could be saved, then why should the individual make any effort on his own behalf? How could one reconcile Christian freedom with the obligations of morality, divine grace with human responsibility, the fatherhood of God with the dogma of predestination? Was it just that all men should inherit the sin of Adam, even infants being held guilty of rebellion against God? And why could sin be canceled only by the death of Christ on the cross? By suggesting such questions, the letters of Paul evoked a dreary and apparently interminable series of controversies, accompanied during the sixteenth and seventeenth centuries by wars and persecutions and all the evils of theological hatred. Yet if one remembers that Pauline theology began not with logic but with subjective experience, and that its primary intention was not to present a rational picture of the universe or to justify God's ways to man but to explain the meaning of the Christian attitude, then it is no longer difficult to understand.

In preaching that all men were sinners Paul was not trying to envelop all human life in a pall of gloom or expressing a vindictive

[8] II Thessalonians, ii, 7-8.

and neurotic hatred of the world and the flesh; he was stating a psychological fact. Man was a divided creature, driven by egotistical passions that conflicted with his own moral principles, capable of envisaging ideals, but unable to realize them. Obviously he fell short of his proper perfection, and this failure was written large in the pages of history with their melancholy record of violence, lawlessness, treachery, and unnatural vice. For Paul, unlike the Hellenic philosophers, the misery of mankind was owing /408/ not merely to evil, but to sin; man was morally responsible for his own shortcomings. But this emphasis on human guilt was a necessary consequence of the Christian exaltation of human destiny. God had originally given man the power of achieving perfection, and man's failure resulted not from the nature of the world but from his own abuse of the freedom with which God had endowed him. The root of evil lay not in matter, as Hellenic philosophy had declared, but in the human will, and this was capable of regeneration. By what means the original sin of Adam had been transmitted to his descendants, and how this doctrine of inherited guilt could be reconciled with the justice and benevolence of God, were questions which perplexed a long succession of theologians, but with which Paul was not concerned.

All men deserved death for their sins, but Christians could enjoy eternal life because the penalty had been paid by the death of Jesus Christ. This doctrine of the atonement was briefly stated in several of Paul's letters, thus transforming the cross, which for all inhabitants of the Roman Empire had been a symbol of the utmost degradation, into the instrument of man's salvation. There have been many different attempts to explain the atonement, most of them fantastic and repugnant. Christ's death has been interpreted as a satisfaction of God's honor or of God's justice or even as the payment of a debt to the devil. According to the "mousetrap" theory developed by Latin theologians of the third and fourth centuries, the devil had acquired power over humanity, but was tricked by the crucifixion into relinquishing it, Christ's flesh serving as the bait of a trap. Christianity has, in fact, never succeeded in rationalizing the atonement; yet it has never found it possible to abandon it. The true *raison d'être* of the doctrine is to be found not in the nature of God, but in the nature of man. The sense of guilt is one of the most potent and destructive forces in the human psyche, and man cannot enjoy spiritual health and security unless he is purged of it. Primitive man had satisfied his sense of guilt by transferring it to a scapegoat who was put to death in atonement for the misdeeds of the community. The Christian could rest assured of the love of God only because of his conviction that Jesus Christ, a man who was himself without sin, had suffered death as a universal scapegoat for the sins of others.

If all men were corrupted from birth, then they could achieve /409/ salvation only through divine grace, not by any effort of their own. The initiative in the process of conversion must come from God, not from man's perverted will, and only those whom God had chosen could be saved. Later theologians expounded these doctrines of predestination and election as exercises in logic, thus making God appear a monster of cruelty. In the fulfillment of his own inscrutable purposes he had decreed that only a tiny fraction of mankind would enjoy salvation while the remainder would be condemned to eternal torment for sins they could not avoid committing. Once again it is necessary to turn from logic to psychology. The Pauline doctrine of election was a deduction from the subjective experience of conversion. A man became a Christian not by making a conscious decision, but by submitting to emotional forces that brought about a transformation of his entire personality and seemed to him to come from an external spiritual power—according to Paul, from divine grace. Paul's own acceptance of Christianity had been brought about by an emotional cataclysm in the form of a vision of the risen Jesus; and the feeling of being called by the Holy Spirit was shared by his converts. Thus, faith appeared as the gift of God to those whom he had chosen; and as the essence of faith was trust in Jesus and an acceptance of his ethical values, it was necessarily followed by good works. Paul occasionally found it advisable to explain that Christian freedom did not mean a repudiation of all morality, but there was no problem in his own mind about the relationship between faith and works. Because the Christian was guided by love, he would spontaneously display goodness. With the transformation of his personality he would no longer feel obligated to obey a legal or moral code, but the sense of moral duty had been transcended rather than abrogated. /410/

from *ANTHROPOLOGY AND HUMAN NATURE*

M. F. ASHLEY MONTAGU

3. MAN—AND HUMAN NATURE

Ideas taught do not have greater power than they receive from those who are taught.

FRANCESCO SANCHEZ (1552-1632)
Quod Nihil Scitur, Lyons, 1581

What is man? What is human nature? These are questions which have exercised the speculative faculty of human beings ever since they became capable of self-reflection. As we examine the cultures of humanity, that is to say, the man-made parts of the human environment, or as Sir John Myres has put it in *Political Ideas of the Greeks,* what remains of men's past working on their present to shape their future, we find that the answers to these questions are usually interrelated in a special way. We find that the answer to the question "What is man?" is usually returned in terms of what man's nature is conceived to be.

In other words, we at once perceive that most cultures begin with a conception of human nature and then proceed to fashion their man according to it. Man is custom made, tailored according to the pattern prevailing in his particular culture. And as students of human society have shown, man's societies are remarkably various. Within the great range of human cultures the views held concerning the nature of man are almost as numerous as the leaves in Vallombrosa. In point of fact we know astonishingly little of the views concerning the nature of man held by non-literate peoples. In most cases we know more about what they think of their supernaturals than we do about what they think of the nature of man. But we do know a little, and together with what we have learned of the views of man held by the literate cultures of the world, we can say that these well-nigh exhaust the envisageable possibilities. A comparative study of such "man-views", as they may be called,

M. F. Ashley Montagu, *Anthropology and Human Nature* (Boston: Porter Sargent, 1957), pp. 28-42. Reprinted by special permission.

has never been made. It would be most revealing. The nearest to it that we have at the present time are the studies in culture and personality that anthropologists have initiated in recent years. Such studies, in which the attention is largely focussed on child-rearing practices and their relation to the development of personality, throw considerable light upon the "man-views" of different cultures, and represent, perhaps, the best means available to us of discovering the nature of those views.

For the cultures of the western world the work of psychoanalytically oriented investigators has proved equally illuminating. There has been not merely a convergence of interest but an increasingly active and fruitful partnership between anthropologists and psychiatrists. There is every promise that this collaboration will grow and /28/ increase, and that it will have the most beneficial effects upon the social and medical sciences to the great advantage of humanity. I am convinced that the healthy course upon which we are now embarked will lead to the discovery that medicine is possibly more of a social science than it is by many at present allowed to be.

I should like here to consider the conceptions of man and of human nature which prevail in the western world. There are several reasons why at this time we should pause critically to examine these beliefs.

In the first place, it is a good practice, from time to time, to hang a question mark on the beliefs we take most for granted, for they may in fact be wholly or partly erroneous. When subjected to such questioning many of our most entrenched beliefs are found to be so encrusted with age and fortified by rationalization that they have become impervious to any but the most critical examination. In the second place, such beliefs may be very damaging without our knowing that they are. In the third place, while it is seldom possible to trace the origins of many cultural traditions, it *is* possible to trace something of the complex history of the "man-view" so widely held throughout the western world, and hence, if we are in error, we may yet learn something of the route by which we arrived at what may be described as our compulsive enslavement to destructive certainties—the very edge of doom. In the fourth place, as a consequence of the labors of many workers in the medical, psychiatric, social, and biological fields, a great deal of largely unintegrated knowledge has been accumulated which renders a revaluation of our traditional "man-view" urgently necessary.

By "traditional" is to be understood not only the beliefs that we have inherited from antiquity, but also those of more recent vintage which have in any way contributed to the traditional complex of beliefs.

Can we give a brief statement which fairly represents the essence of this traditional complex of beliefs?

A very short statement would be that in the western world it is generally believed man is a "cussed" and "ornery" creature. There is good and evil in him, but the good is so shot through with the evil that one must constantly be policing the evil in order to give the good an opportunity to express itself. Child-rearing practices, education, religion, indeed most, if not all, of man's major social institutions testify to the pervasiveness of this view of human nature.

Most of the trouble in which man finds himself is held to be due to his inherent brattishness. Hence the necessity of devising social controls calculated to keep the brute in him in check so that the amount of trouble into which he gets is kept to more or less manageable proportions. /29/

How old are these views in the western tradition? They appear to be as old as the oldest traceable traditions of the west. In the Old Testament the tradition of man's innate iniquity is already established. "Behold, I was shapen in iniquity; and in sin did my mother conceive me." So it is written in *Psalm* 51:5. This tradition was largely reinforced and supplemented in the west with the spread of Christianity which at once brought the teachings of the Old and New Testaments, plus the addition of Greek pessimism, to weigh upon the spirit of western man. This new teaching gave western man a much-needed explanation for the evil he observed within himself and about him. The Hebraeo-Christian-Greek tradition was largely the work of its chief syncretist and architect, the divinely obsessed, Jesus-intoxicated, uncompromising zealot, Saul called Paul. It is to the interpretation given to the teachings of Jesus by St. Paul, rather than to those teachings themselves that Christianity owes its basic form and much of its content. It is to St. Paul that the western world is indebted for the peculiar development of the doctrine of Original Sin and the inherent wickedness of man—a dogma, so far as we know, not even remotely suggested by anything Jesus ever said or did.*

---

* The doctrine of Original Sin, in its various forms, enshrines the belief that the sin of Adam "was the sin of Human Nature (Rom. v. 12-21) and inheres as habitual sin in all who share in that nature by bodily generation." "It must be noted that the Church repudiates and abhors the doctrine that concupiscence [a general propensity towards an uncontrolled love of oneself and of creatures] is itself original sin or that man is wicked by the very condition of his nature as such or that original sin is an essential corruption of the soul." Donald Attwater (editor), *A Catholic Dictionary.* /30/

St. Paul's teaching that the law is spiritual but that man is carnal, sold under sin; that in his flesh "dwelleth no good thing," but that sin dwelleth in him (Rom. 7:14-24), was systematically elaborated by the Church Fathers, to become accepted doctrine throughout the length and breadth of Christendom. Jansenism and Puritanism are two forms, by no means extreme, of this doctrine, the one holding that man becomes progressively more evil as he lives, and the other that the proof of man's inherent evil nature lies in his apparently unlimited capacity for enjoyment. Jonathan Edwards (1703-1758), for example, was quite certain that "In Adam's fall We sinned all", and that from the consequences of this sin there was no escape except by virtue of divine grace.

Charles Wesley (1707-1788), who wrote more than six thousand Methodist hymns, enjoined parents in one of them:

> "To time our every smile or frown
> To mark the bounds of good and ill,
> And beat the pride of nature down,
> And subjugate his rising will." /30/

And Hannah More (1745-1833), the English bluestocking, praised the dictum that children should be taught they are "naturally depraved creatures," and went on to add that a stroll in the public gardens on Sunday evening or attendance at a sacred concert were to be condemned as sinful.

As H. J. Muller has remarked in *The Uses of the Past:*

"Throughout Christian history the conviction that man's birthright is sin has encouraged an unrealistic acceptance of remedial social evils, or even a callousness about human suffering. It helps to explain the easy acceptance of slavery and serfdom, and a record of religious atrocity unmatched by any other high religion."

> "Have 2000 years of saying mass
> Gone as far as poison gas?
> Or taken us further, with aplomb,
> To genuflect before the atom bomb?"

To explain the existence of evil, the common appeal of many early peoples has been to a "fall" from a prior state of perfection. Nothing could be more natural than such an explanation. It is found in early Chaldean legends. And Hesiod in *Works and Days* tells how "the golden race . . . as gods were wont to live;" but Pandora ensnared her husband Epimetheus, in disobedience of the divine command, to open the box with which she had been presented by the gods, whereupon trouble and sorrow escaped into the world, leaving only hope behind.

The early and widespread beliefs in "the fall", in doctrines of inherent natural depravity, or the original sinfulness of human nature, have enjoyed so wide an appeal, we may suspect, because they have served to shift the responsibility for man's evil behavior from himself to his inherent nature. As a self he can strive to be good, but always in the presence of the dangerous undertow of his evil and destructive impulses, which are constantly threatening to pull him under.

The secular experience of humanity during the last 2000 years, the internecine wars, the bloodshed, plunder and treachery, the general inhumanity of man to man, has in almost every way served to confirm the Church Fathers' view of the natural depravity of man.

The "nasty brute" view of man which is developed in Thomas Hobbes' (1588-1679) *Leviathan* (1651) stated the rationalist viewpoint very clearly. Man, argued Hobbes, is simply the motions of the organism, and man is by nature a selfishly individualistic animal at constant war with all other men. Except for the 18th century Enlightenment interlude, this view of man's nature has enjoyed uninterrupted sovereignty up to the present day. What is more, it has re-/31/ ceived the validation of two separate scientific disciplines, Darwinian evolutionary theory and Freudian psychology.

Life in the state of nature, the Darwinians convincingly showed, is a struggle for existence, characterized by ruthless competition. Conflict and combat is the rule, indeed, the law of nature. In the social-economic context of the day, the survival of the fittest was taken to mean not the surival of the fit but the survival of the fightingest (or anyone with an income of over $2500 per annum); the weakest, it was asserted, went to the wall and the strongest took all the prizes. Nature was red in tooth and claw, and though it shrieked against the creed of man, man was still a part and a product of nature.

In a famous article, published in February 1888, which became known as "The Struggle for Life Manifesto," Thomas Henry Huxley put the viewpoint he so ably represented in these forceful words: "From the point of view of the moralist, the animal world is on about the same level as a gladiator's show. The creatures are fairly well treated, and set to fight—whereby the strongest, the swiftest and the cunningest live to fight another day. The spectator has no need to turn his thumbs down, as no quarter is given."

Numberless such statements could be cited from the authorities of the day. In our own time a world famous anthropologist, and one of the kindliest of men, Sir Arthur Keith (1866-1955), could remark in *The Place of Prejudice in Civilization* that: "Nature keeps her orchard healthy by pruning; war is her pruning-hook. We cannot dispense with her services. This harsh and repugnant forecast of man's future is wrung from me. The future of my dreams is a warless world."

Students of the human mind have been no less influenced by Darwinian theory than students of the evolution of the human body. Any competent comparative anatomist could demonstrate the evidences of structures long useless in man but quite functional in his ancestors; and, of course, most of man's anatomical characters he held in common with his nearest living relatives, the great apes. It was to be expected, then, that his psychological endowment would also exhibit some persisting evidences of his lowly origins.

It was true that man was something more than a beast, yet it was equally true that he was not less than a beast, that he was still in part beast, and in spite of such humanity as he was capable of achieving, it was only too evident that the beast in him would keep on creeping out. This viewpoint is still widely held at the present time—whether the beastliness is of the Passionate Pauline or of the Dismal Darwinist variety.

This general viewpoint has received what is perhaps its most striking reinforcement from a source which undoubtedly represents the most insightful contribution to our understanding of human /32/ nature in the history of humanity. I refer to the psychoanalytic theories of Sigmund Freud (1856-1939).

Born three years before the publication of *The Origin of Species,* Freud grew up in the Darwinian age, and was himself a thoroughgoing Darwinist. He was a product of the Hebraeo-Christian tradition, of the period of Franz-Josef and the Victorian age, the chief concern of which was the preoccupation with morality, in which the two elemental forces of Love and Death fought with each other for supremacy. It is not surprising that Freud was unable to avoid structuring what he perceived of the dynamics of the human mind in terms of the dynamics of the human society with which he was familiar, precisely as the Darwinians were unable to avoid seeing nature in terms of the competitive struggle for existence which prevailed in 19th century England. There is nothing new in the discovery that we tend to see the world according to the kingdom that is within us, and the kingdom that is within us is for the most part likely to be the one in which we have been socialized.

Freud conceived of the mental life of man as the expression principally of the reciprocal interplay of two basic instincts, the one Eros or Love, and the other Thanatos or Death. What began, as Freud himself put it in *Beyond the Pleasure Principle,* as a speculative "often far-fetched idea" terminated as an article of faith in Freud's final work. Exploring the "idea out of curiosity to see whither it will lead" Freud became so enamored of the Death Instinct that thereafter he was unable to resist the tendency to see death and destruction wherever he could. This proceeded to such an extent in Freud that he was quite unable to perceive the answer to the question which he said "We do not know how to answer, and therefore we should feel relieved if the whole structure of our arguments were to prove erroneous. The opposition of ego (or death) instincts and sexual (life) instincts would then disappear, and the repetition-compulsion would also lose the significance we have attributed to it."

The problem is again stated in Freud's last published work, *An Outline of Psychoanalysis.* He writes: "If we suppose that living things appeared later than inanimate ones and arose out of them, then the death instinct agrees with the formula that we have stated, to the effect that instincts tend toward a return to an earlier state. We are unable to apply the formula to Eros (the love instinct). That would be to imply that living substance had once been a unity but had subsequently been torn apart and was now tending toward re-union."

In a matrix of divisiveness, death, and destruction, it is understandable why Freud should have failed to see the answer—which almost any elementary student of biology could have given him—to the question he asked. Freud here presents a striking illustration of /33/ the dangers which arise from becoming too enamoured with theory, namely, the resulting insensibility to facts.

Of course living substance had once been a unity, and we see this unity at a complex level in the single cell; the "tearing apart" is seen in the process of fission, in the one cell coming into being from the other, and the "tending toward re-union," we see not merely in the conjugal behavior of organisms but in the tendency of organisms to relate to each other, as exhibited in the innate tendency of one organism or cell to react in a definite manner with another organism or cell—a process which has been called *prototaxis* by I. E. Wallin in *Symbionticism and the Origin of Species.*

Organisms are environmental necessities of each other. The fact that all living organisms tend to form social aggregates, that is, to interact with each other in a mutually beneficial manner, is proof of the deep-seated nature of this universal drive. I have elsewhere suggested that *the fundamentally social nature of all living things has its origin in the reproductive relationship between genitor and offspring;* in the fact that the life of either one or the other is at some time dependent upon the potential or actual being of the other; and that the social relationships existing between organisms up to and including man represent the largely unconscious development of the interdependent relationship between mother and child as experienced in the reproductive state.

Reproduction, in sexual forms, is a result of sexual union. The tendency of life is not to destroy itself but to reproduce and maintain itself. Sexual conjugation and reproduction are related not simply as cause and effect, in that order, but conjugation occurs as an effect of reproduction. The "repetition compulsions" of which Freud speaks, the desire to return to the unitary state, the drive toward union, arises out of the fact that all living things originate from other living things. The drive to be together is an expression of the desire to be united with one's kind, to be unified without being reduced to uniformity.

I wish to suggest here that in our tradition, up to the present time, the basic assumption concerning the nature of human nature, namely, that it is either wholly or partially evil, in reality represents the error of mistaking the effect for the cause. The evidence indicates that the evil in man is not the cause of his behavior but the effect of the behavior of others upon him.

I know of no evidence which will withstand critical examination that any human being is born with the slightest element of evil within him, whether that evil be called "original sin" or a "drive or tendency to destruction." If there is anyone anywhere who can produce such evidence, I challenge him to do so, I do not think it can be produced. /34/

The tradition of inherent human depravity is an unsound one, and it is one that has been extremely damaging in its human and social effects. The day is, perhaps, not far removed when humanity will look back upon its "unregenerate" view of itself as an unfortunate phase of its development during what may be called its trial-and-error period. The first million years, it would seem, are the hardest. We shall do well to recall that in the continuum of life man as a species is but a flash in the pan, the most recent of nature's experiments, a creature that, with somewhat oafish arrogance, has so prematurely named itself *Homo sapiens,* when the more appropriate appelation at the present time would be *Homo sap,* with the *-iens* to be added when it has been earned. Humanity is in the childhood

of its development—it has yet to achieve maturity. Man, a muta-
tional accident, has inherited great riches which he has not yet
learned to use. Nature's most favored child, he behaves like a spoiled
brat. He has to learn to grow up. Will he succeed?

That human beings possess the potentialities for great wisdom
is admitted, even by those who in the searing light of the hydrogen
bomb have concluded that the goose is cooked—or is it vaporized?
As a matter of pure practical common sense I should have thought
that the only philosophically tenable position for a pessimist, these
days, is optimism.

Freud certainly entertained grave doubts as to man's future. Toward the end of his life he grew more pessimistic than ever. In
Civilization and Its Discontents Freud said, almost literally in the
words of Thomas Hobbes: "Men are not gentle friendly creatures
wishing for love . . . a powerful measure of desire for aggression
has to be reckoned as part of their instinctual endowment . . .
Homo homini lupus; who has the courage to dispute it in the face
of all the evidence in his own life and in history? This aggressive
cruelty usually lies in wait for some provocation, or else it steps
into the service of some other purpose, the aim of which might as
well have been achieved by milder measures. In circumstances that
favour it, when those forces in the mind which ordinarily inhibit
it cease to operate, it also manifests itself spontaneously and reveals
men as savage beasts to whom the thought of sparing their own
kind is alien. Anyone who calls to mind the atrocities of the early
migrations, of the invasion by the Huns or by the so-called Mongols
under Jenghiz Khan and Tamurlane, of the sack of Jerusalem by
the pious crusaders, even indeed the horrors of the last world-war,
will have to bow his head humbly before the truth of this view of
man."

It is, perhaps, not unfair to say that the view of man here en-
shrined by Freud has had a powerful influence upon psychiatric
theory and practice. And this Freudian view of man has served, of
/35/ course, to give the final seal of approval to the traditional
conception of human nature.

Must we humbly bow our heads, as Freud suggests, to the truth of
this so frequently reiterated and reinforced tradition concerning the
innate aggressiveness of man? I would suggest that while the scientific attitude should embrace a certain amount of humility, it is by
no means a part of that attitude to bow one's head even in the face
of the so-called facts, for a fact is at best little more than an interpretation, the consensus of those who *should* know. Only too often
facts, and even laws of nature, turn out to be nothing but theories
which have been smuggled across the border without benefit of the

proper customs examination as to their right to enter the realm of fact. The proper attitude in the face of facts or theories is not belief or disbelief, but dispassionate inquiry.

Freud expressed the belief of the greater part of western tradition when he wrote that "men are not gentle, friendly creatures wishing for love," but that they have a "constitutional tendency to aggression against one another." The question we have to ask is: What is the evidence for these statements?

The answer we are given is: The behavior of human beings. Human beings are hostile to one another, they hate, betray, destroy, kill, and murder. The human record, it is alleged, provides a ghastly record of man's constitutional aggressiveness.

Let us examine these allegations. It is beyond dispute that the human record provides abundant proof of human aggressiveness. But what that record does not provide is proof of its innateness. And here it may be pointed out that when Freud uses the word "constitutional" he uses it incorrectly, as many others have done before and since, as equivalent to "innate." Whereas the fact is that constitution represents the realization of the organism as an expression of the interaction between its genetic endowment and the environment. Similarly, heredity is not constituted by genetic endowment, but by genetic endowment as developed under the modifying influence of the environment. What the organism inherits is a genetic endowment *and* an environment.

The genetic endowment of man is unique, for it represents the most plastic system of potentialities for developing capacities which we recognize as uniquely human. In essence, these capacities may be summed up in one word, namely, *educability*. Educability is, indeed, *the* species character of man. The evidence is quite clear that everything we know and do *as human beings* we have had to learn, which means that we have had to be consciously taught by other human beings.

Man is not born with a built-in-system of responses to the environment, as are most other creatures. On the other hand, man is born /36/ with a built in system of plastic potentialities which under environmental stimulation are capable of being caused to respond in a large variety of different ways.

What we have traditionally understood as human nature, and what we understand human nature to be to this day, is not constituted by our genetic endowment, which may be called *primary potential human nature,* but the expression of the potentialities constituting that endowment under the influence of the human environment, that is, *secondary human nature.* It is secondary human nature that we know as *human nature,* and this human nature is not built in but is *bred* into us. Primary human nature we see overtly in the early infant's expression of the basic needs—and generally we see in them only what we are prepared to see.

Is there a basic need for aggression? Is there such a thing as an aggressive drive? Has anyone ever observed "aggressive instincts," as Freud calls them, in human beings or the "love of aggression in individuals" as an expression of primary nature? I know of no one who has done so, for "the tendency to aggression" and the "love of aggression" of which Freud and others speak is not observable at any time in any human being who has not secondarily acquired it.

A distinguished psychiatrist, Karl Menninger, in a widely read book, *Love Against Hate,* has poured scorn upon sociologists, anthropologists, and others whose psychological ground work is relatively deficient" for regarding aggressiveness as "The result of 'the culture' in which the individual lives. They make such nonsensical propositions as that all aggression is the result of frustration. Anyone who has had his toe stepped on, which is certainly not a frustration, knows how inadequate such a formula is. Furthermore, it [we take the "it" here to refer to the sociologist or anthropologist], completely ignores the question of where the aggressive energy comes from which is provoked by the frustration, and this is what the instinct theory attempts to answer."

It is an excellent rule not to step on anyone's toes, for what I had thought were obvious reasons. I shall do my best not to do so. But it seems to me, if I may mix a metaphor, that the writer has, as it were, fallen into his own trap. He denies that aggressiveness is the result of culture, and he calls nonsensical the proposition that all aggression is the result of frustration. Yet the fact is that the relation of culture to the determinance of behavioral response could not be better illustrated than by this example of toe-stepping. For when a person living in a so-called primitive culture steps on the toes of another, he is likely to do so with bare feet, and is thus unlikely to hurt or frustrate the other, and there will be no aggressive behavior. Whereas in a culture in which one wears shoes one is likely to hurt and frustrate the person upon whose toes one has stepped—but wheth-/37/er one will elicit aggressiveness or not will depend upon the manner in which the stepped-upon has learned to respond to his frustrations.* If we accept the generally accepted

---

* I recall here the definitions of a student of mine. She wrote: "A mentally healthy person is one who has learned to live with his frustrations in a satisfactory sort of way. A neurotic is one who has learned to live with his frustrations in an unsatisfactory sort of way." /38/

definition of a frustration as the thwarting of an expected satisfaction, then it may perhaps be acknowledged that having one's toes stepped on may be experienced as a frustration of the expectation of the enjoyment of pursuing the

> ".... noiseless tenor of one's way
> Yet e'en these bones from insult to protect."

We need not go further than our own culture to observe how the response to frustration is bred into one—and is therefore culturally determined. An ill-bred person may react with aggressive behavior to having his toes stepped on, a well-bred person may react with non-aggressive behavior. But this may reflect no more than a difference in the learned ability to control the expression of aggression. On the other hand, the different responses may actually represent a difference in feeling-content—in the one case aggressive feeling being present, and in the other not present.

Other things being equal, we can take this difference in feeling to be an expression of a nervous system that has been socialized in different ways in connection with the frequency of frustration and the training in the kind of responses permitted to them. I have not the least doubt that different cultures produce differently organized nervous systems. The evidence from different cultures of the manner in which response to frustration is trained is most impressive. Anthropologists and paperback books have made the accounts of these differences so widely available that many who would otherwise not even have been familiar with their names know that the Zuñi Indians avoid every form of aggressive behavior, that the expression of behavior is highly institutionalized among the Kwakiutl of the Northwest Pacific Coast, that the Dobuans of the Western Pacific are pathologically aggressive, and that the Arapesh of New Guinea control some forms of aggression but not others.

Where does all the aggressive energy come from which is provoked by frustration? This question is, indeed, a puzzler, for it certainly does not emanate from the store of aggressiveness which man has inherited from his animal ancestors. If we are to judge from man's closest living relatives, the chimpanzee and the gorilla, man is descended from among the least aggressive creatures in the animal kingdom. Under natural conditions these creatures are peaceful vegetarians and will not hurt so much as a fly. It is our own ferocity /38/ that we have projected upon these gentle creatures. And we have conceived of nature in much the same way, having made of it, in our mind's eye, what we have made of the world of man. We are the only species that makes war on its own kind, yet we speak of "the war of nature." But nature does not make war on itself—only certain branches of mankind do. Warlike activities at the present day are unknown to many human groups. All the evidence indicates that war was a very late development in the history of man, not appearing until the Neolithic, some 10,000 years ago.

Where, then, does the aggressive energy of human beings come from if not from the stores of the "far-fetched" notion of a Death Instinct? From all the available evidence it seems to me that the answer is unequivocally clear: The so-called "aggressive energy" of human beings comes from the same source as that which supplies the energy to love. And what is that source? It is the total energy system of the organism, an energy system which is directed toward the achievement of living in growth and development—the birthright of every living thing. The directiveness of the organism's activities is toward life, *not* toward death.

The energy subserving the functions of love is no different from that which supplies the dynamos of aggression; the one is not a transformation of the other, it is the same energy used to achieve the same ends—the maintenance and growth of the self. Aggression *is* love—it is love frustrated. This is the relationship to which, as a student of human nature, I see all the evidence pointing. In *The Origins of Love and Hate,* a work which I regard as the most original and helpfully constructive critique of Freud, Ian Suttie describes aggression as a technique or mode for compelling the attention which one has been denied. Hate, Suttie points out, is not a primal independent instinct, but a development or intensification of separation-anxiety, which in turn is evoked by a threat against love. "Hate is the maximal ultimate appeal in the child's power— the most difficult for the adult to ignore. Its purpose is not death-seeking or death-dealing, but the preservation of the self from the isolation which is death, and the restoration of a love relationship."

Since those words were published, twenty years ago, much confirmation has been brought to them by the researches of such workers as Lowrey, Levy, Goldfarb, Bender, Spitz, Bowlby, Banham, Maslow, and many others. These and other relevant researches prove that the child is dependent for its healthy development upon the love that it is given, and what is quite as important, the love that it is able to give to others. From the moment of birth, the infant seeks to re-establish its connection with the mother. Just as the fertilized ovum seeks to attach itself to the womb, so the newborn seeks to attach itself to the mother, and in relation to her to realize its further /39/ development—a development which is a continuation of that begun in the womb. From the first, mother and child are in a symbiotic relationship in which they confer mutually advantageous benefits upon each other. The child is as necessary for the parents' further development as is the mother for the child's development. And the directiveness of the child's behavior is toward loving others. The child's need for love from others is important principally because that love is the most significant developer of its own capacity to love others.

Indeed, it may unequivocally be stated that every human being is born *good,* good in the sense that every infant is born with all its energies oriented in the direction of conferring and receiving, of exchanging creatively enlarging benefits. The purposes of the infant are constructive—*not* destructive. He desires to live as if to live and love were one.

When the stimulations necessary for the development of his need to love and be loved are withheld, we know that the child will generally suffer proportionately in its capacity to love. We find that when the human organism is satisfied in its expectation of love, then it develops as a loving creature with a maximum tolerance for frustration and a minimum need for aggression. Aggression, it turns out, is an acquired, not a *basic* need. It is a need which is developed in the child that has not had its needs for love adequately satisfied. In such a deprived child, during its critical developmental periods, the need for love may evoke aggressive responses so frequently, that the child may thus be taught aggression instead of the love in which it strives to develop its capacity. Such a child may later, as we know, use aggression whenever it wants anything.

But what is the nature of this behavior customarily called "aggressive"? The usual statement is that it is behavior directed toward the infliction of injury. In this meaning of the term it can safely be said that no human being has ever been born with one iota of aggression in him. In this sense it is doubtful whether any infant under six months of age ever exhibits this kind of hostile aggression. The evidence indicates quite clearly that the destructive element enters, if at all, into the structure of aggression in the later stages of its development. The fact is that Sears and his co-workers found no correlation between early frustration and later preschool aggression in children. They found this not surprising since, by definition, aggression is taken to be "a goal response to instigation to injure" a person; that is, a gratification arising from performing some act causing injury or pain to another. It is absurd to call aggressive or destructive that behavior consisting in the taking of clocks apart, the removal of the wings of insects, and the breaking and tearing of objects, in which small children almost invariably indulge. Seeing /40/ how things work is an enormously important stage in the development of a human being. Its best interests are not advanced by treating that curiosity as if it were a form of aggression.

The evidence indicates that all personal aggression, whether it be of the early undestructive variety or of the later destructive kind, is almost always the response to love frustrated, and the expression of a claim upon others to provide that love. The most extreme forms of destructive aggression, as in murder, are in effect declarations of the position into which the murderer has been forced and caused to say: "If you will not love me, then I will not love you." Almost always when we witness aggressive behavior, we are observing a demand for love. This is certainly the meaning of the aggressive behavior of those small infants who exhibit it—and it is so at all ages.

Thus understood, aggression is not best met with counter-aggression, but with love—for aggression is the expression of the need for love.*

It is not human nature but human nurture that is the cause of human aggression. Human nature is good, and treated as such leads to goodness. It is for us to realize, in the light of the accumulated evidence, that being born into the human species means that the individual so born is capable of becoming whatever it is within the capacity of that individual to become. The social experience through which the individual has passed will largely determine whether he will become a dominantly aggressive or a dominantly loving person or someone betwixt and between. But there can be no doubt that the individual's drives are originally directed toward the achievement of love, however deformed the process of achievement may subsequently become. There can equally be no doubt that the person's drives are never innately oriented in a destructive direction, except in severely disturbed cases, and that such disturbances are produced principally by cultural factors.

Do let us avoid falling into the common error of attributing to innate nature that which has been produced by cultural factors.

---

* Such aggression is not in itself satisfactory. As Sears and his co-workers conclude in their study of aggression and dependency in young children, "it is clear that the initial stages of the acquisition of aggression involve no more than the learning of specific adaptive acts that serve to remove certain kinds of interference. These acts happen to be destructive or injurious; they may be considered as instrumental rather than goal response aggression. That is, they are intended simply to aid in achieving gratification of some other drive; they are not satisfying in and of themselves. Much of the *interpersonal* aggression observed between ages two and four is of this character, and the true *goal response aggression* becomes noticeable, in many children, only gradually during that period." /41/

Above all do let us avoid setting up our prejudices concerning human nature as the ineluctable laws of nature. Premature psychosclerosis is to be deplored in the votaries of any discipline in the process of /41/ becoming scientific. Reverence for father-figures is important, but so is irreverence. The dignity of an inquirer is not best maintained by adorning himself with a halo of authority from whatever source derived; such dignity Laurence Sterne once defined as a mysterious carriage of the body calculated to conceal the infirmities of the mind. Dignity lies in the maintenance of integrity of mind, in the intellectual honesty which enables one to make the necessary distinctions between hypothesis and fact, rhetoric and argument, prejudice and reason, far-fetched speculations and the laws of nature.

In the words of Robert Browning in *Paracelsus:*

"Truth is within ourselves; it takes no rise
From outward things, whate're you may believe:
There is an inmost centre in us all,
Where truth abides in fulness; and around,
Wall within wall, the gross flesh hems it in,
Perfect and true perception—which is truth;
A baffling and perverting carnal mesh
Which binds it, and makes error: and, *"to know"*
Rather consists in opening out a way
Whence the imprison'd splendour may dart forth,
Than in effecting entry for the light
Supposed to be without."

It is up to us to recognize, as students of human nature, that we have an important role to fulfill in the re-education of humanity, in releasing that imprisoned splendor which lies within each one of us.

QUESTIONS FOR DOCUMENTED PAPERS AND ESSAYS

It is generally easier to organize a paper if it is intended to answer a specific question. A good way to begin the research paper is to pose a question which can be answered by the methods available. After the investigation and study, an answer to the question should be formulated. Actually, the answer will probably simply "be" after some point in the investigation. This answer, insofar as it can be expressed briefly, will comprise the thesis of the paper. For example, take a question related to *Lord of the Flies:* Is Golding's view of human nature more like that of Hobbes or that of Rousseau? The answer, after reflection and qualification, might be: Golding's view of human nature is more like that of Hobbes. This statement then becomes the thesis.

The researcher proceeds in an indirect way (because he doesn't know his destination) to his thesis. It is also possible that his discoveries will lead to a modified and better question. He has perhaps explored many blind alleys and unnecessary bypaths along the way. Somewhere among his data are those bits and pieces which were telling and conclusive; and also there are many parts which can be discarded. He can, in short, present to his reader a direct path to the conclusion that he arrived at with difficulty and indirection. The temptation to be resisted is merely to insist upon the conclusion. It is necessary to recapture the process by which he became convinced. The writer who hopes to convince others must assume a position comparable to that of an attorney in a case at law. Both must employ the rules of evidence while presenting all the data available. The writer must reflect the spirit and the letter of his sources, just as the attorney must observe the spirit and the letter of his precedents. For the student, each element of his "case" becomes a major division of the paper, each fact part of its detail. The test of relevancy is always the thesis which is being propounded. For these reasons the topics for papers are presented as questions; the answer to the question becomes the thesis of the ensuing paper.

Not all commentary on literature and ideas is necessarily contained in documented or research papers. Many topics can best be developed in the form of the essay. The essay (in its meaning of attempt or trial) offers a good opportunity to play with ideas in a freer way than is possible in a paper strictly limited by the necessity for documentation or firm proof. Some judgement must be exercised in the elimination of wild assumptions and unlikely speculations, but ordinarily the essay provides an outlet for those ideas which are too tentative for the documented paper. Some propositions are subject to the kinds of proof available to the research paper, but there are others which, very probably, will remain forever speculative. The latter are best contained in the essay. It is a different kind of paper, but not necessarily any less valuable than the more factual research paper. It is hoped that the following questions will provide topics for both kinds.

QUESTIONS

1. Does *Lord of the Flies* express a Christian view of man?
2. How does Golding differ from Ballantyne if both are basically reflecting the Christian view of the universe?
3. How does the Christian doctrine of original sin, mentioned by several critics, find expression in the novel?
4. How does the doctrine of original sin correlate with the findings of Sigmund Freud, C. G. Jung, or Joseph Campbell?
5. What arguments against the central thesis of Golding's book are contained in Ashley Montagu's article?
6. Is Golding in *Lord of the Flies* an "orthodox" Freudian?
7. Does *Lord of the Flies* faithfully reflect pre-civilized modes of worship according to the anthropologists?
8. Does the questionable scientific basis for atavism invalidate the use of this idea in *Lord of the Flies?*
9. Is it possible to find in *Lord of the Flies* a parable of civilized or educated behavior as opposed to emotional or "instinctive" solution to problems?
10. Why is *Lord of the Flies* different from a parody of *The Coral Island?*
11. What are the advantages of Golding's use of the parallels from *The Coral Island?*
12. How does the *Coral Island* view of man differ from that of *Lord of the Flies?*

13. What reasons and advantages are there for a writer to isolate his characters on an island?

14. Is a pre-knowledge of *The Coral Island* desirable for a full appreciation of *Lord of the Flies?*

15. Is there a view of the structure of *Lord of the Flies* that makes the ending more than a 'gimmick'?

16. Mr. Gindin's article indicates a similarity of all of Golding's novels—a 'gimmick' ending. Are there other similarities?

17. What is the significance of the title, *Lord of the Flies?*

18. What are the major symbols that can be identified in Golding's novel?

19. Are there basic divisions among the critics reproduced here on the philosophy expressed by the novel?

20. In what ways does a reading of Golding's other novels enforce or deny the basic assumptions of *Lord of the Flies?*

21. What use does Golding make of such objects as the conch shell, Piggy's glasses, the night noises, and the dead airman's parachute?

22. What elements in *Lord of the Flies* make it more than an allegory of the *Animal Farm* variety?

23. Is *Lord of the Flies* a fiction or a fable according to the views of Miss Walters and Mr. Peters?

24. Does Hughes' novel *A High Wind in Jamaica* share the same view of child nature as *Lord of the Flies?*

25. What are the contrasts between the characters—Ralph, Jack, and Peterkin of *The Coral Island* and Ralph, Jack, and Piggy (or Simon) of *Lord of the Flies?*